Swami Karpatri

The Linga and the Great Goddess

लिङ्गोपासना-रहस्य
श्रीभगवती-तत्त्व

Preface by His Holiness Jagadguru Shankaracharya
Swami Swarupananda Sarasvati

Introduction and edition by
Jean Louis Gabin

Translation by
Gianni Pellegrini,
Girish Chandra Tiwari and Vimal Mehra

INDICA

Cover illustration: Swami Hariharananda Sarasvati, known as Karpatri-ji, ca. 1940.

Published in 2009 by

Indica Books
D 40 / 18 Godowlia
Varanasi - 221 001 (U.P.)
India

Email: indicabooks@satyam.net.in
Web: www.indicabooks.com

ISBN: 81-86569-88-X

Printed in India by *First Impression*, India
011-22481754, 09811224048

श्रीगणेशाय नमः

Contents

Swami Karpatriji during the consecration of H.H. Swami Swarupananda Sarasvati as Shankaracharya of Jyotishpith in 1973.

भूमिका

धार्मिक पुनर्जागरण के प्रस्तुतकर्ता, धार्मिक-आध्यात्मिक मूल्यों को नए आयाम तक पहुँचने वाले तथा भारतीय-संस्कृति एवं परम्परा को एक नई शुचिता प्रदान कर उसे लोकग्राह्य बनाने वाले धर्मसम्राट् स्वामी करपात्री जी महाराज उन महापुरुषों में से थे जिनसे न केवल तत्कालीन समाज अपितु आने वाली पीढ़ियाँ भी निदर्शन प्राप्त करती हैं। आदि शङ्कराचार्य भगवत्पाद परम्परा दीक्षित संन्यासियों के दशनामों में से सरस्वती नामाभिहित पूज्य स्वामी जी ने 'रागद्वेषविमुक्तात्मा' के गीता-सन्देश से प्रेरणा लेकर भारतीय-संस्कृति के स्वत्वसमन्वित स्वरूप को न केवल अपनी व्याख्याओं अथवा उपदेशों के माध्यम से अपितु अपने आचरणों में स्थापित कर दृढ़ता प्रदान की। सनातन-धर्म के आचारपक्ष के प्रबल समर्थक श्री स्वामी जी वर्णाश्रम, खान-पान, तीर्थयात्रा, गङ्गा-स्नान, यहाँ तक कि सत्यनारायणव्रतादि स्वयं करते थे, यात्राओं में भी पूजनादि नियमों का परिपालन तथा गङ्गाजल-पानादि कृत्य उनकी नियम-निष्ठा, शास्त्राज्ञाओं के परिपालन की उनकी दृढ़ता और उनके अन्तस् में छिपे परम्परा-प्रेम को परिलक्षित करते रहे हैं।

वे विचार के रूप में आदि शङ्कराचार्य के "**ब्रह्म सत्यं जगन्मिथ्या**" का प्रतिपादन करते हुए भी भगवान् के सगुण साकार श्रीविग्रह राम और कृष्णादि के प्रति भक्ति का भी वर्णन करते थे। भक्ति-वर्णन के प्रसंग में मिथ्यात्व की उनकी परिभाषा— "**ब्रह्मसत्त्वापेक्षया किञ्चिन्न्यूनसत्ताकं मिथ्यात्वम्**" होती थी। वे उदाहरण देते थे कि जैसे भगवान् के श्रीविग्रह की अपेक्षा उनके अंग की कौस्तुभमणि,

वनमाला आदि को श्रीविग्रह से न्यूनसत्ताक कहा है उसी प्रकार सच्चिदानन्दघन परब्रह्म परमात्मा की अपेक्षा अपनी माया से कलित सौन्दर्य-माधुर्य-सौगन्ध्य सुधारस की भी ब्रह्मसत्तापेक्षया न्यून सत्ता है, पर अन्यत्र जहाँ ब्रह्म समावृत है वहाँ भगवान् के श्रीविग्रह में अनावृत है। अपने ऐसे प्रतिपदन तथा व्यावहारिक सत्ता में उपास्य-उपासक का भेद स्वीकार कर भक्ति-रस को अत्यन्त मधुर शैली में प्रतिपादित करते थे, जिसका दिग्दर्शन भक्तिसुधादि ग्रन्थों में उपलब्ध है।

पूज्य स्वामी जी ने स्वधर्मनिष्ठ रहकर भी समस्तसम्प्रदायसमन्वयसाधन से अपने को पीछे नहीं छोड़ा और सनातन-धर्म की उपासना-पद्धति का सार्वभौम स्वरूप उपस्थित किया। भारतीय चिन्तन-परम्परा में प्राण सञ्चरित कर ज्ञान के साथ ही आराधना का सुगम पथ दिखाने वाले स्वामी जी का कहना था कि शङ्कराचार्य का अद्वैत-सिद्धान्त, शैवों की प्रत्यभिज्ञा, वैष्णवों की रागानुगा भक्ति, योगियों का बिन्दु तथा शाक्तों की कुलकुहरिणी इन सबका अन्तिम लक्ष्य अनन्तकोटिब्रह्माण्डनायक से साक्षात्कार कराना ही है। एतावता ये सब एक ही श्रुतिमाता से उत्पन्न सहोदरों की भाँति परस्पर एक दूसरे के विरोधी न होकर पूरक हैं। उनका समन्वित रूप केवल उनके विचारों में ही नहीं उनके स्वरूप में भी दिखायी देता था। वे स्फटिक माला धारण कर राजराजेश्वरी पराम्बा ललिता और श्रीयन्त्र की पूजा करते समय शाक्त, रुद्राक्ष तथा त्रिपुण्ड धारण कर हाथ में शृंगी ले रुद्राभिषेक में शैव, नित्य शालिग्राम-पूजन, पुरुषसूक्त से तुलसी अर्चन तथा वैष्णवलिङ्ग दण्ड धारण करते ही वैष्णवोत्तम दिखायी देते थे। हमारे विचार से सनातन-जीवन के हर कोने ने उनसे गरिमा, भारतीय संस्कृति के हर केदार ने समृद्धि, देश की हर समस्या ने ग्रन्थों के रूप में लिखित समाधान और प्रत्येक विषयों ने उनकी वाग्मिता से प्रकाश पाया है।

स्वामी करपात्री जी में समाज-सुधारकता, राजनीतिविशारदता, साधुता और नेतृत्व आदि गुणों का वह मनोरम सामरस्य मिलता है, जो अन्यत्र दुर्लभ है। उनकी सिद्धान्तप्रियता राजनीति में भी अक्षुण्ण रही और उसका दर्शन भारत-विभाजन, कैलाश-मानसरोवर पर आक्रमण, हिन्दू कोड बिल, गौहत्या बन्दी, दहेज पर सरकारी नियन्त्रण, जनेऊ तोड़ो आन्दोलन आदि अवसरों पर उनके निर्भीकतापूर्वक व्यक्त किए गए अभिमतों से होता है। धर्म पर प्रहार को वे किञ्चिन्मात्र भी न सह पाते थे और निर्भीकता से उसका प्रतिवाद करते थे।

उनकी दृष्टि में राजनीति और धर्म भारतीय दम्पतियुगल की तरह अनन्य है। धर्म के बिना (राज)नीति और नीति के बिना धर्म; परिणामात्मक अस्तित्त्व खो देते हैं इसीलिए उन्होंने राजनीति के माध्यम से धर्मराज्य — जिसे उन्होंने रामराज्य का नाम दिया था — की स्थापना का प्रयास किया। भारतीय मर्यादा और भारतीयों के कल्याण हेतु वेदशास्त्रानुमोदित राजनीति की प्रतिस्थापना हेतु स्थापित 'अखिल भारतीय रामराज्य परिषद्' के माध्यम से स्वामी जी ने अपने कार्यक्रम जनता के समक्ष रखे और मुझे इस दल का प्रथम अध्यक्ष बनाया।

भारत की आजादी की लड़ाई चूँकि काँग्रेस के मंच से लड़ी गई थी अत: उसका प्रबल प्रभाव देशवासियों में था। परन्तु रामराज्य परिषद् के सिद्धान्त कांग्रेस से मेल न खाते थे, साथ ही तत्कालीन अन्य राजनीतिक दलों से भी परिषद् के सिद्धान्त मिलते न थे। इस तरह परिषद् ने धर्मराज्य का जो बिगुल बजाया था, वह अन्य सभी दलों के सुरों से विशिष्ट और आकर्षक था। परन्तु परिषद् की स्थापना के थोड़े समय बाद ही भारतीय जनसंघ नामक एक नए राजनीतिक दल की स्थापना हुई—जो कि सिद्धान्तत: परिषद से अत्यन्त दूर होते हुए भी बाह्यत: एक जैसा होने का भ्रम उत्पन्न करता था। भारतीय जनसंघ एवं

हिन्दू महासभा दोनों का ही लक्ष्य हिन्दू-राष्ट्र की स्थापना का था, पर इन दोनों के परिषद् से न केवल मतभेद थे अपितु कार्यक्रमों एवं सिद्धान्तों में भी पार्थक्य था। महाराजश्री का मानना था कि धर्मराज्य से ही जनता का कल्याण हो सकता है। रावण भी तो हिन्दू और ब्राह्मण था, परन्तु उसके राज्य से किसी का भला न हुआ। अत: केवल हिन्दू राष्ट्र बना देने से जन-कल्याण असंभव है। फलत: स्वामी जी ने राष्ट्रीय स्वयंसेवक संघ, हिन्दू महासभा और जनसंघ आदि का खण्डन किया और इनकी धार्मिक तथा राजनैतिक चिन्तनधारा की परिषद् से पृथकता को सुस्पष्ट किया। इसके लिए उन्हें गुरु गोलवलकर रचित 'विचार नवनीत', वीर सावरकर लिखित 'भारतीय इतिहास के छ: स्वर्णिम पृष्ठ' का अपने 'विचार-पीयूष' तथा राष्ट्रीय स्वयंसेवक संघ का 'राष्ट्रीय स्वयंसेवक संघ और हिन्दू धर्म' के माध्यम से खण्डन करना पड़ा। उन्होंने उन प्रत्येक हिन्दू, मुसलमान, सिख, ईसाई, जैन, पारसी तथा बौद्ध आदि के लिए परिषद् का द्वार खोल दिया जो अपने धर्म का पालन दीनदारी और ईमानदारी से करते हों।

पूज्य स्वामी जी ने "रामराज्य परिषद् और अन्य दल" नामक अपने ग्रन्थ में अन्य दलों से परिषद् के अन्तर को स्पष्ट करते हुए लिखा कि— "हम देखते हैं कि देश में जितने राजनैतिक दल कार्य कर रहे हैं, वे न तो स्वयं में स्पष्ट हैं और न ही जनता के सामने। लक्ष्य कुछ है, व्यवहार कुछ। इसका फल यह हो रहा है कि देश में राजनीतिक स्थिरता और विश्वास सुनने को नहीं मिलता है। झूठे प्रलोभन देकर वोट प्राप्त करना ही राजनीति का लक्ष्य हो गया है। इस निम्न कोटि की स्थिति से ऊपर उङ्कर स्वस्थ राजनीतिक विचारों को व्यवहार रूप में लाना ही रामराज्य परिषद् का लक्ष्य है। परिषद् अपने साधन तथा लक्ष्य में स्पष्ट है। न किसी प्रकार का धोखा है, न

प्रलोभन । उसका एक मात्र उद्देश्य है ''पक्षपातविहीन धर्मसापेक्ष राजनीति की स्थापना'' ।

पूज्य महाराजश्री अपने एक फ्रांसीसी अनुयायी शिवशरण (आलें दान्येलू) की चर्चा किया करते थे । उनका विश्वास था कि ''वह (अर्थात् दान्येलू) हमारे भावों को समझता और हममें श्रद्धा रखता है ।'' इसीलिए वे शिवशरण द्वारा अपने लेखों के किए गए अंग्रेजी अनुवादों को अपना आशीर्वाद देते थे और हमे भी उसे स्वामी जी के विचारों को पश्चिम में फैलाने वाला समझते थे । वास्तव में उनका यह कार्य अत्यन्त प्रशंसनीय था । इसीलिए जब श्री शिवशरण के सहयोगी श्री गबें स्वामी जी के शिवशरण अनूदित निबन्धों को प्रकाशित करने लगे तो हमें प्रसन्नता हुई । परन्तु अनुशीलन करने पर पता चला कि शिवशरण ने स्वामी करपात्री जी के मूललेखों के साथ छेड़छाड़ की है और समय-समय पर संपादित करते रहा है, मूल लेखों के मिलान करने पर यह बातें और भी स्पष्टता से अंकित हुईं । हम सभी को ऐसी आशा नहीं थी । स्वामी जी होते तो शिवशरण के प्रति उनके विश्वास को अवश्य चोट लगती ।

अस्तु, ''सत्य परास्त हो सकता है, पराजित नहीं'' की उक्ति चरितार्थ हुई । महापुरुषों के वाक्यों में परिवर्तन करने का अधिकार किसी को नहीं है । यदि शिवशरण ने ऐसा किया तो हमारे देखते ही वह समय भी आ ही गया कि उसी के सहयोगी श्रीगवें ने उसकी छेड़छाड़ को अनावृत्त कर सत्य को पुन: प्रतिष्ठित कर दिया है । सूर्य को धूमिल करने के लिए उछाली गई धूल उछालने वाले के ही मुख पर आकर गिरती है, सूर्य का कुछ नहीं बिगड़ता । हम साधुवाद देते हैं, श्री गबें को जिन्होंने कठिन परिश्रम द्वारा हिन्दी सीखते हुए यह प्रकाशन साधना बनाया है ।

पूज्य स्वामी जी के काया-कल्पादि अवसरों पर अत्यन्त सन्निकट रहने का हमें अवसर मिला था, अतएव उनके समस्त सिद्धान्त और विचार हमारे सामने स्पष्ट हैं। यदि उनके द्वारा कहा गया कोई विषय किसी को दुरूह लगे तो हम उसका सारांश प्रकट करने का प्रयास कर सकते हैं।

यह ग्रन्थ आंग्लभाषियों को सनातन-धर्म एवं दर्शन की गहराई को स्वामी करपात्री जी जैसे प्रमाणित परिमाण से परखने का अवसर देगा — ऐसा विश्वास है।

स्वामी स्वरूपानन्द सरस्वती

पूज्यपाद स्वामी स्वरूपानन्द सरस्वती जी महाराज इस समय आदि शङ्कराचार्य द्वारा प्रतिष्ठापित चार आम्नाय पीठों में से दो — ज्योतिष्पीठ, बदरिकाश्रम और शारदापीठ, द्वारका — के जगद्गुरु शङ्कराचार्य हैं और भारत के वरिष्ठतम धर्माचार्य हैं।

Preface

Known as the 'Emperor of *dharma*' (*dharma saṃrāṭ*), the eminent Svāmī Karpātrī was among those great men who provided guidance not only to his contemporary society, but also to future generations. He made religious and spiritual values easily understandable for people by giving them a new perspective on Indian tradition and culture. Initiated into the Sarasvatī lineage, one of the ten lines of *saṃnyāsin* started by the first Śaṅkarācārya, the venerable Svāmījī took his inspiration from the injunction of the *Gītā* that one should be free from attraction and aversion. Through his conduct — and not merely by sermons and expositions — he lent substance to a definitive articulation of Indian culture. An active proponent of the traditional approach to *Sanātana Dharma*, Svāmījī practiced every rule regarding caste (*varṇāśrama*), food, pilgrimage, bathing in the Gaṅgā — so much so that he would even perform the fast of *Satyanārāyaṇa*, usually done only by householders. He was sure to follow the tenets of worship and to ritually drink Gaṅgā water daily, even when on his pilgrimages; this reflects his devotion to the prescribed rules, his obedience to the precepts of the holy texts and the love for tradition he held in his heart.

Though he expounded the dictum of the first Śaṅkarācārya that "*brahma satyaṃ jaganmithyā*" (*brahman* is real, the world is false), he would nevertheless propagate devotion towards the *saguṇa* (having attributes) *sākāra* (having forms) aspects of God in His aspects of Rāma and Kṛṣṇa. In the context of devotion, his definition of *mithyā* (illusion) was "*brahma sattvāpekṣayā kiṃcinnyūnasattākaṃ mithyātvam*" (Compared to the Supreme reality of *brahman*, the level of reality of *mithyā* is somehow inferior). He used to give the example that, just as the ornaments of the Lord have an inferior existence relative to His divine person, similarly the sublimely sweet ambrosiaic fragrance of *brahman* — a veritable ocean of Sublime Bliss — is relatively inferior to the *parabrahman*, *paramātman* (the Supreme Self) itself due to the effect of his *māyā*; but whereas the *brahman* is normally hidden, it is revealed in the divine form of the Lord. In this way he would expound upon the essence of the path of devotion in a very gentle way, after having acknowledged the difference between the worshipper and the worshipped both in his theory as well as in his practice; this is available in such texts as his *Bhakti Sudhā*.[1]

Even though Svāmījī remained loyal to his *svadharma*, he nonetheless was not remiss in striving for coordination among all religious approaches, and he proffered a universal form of the method of worship of *Sanātana dharma*. He infused life into the Indian thought tradition, and along with his wisdom revealed an easy path of worship. Svāmījī used to say that the ultimate objective of the non-duality principle of Śaṅkarācārya, the *pratyabhijñā* (the spontaneous self-recognition of the Absolute) of Śiva worshippers, the supremely ardent devotion of Viṣṇu worshippers, the *bindu* ('drop') of *yogins* and the *kulakuhariṇī* of Śakti worshippers are all to make one come face to face with the Overlord of the infinite universes. Therefore, instead of being opponents of each other, all these approaches are complementary, like brothers born from the same Vedic mother. This all-embracing attitude was seen not only in his ideas but also in his outward appearance. He appeared to be a *śākta* while worshipping Rājarājeśvarī, Parāmbā, Lalitā and *śrīyantra* with a necklace of rock crystals in his hand; while performing *rudrābhiṣeka* (anointing of Śiva) he appeared to be a *śaiva*, with a *śriṅgin* (cow horn-shaped vessel for offering water to the *śivaliṅga*) in his hand, a *rudrākṣa* rosary around his neck and the three marks of Śiva on his forehead; while singing the *puruṣasūkta* hymn, doing his daily *pūjā* (worship) of the *śāligrāma* (Viṣṇu as an an-iconic symbol) with an offering of *tulasī*, wearing the *vaiṣṇava* mark, he had the mien of the best of *vaiṣṇavas*. In our opinion, he has given significance to every corner of *sanātana* life and prosperity to every field of Indian culture; every problem of

[1] The two articles constituting this book, originally published in *Siddhānta*, were also compiled in *Bhakti Sudhā*.

the country has been solved in his texts and every topic has received enlightenment from his acumen.

In Svāmī Karpātrījī we find a valuable blend of social reformism, political astuteness, saintliness and leadership, difficult to find elsewhere. His love for ideals remained intact even in his politics, and we get a glimpse of that in his fearlessly expressed opinions on such occasions as the partition of India, the Chinese attack on Kailāsa Mānasarovara, the Hindu Code Bill, the ban on cow slaughter, government control on dowry, the agitation to break the sacred thread, and so on. He was inflexible towards even the slightest attack on religion, and would strike back fearlessly.

In his view, politics and religion are as inseparable as an Indian couple. Separate, politics without religion or religion without policy lose all reality; for this, he tried to establish politically a *Dharmarājya* (a religious state) which he called *Rāmarājya* (the rule of Rāma). Svāmījī propounded his ideas before the public in the forum of the *All-India Rama Rajya Parishad*; this was established to promote the welfare of Indians and the Indian way of life with the aim of bringing about a governance which would bear the sanction of the *Vedas* and the scriptures. He nominated me the first president of this body.

Since the fight for India's freedom had been fought from the platform of the Congress Party, this party therefore had a very strong influence upon our countrymen. However, the principles of the *Rama Rajya Parishad* corresponded neither with those of the Congress Party, nor with those of the other contemporary parties. Hence, the clarion call of a nation ruled by *dharma* (*dharmarājya*) proclaimed by the *Parishad* was distinct and more attractive than the tunes that were being sung by the other political parties. However, just a short while after the establishment of the *Parishad*, a new political party called the *Bharatiya Jana Sangh* was established, which — though extremely removed from the *Parishad* in its principles — gave the outward illusion of being similar to the *Parishad*. The objective of both the *Bharatiya Jana Sangh* and the *Hindu Mahasabha* was the establishment of a Hindu nation, but these two differed from the *Parishad* not only in their plans of action, but also in their principles. Svāmī Karpātrījī believed that only through a religious state could public welfare come about — however, he pointed out that although Rāvaṇa was both a Hindu and a brahmin, his kingdom still did no one any good. Therefore, public welfare would not be promoted through the mere creation of a Hindu nation. As a result, Svāmījī refuted the arguments of the R.S.S., the *Hindu Mahasabha* and *Jana Sangh*, and he made evident to all how the religious and political ideology of the *Parishad* was different from the ideologies of these other parties. To this end, through his text *Vicārapīyūṣa* (Nectar of Thoughts) he refuted the arguments given in books such as Guru Golvalkar's *Vicāra navanīta* (Bunch of Thoughts) and Veer Savarkar's *Bhāratīya itihāsa ke chaḥ svarṇima pṛṣṭa* (Six Golden Pages of the Indian History); he also refuted the ideology of the R.S.S. through his book *Rāṣṭrīya Svayaṃsevaka Saṃgha aur Hindū Dharma* (The R.S.S. and the *Hindu Dharma*). He opened the doors of the *Parishad* to every Hindu, Muslim, Sikh, Christian, Jain, Parsi, Buddhist and so forth who practiced their religion with honesty and rectitude.

In his book *Rāmarājya Pariṣad aur anya Dal* (The Assembly of the Kingdom of Rāma and Other Groups), the venerable Svāmījī delineated the differences of the other political parties from the *Parishad* with the following words: "It is evident that no political party at work in the country is consistent, neither within itself nor before the public; their aim is one thing, their conduct is something quite different. As a result, one never hears about any political stability or faith in the country. Getting votes through false promises has become the sole objective of politics. The objective of the *Rama Rajya Parishad* is to rise above this lowly state and bring into practice some healthy political ideas. The *Parishad* is clear about its aims and the means to reach them. Neither is there any type of deceit, nor is there any temptation towards any. Its sole aim is 'the establishment of the politics of impartial *dharmasāpekṣa*'." [2]

[2] Politics which takes support in *dharma*, but is not partial to any concrete religion.

His Eminence Svāmī Karpātri used to speak of a French follower named Śiva Śaraṇ (Alain Daniélou). He believed that "he (that is, Daniélou) understands my feelings and has reverence for me". That is why he would give his blessings to Śiva Śaraṇ's English translations of his articles, and we also thought that he was spreading the ideas of Svāmījī through the West. His project was extremely praiseworthy. For this, we were rather pleased when an associate of Śiva Śaraṇ, Mr. J.L. Gabin set about publishing a book comprising some of Svāmījī's essays translated by Śiva Śaraṇ. But, upon examination, it was found that Śiva Śaraṇ had tampered with the original articles of Svāmī Karpātrījī and had even been further, editing them from time to time. With a more extensive inquiry, this became more and more evident. None of us had expected this from him. If Svāmījī had still been alive, his trust in Śiva Śaraṇ would surely have been wounded.

Thus, the saying "the truth can be beaten, but not conquered" has come true. None has the right to alter the words of great people. If Śiva Śaraṇ did so, then the time has indeed arrived when his former associate, Mr. Gabin, would expose this tampering and re-establish the truth. He who kicks dust to sully the sun will find the dust in his own face; this hurts the sun not at all. We praise Mr. Gabin who, learning Hindi with great effort, made this publication possible.

Having stayed in close proximity to the venerable Svāmī Karpātrījī on many occasions, his ideals and ideas are clear to us. If someone finds something in his writings difficult to understand, we will try to make it clear to him.

We hope that this book will give the opportunity to the English-speaking readers to measure the depth of *sanātana dharma* and philosophy in the light of Svāmī Karpātrījī.

Svāmī Śrī Svarūpānanda Sarasvatī

H.H. Svāmī Svarūpānanda Sarasvatī jī Mahārāja is at this time the Jagadguru Śaṅkarācārya of two of the four *pīṭhas* established by Ādi Śaṅkarācārya — Jyotiṣpīṭha, Badarikāśrama and Śāradāpīṭha, Dvārakā. He is the seniormost *dharmācārya* of India.

Introduction

Svāmī Karpātrī and the Protection of Dharma

A century after his birth, at the *Ardha Kumbha Melā* held in Allahabad[1] (Prayag) in 2007, the presence of Svāmī Karpātrī (1907-1982) loomed very large. Most of the five millions of *sādhus* gathered on this occasion used to refer to him with the title of *paramahaṃsa* (the Great Swan), which is, for the Hindus, the highest goal reachable by a living being. In this Kumbha Melā the name of Svāmī Karpātrī, which is practically ignored in the West, echoed and his face shone at several camps of *sādhus*, including those of the four *śaṅkarācārya*s, which are traditionally recognized as the highest authority of Hinduism. During the whole month of this Kumbha Melā celebrating the centenary of Svāmī Karpātrī, *saṃnyāsins* that had known him, *śaṅkarācāryas* that had been his companions or disciples spoke about him in their discourses, invoked his name in their *pūjās*, and discussed his teachings with new generations of brahmins and *saṃnyāsins* and with the public of all castes who came to listen their expositions on *dharma*. Everywhere in the *sādhus*' processions to the sacred bath, at the beginning and the end of discourses, during *pūjās* and in all kind of ceremonies, the slogans composed by Svāmī Karpātrī rose to the sky: *dharma kī jaya ho!* (victory to *dharma*), *adharma kā nāśa ho!* (destruction of injustice), *prāṇiyoṃ meṃ sadbhāvanā ho!* (goodwill for all creatures), *viśva kā kalyāṇa ho!* (welfare for the world), *gomātā kī jaya ho!* (praise to our mother the cow), *gohatyā band ho!* (stop cow slaughter).

---

[1] The names of the places, political parties and organizations are written without diacritical marks.

Three years before this Kumbha Melā, as I will explain hereafter,[2] I had discovered a big mistake concerning Svāmī Karpātrī in the publications of the sole Westerner who had claimed to be his spokesman. But I had been unable to find any book or academic article about the life and the action of Svāmī Karpātrī. Surprisingly, this monk who had been a spiritual leader of first importance for millions of Hindus in the twentieth century remains widely unknown even in many circles in India. The few references to him portray him as a 'reactionary' *saṃnyāsin* who opposed the *Hindu Code Bill* and other 'progressive' policies of the Nehru Government. Having discovered that Svāmī Karpātrī was not the creator of an ultra-nationalist party linked with fundamentalists, as it was printed here and there, but on the contrary a sage of high knowledge revered by traditional monks, as the four *śaṅkarācāryas* and their entourage, I decided to collect information about him. I found this information — the facts and their explanations — from Svāmī Karpātrī's direct disciples and followers whom I was fortunate enough to meet, at Prayag or Banaras. I presented here this information not to justify or condemn anything, but to try to understand.

I have no any other aim in the following pages than to try — for the first time in English — to give some lights about a contemporary *saṃnyāsin* of deep knowledge, author of more than forty books, a sage who became a political leader, and whose slogans, twenty-five years after his death, were spreading in the whole *Ardha Kumbha Melā* in 2007.

According to the disciples of Svāmī Karpātrī, these slogans — which were those of the *Dharma Sangh*, a cultural and religious organisation he created for the defence of *dharma* in 1939, and afterwards of the *Ram Rajya Parishad*, a political party founded in 1950 with a similar goal — were initially opposed to the anti-traditionalist politics of the British Government, then of the leaders of the Independence movement, who had been educated in English

2 See *infra* 'The problem of Alain Danielou's translations'.

universities and wanted to establish a secular state in the exact pattern of Western countries.

Following these disciples, *sādhus* for the most, these slogans did not pretend to set the Hindus in opposition to the other sections of the population, nor India to any other country, but rather confronted the challenges of the 21st century multicultural societies, as well as the political and ecological dangers of a government mostly ruled by economical aims — which are, traditionally, those of the sole third *varṇa.*[3]

Slogans as *dharma kī jaya ho!* (victory to *dharma*), *prāṇiyoṃ meṃ sadbhāvanā ho!* (goodwill for all creatures), *viśva kā kalyāṇa ho!* (welfare for the world), express another political scope than modern nationalist ones as "one country, one people, one language", which consider the earth as mere property to be exploited, reducing humanity to its material needs and trying to abolish the organic differences that form the base of the traditional kingdoms.[4] From a traditional point of view, a 'secular' government desecrates the earth, imperilling its equilibrium, and profanes also human society — no longer organized as it was the case, at least ideally, as communities in balance with other communities and with Nature, but in nations opposed to other nations.

It appears that Svāmī Karpātrī wanted to reassert principles which had been the spinal cord of Indian civilization, as the social traditional order, a traditional government respecting *dharma*, a government taking into account all the different communities and the different aims of life — and not only the economical ones. It can be argued that several centuries of Muslim and British government had put traditional Hinduism in a defensive position, giving a break on his creativity.

---

[3] It is well known that the four *varṇas* composing the traditional Hindu society are the *brāhmaṇas* (scholars and priests), the *kṣatriyas* (kings and warriors), the *vaiśyas* (tradesmen and farmers) and the *śūdras* (craftsmen and servants).

[4] For the Hindus, the traditional model of state, symbol of justice, remains the kingdom of Rāma, the *Rāma rājya*. Due to that, the political party founded by Svāmī Karpātrī was named the *Ram Rajya Parishad.*

However in the opinion of Svāmī Karpātrī, much of its high principles and values were still alive; due to that, Indian civilization remained through millennia, and its principles should guide again the new state that was about to be born. In his perspective, the reformist following western ideologies wanted to "throw the baby with the dirty water".

This is why Svāmī Karpātrī was opposed to the partition of India, as according to him Hindus and Muslims should live together in the mutual respect of their differences, and against the destruction of the *varṇāśrama*, the ancient Indian social organisation called by the westerners 'caste system', that protected the minorities, the tribes, the ascetics, the family life, the children and the aged persons. From a traditional point of view, the joint-family provides a favourable frame for children and people in the *gṛhastha* (householder) stage; the dignity of aged persons is also provided by the conception of *vanaprastha*, where old people can dedicate themselves to religious life; and the last stages, following the traditional way of renouncement[5] (*saṃnyāsa*), could been fully dedicated to spiritual aims — even if the forest of old have been replaced by other environments.

On discussing these matters with disciples of Svāmī Karpātrī, it was pointed out that it is impossible to find anywhere a human society without defaults, but it should be recognized that this traditional organization contrasts sharply, by example, with the place of Western modern society gives to his own old people. Modern society accords to them, of course, material and medical assistance, but segregates them from the rest of the people, stripping them of all knowledge value and role in the society. It was underlined also that modern 'egalitarian' Indian society claims to have progressed from the traditional and 'oppressive' one, by granting equal rights to all. Sometimes, though, fifty years after Independence, its looks that instead it has given everybody equal lack of rights. For example tribes in India had always led an independent life, and mainstream society let them live their own life in their territories, even if giving them a low status. The modern state,

---

[5] Specially, Svāmī Karpātrī gave a new energy to the institution of *sādhus* named *daṇḍī svāmī*, very alive today in North India.

while theoretically granting them all rights, had deprived them of their territories and independence in the name of progress.

Svāmī Karpātrī, in the context of the formation of a secular state in India fought against the interference of the secular government in matters of religion and struggled strongly to defend the holy cow. This is specially expressed by the slogans *prāṇiyoṃ meṃ sadbhāvanā ho!* (goodwill for all creatures), *viśva kā kalyāṇa ho!* (welfare for the world), *gomātā kī jaya ho!* (praise to our mother the cow), *gohatyā band ho!* (stop cow slaughter). For the Hindus, animal and plants are not deprived of consciousness, and the holy cow represents all the animal stage — in fact, the generosity of Nature — with which the human society has to organize a relationship of reciprocity and not despotic exploitation. The mythical cow Kāmadhenu, who provides all the desires, contains symbolically all the gods in her body; the holy cow had been intimately close-knit to Hindu society. Traditional Hindus cannot consider positively the deny of animals' rights to be free, not only in western 'developed' cities, but also in the modern countryside, which appears as a green desert. From a Hindu point of view, the 'rational' western organization of collective jails for cows and other domesticated animals, treated as mere things, killed in a young age for economic reasons, deprived even of the light of the sun, seems a kind of hell. Svāmī Karpātrī fought all his life to ban cow slaughter from India.

In the 20th century, so fertile with war, revolution and conflict, the spiritual way of Svāmī Karpātrī lay not in keeping himself aloof from world matters, as most *sādhus* usually do, but rather to take an active part in them. For millions of Hindus, Svāmī Karpātrī was a clear example for our modern times of the *sthitaprajña* of the *Gītā*, the sage "established in wisdom" who "performs actions while remaining steadfast in *yoga*" (*Bhagavad Gītā*, II.48). He worked only for the benefit of the world, having already obtained the highest spiritual state: "Forsaking attachment to the fruits of action, ever satisfied, depending on nothing; though engaged in action, truly, he does nothing." (*Bhagavad Gītā*, IV.20).

Indeed, Svāmī Karpātrī paid a heavy price, by going fourteen times to jail to defend traditional Indian society, to claim and reaffirm something very ill-treated by the apparently irresistible triumph of materialism: *sanātana dharma*, the timeless and eternal law that had given India its foundation throughout the millennia.

***

According to B.D. Tripathi,[6] the ascetic who was to become famous under the name of Svāmī Karpātrī was born as Hari Nārāyaṇa Ojhā on Sunday, the 11th September 1907 (*śravaṇa śukla dvitīya, vikrama* 1964, according to the Hindu calendar) at Bhatani in what is now Uttar Pradesh, to a traditional Brahmin family. His grandfather, Caṇḍī Prasāda Ojhā, had lived in a village in Barhalganj in Gorakhpur district called Ojhauli, but at the request of the Rājā of Kalakankar, he migrated to Bhatani, where the future Svāmī Karpātrī was born as the third child of his son Rāma Nidhi Ojhā and his daughter-in-law Śiva Rāṇī Devī.

At a young age, Hari Nārāyaṇa showed an irresistible attraction towards the wandering life of the ascetics, and he escaped his family home in several occasions. His father had him married in 1916 when he was only nine years and sent him forcefully to the village school. Hari Nārāyaṇa took only interest in Sanskrit; he hated worldly life and modern education.[7] His father asked him then to give him an heir, after which he would be free to follow his way. In 1924, Hari Nārāyaṇa became the father of a girl named Bhagavatī Devī and, in 1926, at the age of nineteen, he left forever the house of his father to follow his spiritual destiny.

Then, according to the *Karpātra Jīvanajāhnavī*,[8] Hari Nārāyaṇa while wandering along the banks of Ganga, met a highly revered

---

6 These two paragraphs are based on B.D. Tripathi, *Sadhus of India*, 2nd ed., Pilgrims Publishing House, Varanasi, 2004, p. 224.

7 According to disciples of Svāmī Karpātrī, he always refused to speak or to write in English, despite the fact that he understood this language.

8 *Karpātra Jīvanjāhanvī* (*Karpātrī's life, flowing like the Gaṅgā*), compiled in Hindi by K.P. Sharma and published by Dharma Sangh, Durgakund, Varanasi, 1999.

saint, Svāmī Brahmānanda Sarasvatī — who became later *śaṅkarācārya* of Jyotispīṭha —, from whom he asked initiation. Svāmī Brahmānanda accepted him as a disciple, gave him *naiṣṭika dīkṣā* [9] and renamed him Hariharacaitanya Brahmacārī (name of novice). He sent him to Narwar to study Sanskrit grammar, philosophy and metaphysics under the direction of Svāmī Viśveśvarāśrama, and to practice *yoga* as well. Hariharacaitanya mastered these subjects within eleven months, and in another thirteen months the six systems of philosophy (*ṣaḍḍarśana*), completing therefore in only two years an education which usually takes twelve. After that, he began a solitary life of *tapasyā* on the banks of Gaṅgā. He visited Rishikesh and other places renowned for their religious associations, and thereafter lived for several months alone in a cave in the Himalayas. It seems that it was during this period of profound meditation that he received the inspiration that his mission was not to escape the world but rather to return to worldly existence so that his life and actions should serve as an example in the struggle for the reestablishment of *sanātana dharma*.

In 1930, dressed in a simple cotton cloth and having only a *kamaṇḍala* (ceremonial water pot) with him, he returned to Narwar where he was recognized as a *paramahaṃsa*, a sage having reached the supreme spiritual state, liberated from worldly limitations. Because of his habit of eating only once a day directly from his hands without any utensils, he came to be known as 'Karpātrī' ('He who uses his hands for dish'). He returned to Prayag to have the *darśana* of his *guru* Svāmī Brahmānanda and then proceeded to Kashi (Banaras, now Varanasi) where, under the direction of Svāmī Brahmānanda and in presence of the great scholar Śrī Viśveśvarāśrama, he became *saṃnyāsin* at the age of 24 years and was renamed Svāmī Hariharānanda Saraswatī. At the occasion of the Kumbha Melā of Hardwar in 1932, he had his first *śāstrārtha* (religious debate) with Paṇḍita Madan Mohan Malaviya, the founder of Banaras Hindu University. The subject was, "Should the *praṇava* '*OM*' be given to

[9] The first initiation into permanent *brāhmacārya*, which is the first step to *saṃnyāsa*.

the lowest castes or not?" Over two days, Svāmī Karpātrī demonstrated why, according to the *śastras*, *mantras* could be given to the lowest castes, but the *praṇava* '*OM*' ought not. Then, Svāmī Karpātrī started a pilgrimage across India on foot, teaching religious precepts and organising ritual ceremonies (*yajñas*) in towns and villages. In 1935, at Baghpath on the bank of the Yamunā, he met Svāmī Kṛṣ ṇabodhāśrama, another renowned sage, and the two decided to unite their efforts to liberate the country and revitalize Hinduism — they were both to remain close companions for life. During this period, he wrote *Saṃkīrtana Mīmāṃsā aur Varṇāśrama* (Inquiry into the Practice of the Chant of the Names of the Lord and the System of Castes and Stages of Life), a book that presents the elementary aspects of religion.

A saint amidst the conflicts of the world

In 1939 (*vikrama saṃvat* 1996) at Banaras, Svāmī Karpātrī pointed out some mistakes concerning Ādi Śaṅkarācārya in the magazine *Kalyāṇa,* published in Gorakhpur. Piqued by the non-response with regards to his corrigendum, he himself authored an article on the subject (*śaṅkarabhāṣya*). Some time later, he founded the newspaper *Sanmārga* and the periodical *Siddhānta* in Banaras, with the view of promoting and highlighting religious questions and traditional viewpoints. In 1940, to the same end he founded a cultural and religious organization, the *Dharma Sangh*. He became involved with an effort to re-establish the post of *śaṅkarācārya* of Jyotirmaṭha, which was lying vacant for the last 165 years. In 1941 his *guru*, Svāmī Brahmānanda Saraswatī, was installed as *śaṅkarācārya* of this *maṭha*. Also throughout 1941, his work for the revitalization of Hinduism continued through pilgrimages, the organization of rituals in villages and cities, and efforts to reawaken listless Vedic students. Having published important works such as *Samanvaya Saṃrājya Saṃrakṣaṇa* (The Protection of the Kingdom of Harmony) and *Śrī Bhagavatī Tattva*, he returned to Kashi and proceeded to Calcutta via Ghazipur, Gahmar and Patna, giving discourses and establishing branches of the *Dharma Sangh* along the way.

In 1942, he called the first general assembly of the *Dharma Sangh* at Prayag; he then again resumed his pilgrimages on foot in the company of Svāmī Krișṇabodhāśram and organized branches of the *Dharma Sangh* at Dehradun, Sharanpur, Muzaffarnagar, Meerut, Hapud, Pikhuwa, and so on, travelling from village to village up to Delhi, where an important convocation of the *Dharma Sangh* was celebrated.

Svāmī Karpātrī organized at Lahore a four day long meeting which opposed the idea of the creation of Pakistan. More branches of *Dharma Sangh* and schools were established in Panjab and in Kashmir, where Svāmīji performed the Amarnath pilgrimage, facing the cold and a hailstorm with a minimum of warm clothing, continuing the march despite bad health. A *Dharma Sangh* meeting took place at Srinagar on 25th July 1943, and the General Assembly at Amritsar. Proceeding with his pilgrimages, Svāmī Karpātrī organized a *Dharma Sangh* week, with circumambulations, rituals, prayers and meetings, and delegations were sent to the government. From the 30th of January to the 9th of February 1944, the third General Assembly of the *Dharma Sangh* took place at Delhi, with the organization of Vedic and Sanskrit studies, committees for the protection of the cow and a *mahāyajña* (great sacrificial ritual).

According to his disciples, the struggles of Svāmī Karpātrī for world peace and Indian independence were unique, because they were closely attuned to spirituality. He organized many rituals and *mahāyajña*s, like at Kanpur (April 1944) and notably at Banaras (November 1944), with the participation of thousands of pandits offering ghee and grain to a hundred fires constructed for the occasion. After these events, Svāmī Karpātrī's popularity within traditional circles grew immense. However, this popularity never reached the modernized and anglicized Indian society, nor the people interested in Hinduism outside India. This was so because he spoke and wrote only in Sanskrit and Hindi, and never accepted any compromise with reformism, which was then much in vogue.

To keep Sanskrit studies out of government control, Svāmī Karpātrī organized *Dharma Sangh Shiksha Mandala* (schools) in

Banaras, Bithur, Churu, Muzaffarpur, Amritsar Vidisha, as well as in Delhi and Bihar. In order to send representatives of *sanatāna dharma* to the government, he founded a political party, the *Akhil Bharatiya Sanatan Dal*, as well as a youth organization, the *Dharamveer Dal*, and a women organization, the *Mahila Sangh*. In 1946, the Muslim League gave the command of 'Direct Action' to force the partition of India. This resulted in a veritable genocide of Hindus in the state of Bengal. Hearing about these massacres, and about widespread forced conversions, Svāmī Karpātrī went to the affected regions to heal the hearts of the Hindus, helping in the rehabilitation of families, and declaring that whoever would pronounce the name of Lord Rāma with a pure heart would be accepted back as Hindus.

In 1947, when the almost inevitability of the partition of India was becoming evident, Svāmī Karpātrī launched a *satyagraha*, in the Gandhian way, on a religious platform. On 26 April 1947, he inaugurated a 'combat for *dharma*' (*dharmayuddha*) in front of the Assembly. His five-point demands were as follows: India should remain undivided; cow slaughter should be stopped; legislation that is irreligious should be repealed; the sanctity of temples should be safeguarded; the system of governance should be in tune with the principles of the Scriptures. He was arrested and kept in the same cell of the Lahore jail in which Bhagat Singh, a nationalist martyr, had been incarcerated in the past. He was jailed from the 28th of April to the 22nd of May 1947. His movement continued in Mathura and Delhi, were he was imprisoned six months after the independence of India; he thus became the first political prisoner of independent India.

Mahātmā Gāndhī was assassinated in January 1948. Svāmījī, who was his political adversary but not his enemy, publicly expressed his distress. Following a disciple of Svāmī Karpātrī, the principal differences between Svāmīji and Gāndhījī were about the partition of India: Svāmīji was totally opposed; Gāndhījī, finally, accepted the partition. Svāmī Karpātrī was asking the total ban of cow slaughter; Gāndhījī stressed serving the cow more than its protection and believed that laws are not instrumental in serving the cow. Svāmī Karpātrī wished to create an equitable and just society while safeguarding the fourfold division of Hindu society; Mahātmā Gāndhī believed that the caste division is the root of untouchability and his preservation would be the ruin of religion. Svāmī Karpātrī wanted to secure the acceptance of Hindu scriptures for deciding the validity or otherwise of laws, as is done in the case of Muslims and Christians; Gāndhījī had granted freedom to Muslims and Christians to decide the validity of the legislation according to the *sharia* and the *Bible*, respectively, but did not accept the idea of allowing the Hindus to use their scriptures to the same purpose.

From the 19th of February to the 24th of July of that year, Svāmījī was again imprisoned in accordance with the Public Safety Act. During his incarceration, he started to write his famous work *Marksvāda aur Rāmrājya* (the Marxist theory and the Kingdom of Rāma), comparing Marxism and the Kingdom of Rāma, the ideal political regime in traditional Hinduism. Again, he resumed his pilgrimages to awaken people against cow slaughter and the *Hindu Code Bill* of the Nehru government. This new code was meant only for the Hindus, whose rules for marriage, divorce, inheritance and the like were deeply modified, whereas the Muslims continued to be ruled by their own traditional code.[10] Karpātrījī analysed the situation in a book called *Hindu Code Bill — Pramāṇa kī Kasauṭī par* (The Hindu Code Bill in the Light of Proofs), and challenged the man behind the law, B.R. Ambedkar, then Minister of Justice, to a public debate.[11]

---

[10] See C. Jaffrelot: "The Prime Minister [J. Nehru] wanted to reform Hindu custom so as to conform it to Western Law [...], but the *Hindu Code Bill* provoked such a hostility among the most conservative Hindu circles that Nehru had to fraction it [...]. It is true that the Hindu's virulence also arose from the fact that only Hindus [...] were subjected to the *Hindu Code Bill*, whereas the *sharia* remained the Personal Law of Muslims, and Parsis also retained their own law. Nehru did not want to irritate the minorities for whom their personal law was the base of their identity." *in* "La plus grande démocratie du monde à l'heure du système congressiste", *l'Inde contemporaine de 1950 à nos jours*, under the direction of Christophe Jaffrelot, Editions Fayard, Paris, 1993, p. 27.

[11] Ramachandra Guha, *India after Gandhi. The history of the world's largest democracy.* Macmillan Picador, 2007, pp. 231-232.

In 1949-1950, he started a new political party, the *Ram Rajya Parishad*, which became the political wing of the *Dharma Sangh*. The *Ram Rajya Parishad* differed from every other party, including those that pretended to defend Hinduism, in that it was totally in accord with traditional Hindu *dharma*. The *Ram Rajya Parishad* presented 300 candidates at the General Elections of 1952;[12] four obtained a seat at the Lok Sabha (Parliament of India), around fifty were elected at the Vidhan Sabha (regional parliament) in Rajasthan and several in Madhya Pradesh as well.

In 1953, after the demise of Svāmī Karpātrī's guru Svāmī Brahmānanda Saraswatī, who did not clearly appoint a successor, a dispute arose as to whom should be the next *śaṅkarācārya* of Jyotirmaṭha. Svāmī Śāntānanda claimed the post, but Svāmī Karpātrī, several disciples of Brahmānandajī and the other *śaṅkarācāryas* considered him unfit for the position and consecrated Svāmī Kṛṣṇa-bodāśrama as *śaṅkarācārya*. Svāmī Karpātrī, who was widely considered as the most deserving candidate, had declined the post.

In 1954-1955, Svāmī Karpātrī organized large demonstrations against the *Hindu Code Bill*. In 1957, more than 6000 young *dharmveers* (champions of *dharma*) that had arisen across India at the call of Svāmījī were imprisoned. In the month of July, the police *laṭhī*-charged 95,000 demonstrators in front of the Chandigarh Secretariat, resulting in the injury of many, including the president of the *Ram*

---

[12] See C. Jaffrelot: "The first general elections (1951-1952) were for Nehru an occasion for campaigning, in his public meetings, against 'communalism' — a term that designates the chauvinism of religious communities [...]. Nehru, influenced since his youth by the Fabian Society, and undoubtedly also by the Soviet model, tried to engage India in a socialist way. On his initiative, the Congress Party voted in 1955 at the Avadi session a resolution promoting the evolution of the country towards a 'socialist model of society'; later in 1959, at the Nagpur session, the party adopted a resolution planning the creation of a system of agricultural cooperatives inspired on the Chinese experiences. These measures did not have much continuation, mainly because of the reluctance of the Congress barons." "La plus grande démocratie du monde à l'heure du système congressiste", *l'Inde contemporaine de 1950 à nos jours*, sous la direction de Christophe Jaffrelot, Editions Fayard, Paris, 2e édition, 2006, p. 36.

Rajya Parishad Svāmī Svarūpānand Sarasvatī (presently the *śaṅkarācārya* of Jyotiṣpīṭha and Dvārakā Śaradāpīṭha). Later, Svāmī Karpātrī organized in Kanpur a large conference, the *Sarva Vaidika Shakha Sammelana*, to which were invited many scholars from India and abroad, with the purpose of revitalizing *dharma* and fighting the growing threats of materialism, communism and secularism. Also in 1957, Svāmī Karpātrī had a public debate with a Russian communist ideologist; unable to answer some questions on the incompleteness of the communist doctrine, this one promised to send written responses, which he never did.

Svāmī Karpātrī had always criticized the reformism of the *Āryā Samāj*, a deeply reformist organization which did not accept many Hindu tenets such as the *Purāṇas*, etc., and often challenged its thinkers to public debates. He especially opposed their rejection of funeral rites. The *Āryā Samāj* only saw a loss of time and money in post-mortem rituals, of great importance according to Hindu *dharma* for the posthumous destiny of beings. Equally, the traditional *varṇāśrama* (the ancient Indian social organization[13]) represented for Svāmīji the expression of a state of fact: the fundamental inequality not only among human categories, but also between these, animals and plants, and the necessity of intelligent compensations to these inequalities instead of their negation. In the same way, following

---

[13] See, in *L'Inde contemporaine*, the conclusion of a very interesting analysis by Jacquie Assayag of the 'caste system' after the independence of India: "In fact, caste functions as well among the traditionalists than among the modernists, Christians or Muslims. In spite of the anti-caste rhetoric of the politicians and intellectuals [...] caste can today play a democratic role [...]: to defuse the homogenizing forces of fundamentalism in their fascist aspects." *Op. cit.*, 1993, p. 392. Fifty years after the independence of India, this scientific analysis confirms that the *varṇāśrama*, often despicably called 'caste system', considered by Nehru and several leaders of the Congress Party in the fourties as an obsolete weight of the past, remains today an element who protects Indian society against the tyrannical tendencies of the modern concepts of state, specially Marxist, Socialist or Fascist concepts. The analysis quoted here helps to understand why the fundamentalists of the *Jana Sangh* and the R.S.S. were (and are) opposed to the traditional *varṇāśrama* which was supported from 1950 only by the political party founded by Svāmī Karpātrī, the *Ram Rajya Parishad*.

here an oral explanation given by Dr. Girish C. Tiwari [14] "as the surgeon respects certain rules when he prepares the operation theatre which are not the same as those that a housewife does when she receives some guests, the priests follow some purifications and precise rules of life to approach the divinities in the temples which cannot be imposed upon other categories of the people". Svāmī Karpātrī contested the right of the secular state to interfere in religious matters. This is why, followed by a large number of ascetics and *paṇḍits* of Kāśī, he energetically protested when, on February 19, 1954, with the support of the police, the locks of the Viśvanātha Temple in Varanasi were broken and a delegation of harijans (former untouchables), led by Hindu reformists, having openly challenged the priests of the temple on this matter, burst into the *garbhagṛha* (*sanctum sanctorum*).

Following again the *Karpātra Jīvanajāhnavī* (*op. cit.*), Svāmī Karpātrī and his followers were once more imprisoned, this time as per the Untouchable Offence Act. The orthodox continued their movement until December 11, 1957, when the Court finally gave its verdict in favour of the harijans. Here, it is to be remarked that Svāmī Karpātrī had several untouchable disciples to whom he had given *dīkṣā* (initiation). A year later, on 15th December 1958, he declared the old temple to be polluted and consecrated a New Kāśī Viśvanātha Temple at Mir Ghat.

According to a *saṃnyāsin* close to Svāmī Karpātrī's thought: "Svamiji did not want discriminatory behaviour towards the scheduled castes and in his heart he was their well-wisher. He believed that the scriptures have prescribed measures for the well being of all living beings and in accordance with their rights (talent-capability-ingrained nature) have laid down their duties. It is only through this that the genuine welfare of various peoples can come about."

"If a doctor were to say that it is beneficial for a newborn to suck a sugarcane, the parents of the baby will not straightaway put sugar-

---

[14] Disciple of Svāmī Karpātrī and translator of the present edition of *Liṅgopāsanā rahasya*.

cane into its mouth but rather would place cane juice or a sweet made from it. According to the scriptures those born in the lowest castes receive the same religious benefit by merely looking at the apex of a temple from outside as the brahmins etc. receive by performing worship inside it. Therefore he believed that the *sanctum sanctorum* of the Lord inside temples ought to be safeguarded and only the priests authorized by tradition be allowed to enter it, and the rest of the people should have *darśana* only from outside. This would ensure the safety of the icon, the safety of the objects inside the *sanctum sanctorum*, and prevent inconvenience to the people. It is a fact worth remembering that in India there are numerous temples where by tradition Brahmins function as priests and there are also many temples where, again by tradition, dalits and harijans have been officiating as priests historically. He used to say that we should adhere to the local tradition of each temple in such matters."

"Some people spread the propaganda that Karpātrījī was 'averse to harijans', by giving a political twist to this crystal clear and established belief, and they engineered the forced entry of Harijans into the Viśvanāth Temple. They tried to prove that Karpātrījī was anti-Harijan but Svāmījī continued to speak his mind clearly. He established the new Viśvanāth Temple in which even to this day the traditional system of worship and *darśana* is in vogue and no one is discriminated against."

According to S. Sinha and B. Sarasvati, Svāmī Karpātrī gave in this occasion a series of long interviews where "he admitted that the wheel of change had been set in a motion which nobody can stop; social change is inevitable, but the task before him is not to change or compromise but to maintain the core values of *Sanātana Dharma*."[15]

Though this action is difficult to understand in the present context, fifty years later, we have to keep in mind the historical general context of this time, in which the biggest neighbour leaders of India, as Stalin

[15] Surajit Sinha and Baidyanath Saraswati, *Ascetics of Kashi, An anthropological exploration*, Bose Memorial Foundation, 1978, pp. 208-209.

and Mao Zedong were destroying by force, in a bloody way, the traditional values of Russia and China. These leaders — now recognized murderers of millions of their own people — were then seen by many intellectuals and politicians as heroes of freedom and justice. In a less extreme way, the socialist Nehru government was hostile to traditional Hindu religion and had no problem in interfering and attacking it in every possible way.

The same year, according to the *Karpātra Jīvanajāhnavī,* was finished *Marksvāda aur Rāmrājya*, followed by the second volume of *Veda kā Svarūpa aur Prāmāṇya* (1960) (The Nature and Authority of the *Veda*), *Veda Prāmāṇya Mīmāṃsā* (1961) (Inquiry in the Authority of the *Veda*), and *Ahamartha aur Paramārthasāra* (1962) (The Meaning of the Ego and the Essence of the Supreme Principle).

The harmony of all creatures

The harmony between all creatures, their mutual goodwill and compassion, is one of the politico-religious slogans composed by Svāmī Karpātrī: *prāṇiyoṃ meṃ sadbhāvanā ho!* On 18th October 1962, he led a protest march from Akola to Bombay demanding the closure of a slaughterhouse. He was accompanied by *dharamveer*s and he organized a signature and telegram campaign asking for prohibition of cow slaughter. At Meerut in 1964, the then Prime Minister of India, Gulzari Lal Nanda (who was proclaimed temporarily Prime Minister of India after the demise of J. Nehru), came to the general convention of the *dharamveer*s and of the *Ram Rajya Parishad* in the presence of several *śankarācārya*s and gave his assurance that a solution would quickly be found on this matter. On the 7th of November 1966 in Delhi Svāmī Karpātrī led a peaceful demonstration of the 'All-Party Committee for the Protection of the Cow' (*Sarvadaliya Goraksha Mahabhiyan Samiti*), gathering close to one million people. Some agitators tried to sabotage the movement; the police charged and many *sādhus* were wounded, and a few even died from their injuries. Svāmī Karpātrī was again imprisoned for six months. In the Tihar Jail, he was attacked by a group of criminals with metal sticks, and he suffered serious injuries on his head and elsewhere.

Svāmījī wrote several books during that period: *Vedasvarūpa-vimarśaḥ* (Consideration about the Nature of the *Veda*) in 1969, and the next year *Rāṣṭriya Svayaṃsevaka Saṃgha aur Hindū Dharma* (The Union of the National Volunteers and the Hindu *Dharma*), to show that the *Rashtriya Svayamsevak Sangh* (R.S.S.), a nationalist movement that used Hinduism as an identity mark and a political weapon, did not respect the principles of traditional Hinduism. As usual, Svāmī Karpātrī invited his adversaries to publicly debate on the question, but the challenge was not accepted. In 1973 Svāmīji wrote *Caturvarṇya Saṃskṛti Vimarśa*, then *Śrī Vidyāratnākara,* where he described the cult of Goddess Tripurasundarī in the *śrīvidyā* tradition. The same year, after the demise of Svāmī Kṛṣṇabodhāśram, Svāmī Svarūpānanda Sarasvatī[16] was consecrated *śaṅkarācārya* of Jyotirmaṭha in a ceremony conducted by Svāmī Karpātrī in the presence of other *śaṅkarācāryas*.

In 1975, he published *Vicāra Pīyūṣa* (The Nectar of thoughts), an important philosophical and political answer to *Vicāra Navanīta* (The Fresh Butter of Thoughts) by Golwalkar, the leader of the R.S.S. Then, to show his disagreement with *From Sex to Samadhi* by Rajneesh, the popular modern guru and self-proclaimed Bhagwan — 'God'— (later called Osho), he wrote a book called *Kyā Saṃbhoga se Samādhi Sambhāva Hai?* (Is it possible to go from Sex to Samadhi?). In 1977, an important literary work *Rāmāyaṇa Mīmāṃsā* (Investigation on the *Rāmāyaṇa*) clarified some mistakes in the book of Father Kamil Bulke on the *Rāmcaritmanas.*

According to a disciple of Svāmī Karpātrī, Reverend Father Kamil Bulke, in his research work *Rāma-Kathā, Uttpatti Aur Vikāsa*, 1950, had put forth many theses that betray an attempt to demolish the actual beliefs of Hinduism: Śrī Rāma is not an incarnation of Viṣṇu; in the *Rāmāyaṇa*, many places mentioned therein are incapable of being

[16] H.H. Svāmī Svarūpānanda Sarasvatī is the author of the preface of this book.

located; *Rāmāyaṇa* is not authentic history but rather a bundle of fantasies; the ten heads of Rāvaṇa, the jumping across the ocean by Hanumān, His swallowing of the sun, Kumbhakarṇa's sleeping for six months, the appearance of gods like Indra to grant boons, Sītā's ordeal by fire, these are all flights of fantasy. Svāmījī disproved these misguided ideas with the help of rational debate and scriptural evidence, to which end he gave references from as many as 684 texts.

The year 1978, Svāmī Karpātrī was honoured by the Chancellor of the Sampurnanand Sanskrit University, Varanasi, with the honorary degree of *vācaspati*.

In 1979, the Mahārājā of Banaras presented his book *Vedārtha Parijāta* (The Jasmine Flower of the Meaning of the Veda) to the public. The same year, Svāmī Karpātrī established an institute for Vedic research (*Veda Śāstrānusandhāna Kendra*) at Kedarghat, Varanasi, and supported the *Ram Rajya Parishad* candidates at the 1980 elections in Uttar Pradesh, Delhi and Rajasthan. In spite of his poor health, he participated in the Kumbha Melā at Hardwar in April 1980. He continued his activities and travels throughout the country until 1981, when during a discourse in Kanpur, he felt a strong pain in his ear. He understood it as a call from the Lord and asked to be brought to Kashi. In the Hindu tradition, death in Kashi is believed to bring immediate release (*mukti*). For a whole year, he stayed in his *maṭha* in Kedarghat, suffering several ailments. He accepted only ayurvedic remedies and strictly refused all allopathic medicines.

On the 7th February 1982, at 9 a.m., surrounded by his close disciples and devotees, Svāmī Karpātrī breathed his last breath while chanting "Śiva, Śiva, Śiva". For the whole of the next day, his body was exposed at the Town Hall, where *lakhs* of people gathered for his last *darśana*. A day later, on the 9th February, his body, covered with flowers, was submerged in the Gaṅgā (*jalasamadhi*) at Kedarghat by the *śaṅkarācārya*s of Jyotirmaṭha and Puri.

Svāmī Karpātrī displayed an exceptional activity to fight in defence of *dharma*, surrendering all his talents as a scholar, writer, speaker and organizer to the service of this cause. The motives of Svāmī Karpātrī were not personal. He lived all his life in a very frugal way, and he refused any possession, power, or honour, even declining the post of *śaṅkarācārya* when it was repeatedly offered to him. His exceptional qualities emerged from his saintliness; his intelligence, his memory, his qualities as an organizer in the social and political fields, the intellectual heroism that he displayed to defend the traditional values during a century that did not doubt its right to attack and destroy them. Given the frame of time, his capacity of resistance, his energy in the ideological war of the 20th century, the dimensions of his literary work (as the author of about forty books) seem really providential — to the point that many people do not hesitate to compare him to the great Śaṅkarācārya, who also gave a new life to Hinduism at a particularly critical moment of its history; furthermore, many also consider him an *avatāra* of Śiva.

At the most critical times of its history, India has never failed to produce exceptional saints (*mahāpuruṣa*) who have showed the way and brought their teachings and grace to give a new life to *sanātana dharma*. The years before and after Independence (1947) were indeed critical as it was the period when the vision of the new post-colonization India was being born. Many politicians wanted the new country to blindly follow the way of its colonizers, and reformers of every shade wanted to change the traditional religion so as to make it 'compatible' with the modern world that the British represented. The new ideologies of Capitalism, Socialism and Communism seemed to be the new *dharma*, which would — one or the other — very soon conquer the whole world, while the old *dharma* seemed to be only an outdated obstacle in the way of progress.

At this historical juncture, Svāmī Karpātrī gave a new life to the old tradition by reaffirming its eternal principles and instilling new confidence in its elites and representatives. From the beginning, the tradition of the *ṛṣi*s, the oldest among the living traditions of the world, has always sustained Indian civilization and made her so remarkably long-lived.

The saintly character of Svāmī Karpātrī, who was called *dharma saṃrāṭ*, Emperor of Dharma, is still today very much remembered, particularly at Varanasi, among all social strata, even the most humble. People recall that once, as he came back to the sacred city after having organized a large *yajña* at Calcutta (now Kolkata), many Muslims were also keen to participate in his reception, and constructed a welcome gate for him.

Twenty five years after the demise of Svāmī Karpātrī, Indian society has considerably changed and some of Svāmījī's views are difficult to understand; but several of his preoccupations seem much more actual; the ecological situation in the world, the pollution of rivers and oceans, the disappearance of animal species, the social conflicts between human communities and religions, the destruction of family groups, social links, cultural and religious roots, the psychological condition of aged persons, the number of lonely, uprooted and alienated people who can find no sense in life — in fact the lack of '*dhārmika*' values in the western model of global civilization spreading actually in the world — are considered urgent and very important problems by an ever more growing number of intellectuals.

The problem of Alain Daniélou's translations

The first English translation of any of Svāmī Karpātrī's works was made by Alain Daniélou, who translated nine of his articles in the 1940's; these translations were the only ones available before the publication of the present book. Alain Daniélou (1907-1994) was a French artist and musician who, before the Second World War, took refuge in Varanasi where he remained until 1954. He learnt Hindi and Sanskrit, met Svāmī Karpātrī and published some articles in *Siddhānta* under the name of 'Shiva Sharan'. After his return to Europe, Daniélou acquired some reputation as an exponent of Hinduism and Indian music, contributing to its worldwide popularity.

Daniélou claimed that his works on Hinduism were based on traditional doctrines and especially on Svāmī Karpātrī's teachings; he published nearly thirty books related to India, on some speaking with admiration of Svāmī Karpātrī: "Svāmī Karpātrī was a wandering monk — a *saṃnyāsin* — and a man of astounding knowledge. [...] He was considered the spiritual leader of a large part of northern India [...] When he created the Dharma Sangh, a movement for the defence of Hinduism against modern trends, we had many long conversations together [...] I wrote several articles for *Siddhānta*." [17] Several of Daniélou's books, written with clarity and elegance, met with a popular reception and brisk sales. In the USA, the fourth edition of Daniélou's *Myths and Gods of India. The Classic Work on Hindu Polytheism*, from the Princeton Bollingen Series has sold 16,000 copies. More than 140 quotes of Svāmī Karpātrī are included in that book. Many westerners discovered Hinduism, India's traditional music, culture and social structures through Daniélou's teachings.

However, none of Svāmī Karpātrī's books were ever translated in the West.[18] In 1988, meeting Alain Daniélou, I suggested him to bridge this lacuna and collect his translations of Svāmī Karpātrī's articles into a single volume. Daniélou agreed to this idea and in 1992 gave me a revised English translation of three of the nine articles,[19] asking me to find a translator so as to publish a French edition. Due to the difficulties of the metaphysical vocabulary, I was unable to find a qualified translator, and finally Daniélou translated it himself. The book was published a few months before his death, under the title: Swami Karpâtri - Alain Daniélou, *Le Mystère du culte du Linga*.[20]

In 1991, I had been given by Daniélou himself the responsibility to collect and edit his numerous unpublished works, and I was working on this during my holidays. In 2002, the Alain Daniélou Centre of Rome gave me the opportunity to dedicate my full time to that task, and

---

[17] Alain Daniélou, *The Way to the Labyrinth. Memories of East and West*, New Direction Paperbooks, New York, 1987, pp. 137-138.

[18] If we don't take into account the well-known *The Lamp of Non-dual Knowledge* (*Advaita Bodha Dipika*), which is only attributed to him.

[19] The three articles were: "The Inner significance of Linga worship", "The Mystery of the All-powerful Goddess" and "The Ego and the Self".

[20] Swami Karpâtri - Alain Daniélou, *Le Mystère du culte du Linga*, Editions du Relié, Robion, France, 1993.

between 2003 and 2006, I edited five posthumous books of Daniélou.[21]

But in 2004, while I was living in Varanasi, I discovered that Daniélou had committed a significant mistake concerning Svāmī Karpātrī, an error which was published in several of his books:[22] according to him, the Svāmī had created the political party *Jana Sangh*, even though the party that Svāmī Karpātrī founded, the *Ram Rajya Parishad*, was opposed to this very *Jana Sangh*. I later noticed that many people in the West attributed the foundation of *Jana Sangh* to Svāmī Karpātrī based on Alain Daniélou's authority. On discussing this matter with direct disciples of Svāmī Karpātrī, who were surprised by this strange confusion by someone who claimed to know Svāmī Karpātrī's thoughts, some doubts arose concerning the quality and authority of Daniélou's translations.

Even if Svāmī Karpātrī was mainly known in India for his involvement in politics, I was mostly interested in his person not as politician but as a scholar and a sage of the highest level. Even so, it was on my responsibility to clear the political mistake done by Danielou, and I published in 2004 a first clarification,[23] then a second one in 2007, with more historical precisions.[24] I still had not forgot-

[21] Oeuvres posthumes d'Alain Daniélou, collection 'Les Cahiers du Mleccha' dirigée et présentée par Jean Louis Gabin, Editions Kailash, Paris-Pondichéry, France and India, vol. I, *Origines et Pouvoirs de la Musique* (2003, 2006); vol. II, *La Civilisation des différences* (2003, 2005); vol. III, *Shivaïsme et Tradition primordiale* (2004, 2006); vol. IV, *Approche de l'hindouisme* (2005, 2007); vol. V, *Yoga, Kama, le Corps est un temple* (2006). English editions: *Sacred Music, its Origins, Power and Future*, Indica Books, Varanasi, India, 2003; *India, a Civilization of Differences*, Inner Traditions International, Rochester, USA, 2005; *Shiva and the Primordial Tradition*, Inner Tradition International, 2007.

[22] Alain Daniélou, *A Brief history of India*, Inner Traditions International, 2003, p. 315, and *The Way to the Labyrinth*, A New Directions Books, New York, 1987, pp. 139, 152, 185, 219.

[23] "Une erreur a redresser" and "Portraits de Swami Karpatri", *in* "L'orthodoxie d'Alain Danielou", postface to *Approche de l'Hindouisme* by Alain Daniélou, Editions Kailash, Paris-Pondichéry, 2004, pp. 203-210.

[24] "Swami Karpâtri et le vrai visage de l'hindouisme traditionnel", postface to the 2nd edition of *Approche de l'Hindouisme* by Alain Daniélou, Editions Kailash, Paris-Pondichéry, 2007, pp. 181-202.

ten the project of publishing in a single volume Alain Daniélou's translations of Svāmī Karpātrī's works; for this I had collected with some difficulties the nine translated articles. I was preparing their edition under the title: *The Ego and the Self and Other Essential Writings*. I began then to compare the various Daniélou's translations. Immediately, huge discrepancies among them became apparent, sometimes considerably modifying the sense of the text. For example, in "The Inner Significance of Linga Worship", the term '*liṅga*', which appears as such in the 1941's translation, is later frequently replaced by 'phallus' or by 'sexual organ', which can cause the reader to think that this was Svāmī Karpātrī's interpretation. As an example of different English versions published by Daniélou:

A SENTENCE OF SVĀMĪ KARPĀTRI TRANSLATED BY DANIĒLOU IN 1941 AS:	BECAME IN *THE HINDU POLYTHEISM / MYTHS AND GODS OF INDIA* IN 1964:
"A life spent without worshipping the *liṅga* of Śiva is a source of misfortunes; while its worship brings everything; worldly pleasure (*bhukti*) as well as liberation (*mukti*)."	"Those who do not recognize the divine nature of the phallus, who do not measure the importance of the sex-ritual, who consider the act of love as low or contemptible or as a mere physical function, are bound to fail in their attempts at physical as well as spiritual achievement. To ignore the sacredness of the *liṅga* is dangerous, whereas through its worship the joy of life (*bhukti*) and the joy of liberation (*mukti*) are obtained." (Karpātrī, 'Liṅgopāsanā-rahasya').[25]
Journal of the Indian Society of Oriental Art, Calcutta, India, vol. IX, 1941, p. 71.	*The Myths and Gods of India*, Inner Traditions International, Rochester, USA, 1991, p. 227.

[25] The same sentence, attributed to Svāmī Karpātrī, can be found on several Internet sites, as www.tantra.co.nz/lingam/lingampuran.htm

Clearly, there had been changes as well as transpositions in the second and third versions of Daniélou's translation (the first for *Siddhānta* in the 40's, a second one of some quotations from his books, published as *Hindu Polytheism* in the 60's, and the third, a revised edition of three of the *Siddhānta* articles in 1992). At that point, some important questions arose: Why did Daniélou make these additions and changes? Was it to better express the thought of Svāmī Karpātrī? Was his first translation accurate or not? The only way to know the truth was to compare Daniélou's translations with the original articles in Hindi. With great efforts, I finally managed to obtain the original "*Liṅgopāsanā Rahasya*" and a reprint of "*Śrī Bhagavatī Tattva*" as it appeared in *Siddhānta*.[26]

Dr. G.C. Tiwari, a direct disciple of Svāmī Karpātrī, agreed to check the translation of the "*Liṅgopāsanā rahasya*" and, despite the fact that I had only begun to learn Hindi three years before, I also took part in this work. Very soon, we discovered several biased translations — as the singular 'deity' replaced by the plural 'deities' [27] — and transpolations; some paragraphs were arranged differently, falsely emphasizing some sentences and minimizing others. But, above all — to my utter stupefaction — some sentences had been completely omitted by Daniélou, even within some key points of the original reasoning of Svāmī Karpātrī. Finally, the five last pages concluding the article were totally omitted.

Regarding the revised English translation made by Daniélou at the end of his life, more manipulations, twists and inaccurate expressions are revealed when we compare with the 1941 translation and with the original in Hindi. As an example, in the following table, the words omitted by Daniélou appear in bold between brackets, and the additions in italics:

---

[26] "Liṅgopāsanā rahasya", in *Siddhānta*, Kāśī, year II, 1941, n° 20-21, pp. 153-156 & 163-166; "Śrī Bhagavatti Tattva", *in Siddhānta*, Kāśī (Varanasi), year V, 1945, n° 47, pp. 242-278. These articles had been collected in *Bhakti Sudhā*, Sri Radhakrishna Dhanuka Prakashan Samsthan, Kolkata- Delhi-Vrindavan, 4nd Ed., 2003, pp. 74-81 &162-200.

[27] See *infra* p. 61, note 17.

Version 1:Journal of Indian Society of Oriental Art, n° IX, p. 55 (in bold between brackets: sentence omitted by Daniélou)	Version 2: English revised translation done by Daniélou in 1992 and published in French in *Le Mystère du Culte du Linga*, p. 77-78 (in italics: modifications or additions; in bold between brackets: sentences omitted)
"The pleasure and love which is found in things prohibited by religion ('*shastras*') is a fault and should be given up. ***[Useful is that virtuous (puṇya) bliss and love found in things supported by śāstra.]*** But that pleasure and love which is immaterial, free from contingencies, truly belongs to the supreme spirit." [28]	"Pleasure and love found in what is forbidden by *ethics* should be *avoided.* ***[Useful is that virtuous (puṇya) bliss and love found in things supported by śāstra.]*** *As a general rule*, pleasure and love ***[which is unconditioned, free from contingencies]*** *draw us closer to the divine.*" [29]

Other sentences left out by Daniélou were of this type: "Because spiritual and supernatural topics are described within the *Vedas* and the *Purāṇas* in a worldly language, sometimes ignorant people (*ajña*) think that these therefore imply something indecent."[30] Also omitted were several passages concerning the essentiality of the inseparability of Śiva and Śakti.[31] Sometimes, in a single page, a set of similar sentences were eliminated by Daniélou: "It would be a great offence to consider *liṅga* and *yoni*, that are forms of Śiva-Śakti, as merely the worldly penis and vulva, the fleshy organs of urination";[32] "Could

[28] See *infra* p. 61 and notes 18-20.

[29] French version: "Le plaisir et l'amour que l'on trouve dans les choses interdites par la *morale* sont à *éviter. En principe,* le plaisir et l'amour [***immatériels, libres de toute contingence***,] nous *rapprochent du divin.*" *Le Mystére du Culte du Linga*, op. cit., p. 77-78.

[30] See *infra* p. 73 note 43.

[31] See *infra* pp. 57 note 3, 69 note 32, 105 note 85, 107 note 86.

[32] See *infra* p. 85 note 73.

an ordinary *liṅga* be able to roam the various worlds, having fallen and burst into flames? And would Viṣṇu, Rāma, Kṛṣṇa and all the gods and *munis* worship a mere worldly *liṅga* or *yoni*? [33] "Could a worldly *yoni*, a urinary organ, a scrap of leather, support the *jyotirliṅga*, made of fire, that burns everything?" [34] "Therefore it is ignorance to say that, in these and other passages of the Scriptures, the word '*yoni*' denotes the urinary organ", [35] and so forth.

The completely censured five last pages concluding *Liṅgopāsanā rahasya* totally refute Daniélou's main theories about Śaivism's relationship with Hinduism. Some paragraphs of Svāmī Karpātrī, very surprising for a Daniélou reader, underline the final identity between Śiva and Viṣṇu or Śiva and Śakti: "Viṣṇu [is] considered to be [Śiva's] inner essence [....]. In fact Śiva and Viṣṇu are one — as [shown in] the image of Harihara." [36] "The same Lord, having taken the form of Śakti, is called Caṇḍikā, the fearful Goddess." [37]

Daniélou always claimed to represent the point of view of Śaivism, a Śaivism which excluded Visnu and even Śakti. Independently of the correctness of his views from the Śaiva tradition — and a Śaivism without Śakti does not make any sense — he cannot in any case shelter his opinions under the authority of Svāmī Karpātrī, as the present book makes clear enough.

If, following Svāmī Karpātrī, the different gods are the various aspects of the same reality, this denies a characterization of Hinduism as ultimately 'polytheistic'. Svāmī Karpātrī insists on this matter — as to reply to western opinions expressed by Danielou: "Agni, Vāyu, Mātariśvan — and so on — are the various names of the same reality." [38] After having quoted several *ślokas*, Svāmījī adds: "In these

---

[33] See *infra* p. 95 note 74.

[34] See *infra* p. 97 note 76.

[35] See *infra* p. 99 note 78.

[36] See *infra* pp. 121-123. It can be noted that the very *saṃnyāsa* name of Svāmī Karpātrī, Hariharānanda, points to this identity of both deities.

[37] See *infra* p. 123.

[38] See *infra* p. 117.

passages of the *Śruti* (*Vedas*), it is said that the Absolute (*parabrahman*), the Supreme Self (*paramātman*) is none other than Hara (Śiva)."[39] As opposed to Daniélou's presentation of Hinduism, Svāmī Karpātrī demonstrates, in the line of most of Hindu tradition, and specially of *Advaita Vedānta*, that the different 'gods' are only various aspects of the same divine reality.

Another point underlined several times by Svāmī Karpātrī — and omitted by Daniélou — concerns the theory presenting Śiva as a 'non-Aryan' god. Svāmī Karpātrī emphatically refutes this theory which interprets the history — and therefore the religion — of India as divided between that of the Aryans, supposed to have brought Vedism from outside, and of the original non-Aryans inhabitants whose religion would have been Śaivism. Explaining the importance of Śiva-Rudra in the *Vedas*,[40] Svāmī Karpātrī expresses opinions totally opposed to those of Daniélou: "Śiva is frequently claimed to be non-Aryan. However, in the *Vedas*, Śiva-Rudra has been given an important stature."[41] Then Svāmī Karpātrī quotes several passages of the *Ṛg*, *Yajur* and *Atharva Vedas*, *Taittirīya Āraṇyaka*, and the like,[42] which were never mentioned by Daniélou. Svāmī Karpātrī concludes his article thus: "So, what is the basis of saying that the worship of Lord Śiva was taken from non-Aryans?"[43]

A further matter developed in these omitted pages is the error of confusing Śiva and *tamas*: "There are no *tāmasika* ingredients amongst those implements for a Siva *pūjā* used by Vedic priests";[44] "To say that Śiva is [merely] god of *tamas* is great foolishness";[45] "Lord Śiva is the controller of *tamas*; he is not within the power of *tamas*".[46] In fact, the conclusions drawn by Svāmī Karpātrī in this article seem especially written to refute Daniélou's main assertions about Śaivism.

---

[39] See *infra* p. 105 note 83.

[40] See *infra* pp. 117-119. This prominent presence of Śiva-Rudra in the *Vedas* is denied in all Daniélou's books.

[41] See *infra* p. 113.

[42] See *infra* pp. 113-115.

[43] See *infra* p. 125.

[44] See *infra* p. 121.

[45] See *infra* p. 121.

[46] See *infra* p. 121.

The same subject is discussed by Svāmī Karpātrī in a passage of the article, "*Śrī Bhagavatī Tattva*", of which Daniélou translated only the first sentence, omitting the very clear reasoning of Svāmī Karpātrī: "Destroying affliction, protecting life and building strength: these are the respective functions of Śiva, Viṣṇu and Brahmā. Of course, all three are characterised purely with *sattva*; that is why in Śaivite *Purāṇas* even Śiva is known as being replete with *sattva* (*sattvamaya*). *Śaivas*, *vaiṣṇavas* and *śāktas* all consider their respective chosen deity (*iṣṭadeva*) to be the original principle. When the original principle is defined as 'complete omniscience', then it is said to be of a *sāttvic* nature. Since it is devoid of the camouflage represented by the three *guṇas* and is thereby free from their effect, it is then also called *nirguṇa* (non-qualified)." [47]

Daniélou omitted forty percent of the text of "*Śrī Bhagavatī Tattva*" — though it is true that he presented it as an 'adapted translation'. Sometimes the passages left out were sophisticated demonstrations of logic presenting difficulties of comprehension and translation, as Dr. G. Pellegrini explains hereafter.[48] However, sometimes, a few words omitted would have been easy to understand and translate, as this remark in the beginning of a paragraph: "Monotheism (*ekeśvaravāda*) is universally accepted".[49] Alain Daniélou, who became famous with his *Hindu Polytheism* and was known to be a passionate opponent of monotheism, edited out only these four words when translating this page, and never mentioned this opinion of Svāmī Karpātrī, which manifests in fact the practically unanimous current of Hindu thought which, while recognizing many gods (*devatās*), clearly point to their final unity and can be thus designated both as polytheistic and monotheistic — as much as these Western concepts make sense in Hindu thought. Furthermore, the order of the paragraphs was completely rearranged in a very personal patchwork.

---

[47] See *infra 'The icon secret'*, p. 273 note 280.

[48] About *The refutation of Śakti* and *The confirmation of Śakti*, see *infra* p. 335 note 36.

[49] See *infra* p. 229.

Daniélou's translation reflects the original text as a mirror broken into many pieces reflects a landscape. All the reasoning of Svāmī Karpātrī disappears, and what remains are 'tales',[50] 'myths' and 'gods' [51] designated by decorative names — like '*Śiva, The Lord of Sleep*', '*Sarasvati, the Lady of the Lake*',[52] — always colourful, but often wrong.

Daniélou always presented his theories of pre-Aryan Śaivism, his portrayal of Śiva as opposed to Viṣṇu and his undervaluation of the latter, of Śiva as a 'God of love and ecstasy', a 'God of *Tamas*', and his characterisation of Hinduism as exclusively polytheistic, as if these views were taught in traditional Hinduism and were specifically the thoughts of Svāmī Karpātrī — whose teachings he always claimed to have brought to and exposed for the West.

"When I was introduced to Hindu mythology," wrote Daniélou, "it seemed like an incomprehensible jungle. I tried to grasp the significance of the different gods, their relationship to cosmological theories on the nature of the world. I asked the Swami [Karpātrī] many questions, which he answered in writing in a series of articles published by *Siddhānta*. It was on the basis of these questions and articles that I later wrote my book *Hindu Polytheism*." [53] If it was indeed the case, it seems that Daniélou, blinded by his own personal convictions, refused to accept many of Svāmī Karpātrī's clarifications.

Daniélou lived in Varanasi for fifteen years, and became involved to a certain extent in Hindu tradition; he claimed that he had been initiated into Śaivism.[54] But he was apparently not able to understand that personal opinions have no place in traditional thought, which is transmitted in an interrupted chain from master to disciple (*guru-śiṣyaparamparā*); in this view the first requirement is the respect of

[50] See *infra* 'The first deed', p. 333 note 240.

[51] *Myths and Gods of India* is the title of one of the most famous Daniélou's books.

[52] See *JISOA* XIII, 1945 pp. 142, 143, 158, 170.

[53] Alain Daniélou, *The way to the Labyrinth. Memories of East and West*, New Direction Paperbooks, New York, 1987, p. 138.

[54] *Id., ibid.*

the thought of the *guru*. By falsifying Svāmī Karpātrī's thought and attributing to him his own biased views, Daniélou is responsible for the undeserved notoriety and false reputation of such a great *saṃnyāsin*, considered by some scholars, especially in the USA, as a "tantric teacher and practitioner" whose "conjunction of unorthodox erotics and a Hindu nationalist theory of history can be found, further transmuted, in the writings of his disciple, the French Indologist Alain Daniélou."[55]

For many years I was a follower of Alain Daniélou, then an editor of his posthumous books. I always believed him to be a reliable and authoritative exponent of Hinduism, which he claimed to know to a greater depth than academicians and other commentators. His presentation of Hinduism as a non-dogmatic and joy-seeking religion — in which debates on any subject seemed to be permitted — appealed to me, as it did to many other westerners, unhappy with the dogmatic and almost exclusively moralistic modern Christian religion. Being a specialist on French poetry, I was particularly interested by several facts given by Daniélou about *Sāṃkhya*, the nature of languages and universal correspondences, which were in harmony with the theories of Baudelaire and Rimbaud.[56]

Because of Daniélou's books I came to India, where I had the chance to teach French Literature for ten years. As I have mentioned above, after Daniélou's death I continued to edit his unpublished works, for which I also wrote the introductory prefaces. When the Alain Daniélou Centre gave me the opportunity to dedicate all my time to Daniélou's unpublished writings, I came to Varanasi, seeking the roots of Daniélou's knowledge. In the course of this work, the discovery of the historical truth about the *Jana Sangh* was the first shock for me: was it an involuntary mistake perpetrated by Daniélou? But how an author writing a *History of India* could make such a

[55] Lawrence Cohen, *No Aging in India*, Berkeley, University of California press, USA, 1998, p. 201.

[56] See: Jean-Louis Gabin, "Light on *Samkhya* and Poetry", appendix of Alain Daniélou, *Shiva and the primordial Tradition*, Inner Tradition International, 2007, pp. 107-115.

blunder? Later, while editing Daniélou's translations of Svāmī Karpātrī's articles for their publication, I was directly confronted — beyond any doubt — with his many inaccuracies and distortions.

It appears that from the outset in 1941, the translations of Daniélou twisted — and even in several places expunged and inverted — the thoughts of Svāmī Karpātrī. In his 1964 and 1992 revisions, Daniélou added many more interpolations — his own personal opinions presented as translations — and omitted more passages.

Bewildered and confounded, I remembered then with pain several Daniélou's assertions and claims: "After India became independent, Swami Karpatri created a political movement, the Jana Sangh (people's assembly)[57] [...] When the political war waged by the Jana Sangh grew more intense, Swami Karpatri advised me to return to Europe and try to educate people on the basic principles of Hinduism. Being a foreigner, I could not take part in the political struggle of India [...] Swami Karpatri ordered Brahmanand [Daniélou's Hindi teacher] to perform my initiation rites as well as [Daniélou's friend] Raymond's. He and I, it seems, are the only foreigners who were initiated and incorporated into orthodox Hinduism."[58]

Everyone is free to hold his own opinions about everything. But one cannot attribute them to venerable people so as to gain credibility. After coming to Varanasi and contacting circles related to Svāmī Karpātrī, I realized that the Svāmī was still very much remembered and respected as a champion of traditional Hinduism. These people were shocked to hear about Alain Daniélou's interpretations of Svāmījī's thought. I was then confronted with the painful responsibility of making Alain Daniélou's distortions known to the public and dis-

[57] "Throughout the years that preceded and followed the independence of India, I lived in the *milieu* where was founded the Jana Sangh, the Hindu traditional party, in whose birth I participated. The point of view that I express is therefore that of a generally ignored majority, as all sources of information proceed either from Europeans or from English-educated Indians." Alain Daniélou, backcover of *Histoire de l'Inde*, Fayard, Paris, 2nd edition, 1985.

[58] Alain Daniélou, *The Way to the Labyrinth. Memories of East and West*, op. cit. pp. 138-139.

owning the editions I had made of Daniélou's works and the prefaces that I had written for them.

A new translation and an annotated bilingual edition

After these disclosures, there was no question of publishing Alain Daniélou's translation. Svāmī Karpātrī being known in the West only through Daniélou and his numerous quotations and references to his works,[59] I considered it necessary to publish a new translation, a fresh bilingual edition of Svāmī Karpātrī's articles with annotations, to clearly establish the truth and exonerate Svāmījī's thought from Alain Daniélou's misinterpretations.

I therefore present here, besides the original text in *devanāgarī*, two articles: "*Liṅgopāsanā rahasya*", mainly translated by Dr. G.C. Tiwari, and "*Śrī Bhagavatī Tattva*", largely translated by M.V. Mehra. The two translations were discussed in Varanasi by Swami Avimukteshvaranand Sarasvati, Shri Avinash Chandra and myself. Some of the Sanskrit *ślokas* and the philosophical chapters of "*Śrī Bhagavatī Tattva*" were especially translated and enriched with substantial notes by Dr. Gianni Pellegrini (*Vedāntācārya* from the Sampurnananda Sanskrit University of Varanasi), in collaboration with Paṇḍita Prof. Shri Narayana Mishra. Dr. G. Pellegrini also made a final revision of the whole translation. The notes dealing with Danielou's omissions, mistranslations and interpolations (specifying the date: 1941, 1960, 1992) were written by me. My special thanks to Swami Sadananda Sarasvati, called Vedanti Swami, to Dr Om Prakash Sharma, to Mahant Sri Virbhadra Mishra ('Mahantji'), to Purnamba Devi for their help and inspiration, and to Michael Ianuzielo for his English editing.

---

[59] There are many references and quotations of Swāmī Karpātrī in the most famous Daniélou's books as *The Hindu Polytheism / Myths and Gods of India*, 1964, 1985, 1991, 2004; *Shiva and Dionysus*, 1982, 1984, 1992; *While the Gods Play*, 1987, 2003; *The Phallus, Sacred Symbol of Male Creative Power*, 1995, 2001; all books published by Inner Traditions International, USA. In these books, Daniélou spells the name of Svāmī Karpātrī as 'Karapâtra' or 'Karapâtri', as it appears in several Internet quotations based on mistranslated passages of these articles.

Most of the references offered by Svāmī Karpātrī were given without the support of any book, being part of his immense learning. So it was very difficult to us to trace them. Only several passages were identified by us.

Independently of the notes about Daniélou's translation, I hope this edition of two Svāmī Karpātrī's articles — out of a huge literary production — will have a great appeal for persons with a deep interest in *Sanātana dharma*, and will, to an extent, make known to the public the figure of the learned Svāmī.

Translated for the first time in full, the brilliant expositions of one of the greatest metaphysicians of the Twentieth century concerning the mysteries of *liṅga* worship and the importance of the Great Goddess in Hinduism appear at last as they are in Hindi: masterful developments, emphasizing the correspondences between different gods and different texts, *Vedas*, *Purāṇas* and *Tantras*; in remarkable passages, the traditional schools of philosophy, *Vedānta*, *Nyāya*, *Mīmāṃsā* and the great epics *Mahābhārata* and *Rāmāyaṇa* are put in relation in a comparative approach, questioning the origin and the meaning of the universe in connection with the human destiny. Taking into account the differences of time, place and style, the name of the divine Plato often comes to the mind when confronted with such lucid reasoning in which the fertile questions of a lover of truth — the quest of *philo-sophia* — enter in awakened dialogue with the reader in the banquet of the spirit.

The English language has taken an ever-growing place within India since Independence — to the detriment of the sanskritized Hindi used by Svāmī Karpātrī, full of terms with dense meaning — to the point that the original texts are often not comprehensible to later generations brought up with a modern education. May this first English and Hindi book of one of the greatest souls of the Twentieth century be well received by readers and scholars, and be followed by subsequent translations of his works.

Jean Louis Gabin

लिङ्गोपासना-रहस्य

THE SECRET OF LIṄGA WORSHIP

लिङ्गोपासना-रहस्य

सर्वाधिष्ठान, सर्वप्रकाशक परब्रह्म परमात्मा ही ''शान्तं शिवं चतुर्थम्मन्यन्ते'' इत्यादि श्रुतियों से शिवतत्त्व कहा गया है । वे सच्चिदानन्द परमात्मा अपने आप को ही शिवशक्तिरूप में प्रकट करते हैं । वह परमार्थतः निर्गुण, निराकार होते हुए भी अपनी अचिन्त्य दिव्य लीलाशक्ति से सगुण, साकार सच्चिदानन्दघनरूप में भी प्रकट होते हैं । वही शिव-शक्ति, राधाकृष्ण, अर्द्धनारीश्वर आदि रूप में प्रकट होते हैं । सत्ता के बिना आनन्द नहीं और आनन्द के बिना सत्ता नहीं । ''स्वप्रकाश सत्तारूप आनन्द'' ऐसा कहने से आनन्द की वैषयिक सुखरूपता का वारण होता है, सत्ता को आनन्दरूप कहने से उसकी जड़ता का वारण होता है । जैसे आनन्दसिन्धु में माधुर्य्य उसका स्वरूप ही है, वैसे ही पार्वती शिव का स्वरूप किंवा आत्मा ही है । माधुर्य्य के बिना आनन्द नहीं और आनन्द के बिना माधुर्य्य नहीं । दूसरी दृष्टि से

सर्वयोनिषु कौन्तेय मूर्तयः संभवन्ति याः ।
तासां ब्रह्म महद्योनिरहं बीजप्रदः पिता ॥ (गीता)

समस्त प्राणियों में जितनी वस्तुएँ उत्पन्न होती हैं, उन सबकी योनि अर्थात् उत्पन्न करनेवाली माता प्रकृति है और बीज देनेवाला शिव (लिङ्ग) पिता मैं हूँ । अर्थात् मूलप्रकृति और परमात्मा ही उन-उन

The Secret of Liṅga Worship

As the Vedas (*śruti*) tell us, the substratum[1] of everything, the light which illumines everything, the Absolute Reality (*parabrahman*), the Supreme Self (*paramātman*) is the Auspicious Essence (*śiva-tattva*): "the auspicious one, who is absolute peace, is the fourth stage" [*Māṇḍūkya Upaniṣad* 7].[2] The Supreme Self made of Being, Consciousness and Bliss manifests itself in the form of Śiva-Śakti.[3] This Absolute reality (*paramārtha*) is beyond qualification (*nirguṇa*) or form (*nirākāra*), but through its inconceivable divine power of enactment (*divyalīlāśakti*) it appears with qualifications and forms as an entity of Being, Consciousness and Bliss. It is He who manifests Himself in the shape of Śiva-Śakti, Rādhā-Kṛṣṇa, Ardhanārīśvara (the Lord who is half-woman) and others. There is no bliss (*ānanda*) other than being, and no being other than bliss.[4] By speaking of the self-illumined existential form of bliss (*svaprakāśa sattārūpa ānanda*), bliss is shown as distinct from the carnal aspect of pleasure; and by saying that being is the form of bliss, being is freed from the notion of unconsciousness. Just as sweetness is the nature of the ocean of bliss, so too Pārvatī is the form — the soul (*ātman*) — of Śiva. There is no sweetness (*mādhurya*) without bliss (*ānanda*), nor bliss without sweetness.

From another point of view:

> O son of Kunti, whatever forms are born from all the wombs,
> Of them the great sustainer is the womb; I am the father who deposits the seed. [*Bhagavad Gītā* XIV.4] [*5*]

That is, the Universal Womb from which all creatures issue, which is the mother of all, is Prakṛti [*6*] and I am the father, Śiva — the *liṅga* [*7*] —

Numbers sending to endnotes about Alain Daniélou's previous translations — written by Jean Louis Gabin — are set in italics; those of explicative notes — written by Gianni Pellegrini —are signalled by being set in regular or Roman type.

माता-पिता (योनिलिंग) रूप में उन-उन मूर्त्तियों (वस्तुओं) का उत्पादन करते हैं । जैसे लोक में प्रजोत्पादन की कामना से प्राणी नारी में गर्भाधान करता है, वैसे ही "**एकोऽहं बहुः स्यां, प्रजायेय**" इत्यादि श्रुतियों के अनुसार एक ब्रह्मतत्त्व ही प्रजोत्पादन या बहुभवन की कामना से प्रकृति में गर्भाधान करता है । "**सोऽकामयत**" यह प्रजा की सिसृक्षारूप काम ही प्राथमिक आधिदैविक काम है । इसी काम द्वारा प्रकृतिसंसृष्ट होकर भगवान् अनन्त ब्रह्माण्ड को उत्पन्न करते हैं । यह काम भी भगवान् का ही अंश है—"**कामस्तु वासुदेवांशः**" (भागवत) ।

लोक में भी प्रेम, काम या इच्छा का मुख्य विषय आनन्द ही है । सुख में साक्षात् कामना और उससे अन्य में सुख का साधन होने से इच्छा होती है, इसीलिए आनन्द और तद्रूप आत्मा निरतिशय, निरुपाधिक परप्रेम का आस्पद है, अन्य वस्तुएँ सातिशय, सोपाधिक अपर प्रेम के आस्पद हैं । कान्त को कान्ता की कामना, उसको सुखाभिव्यञ्जक अतएव सुखमय समझ कर ही होती है । कामना या तृष्णा से व्यथित हृदय में स्वरूपभूत आत्मानन्द का प्राकट्य नहीं होता । परन्तु, अभिलषित कान्ता की प्राप्ति होने पर क्षणभर के लिए वह तृष्णा निवृत्त हो जाती है, बस तभी अन्तर्मुख किञ्चित् शान्त मन पर आत्मानन्द का प्राकट्य होता है । परन्तु आत्मा में ही आनन्द है अथवा आनन्दाभिव्यञ्जक तृष्णा की निवृत्ति में, इसको तो विवेकी ही जानता है, अविवेकी तो आत्मा के स्वरूपभूत आनन्द को नहीं समझता । तृष्णानिवृत्ति को भी आनन्दाभिव्यञ्जक नही समझता, किन्तु तृष्णानिवर्त्तक सुन्दरी कान्ता में ही आनन्द मानता है । अतएव, उसी की पुनः तृष्णा करता है और फिर कान्ताप्राप्ति की तृष्णारूपव्यथा की निवृत्ति से आनन्दित होकर फिर उसी को चाहता है । विवेकी समझता है कि यद्यपि कान्ताप्राप्ति के अनन्तर आनन्द होता है, तथापि कान्ता साक्षात् आनन्दरूप नहीं

who gives the seed. This means that it is the Primeval Nature (*mūla prakṛti*) united with the Supreme Self (*paramātman*) who, like a mother and father — *yoni* and *liṅga* —, give birth to everything that exists. In the world, living beings inseminate females when they desire progeny; in the same way, according to such words of the Vedas as "I am one, for creation let me be many" [*Taittirīya Upaniṣad* II.6], the Supreme Principle (*brahmatattva*), with the desire of multiplicity, fecundates Prakṛti. "He desired" [*Taittirīya Upaniṣad* II.6, *Bṛhadāraṇyaka Upaniṣad* I.2.4, 6-7]; this desire, which takes the shape of a wish to create, is the primary divine desire (*adhidaivika kāma*). United to Prakṛti by this desire, the Supreme Being gives birth to innumerable worlds. This desire is also a part of God. "Desire is a portion of Vāsudeva" (*Bhāgavata Purāṇa*).

Similarly, in the world, the fundamental concerns of love (*prema*), desire (*kāma*) or volition (*icchā*) are nothing else than bliss (*ānanda*).[8] It is evident that when arises a direct aspiration towards happiness, and identifying in something different the means to fulfil this, there is the desire; for this very reason, bliss (*ānanda*) and the Self who is bliss-natured is the repository seat of the absolute, limitless, supreme love, and the other things are the object of relative, limited, lower love.[9] The [10] desire of the lover for the beloved makes him think her to be the means to, and nature of, his happiness. The Self does not show itself in its own form of bliss when the heart is tormented by desire or longing. However once the desire for the lover is fulfilled, for a moment that longing is completely suppressed; so, in the mind somewhat introverted and pacified appears the bliss of the Self.[11] However, only the sage (*vivekin*) knows that only in the Self bliss is found, or in the cancellation of longing is bliss revealing, but those who are unable to discriminate (*avivekin*) don't understand that the Self is bliss itself. They believe that bliss, which destroys longing, is within a beautiful lover. Thereafter, again and again they desire her and when possessing her they experience the destruction of the anguish of desire — that is bliss — and so they wish for her always. But the discriminating ones understand that even if there a sort bliss following

है, किन्तु तृष्णानिवृत्ति, मनःशान्ति से आत्मा का ही आनन्द प्रकट होता है। आनन्द के प्रति कान्ता दूरतः कारण है, सो भी आनन्दजनकत्व या आनन्दमयत्व की भ्रान्ति से। जैसे विष के प्रभाव से कटु निम्ब में मिठास प्रतीत होती है, वैसे ही भ्रान्ति या मोह के प्रभाव से मांसमयी कान्ता में आनन्द का भान होता है। परन्तु, इसके अतिरिक्त शुद्ध आनन्द या आत्मा में जो प्रेम, आनन्द, कामना है वह तो स्वाभाविक है, आत्मा का अंश ही है।

प्रेम, आनन्द, रस यह सभी आत्मा का स्वरूप है। रसरूप आनन्द से ही समस्त विश्व उत्पन्न होता है, अतः सबमें उसका होना अनिवार्य है। इसीलिए जिस तरह सोपाधिक आनन्द और सोपाधिक प्रेम सर्वत्र है ही, उसी तरह कान्ता भी सोपाधिक आनन्दरूप कही जा सकती है। अतएव वह सोपाधिक प्रेम का विषय भी है। परन्तु निरुपाधिक प्रेम तो निरुपाधिक आत्मा में ही होना ठीक है। जैसे सत् के ही सविशेष रूप में अनुकूलता, प्रतिकूलता, हेयता, उपादेयता होती है, निर्विशेष तो शुद्ध आत्मा ही है, वैसे ही सविशेष आनन्द और प्रेम में भी हेयता, उपादेयता है।

सुन्दर, मनोहर देवता और तद्विषयक प्रेम आदि उपादेय हैं, सुन्दरी वेश्यादि की आनन्दरूपता और तद्विषक प्रेम हेय है। जैसे अतिपवित्र दुग्ध भी अपवित्र पात्र के संसर्ग से अपवित्र समझा जाता है, वैसे ही आनन्द और प्रेम भी अपवित्र उपाधियों के संसर्ग से दूषित हो जाता है। शास्त्रनिषिद्ध विषयों में आनन्द और प्रेम दोष है, हेय है। शास्त्रविहित विषयों में आनन्द और प्रेम पुण्य है, उपादेय है। परन्तु, निर्विशेष, सर्वोपाधिमुक्त प्रेम, आनन्द तो स्पष्ट आत्मा या ब्रह्म ही है।

the possession of the lover, nevertheless the woman is obviously not bliss itself. Still the bliss of *ātman* surely is found in a mind calmed by the destruction of desire.[12] We can consider that woman is only a quite remote cause of bliss and she is only erroneously thought to be a source of bliss or being herself bliss. Just as, under the influence of poison, one finds sweet taste in the bitter leaves of the *nīm* tree, similarly it is under the influence of error (*bhrānti*) or attachment (*moha*) that one sees bliss in a carnal beloved.[13] But, apart from that, the love, the joy, the desire (*kāmanā*) found in the soul is pure bliss, is a part (*aṃśā*) of *ātman*[14] — this is why the non-dual Self (*advaita ātman*) is the repository of unconditioned love; but, there, there is no difference between the object and the receptacle of love.

Love,[15] bliss and enjoyment (*rasa*) are all the essence of the Self (*ātman*). All this universe has arisen precisely from this blissful taste (*rasarūpa*); thus, inevitably, it is in everything. For this, as this type of conditioned (*sopādhika*) bliss and conditioned love are surely everywhere, in the same way, it can be said that a woman is a conditioned form of bliss. Thus, she can also be the object of that conditioned love. However, unconditioned love (*nirupādhika*) ought to remain within the unconditioned *ātman*. Just as in the qualified form of the pure reality there are the approval, the rejection, the possibility to reject it and to hold it, the pure Self, instead, is unqualified, and so the qualified bliss and love can be rejected or held.[16]

Beautiful and charming is the deity,[17] and our love for Him is fruitful, while the pleasure arising from beautiful prostitutes, etc. is harmful and their love is to be rejected. Just as the purest milk kept in contact with an impure pot is known to be polluted, so too do bliss and love acquire impure characteristics from contact with depravity (*dūṣita*). The bliss and love found in things prohibited by Scriptures (*śāstra*)[18] is flawed (*doṣa*) and should be rejected. Useful is that virtuous (*puṇya*) bliss and love found in things supported by *śāstra*.[19] But that bliss and love which is unconditioned, free from contingency, is truly the soul (*ātman*) and the Absolute (*brahman*). In spite of this caveat, every one of these are bliss and love.[20] Love, which is part of

इतने पर भी आनन्द और प्रेम सभी हैं । आत्मा के ही अंश अपवित्र विषय के दूषण से ही कामिनी आदि विषयक प्रेम को काम या राग आदि कहा जाता है, देवताविषयक प्रेम को भक्ति आदि कहा जाता है । सजातीय में ही सजातीय का आकर्षण होता है । बस यह आकर्षण ही प्रेम या काम है । कान्ता कान्त दोनों ही में रहनेवाले तत्तदवच्छिन्न रस या आनन्द में ही जो परस्पर आकर्षण है, वही काम है ।

समष्टि ब्रह्म का प्रकृति की ओर झुकाव आधिदैविक काम है । परन्तु जहाँ शुद्ध, सच्चिदानन्दघन परब्रह्म का स्वरूप में ही आकर्षण होता है, किंवा आत्मा का अपने ही अत्यन्त अभिन्न स्वरूप में ही जो आकर्षण या निरतिशय, निरुपाधिक प्रेम है, वह तो आत्मस्वरूप ही है । यही राधाकृष्ण, गौरीशङ्कर, अर्द्धनारीश्वर का परस्पर प्रेम, परस्पर-आकर्षण है और यह शुद्ध प्रेम ही शुद्ध काम है । यह कामेश्वर या कृष्ण का स्वरूप ही है । अनन्त ब्रह्माण्ड में विस्तीर्ण कामबिन्दु मन्मथ है । अनन्तब्रह्माण्डनायक का प्रकृति मे वीर्याधान का प्रयोजक कामसागर साक्षान्मन्मथ है । परन्तु, सौन्दर्य-माधुर्यसार-सर्वस्व, निखिलरसामृतमूर्त्ति कृष्णचन्द्र का जो अपनी ही स्वरूपभूता माधुर्य्याधिष्ठात्री राधा में आकर्षण है, वह तो साक्षान्मन्मथमन्मथ ही है । उनका पूर्णतम सौन्दर्य ऐसा अद्‌भुत है कि उन्हें ही विस्मित कर देता है । काम उनकी पदनख-मणि-चन्द्रिका की रश्मिच्छटा को देखकर मुग्ध हो गया । उसका स्त्रीत्व-पुंस्त्वभाव ही मिट गया, उसने अपने मन मे यह ठान लिया कि अनन्त जन्मों तक भी तपस्या करके व्रजाङ्गनाभाव प्राप्त कर श्रीकृष्ण के पद-नख-मणि-चन्द्रिका का सेवन प्राप्त करूँगा । परन्तु, यहाँ तो कृष्ण ने ही अपने स्वरूप पर मुग्ध होकर उस रस के समास्वादन के लिए ब्रजाङ्गनाभावप्राप्त्यर्थ तपस्या का विचार कर लिया । यहाँ शुद्ध आकर्षण प्रेम या काम है । सत्‌रूप गौरी एवं चित्‌रूप शिव

the soul (*ātman*), due to the flaw of impure objects, is called attachment (*rāga*) or passion (*mana*) when it is directed towards pretty women or worldly things and the like, while the love for the deity is called devotion (*bhakti*). Attraction can exist only between two homogenous things. Love or desire is only such an attraction. The mutual attraction in both lovers is only to taste that bliss (*ānanda*) which resides within the other, that is *kāma*.

The universal *kāma* (*adhidaivika kāma*) is the inclination of the all-encompassing *brahman* (*samaṣṭi brahman*) towards *prakṛti*. But when the attraction is towards the essence of the pure-natured Being-consciousness-bliss Absolute (*parabrahman*), or better, the attraction or the supreme unconditioned love of the Universal Soul for its own nature — which is in no way distinct from itself — it is the selfsame *ātman* (*ātmasvarūpa*). Hence, the mutual love, the mutual attraction of Rādhā-Kṛṣṇa, Gaurī-Śaṅkara or Ardhanārīśvara is pure love that is pure desire. The real nature of Kṛṣṇa or Kāmeśvara is precisely this. The god of Love (Manmatha) is the seed of desire (*kāmabindu*) that spreads over the infinite universe. It is Manmatha directly (*sākṣātmanmatha*), the ocean of desire, who instigates the insemination of Prakṛti by the Lord of the Countless Universes. Moreover, the attraction of Kṛṣṇa — the very embodiment of the universal essence of beauty and sweetness, the incarnation of the sweet nectar taste of infinity — for his own nature made manifest as Rādhā, the guiding principle of this sweetness, is the turbulence of the mind of Manmatha himself. His own perfect beauty is so astonishing that even he is taken aback. Kāma was fascinated, having seen the beams of light from the jewel-like crescents of his toenails. All feelings of masculinity or feminity in him were obliterated, and in his mind he resolved that he would do austerities (*tapas*), even for countless infinite lifetimes, until he would obtain the existence of a *gopī* in order to serve to the jewel-like crescent moons of his toenails. However, having already been enthralled by his own essence, Śrī Kṛṣṇa had come to the idea of performing *tapas* in order to assume the nature of a *gopī* for the purpose of fully imbibing that sensation. The relation of Śiva-

दोनों ही जब अर्द्धनारीश्वर के रूप में मिथुनीभूत (सम्मिलित) होते हैं, तभी पूर्ण सच्चिदानन्द का भाव व्यक्त होता है, परन्तु यह भेद केवल औपचारिक ही है, वास्तव में तो वे दोनों एक ही हैं।

कुछ महानुभावों का कहना है कि पूर्ण सौन्दर्य अपने में ही अपने प्रतिबिम्ब को अपने आप देख सकता है, भगवान् अपने स्वरूप को देखकर स्वयं विस्मित हो जाते हैं—

विस्मापनं स्वस्य च सौभगर्द्धेः ।

बस इसी से प्रेम या काम प्रकट होता है। इसी से शिवशक्ति का संम्मिलन होता है। वही शृङ्गाररस है। कामेश्वर-कामेश्वरी, श्रीकृष्ण-राधा, अर्द्धनारीश्वर वही है। पूर्ण सौन्दर्य अनन्त है, अप्सराओं का सौन्दर्य उसके सामने नगण्य है। उसी सौन्दर्य के कणमात्र से विष्णु ने मोहिनीरूप से शिव को मोह लिया। उसी के लेश से मदन मुनियों को मोहता है। वही सगुण रूप में कहीं ललिता, कहीं कृष्णरूप में प्रकट होता है—

षोडशी तु कला ज्ञेया सच्चिदानन्दरूपिणी (सुभगोदय)

नित्यं किशोर एवासौ भगवानन्तकान्तकः ॥

कभी आद्या ललिता ही पुंरूपधारिणी होकर कृष्ण बनती है, वही वंशीनाद से विश्व को मोहित करती है—

कदाचिदाद्या ललिता पुंरूपा कृष्णविग्रहा ।
वंशीनादसमारम्भादकरोद्विवशं जगत् (तन्त्रराज)

प्रकृतिपार, सौन्दर्य-माधुर्यसार, आनन्दरससार परमात्मा में भी शिवपार्वतीभाव बनता है। अनन्तकोटिब्रह्माण्डोत्पादिनी अनिर्वचनीय शक्तिविशिष्ट ब्रह्म में भी शिव-पार्वतीभाव है। उस परमात्मा में ही लिङ्गयोनिभाव की कल्पना है।

Śakti, the relation of Ardhanārīśvara and the pure attraction that is love or desire, are precisely here, within the purest, Supreme Essence[21] (*paramatattva*). Only when Gaurī who is being (*sat*) and Śiva who is consciousness (*cit*) couple [are united] in the form of Ardhanārīśvara, then the reality of the fundamental Being-Consciousness-Bliss (*saccidānanda*)[22] finds expression — however this differentiation is only apparent: in reality, both are one and the same.

It is said by some realized persons that perfect beauty can by itself see its own reflection within itself; God, seeing his own self, is amazed.

Astonishment for His own perfect beauty

In this way love or desire appears. In this way, Śiva and Śakti unite. That is the real passion of love (*śṛṅgārarasa*). Kāmeśvara-Kāmeśvarī, Śrī Kṛṣṇa-Rādhā and Ardhanārīśvara are that one. Perfect beauty is infinite; the beauty of the *apsaras* is nothing compared to it. With but a mere fragment of that very beauty, in the form of Mohinī, Viṣṇu charmed Śiva. With just a small piece of it, Madana (Kāmadeva) bewitched the *munis*. Then, in its qualified form he is revealed sometimes as Lalitā, sometimes as Kṛṣṇa.

> The sixteenth digit[23] is considered as representing Being, Consciousness, Bliss. [*Subhagodaya*][24]
>
> The Lord who kills also the death giver (Yama) is eternally a boy of sixteen (*kiśora*).

[Following the] *Tantrarāja*:

> Once upon a time the primeval[25] Lalitā, with a male-form, took the shape of Kṛṣṇa,
> And by the melody of the flute, she enchanted the universe.

Beyond Nature (*prakṛtipāra*) in the Supreme Self, which is the essence of all beauty, sweetness and pure bliss, appears the relation of Śiva-Pārvatī. In the omnipotent, indescribable *brahman* too, manifestator of infinite universes, qualified by an indescribable potency, arises the feeling of Śiva-Pārvatī. In that *paramātman* lies the imagination (*kalpanā*) of *liṅga-yoni*.[26]

निराकार, निर्विकार, व्यापक दृक या पुरुषतत्त्व का प्रतीक ही लिङ्ग है और अनन्तब्रह्माण्डोत्पादिनी महाशक्ति प्रकृति ही योनि, अर्घा, या जलहरी है। न केवल पुरुष से सृष्टि हो सकती है, न केवल प्रकृति से। पुरुष निर्विकार, कूटस्थ है, प्रकृति ज्ञानविहीन जड़ है। अत: सृष्टि के लिए दृक्-दृश्य, प्रकृति-पुरुष का सम्बन्ध अपेक्षित होता है। 'गीता' में भी प्रकृति को परमात्मा की योनि कहा गया है—

मम योनिर्महद्ब्रह्म तस्मिन् गर्भं दधाम्यहम्।
सम्भवः सर्वभूतानां ततो भवति भारत॥

भगवान् कहते हैं— महद्ब्रह्म-प्रकृति-मेरी योनि है, उसी में मैं गर्भाधान करता हूँ, तभी उससे महदादिक्रमेण समस्त प्रजा उत्पन्न होती है। प्रकृतिरूप योनि में प्रतिष्ठित होकर ही पुरुषरूप लिङ्ग विश्व का उतपादन करता है। अतएव बिना योनि-लिङ्ग-सम्बन्ध के कहीं भी किसी की सृष्टि ही नहीं होती, हाँ, यह बात अवश्य समझ लेनी चाहिए कि लोक-प्रसिद्ध मांसचर्ममय ही लिङ्ग और योनि नहीं है, किन्तु वह व्यापक है। उत्पत्ति का उपादानकरण पुरुषत्व का चिह्न ही लिङ्ग कहलाता है। दृश्य अण्डरूप ब्रह्म भी अदृश्य पुरुष ब्रह्म का चिह्न है और वही संसार का उपादान भी है, अत: वह लिङ्गपदवाच्य है। लिङ्ग और योनि पुरुष-स्त्री के गुह्याङ्गपरक होने से ही इन्हें अश्लील समझना ठीक नहीं है। गेहूँ, यव आदि में भी जिस भाग में अङ्कुर निकलता है उसे योनि माना जाता है, दाने निकलने से पहले जो छत्र होती है वह लिङ्ग है। ब्रह्मा या देवताओं के सङ्कल्प से उत्पन्न सृष्टि का भी लिङ्ग-योनि से सम्बन्ध है अर्थात् शिव-शक्ति ही यहाँ लिङ्ग-योनि शब्द से विवक्षित हैं।

उत्पत्ति का आधारक्षेत्र भग है, बीज लिङ्ग है। वृक्ष, अङ्कुरादि सभी

The symbol of the essence of *puruṣa*, the formless, the changeless pervasive witness, is exactly the *liṅga*; and the symbol of the great power, *prakṛti*, the source of the infinite universes, is none other than the *yoni*, the *arghā* or *jalaharī*.[27] There cannot be creation from *puruṣa* only, nor from *prakṛti* only. *Puruṣa* is changeless and immovable, *prakṛti* unconscious and passive. Therefore the union of the seer and the seen (*dṛk dṛśya*), of *puruṣa* and *prakṛti*, is necessary for manifestation.[28] Even in the *Gītā*, the highest reality of *prakṛti* is said to be the *yoni*.

> My womb is the great sustainer. In that I place the seed. From that, O scion of the Bhārata dynasty, occurs the birth of all things. [*Bhagavad Gītā* XIV.3] [29]

The Lord affirms: "The universal Principle (*mahadbrahman*) — *prakṛti* — is my *yoni*; into that I place the seed; then, from her, taking by succession from the universal intellect (*mahat*), etc., all the offsprings take birth (*mahadādikrameṇa*)". Only when the *liṅga*, form of *puruṣa*, is established in the *yoni*, aspect of *prakṛti*, it can manifest. Indeed, without any contact between the *yoni* and the *liṅga* nothing can be created. Without fail, this topic must be understood as not referring to the worldly meat-and-leather *liṅga* and *yoni*; still, [its scope] is extensive. It is said that the symbol of masculinity, the material cause of origination is *liṅga*. The seen, egg-shaped reality (*dṛśya aṇḍarūpa brahman*)[30] is a symbol of the invisible universal *puruṣa* [31] (*puruṣabrahman*), and indeed is the origin of *saṃsāra*; thus, this is said to be the direct meaning of the word *liṅga* (*liṅgapada*). It is not proper to think indecently about these, even if the hidden organs of man and woman can be called *liṅga* and *yoni*. Wheat also originally sprouted from such a place, which is also considered to be a *yoni*, a mushroom before the sprouting of the seed is a *liṅga*. From contact between the *yoni* and the *liṅga* comes the creation that arises from the will of Brahmā or the gods; this means that Śiva and Śakti are implied by the words '*liṅga*' and '*yoni*'.

प्रपञ्च की उत्पत्ति का क्षेत्र भग है, बीज पुरुष लिङ्ग है। जैसे दृकतत्त्व व्यापक है, वैसे ही दृश्य प्रकृतितत्त्व भी। तभी तो कभी लोकप्रसिद्ध योनि-लिङ्ग के बिना भी मानसी सङ्कल्पजा सृष्टि होती थी। कहीं दर्शन से, कहीं स्पर्श से, कहीं फलादि से भी सन्तान होती थी। कहीं भी, कैसी भी सृष्टि क्यों न हो, परन्तु वहाँ सृष्टि के उत्पादनानुकूल शिव-शक्ति का सम्बन्ध अवश्य मानना पड़ता है। वृक्ष, लता, दूर्वा, तृणादि सभी तत्त्वों की उत्पत्ति में तदुपयुक्त शिव-शक्ति का सम्बन्ध अनिवार्य है। योग-सिद्ध महर्षियों का प्रकृति पर अधिकार होता था। अतः ये सङ्कल्प, स्पर्शन, अवलोकन आदि से ही सृष्टि के उपयुक्त लिङ्ग-योनि-सम्बन्ध स्थापित कर सकते थे। प्रसिद्ध लिङ्ग और योनि ही असली लिङ्ग योनि नहीं है। किन्तु यह तो उनकी अभिव्यक्ति का स्थान, केवल गोलक है। सर्वसाधारण लोग जिसे नेत्र समझते हैं वह नेत्र नहीं है, किन्तु वह तो अतीन्द्रिय नेत्र इन्द्रिय की अभिव्यक्ति का स्थान गोलक है, इन्द्रिय उससे पृथक् सूक्ष्म वस्तु है। प्रसिद्ध नासिका या कान ही घ्राण और श्रोत्र नहीं, किन्तु यह सब तो गोलक है। घ्राण, श्रोत्र आदि इन्द्रियाँ तो अतिसूक्ष्म हैं, वे नेत्रादि के विषय नहीं हैं। फिर भी विशेषरूप से उनका इन गोलकों में प्राकट्य होता है, अतएव कभी जब इन गोलकों के ज्यों के त्यों बने रहने पर भी इन्द्रियशक्ति क्षीण हो जाती है, तब दर्शन, श्रवण, आघ्राण आदि नहीं होते। योगियों को घ्राण, श्रोण, नेत्र-सम्बन्ध बिना भी दूरदर्शन-श्रवणादि होते हैं। उसी तरह लौकिक प्रसिद्ध लिङ्ग-योनि आदि केवल गोलक हैं, उनमें व्यक्त होनेवाला योनि-लिङ्ग तो अतीन्द्रिय ही है। वैसे ही प्रजनन इन्द्रिय, वीर्य्य, रज आदि भी उसके मुख्यरूप नहीं, किन्तु उनसे भी सूक्ष्म, उनमें विशेषरूप से व्यक्त दृक्-दृश्य ही शिव और शक्ति है।

यद्वा जैसे अग्नितादात्म्यापन्न लौह-पिण्ड में दाहकत्व, प्रकाशकत्व हो सकता है, वैसे ही पुरुष-प्रतिबिम्बोपेत हो अचेतन प्रकृति चेतित

The basic field of manifestation is *bhaga* (womb), and the seed is the *liṅga*. *Bhaga* is the ground from which springs a tree, a sprout, or what have you, every manifestation; the seed is the *liṅga*, *puruṣa*. The reality of the Seer is all-pervading, so is the principle of the seen (*prakṛti*). This is why there are commonly-known cases when manifestation springs up from a mental projection without relationship between *yoni* and *liṅga*. Sons were born from a glance, from a touch, from the eating of a fruit. Nevertheless wherever and whenever there is manifestation, the relation of Śiva and Śakti is absolutely necessary. We find the essential connection of Śiva and Śakti in absolutely every aspect of manifestation, in trees, creepers, buds, grasses, and so on.[32] The great *ṛṣis*, perfected by *yoga*, could master over Nature. This means that by will, touch or look they could produce one relation similar to that of *liṅga* and *yoni* necessary for any production. The commonly known *liṅga* and *yoni* are not the real ones. On the contrary, there are only their places of manifestation, their 'seats' (*golaka*). What ordinary people believe to be the eye is not the eye, but the organ in which the invisible eye manifests itself as a sense; the subtle sense of sight is something different from it.[33] Similarly, the physical nose or ear are not the senses of smelling or hearing, but are rather the seats thereof. The senses of smelling or hearing are very subtle, they cannot be seen by the eyes. Nevertheless they are more specially manifested in these particular seats. Therefore, when the power of the faculties decreases, although there may be no change in the organs, there still will be no sight, no hearing, and no smelling. *Yogins* can see and hear from afar without any connection with their noses, ears or eyes. Similarly are the things generally considered '*liṅga*' and '*yoni*' merely organs; the *liṅga* and *yoni* which are manifested in them are invisible. And therefore the organ of procreation is not the main form, but it is the seer and what is seen which, much more subtle, are manifested in them, and which are Śiva and Śakti.[34]

Just as a piece of iron which held in the fire becomes hot and luminous, the unaware *prakṛti*, having been in contact with the reflec-

होकर विश्व का निर्माण करती है। जैसे पुरुष के सर्वाङ्गसार वीर्य्य को पाकर ही योनि सन्तान रचती है, वैसे ही पुरुष-प्रतिबिम्ब भी पुरुष समानाकार पुरुष की प्रतिकृति ही होता है, उसी से अचेतन प्रकृति में भी चेतनता का सञ्चार होता है। इधर मूर्तिपूजा का भी भाव यही होता है कि दृश्य से अदृश्य की पूजा हो। शालग्राम में विष्णु की भावना होती है। केवल काष्ठ, पाषाण, धातु की पूजा नहीं होती, किन्तु मन्त्र और विधानों की महिमा से आहूत, संनिहित व्यापक दैवततत्त्व ही मूर्ति मे आराध्य होता है। व्यष्टि के द्वारा ही प्राणियों के मन में समष्टिभाव का आरोहण होता है। अतएव, समस्त व्यष्टि लिङ्गों एवं अन्यत्र भी व्यापक शिवतत्त्व की समष्टि मूर्ति महादेव-लिङ्ग है। जैसे व्यष्टि नेत्रों का अधिष्ठाता समष्टिनेत्र सूर्य्य है, वैसे ही व्यष्टि प्रजननशक्तियों में व्याप्त शिवतत्त्व का समष्टिरूप शिवलिङ्ग है। जैसे व्यष्टि नेत्र की उपासना न होकर समष्टिनेत्र सूर्य्य की ही आराधना होती है और प्रतिमा भी उन्हीं की बनती है, वैसे ही समष्टि शिवमूर्ति की ही उपासना और प्रतिमा होती है। जैसे जाग्रत, स्वप्न की उत्पत्ति और लय सौषुप्त तम से ही होता है, वैसे ही तम से ही सबका उद्भव और उसी में सबका लय होती है। तम को वश में रखकर उसके अधिष्ठाता शिव ही सर्वकारण हैं। कार्यों को कारण का पता आद्यन्त नहीं लगता।

यह कहा जा चुका है कि समस्त योनियों का समष्टि रूप प्रकृति है, वही शिवलिङ्ग का पीठ या जलहरी है। योनि में प्रतिष्ठित लिङ्ग आनन्दप्रधान, आनन्दमय होता है। जैसे समस्त रूपों का आश्रय चक्षु, समस्त गन्धों का आश्रय-एकायतन-घ्राण है, वैसे ही समस्त आनन्दों का एकायतन लिङ्ग-योनिरूप उपस्थ है। अतएव, प्रकृतिविशिष्ट दृक रूप परमात्मा आनन्दमय कहलाता है। सुषुप्ति में भी उसी के अंशभूत व्यष्टि आनन्दमय का उपलम्भ होता है। प्रिय, मोद, प्रमोद,

tion of *puruṣa*, becomes conscious and manifests the universe. A *yoni* creates offspring after receiving semen, the essence of *puruṣa*; in the same way, the reflection of *puruṣa* is the duplicate of *puruṣa*, taking the same appearance, and only through it does a flow of consciousness spread into the unconscious *prakṛti*. The same process is found in worshipping images, that is to worship the invisible through the visible. The presence of Viṣṇu is felt in the *śālagrāma*.[35] People never worship wood, stone or metal; they worship the all-pervading divine element invoked in the image by the power of *mantras* and rites. Through a fragment, the presence of the totality is felt in the mind. Therefore the Mahādeva-*liṅga*[36] is the universal essence of Śiva (*śivatattva*) which pervades all individual *liṅgas* as well as everything else. Just as the sun is the universal eye by whose power all individual eyes see, similarly the *śivaliṅga* is the universal form of *śivatattva*, which pervades all the individual powers of generation. People do not worship individual eyes nor do they make idols of them but they do so of the Sun, the sum of all eyes;[37] similarly it is the total Śiva who is worshipped and of whom images are made. Just as wakefulness and dream spring up from and merge back into the darkness of the dreamless sleep (*suṣupti*), similarly everything arises from darkness (*tamas*) and disappears into it. Because he rules over obscurity (*tamas*) and controls it, Śiva is the universal cause. The effects do not become aware of their cause either at the beginning or at their end.

It has already been said that the collective form of the sum of all *yonis* is *prakṛti*, who is the pedestal (*pīṭha*) or water receptacle (*jalaharī*) of the *śivaliṅga*. The *liṅga* established in the *yoni* is predominantly bliss,[38] which consists of delightfulness (*ānanda-maya*).[39] Just as all forms are to be grasped by the eye, and all fragrances are so dependent on the nose — their unique seat — just so every [sexual] pleasure (*ānanda*) has its sole ground in the sex-organ (*upastha*) *liṅga-yoni*.[40] Therefore it is said that the Supreme Self, as the Seer qualified by Nature, is called 'Made of Bliss' (*ānandamaya*). We, parts of the 'bliss made', also experience a part of it in deep

आनन्द यह आनन्दमय के अवयव हैं, शुद्ध ब्रह्म इन सबका आधार है। जब अनन्तब्रह्माण्डोत्पादिनी प्रकृति समष्टि योनि है, तब अनन्तब्रह्माण्डनायक परमात्मा ही समष्टि लिङ्ग है और अनन्त ब्रह्माण्ड प्रपञ्च ही उनसे उत्पन्न सृष्टि है। इसीलिए परमप्रकाशमय, अखण्ड, अनन्त शिवतत्त्व ही वास्तविक लिङ्ग है और वह परम प्रकृतिरूप योनि-जलहरी-में प्रतिष्ठत है। उसी की प्रतिकृति पाषाणमयी, धातुमयी जलहरी और लिङ्गरूप मे बनायी जाती है।

अदीर्घदर्शी, अज्ञ प्राणी के लिए सांसारिक सुखों में सर्वाधिक सुख प्रियाप्रियतमपरिष्वङ्ग मैथुन में है। अत: उसके उदाहरण से भी श्रुतियों ने अनन्त, अखण्ड, परमानन्द ब्रह्म और प्रकृति के आनन्दमय स्वरूप को दिखलाया है। कहीं-कहीं जीवात्मा के परमात्मसंम्मिलन-सुख को इसी दृष्टान्तसुख से दिखलाया गया है—

तद्यथा प्रियया भार्य्यया सम्परिष्वक्तो नान्तरं किञ्चन वेद न बाह्यम्।
एवमेव प्राज्ञेनात्मना सम्परिष्वक्तो नान्तरं किञ्चन वेद न बाह्यम्॥

जैसे प्रियतमा के परिरम्भण में कामुक को आनन्दोद्रेक से बाह्य, आभ्यन्तर विश्व विस्मृत होता है, वैसे ही जीव को परमात्मा के संम्मिलन में प्रपञ्च का विस्मरण होता है। श्रुतियों एवं पुराणों में आध्यात्मिक, आधिदैविक तत्त्वों का ही लौकिक भाषा में वर्णन किया जाता है, जिससे कभी-कभी अज्ञों को उसमें अश्लीलता झलकने लगती है। गोलोकधाम में एक पूर्णतम पुरुषोत्तम श्रीकृष्ण ने अकेले अरमण के कारण अपने आप को दो रूप में प्रकट किया—एक श्याम तेज, दूसरा गौर तेज। गौर तेज राधिका में श्यामल तेज कृष्ण से

sleep. In the pure *brahman* rests every part of that which is of the form of bliss, as well as of [that which is of the form of] dearess (*priya*), delight (*moda*), joy (*pramoda*) and bliss (*ānanda*).[41] If *prakṛti*, who gives birth to infinite universes is the universal *yoni*, so also the Supreme Spirit who rules over these infinite universes is the universal *liṅga*, and the eggs of the infinite universes which spring forth from them are the manifestation (*sṛṣṭi*). Consequently, the indivisible, infinite *śivatattva* of supreme light is the real *liṅga*; it is established[42] in the *yoni* (*jalaharī*), which is the form of the supreme *prakṛti*. The *jalaharīs* and the *liṅgas* made of stone or metal are copies of these.

For short-sighted, ignorant beings, the sexual embrace (*maithuna*) of lover and beloved appears as the hightest of all worldly pleasures. Therefore, even the *Vedas* (*śruti*) show this example to describe the infinite indivisible supreme joy of *brahman* and *prakṛti*, the essence of which is bliss itself. Sometimes, the bliss of the individual soul (*jīva*) which unites with the Supreme Being (*brahman*) is shown to be comparable to this pleasure.

> As someone embraced with his beloved wife perceives neither inside, nor outside, so who is united with the Self, in the *prājña* condition [during the dreamless sleep] does not know anything internal or external. [*Bṛhadāraṇyaka Upaniṣad* IV.3.21].

"Like the passionate man who, in the arms of his beloved, forgets the world, both internal and external, the soul (*jīva*) when it unites with the Supreme Self (*paramātman*) forgets all worldly matters" (*Bṛhadāraṇyaka Upaniṣad*). Because spiritual and supernatural topics are described within the *Vedas* and the *Purāṇas* in a worldly language, then, sometimes, ignorant people (*ajña*) think that these therefore imply something indecent.[43] Because the perfect (*pūrṇatama*) absolute Supreme Being (*puruṣottama*)[44] Śrī Kṛṣṇa was alone[45] in his world (Kṛṣṇa's sphere, *golokadhāma*), he manifested himself in two forms, one of black light, the other of white light. The white light, Rādhikā, was inseminated by the black light, Kṛṣṇa, and from this arose the Golden Embryo (*hiraṇyagarbha*) in which is predominant the

गर्भाधान होने पर महत्तत्व, प्रधान, हिरण्यगर्भ उत्पन्न हुए। यह भी प्रकृति-पुरुष के संयोग से महत्तत्वादि प्रपञ्च की उत्पत्ति रूपक से कही गयी है।

इसी को यों भी समझ सकते हैं— जाग्रत, स्वप्न के अभिमानी विश्व, तैजस और विराट, हिरण्यगर्भ ये सभी सावयव हैं। किन्तु सर्वलयाधिकरण ईश्वर निरवयव है, वह माया से आवृत होता है। अविद्या के भीतर ही रहनेवाला तो जीव है, परन्तु जो '**अत्यतिष्ठद्दशाङ्गुलम्**', के सिद्धान्तानुसार अविद्या का अतिक्रमण कर स्थित है, वही ईश्वर है। निरावरण तत्त्व शिव है। ईश्वरभाव माया से आवृत और शिवभाव अनावृत है। माया जलहरी है और उसके भीतर आवृत ईश्वर है, जलहरी के बाहर निकला हुआ शिवलिङ्ग निरावरण ईश्वर है। जिसका पृथक्-पृथक् अङ्ग न व्यक्त हो, वह पिण्ड के ही रूप में रहेगा। सुषुप्ति में प्रतीयमान विशिष्ट आत्मभाव का सूचक पिण्डी है। शिव के सम्बन्धमात्र से प्रकृति स्वयं विकाररूप में प्रवाहित होती है। इसलिए अर्घा गोल नहीं, किन्तु दीर्घ होता है। लिङ्ग के मूल मे ब्रह्मा, मध्य में विष्णु, ऊपर प्रणवात्मक शङ्कर हैं। लिङ्ग महेश्वर, अर्घा महादेवी हैं—

मूले ब्रह्मा तथा मध्ये विष्णुस्त्रिभुवनेश्वरः।
रुद्रोपरि महादेवः प्रणवाख्यः सदाशिवः॥
लिङ्गवेदी महादेवी लिङ्गं साक्षान्महेश्वरः।
तयोः सम्पूजनान्नित्यं देवी देवश्च पूजितौ॥ (लिङ्गपुराण)

Universal Intellect. This can also be called the union of *puruṣa* and *prakṛti*, from which arose first the Universal Intellect and then the worldly forms.[46]

It can also be understood in the following way. The consciousness identified with the waking and dream conditions, which is called *viśva* and *taijasa* [in the individual realm], *virāṭ* and *hiraṇyagarbha* [in the universal realm], these all are composites. But the Lord — into whom everything merges — is not composite; He is veiled by *māyā*. All living beings dwell in ignorance (*avidyā*), but according to the doctrine of *atyatiṣṭhaddaśāṅgulam* ("He overpasses it by the breadth of ten fingers") [*Ṛgveda* X.90.1],[47] that which exists beyond ignorance is God (*īśvara*). The unveiled principle is Śiva. The condition of God (*īśvarabhāva*) is veiled by *māyā* and the condition of Śiva (*śivabhāva*) is unveiled.[48] *Māyā* is the water vessel (*jalaharī*), and within it is *īśvara* enclosed. The *śivaliṅga* which comes out of the *jalaharī* is *īśvara* unveiled. Of that, wherein separate parts might not be evident, it will keep this appearance, of a formless mass (*piṇḍa*). The shapeless form (*piṇḍin*) of the *liṅga* purportedly represents the distinctive nature of the *ātman* when in deep sleep (*suṣupti*). With a mere touch of Śiva, Prakṛti itself drifts into a modified form[49] (*vikāra*). That is why the water vessel[50] (*arghā*) is elongated and not round. At the root of the *liṅga* resides Brahmā, in the middle Viṣṇu and in the upper portion Śaṅkara (Śiva) of the nature of *AUM* (*praṇava*). The *liṅga* is the supreme God, the *arghā* is the supreme Goddess.

> At its root is Brahmā, in the middle Viṣṇu, the Lord of the Triple Sphere,
> Above is Rudra, the Great Lord called Praṇava (*AUM*), who is Sadāśiva.
> The basement of the *liṅga* is the Great Goddess, and the Great God himself is the *liṅga*.
> By worshipping daily both of them [*liṅga-yoni*], the Goddess and the Lord are worshipped. [*Liṅga Purāṇa,* I.73.19-20]

चैतन्यरूप लिङ्ग सत्ता और प्रकृति से ही ब्रह्माण्ड बना। उनके सहारे ही वह लय की ओर जा सकेगा। अर्थात् शुद्ध मोक्ष के लिए उसी के द्वारा पहुँचना होगा।

यद्वा प्रणव में अकार शिवलिङ्ग है, उकार जलहरी है, मकार शिवशक्ति का सम्मिलित रूप समझ लिया जाता है। शिवब्रह्म का स्थूल आकार विराट-ब्रह्माण्ड है, ब्रह्माण्ड आकार का ही शिवलिङ्ग होता है। निर्गुण ब्रह्म का बोधक होने से यही ब्रह्माण्ड लिङ्ग है। अथवा उकार से जलहरी, अकार से पिण्डी और मकार से त्रिगुणात्मक त्रिपुण्ड कहा गया है। अथवा निराकार के आकाशरूप आकार, ज्योति:स्तम्भाकार तथा ब्रह्माण्डाकार आदि सभी स्वरूपों में शक्तिसहित शिवतत्त्व का ही निवेश है। सर्वरूप, पूर्ण एवं निराकार का आकार अण्ड के आकार का ही होता है। मैदान में खड़े होकर देखने से पृथ्वी पर टिका हुआ आकाश अर्द्ध अण्डाकार ही मालूम होता है। पृथ्वी के ऊपर जैसे आकाश है, वैसे ही नीचे भी दोनों को मिलाने से वह भी अण्डाकार ही होगा। आत्मा से आकाश की उत्पत्ति है, यही निराकार का ज्ञापक लिङ्ग उसका स्थूल शरीर है। पञ्चतत्वात्मिका प्रकृति उसकी पीठिका है। आकाश भी अमूर्त्त और निराकार होने से विशेषरूप से तो प्रत्यक्ष होता नहीं, फिर भी वह कुछ है ऐसा ही निश्चय होता है। उसी का सूचक भावमय गोलाकार है। शिवब्रह्म निराकार होता हुआ भी सब कुछ है, निर्विशेष ही सर्वविशेषरूप होता है। चिदाकाश में भी इसी तरह शिवलिङ्ग की भावना है। इसी अण्डाकार रेखा से सब अङ्क उत्पन्न होते हैं। यही किसी अङ्क के आगे आकर उसे दशगुनी अधिक करता है।

ज्योतिर्लिङ्ग का स्वरूप इस तरह समझना चाहिए—

The Universe — the Egg of Brahmā — was created precisely by *prakṛti* and the supreme *liṅga*, which is consciousness; only through them can it be destroyed. In other words, the pure liberation (*śuddha mokṣa*) will be attained through them.

It is also been understood that in the *praṇava AUM*, the letter '*A*' is the *śivaliṅga*, '*U*' the *jalaharī* (*yoni*) and '*M*' is the united form of Śiva and Śakti. The vast Universe (*virāṭ brahmāṇḍa*) is the gross appearance of *śivabrahman*; the *śivaliṅga* is the very form of the universe (*brahmāṇḍa ākāra*). The universe is a sign (*liṅga*), thereby through it the *nirguṇa brahman* can be known. Otherwise, it is said that the letter *U* means the water vessel (*jalaharīyoni*), the letter *A* is the aniconic form (*piṇḍin*) and the letter *M* the three horizontal lines [drawn on one's forehead, which represent] the essence of the three fundamental tendencies (*guṇas*). Be it the manifestation of the formless as space, the appearance of the pillar of light (*jyotirliṅga*), or the manifestation of the universe (*brahmāṇḍa*), the fundamental identity of everything is that of the *śivatattva* abiding with Śakti. The manifestation of the absolute, of the totality, of the formless, has the appearance of an egg. If we stand on a field, the sky seems to have the shape of half an egg, sticking up out of the ground. The sky below the earth having the same shape, both together would have the shape of one egg. Ether (*ākāśa*) arose from the Universal Soul (*ātman*); hence its gross body is the *liṅga*, and through it the formless can be known. Its pedestal is Nature (*prakṛti*) made of five elements. Ether is imperceptible, having no appearance and no form. Nevertheless, there still is some proof to ascertain its existence. One empty existent object indicates it. The principle Śiva is formless; its indicator too is an empty positive entity. Even if it is formless, it is everything; having no characteristics, it is the sum of all characteristics. In the ether of the consciousness (*cidākāśa*) we have to meditate in this way on the *śivaliṅga*. All numbers have arisen from this egg-shaped sign. Thus, when this shape is placed after any number it multiplies it by ten.

The nature of the *liṅga* of light (*jyotirliṅga*) ought to be understood in this way:

नासदासीन्नो सदासीत्तदानीं नासीदजो न व्योमापरो यत्
।(ऋ० ८ ।७ ।७)

न सन्न चासच्छिव एव केवलः ।

अर्थात् पहले कुछ भी नहीं था, केवल शिव ही था ।

सर्वे निमेषा जज्ञिरे विद्युतः पुरुषादधि ।
नैनमूर्ध्वं न तिर्य्यञ्चं न मध्ये परिजग्रभन् ॥

उसी से विद्युत् पुरुष और फिर उससे निमेषादि काल-विभाग उत्पन्न हुए । वही विद्युत पुरुष ज्योतिर्लिङ्ग हुआ, उसका पार, आदि, अन्त, मध्य कहीं से किसी को नहीं मिला । वही "**तदण्डमभवद्धैमं सहस्रांशुसमप्रभम्**" (मनु०) है । अर्थात् सूर्य के समान परम तेजोमय अण्ड उत्पन्न हुआ ।

तल्लिङ्गसंज्ञितं साक्षात्तेजो माहेश्वरं परम् ।
तदेव मूलप्रकृतिर्माया च गगनात्मिका ॥ (शिवपुराण)

ब्रह्माण्डपिण्ड सप्तावरण प्रकृतिरूप योनि से आवृत-परिवेष्टित है । 'शिवपुराण' में लिङ्ग शब्द की व्युत्पत्ति इस प्रकार बतलायी गयी है—

भगवन्तं महादेवं शिवलिङ्गं प्रपूजयेत् ।
लोकप्रसविता सूर्यस्तच्चिह्नं प्रसवाद् भवेत् ॥
लिङ्गे प्रसूतिकर्त्तारं लिङ्गिनं पुरुषो यजेत् ।
लिङ्गार्थगमकं चिह्नं लिङ्गमित्यभिधीयते ॥
लिङ्गमर्थं हि पुरुषं शिवं गमयतीत्यदः ।
शिवशक्त्योश्च चिह्नस्य मेलनं लिङ्गमुच्यते ॥

> The non-existent was not, the existent was not; then, the unborn was not,
> Not the firmament, nor that which is above [that firmament].
> [*Ṛg Veda* X. 121.1]

> There was neither being nor non-being; Śiva alone was there.
> [*Śvetāśvatara Upaniṣad* IV.18]

In other words, in the beginning there was nothing, there was only Śiva.

> In the beginning all the twinkling units of time were born out from the lighting being.
> Not his top, nor his bottom and neither his middle part they discovered. [*Śvetāśvatara Upaniṣad* IV.19].

That was a Golden Embryo, having the same splendour of thousands of suns. This is "the egg of resplendent light having arisen like a sun" [*Manusmṛti* I.9]. What is directly called the symbol of it, is the supreme splendour of the Great Lord.[51]

> What is directly called the symbol of it is the supreme splendour of the great Lord.
> It is also taken as a symbol of Primeval Nature — which is illusion — made up of space. (*Śiva Purāṇa*)

The body (*piṇḍa*) of the world (*brahmāṇḍa*) is enclosed — covered — by the *yoni*, appearing as the seven-veiled *prakṛti*. In the *Śiva Purāṇa* the etymology of the word *liṅga* has been explained in this way:

> Man should worship the Lord Mahādeva as the *śivaliṅga*.
> Sūrya is the creator of the world. [So, the *liṅga*] is his symbol, because of creation of the world.
> Man should whorship *puruṣa* in the *liṅga*,who is symbolized there, the creator of the world.
> The *liṅga* is said to be the sign that indicates a symbolic sense
> So it conveys the meaning who is the *puruṣa*, Śiva:

अर्थात् शिवशक्ति के चिह्न का सम्मेलन ही लिङ्ग है। लिङ्ग में विश्वप्रसूतिकर्त्ता की अर्चा करनी चाहिये। यह परमार्थ शिवतत्त्व का बोधक होने से भी लिङ्ग कहलाता है। प्रणव भी भगवान् का ज्ञापक होने से लिङ्ग कहा गया है। पञ्चाक्षर उसका स्थूल रूप है—

तदेव लिङ्गं प्रथमं प्रणवं सार्वकामिकम्।
सूक्ष्मप्रणवरूपं हि सूक्ष्मरूपन्तु निष्कलम्॥
स्थूललिङ्गं हि सकलं तत्पञ्चाक्षरमुच्यते।

माघ कृष्ण चतुर्दशी महाशिवरात्रि के दिन कोटिसूर्य्य के समान परम तेजोमय शिवलिङ्ग का प्रादुर्भाव हुआ है—

माघकृष्णचतुर्दश्यामादिदेवो महानिशि।
शिवलिङ्गस्समुद्भूतः कोटिसूर्य्यसमप्रभः॥

'शिवपुराण' में लिखा है कि एक शिव ही ब्रह्मस्वरूप होने से निष्कल हैं, दूसरे देव सभी रूपी होने से सकल कहे जाते हैं। निष्कल होने से ही शिव का निराकार (आकारविशेषशून्य) लिङ्ग ही पूज्य होता है, सकल होने से ही अन्य देवताओं का साकार विग्रह पूज्य होता है। शिव सकल, निष्कल दोनों ही हैं, अतः उनका निराकार लिङ्ग और साकार स्वरूप दोनों ही पूज्य होते हैं। दूसरे देवता साक्षात् निष्कल ब्रह्मरूप नहीं हैं। अतएव, निराकार लिङ्गरूप में उनकी आराधना नहीं होती (विद्येश्वरसंहिता, शि० पु० ३ अध्याय)।

> *Liṅga* is said to be the symbol of the union of Śiva and Śakti.
> The combined form of Śiva and Śakti is called *liṅga.*[52]
> [*Śiva Purāṇa*, I.16.105-107]

This means that the *liṅga* is the 'sign' of the union of Śiva and Śakti. In the *liṅga* we ought to perform worship for that (one who) gives birth to the universe.[53] It is called a sign (*liṅga*) because by it we know he is the indicator (*bodhaka*) of *śivatattva*, the highest reality.[54] The *liṅga* is also said to be the syllable *AUM* (*praṇava*), the herald of God. Its gross form is the five syllabed *mantra*.

> That is the first *liṅga* (symbol), *praṇava* (*AUM*), bestower of every desire.
> The form of praṇava is subtle and that subtle form is undivided (*niṣkala*).
> The gross form of the symbol, endowed with parts, (*sakala*) is called the Five-Syllabed *mantra*.

On the fourteenth of the waning moon of Māgha [January-February], on the day of Mahā Śivarātri, there was the origin of the *liṅga* filled with the greatest light, as of ten million suns.

> In the great night of the fourteenth dark fortnight of the month of Māgha
> The primordial deity appeared as the symbol of Śiva, endowed with a splendour as of millions of suns.

In the *Śiva Purāṇa* it is written that only Śiva, being the Absolute (*brahman*), is undivided (*niṣkala*). The other gods, all having form, are said to be conditioned (*sakala*). Śiva unconditioned is worshipped in the *liṅga*, in a form without shape, while other gods, being conditioned, are worshipped in icons with form. Śiva is both conditioned and unconditioned (*sakala, niṣkala*); therefore he is worshipped both as a shapeless *liṅga* and as an icon with form. The other gods are not directly formless manifestations of the *brahman*, therefore they are not worshipped through the formless manifestation of the *liṅga* (see: *Śiva Purāṇa*, *Vidyeśvara Saṃhitā*, 3rd chapter).[55]

यहीं आगे निष्कल स्तम्भ रूप मे ब्रह्मविष्णु का विवाद मिटाने के लिए शिव का प्रादुर्भाव वर्णित है। श्री शिवलिङ्ग ही से समस्त विश्व की उत्पत्ति, स्थिति और अन्त में सब के लय का अधिष्ठान होने से भगवान् ही लिङ्ग कहलाते हैं। अथवा कार्य्यद्वारा कारणरूप से लिङ्गित-अवगत-होने से ही भगवान् लिङ्गशब्दवाच्य है। इसलिए जब सब सृष्टि का आधार ही शिवलिङ्ग है, तब तो फिर सर्वत्र शिवलिङ्ग की पूजा पायी जाय, यह ठीक ही है। अत: यह पहले अनार्य्यों की पूज्य मूर्ति थी यह सब कहना निराधार ही है।

दूसरी दृष्टि से कूटस्थ स्थाणु परब्रह्म ही शिव है। श्रीपार्वती शक्ति अपर्णा लता के संसर्ग से यह पुराण स्थाणु कैवल्यपदवी देता है जो कि कल्पवृक्षों के लिए देना भी अशक्य है। स्थाणु (ठूँठ) लिङ्गरूप में व्यक्त शिव हैं, अपर्णा जलहरी है। शिवलिङ्ग का कुछ अंश जलहरी से ग्रस्त है, यही योनिग्रस्त लिङ्ग है, प्रकृतिसंस्पृष्ट पुरुषोत्तम है—

पीठमम्बामयं सर्वं शिवलिङ्गस्य चिन्मयम्।

ऊपर महान् अंश योनिबहिर्भूत प्रकृति से असंस्पृष्ट है—

पादोऽस्य विश्वा भूतानि त्रिपादस्यामृतं दिवि।

प्रकृतिविशिष्ट परम ब्रह्म ही सर्वकर्त्ता, सर्वफलदाता है, केवल तो उदासीन है। शुद्ध शिवतत्त्व त्रिगुणातीत है, त्रिमूर्त्यन्तर्गत शिव भी परम बीज, तमोगुण के नियामक है। सत्व के नियमन की अपेक्षा भी तम का नियमन बहुत कठिन है। सर्वसंहारक तम है, पर उसको भी वश में रखनेवाले शिवकी विशेषता स्पष्ट ही है।

The explanation of the arising of Śiva as an unlimited pillar to put an end on the quarrel between Brahmā and Viṣṇu is given later here. From the sacred *śivaliṅga* has the universe arisen, [by it] all is maintained, and into it, in the end shall all things be reabsorbed; since it is the substratum of everything and the support of the destruction of everything, the Lord is thereby said to be the *liṅga*. In other words, the cause is inferred (*liṅgita*)[56] by means of the effect; the direct meaning of the word *liṅga* is understood to be God. For this, the *śivaliṅga* being the basis of all creation, it is right to find its worship everywhere.[57] Thus, it is baseless to say that it was first a symbol worshipped by the non-Aryans.

From another point of view, the transcendental and changeless Absolute reality is Śiva because he is like a changeless tree trunk. With the contact of a leafless creeper — Śrī Pārvatī-Śakti — this dry tree trunk gives total liberation (*kaivalya*), which is beyond the power of the wish-fulfilling tree (*kalpavṛkṣa*) [of Indra]. Śiva is manifested as a trunk in the form of a *liṅga*, the leafless (*aparṇā*) Pārvatī is the *yoni* (*jalaharī*). The *jalaharī* holds a few limbs of the *śivaliṅga*, hence the *liṅga* is held by the *yoni* just as the Universal Man (*puruṣottama*) in contact with Prakṛti.

> The entire basement is of the nature of the mother, and *śivaliṅga* is of the nature of consciousness. [*Śiva Puraṇa*, I.11.22]

Above, the greater part, separate from the *yoni*, is untouched by *prakṛti*.

> All beings [together comprise] are one quarter of him; his other three quarters, [being] immortal, [abide] in heaven.
> [*Ṛgveda*, X.90.3]

The Supreme *brahman* qualified by *prakṛti*, the all-doer, is the giver of every actions' results, but alone stays detached (*udāsīn*). Pure *śivatattva* is beyond the three *guṇas*; within the *trimūrti* Śiva is the supreme seed, the controller of *tamas*[58] (*tamo guṇa*). Compared to controlling *sattva*, it is more difficult to restrain *tamas*. *Tamas* is the

एक दृष्टि से लिङ्ग चिह्न को भी कहा जाता है। चिह्नशून्य निर्गुण, निराकार, निर्विकार ब्रह्म अलिङ्ग है। श्रुतियाँ उसे अशब्द, अस्पर्श, अरूप बतलाती है। परन्तु, लिङ्ग का अधिष्ठान मूल वही है। अव्यक्त तत्त्व लिङ्ग है। माया द्वारा एक ही परब्रह्म परमात्मा से ब्रह्माण्डरूप लिङ्ग का प्रादुर्भाव होता है। चौबीस प्रकृति-विकृति, पच्चीसवाँ पुरुष, छब्बीसवाँ ईश्वर यह सब कुछ लिङ्ग ही है। प्रकृति के सत्व, रज, तम इन तीनों गुणों से त्रिकोण योनि बनती है। प्रकृति में स्थित निर्विकार बोधरूप शिवतत्व ही लिङ्ग है। इसी को विश्व-तैजस-प्राज्ञ, विराट्-हिरण्यगर्भ-वैश्वानर, जाग्रत्-स्वप्न-सुषुप्ति, ऋक-साम-यजु, परा-पश्यन्ती-मध्यमा आदि त्रिकोणपीठों में तुरीय, प्रणव, परा वाकस्वरूप लिङ्गरूप में समझना चाहिये। "अ, उ, म" इस प्रणवात्मक त्रिकोण में अर्द्धमात्रास्वरूप लिङ्ग है। परमेश्वर समष्टि-व्यष्टि लिङ्गरूप से प्रत्येक योनि में प्रतिष्ठित होकर पञ्चकोशात्मक देहों को उत्पन्न करता है—

अधितिष्ठति योनिं यो योनिं वाचैकं ईश्वरः।
देहं पञ्चविधं येन तमीशानं पुरातनम् ॥

(लिं० पु० ११८)

लिङ्ग-भग से ही समस्त विश्व की उत्पत्ति है, अतएव सभी लिङ्ग और भग से अङ्कित हैं। वेद, उपनिषद, भारत, रामायण, पुराण, तन्त्र सर्वत्र ही शिव की महिमा गायी गयी है। विष्णु, ब्रह्मा, कृष्ण, राम आदि देवाधिदेवों ने भी शिवलिङ्ग की अर्चा की है। सृष्टि-विस्तार की

annihilator of everything, therefore the nature of Śiva, the possessor of this power, is clear.

From one point of view, *liṅga* means also a 'sign' (*cihna*). The Absolute Principle (*brahman*) having no sign, no qualities, no form, no change, is *aliṅga*. The *Vedas* describe it as beyond words, untouchable, without form, and so on. However *brahman* itself is the root substratum of the *liṅga*. The *liṅga* is the 'unmanifested principle of manifestation' (*avyakta tattva*). Under the influence of *māyā,* a perceivable sign (*liṅga*) as the egg-shaped universe was manifested from the Supreme Self, the Supreme *brahman*. The twenty-four elements which are cause and effect (*prakṛti-vikṛti*), as well as the twenty-fifth which is the Cosmic Man (*puruṣa*) and the twenty-sixth which is God (*īśvara*), are nothing else than *liṅga*. From it Brahmā, Viṣṇu and Rudra are manifested; its triangular *yoni* is made of the three qualities (*guṇas*) of *prakṛti*: *sattva*, *rajas* and *tamas*.[59] The *liṅga* is the changeless principle of *Śiva*, the unchanging knowledge which dwells in *prakṛti* in the form of the *liṅga*. It should be understood as the fourth condition in all the triadic bases (*pīṭha*); in the [triad of the individual] gross body, subtle body and causal body (*viśva-taijasa-prājña*); in the [triad of the universal] gross body, subtle body and causal body (*virāṭ-hiraṇyagarbha-vaiśvānara*); in [the triad of the states of limited consciousness, comprised by] waking, dreaming and deep sleep (*jāgrat-svapna-suṣupti*); in the *Ṛk*, *Sāma* and *Yajur Vedas* it is *praṇava* (*AUM*), and in the triad of the words, the spoken, mental, and unmanifested one (*paśyantī-madhyamā-vaikharī*) it is the supreme Word (*parāvāk*), etc. In the *A-U-M* shaped triadic *praṇava AUM* the *liṅga* is the half-letter (*ardhamātrā*). The Supreme God (*parameśvara*), having established itself in every *yoni,* universal or individual, gives birth to the fivefold-sheathed bodies.

> The only one Lord who presides over every womb,
> Through whom the fivefold bodies merge, he, the primeval controller. (*Liṅga Purāṇa* 118)

दृष्टि से लिङ्ग-भग का महत्त्व समझ में आ सकता है, कामप्रयुक्त भोगमात्र की दृष्टि से देखना और बात है । शङ्कर ने काम को जलाकर सृष्टि की बुद्धि से ही मैथुन द्वारा सृष्टि की है, ऐसा ही औरों को भी करना युक्त है । किसी अवसर में दृक् और दृश्य दोनों एक ही रूप होते हैं ।

आसीज्ज्ञानमथो ह्यर्थ एकमेवाविकल्पितम् ।

सृष्टि से पहले ज्ञान और अर्थ (दृश्य) एकमेक हो रहे थे । दृश्यशक्ति के उद्भव बिना सर्वसंद्रष्टा चिदात्मा भी अपने को असत् ही मानने लगता है—

मेनेऽसन्तमिवात्मानं सुप्तशक्तिरसुप्तदृक् । (भागवत)

वह अन्तर्मुख विमर्शरूप सुप्त शक्ति ही माया पद से कही जाती है—

सा वा एतस्य संद्रष्टुः शक्तिः सदसदात्मिका ।
माया नाम महाभाग ययेदं निर्ममे विभुः ॥

निरधिष्ठान शक्ति नहीं और अशक्त अधिष्ठान नहीं, अतः उभय-उभयस्वरूप ही है । इसीलिए शिव ही शक्ति और शक्ति ही शिव, इस दृष्टि से योनि लिङ्गात्मक एवं लिङ्ग योन्यात्मक है । फिर भी इस द्वैत में अद्वैत तत्त्व अनुस्यूत है । ईश्वर और महाशक्ति की अधिष्ठानभूत

From the relation of *liṅga* and *yoni* the whole world arises, and thereby the mark of *liṅga* and *yoni* is found on everything; the greatness of Śiva is sung everywhere, in the *Vedas* and in the *Upaniṣads*, in the *Mahābhārata* and in the *Rāmāyaṇa*, in the *Purāṇas* and in the *Tantras*. The *śivaliṅga* was worshipped by Viṣṇu, Brahmā, Kṛṣṇa, Rāma — the gods of the gods. With regards to the expansion of manifestation, the importance of the male and female organs can be understood; it is quite another matter if one envisages them merely as instruments of lust or pleasure. With a view to create the world, Śaṅkara (Śiva) first destroyed lust — and only thereafter copulated to bring about creation;[60] others should do likewise.[61] In some cases, the seer and the object seen can be even of one form.

> The meaning was made up of knowledge, unique, undivided.

Before manifestation, cognition (*jñāna*) and its object (*artha*) — that is, the seen (*dṛśya*) — were one. Without the origination of the power of sight, even the all-seeing Absolute Consciousness (*cidātman*) thought Himself to be non-existent (*asat*).

> When his *śakti* was asleep, the waking seer considered himself as non-existent. (*Bhāgavata Purāṇa*)

It is this internal reflexion, the asleep power *śakti,* which is known by the word (*pada*) *māyā*.

> She, the power of the conjunct nature of being and not-being of the Seer, whose name is Māyā, oh you Great Person, through this Māyā, the omni-pervading Lord manifests this universe.

There is no power (*śakti*) without a governing principle, nor is there any substratum (*adhiṣṭhāna*) without a power; so of the nature of both. In this way Śiva is none other than his own power (*śakti*) and this power (*śakti*) is He Himself (Śiva); from this point of view, it can be said that the *yoni* is the essence of the *liṅga*, and the *liṅga* [is the essence] of the *yoni*. Anyway in this dualism is pervaded the non-dualism. The pure, non-dual substratum of Īśvara and the great Śakti

अद्वैतसत्ता भी निरञ्जन, निष्कल सत्ता के साथ एकीभूत है। यह सृष्टि का बीज होने पर भी निःस्पन्द शिवमात्र है। अव्यक्त अवस्था अलिङ्गावस्था भी है। इसे महालिङ्गावस्था भी कहा जा सकता है। अव्यक्त से तेजोमय, ज्योर्तिमय तत्त्व आविर्भूत होता है। वह स्वयं उत्पन्न होने से स्वयम्भू लिङ्ग है। वह अव्यक्त अवस्था का परिचायक होने से लिङ्ग है। परमार्थतः द्वैतशून्य तत्त्व है। योनि त्रिकोण है, केन्द्र या मध्यबिन्दु लिङ्ग है—

मूलाधारे त्रिकोणाख्ये इच्छाज्ञानक्रियात्मके।
मध्ये स्वयम्भुलिङ्गन्तु कोटिसूर्य्यसमप्रभम्॥

इस वचन में इच्छा-ज्ञान क्रियात्मक योनि में कोटिसूर्यसमप्रभ स्वयम्भू चिज्जयोतिस्वरूप शिवलिङ्ग माना गया है। मूलाधार आदि षट्चक्र भी योनि ही हैं। सर्वत्र यही लिङ्ग भी भिन्न-भिन्न रूप में विराजमान है। योनि से अतीत होकर बिन्दु अव्यक्त और लिङ्ग अलिङ्ग हो जाता है। कोई गुण, कर्म, द्रव्य बिना योनि-लिङ्ग के नहीं बन सकते। याज्ञिकों के यहाँ भी वेदी की स्त्रीरूप में, कुण्ड की योनिरूप में और अग्नि रुद्र की लिङ्गरूप में उपासना होती है।

एक समय देवी ने शङ्कर से प्रश्न किया कि 'इन्द्रियों से रहित देव शून्यरूप है, उसका कोई आकार नहीं है, उस शून्य के पूजन से क्या फल? शिवजी ने कहा— "महेशानि! शक्तिशून्य शिव शव या प्रेत के ही समान है। उसकी पूजा नहीं बन सकती, किन्तु रौद्री शक्तिसहित ही उनकी पूजा होनी चाहिए। वही ब्रह्मा-विष्णु-शिवात्मिका आद्या

is a single reality, with no divisions. Although He is the seed of creation, the measure that is Śiva is motionless (*niḥspanda*). The unmanifested (*avyakta*) condition is without any distinguishing mark (*aliṅga*). It can even be said to be the condition which transcends differentiation (*mahāliṅga*). From the Unmanifest (*avyakta*) emerges first a state (*tattva*) consisting of radiance and light. As it arises of its own accord, it is said to be a self-manifesting symbol (*svayambhu liṅga*). This 'sign' (*liṅga*) is the indicator of the unmanifested condition (*avyakta avasthā*). That reality which is devoid of duality (*dvaitaśūnya*) is the highest truth. The *yoni* is triangular, in the middle, the *liṅga* is the central point (*madhyabindu*).

> In the *mūlādhāra*, which is said to be a triangle, with the nature of desire, knowledge and action
> In the middle part there is the self-born *liṅga*, with the same radiance of millions of suns.

According to this definition, it has been thought that the self-generated *śivaliṅga*, whose nature is that of the light of consciousness (*cijjyotisvarūpa)*, within the *yoni*[62] whose nature is [the triad of] desire-knowledge-action, shines like million suns. Even within the six *cakra*s, there is a *yoni*, in the *mūladhāra*. Everywhere, this very *liṅga* is resplendent in various forms. Having gone beyond the *yoni*, the *bindu* becomes unmanifest and the *liṅga*, indistinct (*aliṅga*). No quality (*guṇa*), no action, no substance (*dravya*) can be brought into existence without the *yoni-liṅga*. Even the sacrificers worship the altar as a female form, the hearth of the fire as a *yoni*, and the fierce fire in the form of the *liṅga*.

Once the goddess (Pārvatī) asked Śaṅkara (Śiva): "God is devoid of senses and formless — indeed, He has no appearance whatsoever; what fruit [comes] from the worship of that emptiness?" Śiva answered: "Oh Great Goddess! Devoid of Śakti, Śiva is no more than a corpse (*śava*), or a ghost (*preta*). You cannot worship this; however, he together with his fearsome power (*raudrī śaktisahita*) should be worshipped. She is the essence of Brahmā, Viṣṇu and Śiva, and appears

शक्ति सार्द्धत्रिवलया (साढ़े तीन फेरे की) कुण्डलिनीरूपा है। वह शिवतत्व को अपने साढ़े तीन फेरे से वेष्टित किये हुए है। उसी शक्ति के संयोग से शिव अनन्त ब्रह्माण्ड का उत्पादनादि कार्य करते हैं। वही कुण्डलिनी योनि है, उससे परिवेष्टित शिव लिङ्ग है। यही अपर्णालतापरिवेष्टित स्थाणु भी है, अपर्णा पार्वती योनि है, कूटस्थ ब्रह्म ही स्थाणु, ठूँठ य लिङ्ग है—

देव्युवाच–

इन्द्रियै रहितो देवः शून्यरूपः सदाशिवः।
आकारो नास्ति देवस्य किं तस्य पूजने फलम्॥

शिव उवाच–

प्रेते पूजा महेशानि कदाचिन्नास्ति पार्वति।
रुद्रस्य परमेशानि रौद्री शक्तिरितीरिता॥
रौद्री तु परमेशानि आद्या कुण्डलिनी भवेत्।
वर्त्तते परमेशानि ब्रह्मविष्णुशिवात्मिका॥
सार्द्धत्रिवलयाकारै-शिवं वेष्ट्य सदा स्थिता।
शक्तिं विना महेशानि प्रेतत्वं तस्य निश्चितम्॥
शक्तिसंयोगमात्रेण कर्म कर्त्ता सदाशिवः।
अतएव महेशानि पूजयेच्छिवलिङ्गकम्॥

(लिङ्गार्चनतन्त्र २ पटल)

'स्कन्दपुराण' के अनुसार लिङ्गपूजन के बिना महान् अमङ्गल होता है और उसके पूजन से भुक्ति, मुक्ति सब कुछ मिलती है—

विना लिङ्गार्चनं यस्य कालो गच्छति नित्यशः।
महाहानिर्भवेत्तस्य दुर्गतस्य दुरात्मनः॥

as *kuṇḍalinī*, the sacred three-ringed [as she has three and a half coils] primordial energy (*ādyā śakti*). That principle of Śiva is enclosed by her, through her three and a half coils. Out of the union with that Śakti, Śiva performs the initial act of the creation of the world (*brahmāṇḍa*), etc. That *kuṇḍalinī* is the *yoni*; the *śivaliṅga* is enclosed within her. This too is "the tree-stump embraced by the leafless creeper": The leafless Pārvatī is the *yoni*, the enigmatic *brahman* is the stump, denuded tree-trunk or *liṅga*."[63]

> The Goddess spoke:
> Sadāśiva is a God without any senses, free from attributes.
> What is the result of worshipping this formless deity?
> Śiva spoke:
> O Great Goddess (Maheśāni), O Daughter of the Mountain, to worship a dead thing is not possible.
> O Supreme Goddess, Rudra is said to be of wrathful power (*raudriśakti*).
> O Supreme Goddess, Raudrī is the original *kuṇḍalinī*, she is of the nature of Brahmā-Viṣṇu-Śiva.
> She is ever motionless, having covered Śiva with her three and a half veils.
> Without Śakti the deadness of the Great God (Maheśa) is certain.
> Only through the contact with his potency, Sadāśiva becomes active.
> So, O Great Goddess, the supreme God should be worshipped under the symbol of the *liṅga*.
> (*Liṅgārcaṇa Tantra, 2 paṭalam*)[64]

According to the *Skanda Purāṇa*,[65] a life spent without worshipping the *śivaliṅga* is a source of misery, while its worship brings everything — worldly pleasures (*bhukti*) as well as liberation (*mukti*).[66]

> Who always passes his time without worshipping the *liṅga*
> This miserable wicked [person] encounters considerable suffering.

एकतः सर्वदानानि व्रतानि विविधानि च ।
तीर्थानि नियमा यज्ञा लिङ्गाराधनमेकतः ॥
भुक्तिमुक्तिप्रद लिङ्गं विविधापन्निवारणम् ।

यद्यपि शिवलिङ्ग और उसकी पूजा अनादि काल से ही है, तथापि उनके आविर्भाव का, पुराणों में वर्णन है—ब्रह्मा, विष्णु दोनों ही 'मैं बड़ा हूँ' ऐसा कहकर परस्पर लड़ रहे थे । उनका विवाद मिटाने के लिये परम ज्योतिर्मय लिङ्ग का आविर्भाव हुआ । ब्रह्मा भगवान् के उस ज्योतिर्मय लिङ्ग का पता लगाने के लिए हंस पर आरूढ़ होकर ऊपर की ओर गये और विष्णु वराहरूप धारण कर नीचे गये । हजारों वर्ष तक घोर परिश्रम करने पर भी दोनों को उसका कहीं आद्यन्त न मिला । शिवलिङ्ग के मस्तक से गिरती हुए केतकी ने कहा कि 'मैं दश कल्प से चलते चलते यहाँ तक पहुँची हूँ, अभी कुछ ठिकाना नहीं कि कितना जाना पड़ेगा ।" इससे शिवलिङ्ग की अनन्तता मालूम पडती है । दिव्यवाणी से भगवान् ने ब्रह्मा, विष्णु दोनों ही को प्रबोध कराया ।

अन्यत्र पृथ्वी को पीठ और आकाश को लिङ्ग कहा है । जैसे वेदी पर लिङ्ग विराजता है वैसे ही पृथ्वी पर आकाश है । जैसे ब्रह्म का एक देश ही प्रकृति-संस्पृष्ट है, वैसे ही आकाशलिङ्ग का भी एक देश ही पृथ्वीसंस्पृष्ट है । इसीलिए कहीं लिङ्ग ठीक पुरुष के जननेन्द्रिय के समान ही होता है, कहीं ब्रह्माण्ड के आकार का, कहीं पिण्ड के आकार का । केदारेश्वर की नित्यसिद्ध स्वयम्भू मूर्ति कहीं भी लिङ्ग के आकार की नहीं है । वही कारणावस्था या पिण्डावस्था का चिह्न ही लिङ्ग समझना चाहिए । वस्तुदृष्टि से फिर भी वह लिङ्ग ही है ।

आधुनिक वैज्ञानिकों की भी दृष्टि से आकाश वक्र है जैसा कि लिङ्ग का स्वरूप है । किं बहुना, देश-काल-वस्तु सभी वक्र हैं, ब्रह्म को भी वक्र और स्तब्ध कहा है । फिर उससे उत्पन्न सबको वक्र होना

On one side all the offerings and numerous vows, pilgrimages, obedience to rules,
And on the other side, *liṅga* worship:
The *liṅga* bestows prosperity, liberation
And removes many kinds of misfortune."[67]

Although the *śivaliṅga* and its worship have always existed, the *Purāṇas* tell of their first appearance. Brahmā and Viṣṇu had met, each having said to the other, "I am the greatest". To settle their argument, a *liṅga* of the most resplendent light appeared. The god Brahmā, having mounted his swan, went upwards to investigate this *liṅga*, while Viṣṇu, having assumed the shape of a boar, went downwards. Even after thousands of years of intense effort, they could find neither its beginning nor its end. A *keṭakī* flower which had fallen from the top of the *śivaliṅga* told them: "For ten aeons I have been falling and have reached here and no one can say with certainty how far I have still to fall". This was meant to show the endlessness of the *śivaliṅga*. God (*bhagavān*) then imparted knowledge to Brahmā and Viṣṇu by means of a divine disembodied voice.

Elsewhere, the earth (*pṛthivī*) is said to be the pedestal, and space (*ākāśa*) the *liṅga*. The *liṅga* stands on its pedestal as does the atmosphere upon the earth. Just as only one part of *brahman* is in contact with *prakṛti*, similarly only one area of the *ākāśaliṅga* touches the earth. For these reasons, in some places the *liṅga* is said to be similar to the male organ of generation, elsewhere it is said to have the form of the egg shaped world, and in still another place it is said to appear as a formless mass (*piṇḍa*). The eternally famous self-manifest image of Kedāreśvara [68] in no way resembles a *liṅga*. The *liṅga* should be understood to be the sign (*cihna*) of the causal state (*kāraṇa avasthā*), or of the condition of formlessness (*piṇḍa avasthā*). In any event, from the objective point of view, it is a *liṅga*.

From the point of view of modern scientists, space is curved, as is the nature of the *liṅga*. Moreover, time, space, things all are curved;[69] even the Absolute Reality (*brahman*) is said to be curved as well as

ही चाहिए । अनन्तकोटि विश्व सब लिङ्गमय ही है । विश्वों से परे सगुण ब्रह्म का भी लिङ्ग ही आकार है ।

शिवशक्ति के सहवास में अवकाश न मिलने से शुक्राचार्य ने उन्हें शाप दिया कि तुम योनिस्थ लिङ्ग के रूप में पूजित होगे । एकबार शङ्कर दिगम्बर वेष से स्वलिङ्ग अपने हस्त में लेकर दारुक वन मे गये । उन्हें देखकर ऋषि पत्नियाँ मोहित हो गयीं, यह देखकर ऋषियों ने शङ्कर को शाप दिया कि तुम्हारा लिङ्ग गिर जाय । ऐसा ही हुआ, किन्तु लिङ्ग के पृथ्वी पर गिरते ही वह प्रज्वलित होकर अपने तेज से लोक को जलाने लगा । अन्त में शिवा ने उसे योनि मे स्थापित किया और सब ऋषियों और देवताओं ने उसकी पूजा की । यहाँ लिङ्ग, योनि दिव्य प्रकृति और परम पुरुष ही हैं । शिवशक्तिरूप लिङ्ग-योनि को प्राकृत स्त्री-पुरुष के समान चर्मखण्ड मूत्रेन्द्रिय मात्र मान लेना बड़ा अपराध होगा । कहीं यह भी कथा है कि मुनियों के शाप से गिरा हुआ शिवलिङ्ग अग्नि के समान जाज्वल्यमान होकर भूमि, स्वर्ग एव पाताल में फिरा, सभी लोक बड़े दुःखी हुए । ब्रह्मा जी ने कहा कि—

> **गिरिजा की प्रार्थना करो, वही योनिरूप से परमज्योतिर्मय लिङ्ग को धारण कर सकती है ।**

फिर सब देवताओं एवं मुनियों ने जब आराधना की, तब भगवान् और गिरिजा प्रसन्न हुईं और गिरिजा में शिव की प्रतिष्ठा हुई । क्या साधारण लिङ्ग का गिरकर अग्निमय होकर सर्वलोकों में घूमना बन सकता है? और विष्णु, राम, कृष्ण तथा सभी देव, दैत्य, मुनि क्या केवल साधारण लिङ्ग-योनि की ही पूजा करते थे? यदि यही बात थी, तो कृष्ण की उपमन्यु के यहाँ जाकर दीक्षापूर्वक घोर तपस्या करने की क्या आवश्यकता थी?

stable. Therefore, all that issues forth from it ought to be curved as well. The countless millions of worlds are all comprised of that *liṅga*. Beyond the extent of the worlds, even the qualified Principle (*saguṇa brahman*) manifests in the form of *liṅga*.

Śiva and Śakti were always joined in intercourse; as Śukrācārya had no opportunity to meet them, he cursed them, saying: "You shall be worshipped in the form of a *liṅga* within a *yoni*". Once, Śaṅkara (Śiva) went naked into the forest of Dāruka, with his *liṅga* [70] in his hand. Having seen him, the wives of the *ṛṣis* were fascinated; noticing this, the *ṛṣis* cursed Śaṅkara, saying: "Your *liṅga* [71] shall fall".[72] Exactly this happened, but once the *liṅga* fell to the earth it burst into flames and its heat began to incinerate the world. In the end, Śivā (i.e. Pārvatī) fixed it within her *yoni* and all the *ṛṣis* and gods worshipped it. Here, the *yoni* and the *liṅga* are the divine *prakṛti* and the supreme *puruṣa*. It would be a great offence to consider *liṅga* and *yoni* that are forms of Śiva-Śakti, as merely the worldly penis and vulva, the fleshy organs of urination.[73] Thereafter, the story is told of the *śivaliṅga* which, having fallen down due to the curse of the *munis*, became like a raging fire and, roaming the earth, heavens and hells (*pātāla*), bringing great distress to all the worlds. Brahmā then said:

> Supplicate Girijā (i.e. Pārvatī). Only she can bear this *liṅga* of supreme radiance, in her form of the *yoni*.

All the gods and *munis* began to pray; this pleased the Lord and Girijā, and so in the end Śiva was installed within Girijā. Could an ordinary *liṅga* be able to roam the various worlds, and having fallen burst into flames? And would Viṣṇu, Rāma, Kṛṣṇa, and all the gods and *munis* worship a mere worldly *liṅga* or *yoni*? And even were this be so, what would be the need for Kṛṣṇa to go to Upamanyu for initiation to do *tapas*? [74]

Some people [75] say that the aforementioned *śivaliṅga* of the story is just the universe (*brahmāṇḍa*); holding it in his hand, God (*bhagavān*) had gone to play in the forest of Dāruka where, by the curse of the *munis*, this *liṅga* fell out of his grasp. For this reason it is

कुछ लोग कथा में आये हुए उक्त शिवलिङ्ग को केवल ब्रह्माण्ड कहते हैं, उसी को हाथ में लिये हुए भगवान् लीलया दारुक वन में गये थे, वहीं मुनियों के शाप से उनके हाथ से लिङ्ग गिर पड़ा। अतएव वहाँ उसका 'गिरना' कहा गया है, 'कटना' नहीं। उस ज्योतिर्लिङ्ग ब्राह्म तेज का आधार पञ्चतत्त्वात्मिका प्रकृति ही योनि है। अत: पार्वती ने योनिरूप से उस लिङ्ग को धारण किया अर्थात् पञ्चतत्त्वात्मिका प्रकृति बन कर उन्होंने ब्रह्माण्ड को धारण किया। अग्निमय सर्वदाहक लिङ्ग को योनि-प्राकृत चर्मखण्ड मूत्रेन्द्रिय में कौन धारण कर सकता था?

बाणरूपा श्रुता लोके पार्वती शिववल्लभा।

योनिरूपा का अर्थ ही बाणरूपा है। 'बाण' शब्द पाँच संख्या का बोधक होता है, पञ्चशर के अभिप्राय से काम में, पञ्चमुख के अभिप्राय से शिव में, पञ्चतत्त्वात्मिका की दृष्टि से पार्वती में 'बाण' शब्द का प्रयोग होता है। जैसे विद्युत-पुञ्ज पञ्चतत्त्व में व्याप्त होते हुए भी जल और पर्वतश्रेणी में अधिकता से रहता है, वैसे ही पार्वती बाणरूपा हुईं अर्थात् पर्वतश्रेणीरूपा हुईं और उन्हीं में वह तेजोमय लिङ्ग समा गया। विद्युत्पुञ्ज यदि अपनी योनि पृथ्वी या जल में पड़े, तो स्थिर होता है, अन्यथा वृक्ष, मनुष्य सबको भस्म ही करता है। यही बात शिवजी ने कही है—

पार्वतीञ्च विना नान्या लिङ्गं धारयितुं क्षमा।
तया धृतञ्च मल्लिङ्गं द्रुत शान्तिं गमिष्यति॥

अर्थात् पार्वती के बिना कोई इसे नहीं धारण कर सकता, उनके धारण से वह शीघ्र ही शान्त हो जायगा।

सतश्च योनिमसतश्च। (यजु:)

यो योनिं योनिमधितिष्ठत्येक:। (श्वेता०)

said that 'it fell down' and not that 'it was cut down'. *Prakṛti*, made up of the fivefold elements (*pañcatattvātmakā*), is the *yoni*, the support for the brilliant energy of the Absolute (*brahma teja kā ādhāra*), this *liṅga* of light. Therefore, to say that Pārvatī took the shape of a *yoni* to hold the *liṅga* means that, becoming *prakṛti* — in the form of the five elements — she supported the Universe. Could a worldly *yoni,* a urinary organ, a scrap of leather, support the *jyotirliṅga*, made of fire, that burns everything? [76]

> In the world it is heard that Pārvatī, the beloved of Śiva, is of the form of an arrow (*bāṇa*).[77]

The meaning of the form of the *yoni* is the same as that of the form of the arrow. The word 'arrow' (*bāṇa*) is indicative of the number five: it is applied with regards to Kāma, by reason of his five arrows; when addressed towards Śiva, it regards his five faces and when to Pārvatī, the perspective is her nature comprised of by the five elements. Just as a mass of electricity (*vidyut puñja*) pervades the five elements, yet is more predominant within water and in mountain ranges, similarly did Pārvatī become arrow-shaped, that is of the form of a mountain range, and into her the effulgent *liṅga* (*tejomaya liṅga*) entered. If the mass of electricity were to fall into her *yoni* — that is, into earth or water — it would become stable; otherwise, it would reduce trees, men and everything else to ashes. It was said by Śiva:

> Except Pārvatī, no one is able to sustain the *liṅga*; my *liṅga*, supported by her, quickly will find peace.
>
> The womb of the manifest (*sat*) and the unmanifest (*asat*).
> (*Yajur Veda*)
>
> That one who presides over every womb.
> [*Śvetāśvatara Upaniṣad* IV.11]
>
> The cause of the universe which ripens one's own nature.
> [*Śvetāśvatara Upaniṣad* V.5]

यच्च स्वभावं पचति विश्वयोनिः । (श्वेता०)

इत्यादि मन्त्रों में योनि का अर्थ मूत्रेन्द्रिय ही है, यह कहना अज्ञता ही है । श्रीविष्णु आदि देवाधिदेवों का भी पूज्य यह योनिप्रतिष्ठित लिङ्ग प्राकृत वस्तु कथमपि नहीं हो सकता । यदि विष्णुकर्त्तृक पूजा आदि को क्षेपक कहें, तब तो समस्त कथा को ही क्षेपक मान सकते हैं ।

अव्यक्त का लिङ्ग (व्यक्त ब्रह्माण्ड) भृगु (प्रकृति) के आकर्षण-विकर्षण विशेष के तारतम्य से द्यावापृथ्वीरूप में दो टूक हो गया—

वायुरापश्चन्द्रमा इत्येते भृगवः । (गोपथ पूर्व०२ ।८)

शंभो पपात भुवि लिङ्गमिदं प्रसिद्धम् ।
शापेन तेन च भृगोर्विपिनं गतस्य ॥

श्रीशङ्कर ने भी विश्वेश्वरलिङ्ग की प्रतिष्ठापना और पूजा की है—

ब्रह्मणा विष्णुना वापि रुद्रेणान्येन केन वा ।
लिङ्गप्रतिष्ठामुत्सृज्य क्रियते स्वपदस्थितिः ॥
किमन्यदिह वक्यव्य प्रतिष्ठां प्रति कारणम् ।
प्रतिष्ठितं लिङ्ग वैश्वेश्वरं यतः ॥

'नारद पञ्चरात्र' के तीसरे रात्र में, जो कि वैष्णवों का सर्वस्व है, लिखा है कि एक शङ्कर के सिवा सभी स्त्रैण थे । ब्रह्मा, विष्णु, दक्ष आदि ने तपस्या से कालिका देवी को प्रकट किया । देवी ने कहा-'वर माँगो ।' देवों ने कहा कि "आप दक्ष-कन्या होकर शिव को मोहित करो ।' जगदीश्वरी ने कहा— 'शम्भु तो बालक हैं' । ब्रह्मा ने कहा—'शंभु के समान दूसरा कोई पुरुष हो नहीं सकता' । यह सुन कर दक्ष के यहाँ देवी सतीरूप से प्रकट हुईं । देवताओं ने विवाह कराया । सती-शिव

Therefore, it is ignorance to say that, in these and other passages of the Scriptures, the word *'yoni'* denotes the urinary organ. The *liṅga* supported by the *yoni*, worshipped even by Śrī Viṣṇu, the pre-eminent God of gods, cannot be said to be a mundane object. If we say that the worship performed by Viṣṇu and the others originally was a textual interpolation (*kṣepaka*), then the whole narration could be thought to be such an interpolation.[78]

The sign of the unmanifest [the visible universe] was split into two parts, sky and earth, due to the disproportion (*tāratamya*) of the qualities of attraction and repulsion within Bhṛgu (*prakṛti*).

> These are the Bhṛgus: air (*vāyu*), water (*apa*), and moon.
> (*Gopatha Pūrvatapinīya Upaniṣad* II.8)

> This fact is well known that the *liṅga* of Śiva, who went in the forest, fell down to the earth due to that curse of Bhṛgu.

Śrī Śaṅkara himself installed the *liṅga* of the Lord of the Universe (*viśveśvara*) and worshipped it.

> It is only after having worshipped the *liṅga* that Brahmā, Viṣṇu or Rudra or any one else can officiate.
> For the installation [of the *liṅga*] what other reason is possible to say? In fact, the Viśveśvara *liṅga* was installed by Śiva himself.

In [79] the third night of *Nārada Pañcarātra*, a fundamental book of Vaiṣṇavism, it is written that [in the beginning] everything was female except Śaṅkara. Brahmā, Viṣṇu, Dakṣa and others performed *tapas* to evoke the Goddess Kālikā. The Goddess said: "Ask for a boon". The gods then said: "Become the daughter of Dakṣa and seduce Śiva". The Goddess of the universe said: "Śambhu is a child", Brahmā said: "There can be no man comparable to Śambhu". Hearing this, the Goddess was born into the house of Dakṣa as Satī. The gods arranged the marriage. When Satī and Śiva dallied, both their seed fell on the earth; thence arose everywhere the *śivaliṅgas* with their

के रमण से दोनों का तेज भूमण्डल में पड़ा, वही पाताल, भूतल, स्वर्ग सर्वत्र योनिसहित शिवलिङ्ग हुए। लिङ्गपूजा शाक्त, वैष्णव, सौर, गाणपत्य सभी के लिए है—

शाक्तो वा वैष्णवो वापि सौरी वा गाणपोऽथवा।
शिवार्चनविहीनस्य कुतः सिद्धिर्भवेत् प्रिये॥ (उत्पत्तितन्त्रे)

शिव की पूजा के बिना अन्य देवता की पूजा करने से वह देव शाप देकर चला जाता है—

अनाराध्य च मां देवि योऽर्चयेद्देवतान्तरम्।
न गृह्णति महादेवि शापं दत्वा व्रजेत् पुरम्॥

यद्यपि शुद्ध दार्शनिक और आध्यात्मिक विवेचनों से शिवलिङ्ग अनादि ही है, उसकी पूजा भी अनादि ही है तथापि अर्थवादरूप में अनेक प्रकार से शिवलिङ्ग की उत्पत्ति और पूजा का आरम्भ लिखा गया है। जैसे यद्यपि नित्यसिद्ध ही राम, कृष्ण का अवतार माना जाता है, तथापि अवतार से पहले भी वे पूज्य थे ही, क्योंकि कल्प-कल्प में उनके अवतार होते रहते हैं, कोई अवतार नया नहीं है। वैसी ही बात शिवलिङ्ग के विषय में भी समझनी चाहिए। नित्य होने पर भी भिन्न-भिन्न कल्प में उसके आविर्भाव के क्रम भिन्न हैं। समष्टि प्रजननशक्तिसम्पन्न शिवतत्त्व ही समष्टि लिङ्ग है उसी से समस्त व्यष्टि योनि और लिङ्गों का आविर्भाव हुआ है। यही सती-शिव के मैथुन से प्रादुर्भूत तेज से सयोनि लिङ्गों की उत्पत्ति का रहस्य है। प्रकृति-पुरुष का संयोग ही शिव-सती का मैथुन है। प्रकृति मिश्रित अनन्त पुरुषों का प्रादुर्भाव ही उनका मिश्रित तेज है। समष्टि लिङ्ग से ही उत्पन्न होकर व्यष्टि लिङ्ग बनते हैं। अतः सभी व्यष्टि लिङ्गों की योनि भी समष्टि लिङ्ग की ही योनि है। यही शिव के दारुकावन-विहार का रहस्य है।

yonis: in hell, on earth, in heaven. *Liṅgapūjā* is for everyone, for the Śāktas, Vaiṣṇavas, Sauras [Sun-worshippers] and Gāṇapatyas.

> O Beloved one, how can the attainment of perfection be possible for those who don't worship Śiva,
> Be they worshippers of Śakti, of Viṣṇu, of the Sun or of Gaṇapati? (*Utpatti Tantra*).

When one worships any other deity without worshipping Śiva, that deity departs, after giving a curse.

> O Goddess, who not having worshipped me, worships another deity,
> That deity does not accept [the adoration] and having cursed him, returns to his abode.

Although the *śivaliṅga* is beginningless according to philosophers and spiritual investigators, its worship has always existed as well; nevertheless, the first appearance of the *śivaliṅga* and the origins of its worship have been written about in many different ways, as a laudative statement (*arthavādarūpa*).[80] Similarly, the *avatāra*s Rāma and Kṛṣṇa are also considered to be eternal, and consequently were worshipped even before their descents actually took place. This is because, aeon (*kalpa*) after aeon, the *avatāra*s exist again and again; no *avatāra* is new. Similarly should it be understood for the topic of the *śivaliṅga*. While eternal, the order of its manifestation may be different in different aeons. The universal *liṅga* is the principle of Śiva possessing the totality of the powers of procreation. From that very totality comes the manifestation of all the individual *yonis* or *liṅgas*. This is the mystery related to the *liṅgas* and their *yonis* who arose from the seed which fell when Śiva and Satī copulated. The copulation (*maithuna*) of Śiva and Satī is none other than the union of *puruṣa* and *prakṛti*. From their mingled seed have arisen innumerable human beings, and the composite *prakṛti*. Individual manifested *liṅgas* issue from the universal *liṅga*. Therefore the *yoni* of each individual *liṅga* is also (one with) the *yoni* of the universal *liṅga*. This is the mystery of Śiva roaming the forest of Dāruka.

अनन्त अनङ्ग (कामदेव) जिनके श्रीअङ्ग के सौन्दर्य-बिन्दु पर मोहित हो जाते हैं, उन भगवान् परम शिव की ओर समष्टि-व्यष्टि प्रकृतिरूप योनियों का आकर्षण होना स्वभाव ही है। यही मुनिपत्नियों का शिव की ओर आसक्ति का रहस्य है। मुनियों या शुक्राचार्य के शाप से भगवान् का योनिस्थ लिङ्गरूप से पूजित होना या शिव के लिङ्ग का गिर जाना, पुनः उससे जगत्ताप होना, शिवा का योनि में स्थापन करना, ब्रह्मा, विष्णु अदि देवताओं और ऋषि, मुनि, गन्धर्व, असुरादि द्वारा पूजित होना, यह सभी स्वतन्त्रेच्छ, निरङ्कुश भगवान् की लीला है, जैसे विष्णु परमात्मा का शापवश मनुष्य बनना, मत्स्य, वराह आदि रूप धारण करना केवल लीला है। शापादि भी उनकी इच्छा से ही निमित्तरूप में उपस्थित होते हैं।

प्रकृति के साथ परमात्मा का खेल या जीवरूपा परा प्रकृतियों में परमात्मा का रमण किंवा स्वरूपभूत माधुर्याधिष्ठात्री शक्ति में परमेश्वर का रमण रहस्यमय है। जैसे कृष्ण के चीरहरण, रासलीला में अज्ञों को अश्लीलता प्रतीत होती है, वैसे ही भगवान् शिव की लीलाएँ भी परमरहस्यमयी है। अज्ञों को उनमें अश्लीलता का भान हो सकता है—

निर्गुण रूप सुलभ अति, सगुण न जाने कोह।
सुगम अगम नाना चरित, सुनि मुनिमन भ्रम होई॥

राम देखि मुनि चरित तुम्हारे।
जड़ मोहहिं बुध होहिं सुखारे॥

लिङ्गरूप से अतिरिक्त भी भगवान् का गङ्गाधर, चन्द्रशेखर, त्रिलोचन, पञ्चवक्त्र, नीलकण्ठ, कृत्तिवास, व्याघ्रचर्मासन, त्रिशूलधारी,

Innumerable Bodiless Ones [81] (Kāmadeva) would be enthralled by a drop of the beauty of His lovely body; it is only natural that — both universaly and individually — every *yoni* [within] the form of *prakṛti* should be attracted to this supreme Lord Śiva. This is the secret of why the wives of the *munis* were fascinated by Śiva. After being cursed by the sages (*munis*) or by Śukrācārya, God is worshipped under the shape of a *liṅga* established within a *yoni*, or when the *liṅga* of Śiva falls and begins to burn the world until it is grasped by the *yoni* of Śivā (Pārvatī), and is worshipped by Brahmā, Viṣṇu and the other gods along with the *ṛṣis*, *munis*, *gandharvas*, *asuras* and everyone else — all this is the play of the unfettered will of the unbound God; similarly when Viṣṇu, the Supreme Being, was cursed to take the form of a man, a fish, a boar, and other shapes — this is only a divine game. A curse can only be given if He, the cause of everything, wishes it to be given.

The play of the Supreme Being (*paramātman*) with *prakṛti*, or the copulation of this Supreme Being with higher worldly principles (*parā prakṛti*) manifested as individual beings (*jīvarūpā*) — or, more exactly, the copulation of the Lord with Śakti, part of himself, the sweetness which presides over his manifestation — all of these comprise a profound secret. Just like Kṛṣṇa's theft of clothes, or like the *rāsalīlā*, the play of the God Śiva is mysterious and can easily appear obscene to the ignorant. For the ignorant, indecency can appear within them.

> His unqualified aspect is easily understandable, but no one knows the qualified one.
> Innumerable are his simple, but inconceivable deeds; having heard about them, the mind of the seers is confused as well. [Tulasī Dāsa]

> O Rāma, when they see and hear of thy behaviour, the wise rejoice but the fools are embarrassed. [Tulasī Dāsa]

In addition to the form of the *liṅga,* there are other forms of *bhagavān* of transcendental beauty and sweetness: Gaṅgādhara (bearing

वृषभध्वज, साम्ब, सदाशिव रूप है, जिसका लोकोत्तर सौन्दर्य, माधुर्य्य है ।

नान्तःप्रज्ञं न बहिःप्रज्ञं ।

प्रपञ्चोपशमं शान्तं शिवमद्वैतं चतुर्थं मन्यन्ते ।

तमीश्वराणां परमं महेश्वरं, क्षरं प्रधानममृताक्षरं हरम् ।

तमीशानं वरदं समीड्यम् ।

मायिनन्तु महेश्वरम् ।

इन श्रुतियों में परब्रह्म परमात्मा को ही हर और माया को ही प्रकृति या गौरी कहा गया है । सभी जगह संसार में देह-देही आदिकों में आधार-आधेय-भाव देखा जाता है । अनन्त चैतन्य परमात्मा शिव हैं, वही सृष्ट्युन्मुख होने पर लिङ्ग ही है । उन्हीं का आधार योनि प्रकृति है, शिव लिङ्ग रूप में पिता, प्रकृति योनिरूप में माता है—

मम योनिर्महद्ब्रह्म ।

द्विधा कृत्वात्मनो देहमर्द्धेन पुरुषोऽभवत् ।
अर्द्धेन नारी तस्यां स विराजमसृजत्प्रभुः ॥

Gaṅgā), Candraśekhara (bearing the moon), Trilocana (three-eyed), Paṃcavaktra (five-headed), Nīlakaṇṭha (with a blue neck), Kṛttivāsa (wearing the elephant skin), Vyāghracarmāsana (seated on a tiger's skin), Triśūladhārī (bearing the trident), Vṛṣabhadvaja (whose banner is the bull), Sāmba (together with Universal Mother), Sadāśiva (ever benevolent).[82]

Aware of neither inside nor outside. [*Māṇḍūkya Upaniṣad 7*].

They consider it to be the extinction of the universe, peaceful, benevolent, non-dual, the fourth. [*Māṇḍukya Upaniṣad* 7]

The Primeval Nature is perishable, but the Supreme Great Lord of the Lords, Hara is immortal and imperishable.
[*Śvetāśvatara Upaniṣad* I.10]

That Lord, bestower of boons, who is worthy to be adored.

The controller of *māyā* is the Great Lord.
[*Śvetāśvatara Upaniṣad* IV.10]

In these passages of the *Vedas* (*śruti*), it is said that the Supreme Reality (*parabrahman*), the Supreme Self (*paramātman*) is none other than Hara (Śiva), and *māyā* is nothing but *prakṛti* and Gaurī. In every place in the world, between any body and its possessor (*deha-dehin*), is seen a relation like that of a thing which is based [on something] and its basis (*ādhāra-ādheya*).[83] The Supreme Self (*paramātman*), the infinite consciousness, is Śiva. It is he who, when inclined towards manifestation, is the *liṅga*.[84] His support is the *yoni-prakṛti*. Śiva, in the form of *liṅga*, is the father. *Prakṛti*, in the form of *yoni*, is the mother.

My womb is the great substainer. [*Bhagavad Gītā* XIV.3]

Having divided in two parts his own body, with half he became a man and with the other half
A woman. In that woman the Lord created the immense-splendent Being (Virāj).

शिव का लिङ्गयोनिभाव ही अर्द्धनारीश्वर का भाव है। सृष्टि के बीज को देनेवाले परम लिङ्गरूप श्रीशिव प्रकृतिरूपा नारीयोनि में आधाराधेयभाव से संयुक्त होकर उससे आच्छादित होकर व्यक्त होते हैं। यही जगन्माता-पिता के आदि सम्बन्ध का द्योतक है। काम-वासनारहित शुद्ध मैथुन भी पितृऋण से उऋण होने का साधन है। 'शिवपुराण' में लिखा है— बिन्दु देवी और नाद शिव हैं। बिन्दुरूपा देवी माता और नादरूप शिव पिता हैं, अतः परमानन्द-लाभार्थ शिवलिङ्ग का पूजन परमावश्यक है।

भं वृद्धिं गच्छतीत्यर्थाद्भगः प्रकृतिरुच्यते।

वृद्धि को प्राप्त होने वाली प्रकृति ही भग है।

मुख्यो भगस्तु प्रकृतिर्भगवान् शिव उच्यते।
भगवान् भोगदाता हि नान्यो भोगप्रदायकः॥

भग के सहित लिङ्ग और लिङ्ग के सहित भग पूजित होकर इहलोक-परलोक में विविध सुख देने वाला है। सदाशिव से उत्पन्न चैतन्यशक्ति द्वारा जायमान चिन्मय आदि पुरुष ही शिवलिङ्ग है। समस्त पीठ अम्बामय हैं, लिङ्ग चिन्मय है। भगवान् शङ्कर कहते हैं कि जो संसार के मूल कारण महाचैतन्य को और लोक को लिङ्गात्मक जानकर लिङ्गपूजा करता है, मुझे उससे प्रिय अन्य कोई नर नहीं—

लोकं लिङ्गात्मकं ज्ञात्वा लिङ्गे योऽर्चयते हि माम्।
न मे तस्मात्प्रियतरः प्रियो वा विद्यते क्वचित्॥

लिङ्ग चिह्न है, सर्वस्वरूप की पूजा कैसे हो, इसलिए लिङ्ग की कल्पना है। आदि एवं अन्त में जगत् अण्डाकृति ही रहता है। अतएव, ब्रह्माण्ड की आकृति ही शिवलिङ्ग है। शिव-शक्ति के सहवास से ही पशु, पक्षी, कीट, पतङ्गादिकों की भी उत्पत्ति होती है।

This presence of Śiva as *yoni* and *liṅga* is equivalent to that of Ardhanārīśvara. Śiva, the supreme *liṅga*, who looks after the seed of the manifestation (*sṛṣṭi*), having being united with the woman's womb in the form of *prakṛti* through a relation of basis-based, becomes manifest when he is veiled by her. The titles of 'Father' or 'Mother of the Universe' also indicate such a relation. The pure sexual union whose purpose is not lust is a means of repaying the debt one has towards one's ancestors. In the *Śiva Purāṇa*, it is written that the *bindu* represents the Goddess, and the *nāda* is Śiva. The Goddess in this form of the dot (*bindu)* is the Mother and Śiva as the sound (*nāda*) is the Father. This is why, to attain the highest bliss, the worship of the *liṅga* is of the utmost importance.[85]

> 'Bha' means increasing (prosperity), so what increases is bhaga; so it is thereby called 'Nature'. [*Śiva Purāṇa*, I.16.101]

The Nature, which increases, is called *bhaga.*

> The principal glory is *prakṛti* and Śiva is called Glorious (*Bhagavān*).
>
> The glorious Lord is the giver of the enjoyment (*bhoga*): there is no other bestower of enjoyment.
> [*Śiva Purāṇa,* I.16.102, 103]

The *bhaga* worshipped with the *liṅga* and the *liṅga* worshipped with the *bhaga* give various kinds of pleasures, in this world and in other worlds. The *śivaliṅga* is the Primordial Man (*ādi puruṣa*) himself, transcendent and having the nature of knowledge, having issued from Sadāśiva through the *śakti* of the Supreme Consciousness.The whole of the base of the nature is the [divine] mother (*ambā*); the *liṅga* is the essence of consciousness.[86] Lord Śankara says: "The man who is dearer to me than any other is he who worships the *liṅga,* knowing it to be the absolute consciousness which is the root cause of *saṃsāra*, and who knows the essence of the world to be the *liṅga*."

शिव स्वयं अलिङ्ग हैं, उनसे लिङ्ग की उत्पत्ति होती है, शिव लिङ्गी और शिवा लिङ्ग हैं। ज्ञापक होने से, प्राणियों का आलय होने से एवं लयाधिकरण होने से भी वही लिङ्ग हैं—

लीयमानमिदं सर्वं ब्रह्मण्येव हि लीयते।

भिन्न-भिन्न कामना से शिवलिङ्ग के विधान भी पृथक्-पृथक् हैं— यवमय, गोधूममय, सिताखण्डमय, लवणज, हरितालमय, त्रिकटुकमय (शुण्ठी, पिप्पली, मरीचमय) ऐश्वर्य-पुत्रादिकामप्रदायक लिङ्ग है। गव्यघृतमय लिङ्ग बुद्धिवर्द्धक है। पार्थिव लिङ्ग सर्वकामप्रद है। तिलपिष्टमय, तुषज, भस्मोत्थ, गुडमय, गन्धमय, शर्करामय, वंशाङ्कुरज, गोमयज, केशमय, अस्थिमय, दधिमय, दुग्धमय, फलमय, धान्यमय, पुष्पमय, धात्रीफलोद्भव, नवनीतमय, दूर्वाकाण्डसमुद्भव, कर्पूरज, अयस्कान्तमय, वज्रमय, मौक्तिकमय, महानीलमय, महेन्द्रनीलमणिमय, चीरसमुद्भव, सूर्यकान्तामणिज, चन्द्रकान्तमणिमय, स्फाटिक, शूलाख्यमणिमय, वैडूर्य, हैम, राजत, अरकूटमय, काँस्यमय, सीसकमय, अष्टधातुनिर्मित, ताम्रमय, रक्तचन्दनमय, रङ्गमय, त्रिलौहमय, दारुज, कस्तूरिकामय, गोरोचनमय, कुङ्कुममय, श्वेतागुरुमय, कृष्णागुरुमय, पाषाणमय, लाक्षामय, वालुकामय, पारदमय लिङ्ग भिन्न-भिन्न कामनाओं की पूर्ति के लिए पूजनीय बतलाए गये हैं। पार्थिव-पूजन के लिए ब्राह्मणादि वर्णों को क्रम से शुक्ल, पीत, रक्त, कृष्णवर्ण की मृत्तिका से शिवलिङ्ग बनाना चाहिए। तोलाभर मिट्टी से अङ्गुष्ठपर्व के परिमाण का लिङ्ग बनाना चाहिए। पूजा भी वैदिक, तान्त्रिक एवं मिश्र विधि या नाममन्त्रों से करनी चाहिए। किं बहुना, शिवलिङ्ग की विशेषताओं, पूजाओं एवं विधियों पर शास्त्रों में बहुत ही बड़ी सामग्री भरी पड़ी है।

> Having known the world as *liṅga*-substantiated, who worships me in the *liṅga*,
> For me there is nowhere someone dear or dearer than him.[87]
> [*Śiva Puraṇa,* I.9.43-44]

The *liṅga* is a symbol; how could otherwise the worship of the universal essence be possible? In order to accomplish this purpose, there is the concept of *liṅga*. In the beginning and at the end, the world retains its appearance of an egg. In any event, the appearance of the world (*brahmāṇḍa*) is precisely that of the *śivaliṅga*. Through the intercourse of Śiva and Śakti, animals, worms, birds, and insects are born. Śiva himself is ungendered (*aliṅga*) — symbol (*liṅga*) arises from him: Śiva is the 'symbolized' (*liṅgin*)[88] [i.e. not the visible denotation], and it is Śivā (Pārvatī) who is the [visible] *liṅga*. Being the indicator of it, being the abode of all living creatures and being the sole support of their destruction, it is called the sign (*liṅga*).

> All this universe, which is about to disappear, merges into *brahman*.

Different[89] kinds of *śivaliṅgas* are worshipped for different desires: *yavamaya* (made of barley), *godūmamaya* (made of wheat), *sitākhaṇḍamaya* (made of lump sugar), *lavaṇaja* (born from salt), *haritālamaya* (made of sulfure), *trikaṭukamaya* (*śuṇṭhī, pippalī, marīcamaya*) (made of dry ginger, pipper longum and black pepper): the worship of these *liṅga*s provide wealth, sons, and the like. *Gavyaghṛtamaya* (with cow ghee) *liṅgas* bestow wisdom, *pārthiva liṅgas* (made with clay) fulfil every desire. *Tila-piṣṭamaya* (made of sesame powder), *tuṣaja* (born from the chaff of grains), *bhasmottha* (made of ashes), *guḍamaya* (made of jaggery), *gandhamaya* (made of perfume), *śarkarāmaya* (made of sugar), *vaṅśākuraja* (made of bamboo sprout), *gomayaja* (made of cow dung), *keśamayaja* (made of mane or a kind of mineral), *asthimayaja* (made of bones), *dadhimaya* (made of curd), *dugdhamaya* (made of milk), *phalamaya* (made of fruit), *dhānyamaya* (made of paddy), *puṣpamaya* (made of flowers),

बाण और नार्मद लिङ्ग की परीक्षा के लिए उसे तण्डुलादि से सात बार तौला जाता है। यदि दूसरी बार तौलने में तण्डुल बढ़ जायँ, लिङ्ग हलका हो जाय, तो वह गृहियों को पूज्य है। यदि लिङ्ग अधिक ठहरे, तो वह विरक्तों के पूजने योग्य है और सातबार तौलने पर भी बढ़े ही, घटे नहीं, तो उसे बाण लिङ्ग, अन्यथा नार्मद लिङ्ग जानना चाहिए।

प्राय: शिव को अनार्य देवता बतलाया जाता है परन्तु वेदों में शिव का बहुत प्रधानरूप से वर्णन है।

dhātrīphalodbhava (born from the fruit of *emblica officinalis*), *navanītmaya* (made of butter), *dūrvākāṇḍasamudbhava* (made of the root of the *dūrvā* grass), *karpūraja* (made of camphor), *ayaskāntamaya* (made of magnet), *vajramaya* (made of adamant), *mauktikamaya* (made of pearls), *mahānīlamaya* (made of sapphire), *mahendranīlamaṇimaya* (made of the great lord among the sapphire gems), *cīrasamudbhava* (made of clothes), *sūryakāntāmaṇija* (made of the *sūryakānta* gem), *candrakāntāmaṇimaya* (made of the *candrakānta* gem), *sphāṭika* (made of crystal), *śūlākhyamaṇimaya* (made of the gem called *śūla*), *vaidūrya* (brought from Vidūra), *haima* (golden), *rājata* (silver), *ārakūṭamaya* (made of a kind of brass), *kāṃsyamaya* (made of bronze), *sīsakamaya* (made of glass), *aṣṭadhātunirmita* (made of eight metals), *tāmramaya* (made of copper), *raktacandanamaya* (made of red sandal), *raṅgamaya* (made of tin), *trilokamaya* (made of three worlds), *dāruja* (made of wood), *kastūrikāmaya* (made of musk), *gorocanamaya* (made of a bright-yellow orpiment prepared from the bile of cattle), *kuṅkumamaya* (made of vermillion), *śvetāgurumaya* (made of a kind of white aloe wood), *kṛṣṇāgurumaya* (made of a kind of black aloe wood), *pāṣāṇamaya* (made of stone), *lākṣāmaya* (made of red lac), *vālukāmaya* (made of sand) and *pāradmaya* (made of mercury) are said to be worshipped to fulfil different desires. To perform *pārthiva* [90] worship, Brahmins and the other castes should make *śivaliṅgas* with white, yellow, red and black-coloured clay respectively. One should make *pārthiva liṅgas* with approximately eleven grams [one *tola* of clay], measuring one half-finger's length. *Pārthiva pujā* should be performed according to vedic, tantric or mixed methods, or by *mantras* of praise. What more? More details, characteristics and methods to worship the *śiva liṅga* are explained in the *Śāstras*.

To test whether it is a *bāṇa* [91] or a *nārmada liṅga*,[92] we should weight it seven times with rice and other [materials]. If the second time [it is weighted] the measure of rice increases and [that of the] *liṅga* decreases, then it is fit to be worshipped by householders. If the *liṅga* weights more [the second time], it fit to be worshipped by *yogins*

एको रुद्रो न द्वितीयाय तस्थुर्य इमांल्लोकानीशत ईशनीभिः । प्रत्यङ्जनास्तिष्ठति सञ्चुकोचान्तकाले संसृज्य विश्वा भुवनानि गोपाः ॥ (श्वेताश्वर ३।२)

समस्त भुवनों को अपनी ईशनी शक्ति से ईशन करते हुए सब में विराजमान शिव ही अन्त में सबका संहार करते हैं । बस, वही परमतत्त्व सर्वस्व हैं, उनसे भिन्न दूसरी वस्तु थी ही नहीं ।

यदा तमस्तत्र दिवा न रात्रिर्न सन्न चासच्छिव एव केवलः ।

जब प्रलय में दिन-रात, कार्य-कारण कुछ भी नहीं था, तब केवल एक शिव ही थे ।

स्वधया शम्भुः ।

उमासहायं परमेश्वरं प्रभुं त्रिलोचनं नीलकण्ठं प्रशान्तम् ॥

नमो नीलग्रीवाय शितिकण्ठाय । (यजुः)

यहाँ रुद्र के नील और श्वेत दोनों ही तरह के कण्ठ कहे गये हैं ।

ऋतं सत्यं परं ब्रह्म पुरुषं कृष्णपिङ्गलम् ।
ऊर्ध्वरेतं विरूपाक्षं विश्वरूपाय वै नमो नमः ॥

(तैत्तिरीयाण्यक)

and the like; if after weighting it seven times it increases, and does not diminish, then it is a *bāṇa liṅga*. Otherwise, it ought to be known to be a *nārmada liṅga.*

Śiva is frequently claimed to be non-Aryan. However, in the *Vedas*, Śiva has been given a very predominant stature.

> One is Rudra, there is no second. He controls through his power all these worlds,
> He dwells in the interior of the beings, the substainer; having manifested all the worlds, in the end of the time, withdrew them. (*Śvetāśvatara Upaniṣad* III.2)

In the whole universe, Lord Śiva reigns over all through his power of sovereignty (*īśānīśakti*), and, in the end, that very Śiva, presiding over all, will destroy everything. What more? This ultimate reality (*paramatattva*) is everything; apart from Him there was no other thing.

> When darkness was, there no day or night were, nor being, neither not-being, indeed Śiva alone was.
> [*Śvetāśvatara Upaniṣad* IV.18]

During the *pralaya* when there was absolutely nothing, neither day nor night, neither cause nor effect — at that time, there was only Śiva.

> Through *svadhā*,[93] Śambhu.
>
> United with Umā, the Supreme Lord, the All-Mighty, with three eyes, blue-throated, absolutely peaceful.
>
> Salutation to the blue-necked, to the white-throated.
> (*Yajur Veda*)

Here, it is mentioned that the neck of Rudra is both blue and white.

> The Cosmic Order, the Truth, the Supreme *brahman*, the Dark-Brown Being, whose semen rises upward, who has altered [or

यहाँ भी कृष्ण-पिङ्गल,ऋत-सत्य, ऊर्ध्वरेता विरूपाक्ष को नमस्कार किया गया है ।

भुवनस्य पितरं गीर्भिराभी रुद्रं दिवा वर्धया रुद्रमत्यौ ।
बृहन्त मृष्वमजरं सुषुम्नमृग्धुवेम कविनेविता सः ॥

(ऋ० ६ ।४९ ।१०) ।

यो देवानां प्रभवश्चोद्भवश्च विश्वाधिपो रुद्रो महर्षिः ।
हिरण्यगर्भं जनयामास पूर्वं स नो बुद्ध्या शुभया संयुनक्तु ॥

(श्वेता० ३। ४)

यो अग्नौ रुद्रो योऽप्स्वन्तर्य ओषधीर्वीरुध आविवेश ।
य इमा विश्वा भुवनानि चाल्लपे तस्मै रुदराय नमोऽस्त्वग्नये ॥

(अथर्व० ७ ।९२ ।१)

एको रुद्रो न द्वितीयाय तस्थुः ॥ (श्वेता०)

एक एव रुद्रो न द्वितीयाय तस्थुः ॥ (तै० सं० १ ।८ ।६ ।१)

अर्थात् अन्य देवों का कारण, विश्व का एकमात्र स्वामी, अतीन्द्रियार्थ-ज्ञानी और हिरण्यगर्भ को उत्पन्न करनेवाला रुद्र हमें शुभ बुद्धि दे, जो अग्नि में, जल में, ओषधि एव वनस्पतियों में रहता है और जो सब का निर्माता है, उसी तेजस्वी रुद्र को हमारा प्रणाम हो। जो भुवन का पिता है, बड़ा है, प्रेरक और ज्ञानी है, उस अजर की हम स्तुति करते हैं इत्यादि । जो कहते हैं कि अग्नि ही वेद के रुद्र है, उन्हें इस बात पर ध्यान देना चाहिए कि अग्नि, जल, क्या सभी प्रपञ्च में रुद्र रहते हैं । जब रुद्र से भिन्न दूसरा तत्त्व ही नहीं है, तब अग्नि आदि सभी रुद्र हों यह ठीक ही है ।

half-closed] eyes, to the form of every thing, to Him do I pledge my obedience. (*Taittirīya Āraṇyaka*)

Here, praise is given to He who is black-yellow (*kṛṣṇapiṅgala*), He who is [of the nature of] the ultimate universal truth (*ṛta-satya*), He whose semen rises upward (*ūrdhvareta*), and He whose eye is misshapen (*virūpākṣa*).

> Exalt Rudra, the father of the world, with these hymns by day; [exalt] Rudra [with them] by night; animated by the far-seeing, we invoke him, mighty, of pleasing aspect, undecaying, endowed with bliss, [the source of] prosperity. (*Ṛg Veda* VI.49.10)
>
> Rudra, the ruler of the universe, who is the power and the origin of the deities, who, in the beginning, generated the Golden Embryo (Hiraṇyagarbha), he should endow us with an auspicious intellect. (*Svetāśvatara Upaniṣad* III.4)
>
> To the Rudra that is in the fire, that is within the waters, that entered the herbs, the plants, that shaped all these beings, to that Rudra, to Agni, salutations. (*Atharva Veda*, VII.92.1)
>
> One is Rudra, there is no second. [*Śvetāśvatara Upaniṣad* III.2]
>
> One only is Rudra indeed, there is no second.
> (*Taittirīya Saṃhitā* I.6.8.1)

In other words, may goodwill be given by Rudra, the cause of the gods, the only master of the universe, who has the knowledge of the objects beyond the range of the senses (*atīndriyārthajñānin*), and the cause of the Hiraṇyagarbha: give us pure intellect, O one who dwells in the fire, in the water, in the medicinal herbs, in the vegetation; we give our salutation to that resplendent Rudra. We praise this one, the unchanging one who is the Father of the world, the great, the impeller, the learned. Some people say that Agni is the Rudra of the *Vedas*; they should give attention to this point that Rudra resides in every manifestation (*prapañca*), in fire, in water, in everything. When

एक ही परमात्मा के अग्नि, वायु, मातरिश्वा आदि अनेक नाम होते ही हैं ।

एकं सद्विप्रा बहुधा वदन्ति ।
अग्निं यमं मातरिश्वानमाहुः ॥

परन्तु, अग्नि से भिन्न रुद्र हैं ही नहीं, यह कहना सङ्गत नहीं है ।

ईशानादस्य भुवनस्य भूरेर्न वा उ योषद्रुद्रादसुर्य्यम् ।
(ऋ० २ ।३३ ।९)

इस भुवन के स्वामी रुद्रदेव से उनकी महाशक्ति पृथक् नहीं हो सकती ।

अन्तरिच्छन्ति तं जने रुद्रं पोरो मनीषया ॥ (ऋ० ९ ।७३ ।३)

मुमुक्षु उस रुद्र परमात्मा को मनुष्य के भीतर बुद्धि द्वारा जानना चाहते हैं ।

असंख्याताः सहस्त्राणि ये रुद्रा अधिभूम्याम् ।

रुद्रस्य ये मील्हुषः पुत्राः । (ऋ० ९ ।७३ ।३)

अज्येष्ठासो अकनिष्ठास एते संभ्रातरो वावृधुः ।
सौभगाय युवा पिता स्वया रुद्र एषाम् ॥ (ऋ० ५ ।६० ।५)

रुद्र से उत्पन्न सब रुद्र ही हैं । तत्त्वमस्यादि महावाक्यों के अनुसार उनको भी एक दिन महारुद्र परमात्मा होना पड़ेगा ।

स रुद्रः स महादेवः ।

there is absolutely no other reality except Rudra, at that time would it be proper to say that Agni, and everything else, is Rudra.

Agni, Vāyu, Mātariśvan — and so on — are the various names of the same Supreme Self (*paramātman*).

> The Sages call that real One in many ways
> Agni, Yama, Vāyu, they call Him. [*Ṛg Veda* I.164.46]

But it is not correct to say that there is no Rudra apart from Agni.

> Indeed, from Rudra, the Lord of this immense universe the female (*śakti*) Principle (*yoṣad*) is inseparable. [*Ṛg Veda* II.33.9]

Rudra Deva, the master of this world, cannot be isolated from his great power (*mahāśakti*).

> They seek by their intellect to place that Rudra in the forefront, for the sake of the offerer. [*Ṛg Veda* VIII.72.3]

Those who desire liberation (*mumukṣu*) must understand intellectually that Rudra is that Supreme Self (*paramātman*) within man.

> Innumerable, thousands, the Rudras wander about the earth.

> They are the liberal sons of Rudra. [*Ṛg Veda* VI. 66. 3]

> They are brothers, of whom no one is the elder, no one the younger, but who grew up together for their mutual prosperity. Their father is Rudra, ever youthful, the doer of good deeds, and Pṛṣṇi [their mother], easy to be milked; may they grant favourable days for [the sake of] the Maruts. [*Ṛg Veda* V. 60. 20]

All those arising from Rudra are also Rudra. According to such great sayings as '*tat tvam asi*' ('you are that') [*Chāndogya Upaniṣad* VI.8.6] and the like, those who are born of Rudra shall surely one day become one with the supreme reality, Mahārudra.

> He is Rudra, He is the Great Divinity.

रुद्रः परमेश्वरः । (अथर्व० ११ ।२ ।३)

इत्यादि मन्त्रों में भी परमात्मा को ही रुद्र, महादेव आदि कहा गया है । जो कहते हैं कि शिव से पृथक् रुद्र हैं, उन्हें वेदों के ही अन्यान्य मन्त्रों पर ध्यान देना चहिए, जिनमें स्पष्टरूप से परमेश्वर के लिए ही शिव, त्र्यम्बक, महादेव, महेशान, परमेश्वर, ईशान, ईश्वर आदि शब्द आये हैं ।

त्र्यम्बकं यजामहे सुगन्धिं पुष्टिवर्द्धनम् ।
उर्वारुकमिव बन्धनान्मृत्योर्मुक्षीय मामृतात् ॥ (ऋक्)

ये भूतानामधिपतयः कपर्दिनः । (यजुः)

असंख्याताः सहस्राणि ये रुद्रा अधिभूम्याम् ।

नील ग्रीवाः शितिकण्ठाः । (यजुः)

तमु ष्टुहि यः स्विषुः सुधन्वा यो विश्वस्य क्षयति भेषजस्य ।
यक्ष्वामहे सौमनसाय रुद्रं नमोभिर्देवमसुरं दुवस्य ॥
(ऋ० ५ ।४२ ।११)

क्षरं प्रधानममृताक्षरं हरं क्षरात्मानावीशते देव एकः ।
(श्वेता० १ ।१०)

सर्वव्यापीस भगवांस्तस्मात् सर्वगतः शिवः । (श्वेता० ३ ।११)

आवो राजानमध्वरस्य रुद्रं होतारं सत्ययजं रोदस्योः ।
अग्निं पुरा तनयित्नोरचित्ताद्धिरण्यरूपमवसे कृणुध्वम् ॥
(साम-कौथुम, १ ।७ ।७)

Rudra is the Supreme Lord. (*Atharva Veda* XI.2.3)

Even in these very *mantras*, the Supreme Self itself has been called Rudra, Mahādeva, and the like. Those who say that Rudra is distinct from Śiva should pay heed to the various *mantras* of the *Vedas*, in which the words Śiva, Tryambaka, Mahādeva, Maheśāna, Īśāna, Īśvara and the like have clearly been used only to denote the Supreme Lord (*parameśvara*).

> We offer oblations to the triple-eyed Lord, to the Fragrant one [or: to the Auspicious Thinker], to the Increaser of welfare; like a mature pumpkin from its stalk, might I be free from death, not from immortality. (*Ṛg Veda*)
>
> They are the rulers of the living beings, they the knotted-haired [like the cowrie shell]. (*Yajur Veda*)
>
> Innumerable thousands of Rudras wander about the earth.
>
> The blue-necked, the dark-throated. (*Yajur Veda*)
>
> Praise to him who has the sure arrow, the strong bow, who presides over all herbal medicines; worship Rudra for a comprehensive and sound understanding; adore the powerful divinity with prostrations. (*Ṛg Veda* V.42.11)
>
> The Primeval Nature is perishable, Hara, is immortal and imperishable. The one deity rules over the perishable (*prakṛti*) and her essence (*puruṣa*). (*Śvetāśvatara Upaniṣad* I.10)
>
> The Glorious Lord, all-pervasive, therefore omnipresent and auspicious. (*Śvetāśvatara Upaniṣad* III.11)
>
> Win, to protect you, Rudra, Lord of worship, priest of both worlds, effectual sacrificer, Agni, invested with his golden colours, before the thunderstrikes and lays you senseless.
> (*Sāma Veda Kauthumīya* I.7.7)

त्वमग्ने रुद्रो असुरो महादिवस्त्वं शर्द्धो मारुतं पृक्ष ईशिषे ॥
(ऋ० २ ।१ ।६)

इत्यादि मन्त्रों में अग्नि को ही रुद्र कहा गया है ।

स्थिरैङ्गैः पुरुरुप उग्रो बभ्रुः शुकेभिः पिपिशे हिरण्यैः ।

यहाँ रुद्र को पुरुरुप, असाधारण तेजस्वी और वभ्रुवर्ण कहा गया है ।

वैदिकों के यहाँ शिवपूजा की सामग्रियों में कोई भी तामस पदार्थ नहीं हैं । बिल्वपत्र, पुष्प, फल, धूप, दीप, नैवेद्य आदि से ही भगवान् की पूजा होती है । मद्य, मांस का तो शिवलिङ्गपूजा में कभी भी उपयोग नहीं होता । अतः शिव तामस देवता हैं यह कहना अनभिज्ञता है । हाँ, त्रिमूर्त्यन्तर्गत शिव कारणावस्था के नियन्ता माने जाते हैं । कारण या अव्यक्त की अवस्था अवष्टम्भात्मक होने से तमःप्रधाना कही जा सकती है । "**तम आसीत्तमस्यगूढ़मग्रे**" इस श्रुति में तम को ही सबका आदि और कारण कहा गया है । उसी में वैषम्य होने से सत्व, रज का उद्भव होता है । तम का नियन्त्रण करना सर्वापेक्षयाऽपि कठिन है । भगवान् शिव तम के नियन्ता हैं, तम के वश नहीं है । शिव भयानक भी हैं, शान्त भी हैं । सर्वसंहारक, कालकाल, महाकालेश्वर, महामृत्युञ्जय भगवान् में उग्रता उचित ही है । ब्रह्मक्षत्रोपलक्षित समस्त प्रपञ्च जिसका ओदन है, मृत्यु जिसका दालशाक है, मृत्युसहित संसार को जो खा जाता है, उसका उग्र होना स्वाभाविक है । शिव से भिन्न जो भी कुछ है, उस सबके संहारक शिव हैं । इसीलिए विष्णु को उनका स्वरूप ही माना जाता है । अन्यथा भिन्न होने पर तो उनमे भी

> Agni, you are Rudra, the expeller [of foes] from the expanse of heaven; you are the strength of the Maruts; you are supreme over [sacrificial] food. [*Ṛg Veda* II.1.6]

In these *mantras* and the like, Agni has been called Rudra.

> O you of multifarious aspect, terrible one, you are of a brown-reddish colour, you want to drink with your stable bright, golden arms.

Here, Rudra has been called *pururūpa* ('of innumerable aspects'), *asādhāraṇa tejasvin* ('the exceptionally aglow') and *babhruvarṇa* ('He of the greyish-brown colour').

There are no *tāmasic* ingredients amongst those implements used by Vedic priests for a *Śiva pūjā*. Only *bilva* leaves, flowers, fruits, grass, lamps and consecrated foods are used to worship God. Wine and meat are never used in *śivaliṅga pūjās*. For these reasons, to say that Śiva is [merely] god of *tamas* is great foolishness. Yes, within the Trimūrti, Śiva is thought to be the condition of causation (*kāraṇā-vasthā*). The primary cause (*pradhāna*) can be said to be *tamas*, from the standpoint of the causation or of the condition of the unmanifest. "In the beginning there was darkness, covered by darkness" [*Ṛg Veda* X.129.1]. In this Vedic passage, *tamas* has been said the prime cause of everything. *Sattva* and *rajas* arise from the disharmony within *tamas*. In comparison to the others, it is rather difficult to rule *tamas*. Lord Śiva is the controller of *tamas*; he is not within the power of *tamas*. Śiva is terrifying (*bhayānaka*), and totally peaceful (*śānta*) as well. To be terrifying is quite natural for the God who is the destroyer of everything (*sarvasaṃhāraka*), the Death of death (*kālakāla*), Mahākāleśvara, Mahāmṛtyuṃjaya. The whole world seems to be his food; he eats the whole of *saṃsāra* including death, which are like vegetables with lentils to Him — so it is quite natural for him to be terrifying. Everything is apart from Śiva; he is the destroyer of all. Only because of this, Viṣṇu is considered to be his inner essence

संहार्यता आ जायगी। वस्तुतः हरिहर, शिवविष्णु तो एक ही हैं। उनमे अणुभर भी भेद है ही नहीं। "**भीषास्माद्वातः पवते**"। भगवान् के भय से ही वायु, अग्नि, सूर्य्य, मृत्यु अपना काम करते हैं। "**महद्भयं वज्रमुद्यतम्**" समुद्यत महावज्र के समान भगवान् से सब डरते हैं, तभी भगवान् को मन्यु या चण्ड कोपरूप माना गया है। "नमस्ते रुद्र मन्यवेङ्ग हे रुद्र! आपके मन्युस्वरूप की मैं वन्दना करता हूँ। वही शक्तिरूपधारिणी होकर चण्डिका कहलाते हैं, फिर भी वह ज्ञानियों और भक्तों के लिए रसस्वरूप है।

रसो वै सः।

एष ह्येवानन्दयाति। (श्रुति)

भगवान् रसस्वरूप हैं, निखिल रसामृतमूर्त्ति भगवान् से ही समस्त विश्व को आनन्द प्राप्त होता है, इसीलिए भगवान् की अघोरा, शिवा तनु घोर तनु से पृथक् वर्णित है—

या ते रुद्र शिवा तनूरघोरा पापकाशिनी।
तया नस्तन्नुवा शन्तमया गिरिशन्ताभिचाकशीहि॥

भगवान् की कल्याणमयी, शन्तमा, शिवा, तनू, परम कल्याण-मयी है।

शान्तं शिवम्।

अघोरेभ्योऽथ घोरेभ्यो घोरघोरतरेभ्यः।
सर्वेभ्यः सर्वशर्वेभ्यो नमस्ते अस्तु रुद्ररूपेभ्यः॥

(*svarūpa*); otherwise, being apart from him, he would also be fit to be destroyed. In fact, Śiva and Viṣṇu are one — as [shown in] the image of Harihara. There is not even a single atom of difference between them: "*Out of the fear of him blows the wind*" [*Taittirīya Upaniṣad* II.8.1]. Out of their fear of God, air (*vāyu*), fire (*agni*), the sun (*sūrya*) and death (*mṛtyu*) all perform their duties. "*The great fear, alike a thunderbolt uplifted.*" [*Kaṭha Upaniṣad* II.3.2]. All fear the Lord, like an uplifted thunderbolt; then has God been said to be of the form of rage, as Manyu or Caṇḍa. "*Namaste rudra manyave.*" [Yajur Veda] "Hail Rudra! I give praise to your most furious form" (*manyusvarūpa*). That same Lord, having taken the form of Śakti, is called Caṇḍikā, the fearful Goddess (*śaktirūpadhāriṇī*); nevertheless, for the sages and for his devotees, he is of the very nature of delight (*rasasvarūpa*).

> Indeed He is the flavour
>
> Who indeed bestows bliss. (*Śruti*)

God is of the nature of bliss; the whole world receives bliss from God's form as the perfect nectar of pleasure (*nikhilarasāmṛtamūrti*); this is why the Lord has been described variously as Aghora (unterrifying), Śivātanu (with a benevolent form) and Ghoratanu (with a tremendous form).

> O Rudra, that which is your auspicious (śiva) form, non-tremendous, illuminator of the virtues, through that peaceful form, O benevolent, please look at us.
> [*Śvetāśvatara Upaniṣad* III.5]

The Lord's aspect is associated with welfare, peaceful, auspicious, and the greatest good (*paramakalyāṇamayī*).

> *Śāntam śivam* (peaceful, auspicious). [*Māṇḍūkya Upaniṣad* 7]
>
> To the unterrifying aspects and to the terrifying ones, to the dreadful and to the even more dreadful,

इस तरह रुद्राध्याय में उग्र, श्रेष्ठ, और भीमरूप वर्णित हैं ।

नमः शम्भवाय च मयोभवाय च नमः शङ्कराय च भयस्कराय च नमः शिवाय च शिवतराय च। (यजु० १६ ।४१)

इस मन्त्र में शिव को शिवस्वरूप, कल्याणदाता, मोक्षदाता कहा गया है ।

इस तरह जब अनादि, अपौरुषेय वेदों एवं तन्मूलक इतिहास, पुराण, तन्त्रों द्वारा शिव का परमेश्वरत्व, शान्तत्व, सर्वपूज्यत्व सिद्ध होता है, तब शिव की पूजा अनार्य्यों से ली गयी है इन बेसिर-पैर की बातों का क्या मूल्य है?

> To all the archers, let all obedience be for you, to you, having a fearful aspect [or: to the aspect of Rudra].[94] [*Yajur Veda*]

There, in the Rudra chapter, the great, terrible and powerful forms are described.

> Obedience to the benevolent and to who causes delight, so to the benevolent one,
> To the bliss giver, to the auspicious one and to the even more auspicious. [*Yajur Veda* XVI.41]

In these *mantras*, Śiva has been called the nature of auspiciouness (*śivasvarūpa*), the giver of welfare (*kalyāṇadātā*), the giver of liberation (*mokṣadātā*).

In this way, the eternal and of non-human [origin] (*apauruṣeya*) *Vedas*, *Purāṇas*, *Tantras* and the stories concerning them have proved the reality of Śiva having the nature of the ultimate lordship (*parameśvaratva*), peacefulness (*śāntatva*), the all-praised (*sarvapūjyatva*); so, what is the basis to say that the worship of Śiva was taken from non-Aryans? What is the value of such baseless talk?

Notes

Abbreviations: A.D.: Alain Daniélou; *JISOA*: *Journal of the Indian Society of Oriental Art*; *MCL*: *Le Mystère du culte du Linga*; ms.: manuscript.

1 The concept of *adhiṣṭhāna*, substratum, is of primary importance in *Vedānta*. The substratum is technically that real basis on which the erroneous perception takes place; so the rope is the *adhiṣṭhāna* for the snake, as the *adhiṣṭhāna* of the world is the Supreme Lord.

2 All the words between square brackets were added by the editor.

3 This sentence joining Śiva-Śakti was omitted by Daniélou from his first translation in the *JISOA IX*, 1941, p. 52, and was never mentioned later; see also *MCL*, 1993, p. 73.

4 This precision is to clarify that these expressions do not refer to any attribute or accident, but to the inner nature (*svarūpa*) of the Supreme Being. The Absolute is, according to metaphysic, without qualities and attributes. All these words do not express different entities, but the selfsame inherent nature of *brahman* absolutely free from any kind of differentiation. If the words 'being, consciousness and bliss' would be interpreted as qualities, they should be one different from the other, but in this context they are considered as synonyms of the *brahman* itself, so the being of *brahman* is not different from its absolute consciousness, and its consciousness is identical with its essential bliss.

5 Transl. Svāmī Gambhīrānanda, *Bhagavad Gītā*, Advaita Ashrama Publisher, Kolkata, 2003, p. 570.

6 In the translation we decided to keep the doctrinal terms in italics and the proper names in roman with a capital initial letter.

7 Here Svāmī Karpātrī considers the 'father' mentioned in this *śloka* of the *Bhagavad Gītā* as 'Śiva' and he adds '*liṅga*' in brackets (we put it between dash to avoid confusion with editor's brackets). Daniélou, in the *JISOA IX*, 1941, p. 53, translated *liṅga* by 'Phallus' in brackets. After 1964, in several quotations of this passage, Daniélou wrote again 'Phallus', but within brackets, which thus wrongfully appeared as an interpretation given by Svāmī Karpātrī. See also, French version, *MCL*, 1993, p. 74: "Je suis le père, Shiva, le phallus, qui donne la semence".

8 Addition of A.D., ms. 1992: "This desire finds its end in erotic enjoyment". French version, *MCL*, 1993, p. 75: "Ce désir trouve sa finalité dans la jouissance érotique".

9 In 1964, several Daniélou's interpolations have modified totally the meaning of these four sentences: "Pleasure dwells in the sex-organ (*upastha*), in the cosmic *liṅga* and *yoni* whose union is the essence of enjoyment. In the world also all love, all lust, all pleasure, is a search for enjoyment. Things are desired for the pleasure

they contain. Divinity is the object of love because it is pure enjoyment. Other things are objects of temporary love since they bring us only a temporary satisfaction (Karapātrī, '*Liṅgopāsanārahasya*', p. 153)." Alain Daniélou, *Hindu Polytheism*, 1964, *The Myths and Gods of India*, 1991, p. 225. The term '*upastha*' does not occur in this passage.

10 In 1941, Daniélou makes here a new paragraph to emphasize his one-sighted translation of *kānta kānti kāmanā* as 'The lust of sexual man for the sexual woman' (JISOA IX, p. 53); 'The desire of a lustful man for a woman' (*Hindu Polytheism,* 1964, *The Myths and Gods of India*, 1991, p. 225).

11 In his quotation of this passage in *Hindu Polytheism*, Daniélou ends here the paragraph and omits — without any indication — the twelve following sentences (*Hindu Polytheism, 1964, The Myths and Gods of India*, 1991, p. 225).

12 A.D., *ms.* 1992 : "It is in the mind pacified by the relief from desire that the bliss, that sensual pleasure of the soul appears."

13 In all this paragraph and generally in the whole text, the Daniélou's translation eroticises the vocabulary, translating '*ānanda*' by 'pleasure' or lover and beloved by 'sexual man' and 'sexual woman' (*JISOA IX*, p. 53).

14 Mistranslation of A.D., *ms.* 1992: "The true object of love, pleasure and desire is pure sensual pleasure, which is the nature of the Divine Being". *MCL*, 1993, p. 77: "L'objet réel de l'amour, du plaisir et du désir, est la volupté pure qui est la nature de l'Etre divin".

15 After having omitted the twelve previous sentences, Daniélou, in *Hindu Polytheism,* translates this passage as follows: "All enjoyment, all pleasure, is experience of divinity. The whole universe springs forth for enjoyment; pleasure is found at the root of everything. But perfect love is that whose object is not limited, love without attributes, the pure love of love itself, of the transcendent being-of-joy. (Karapātri, 'Lingopasana-rahasya', p. 153)", *Hindu Polytheism, 1964, The Myths and Gods of India*, 1991, p. 225.

16 This discussion makes remember us the passage of the *Bṛhadāraṇyaka Upaniṣad* II.4.5, which reverbers on the advaitic assumption that only the Supreme Being is the reservoir of the absolute love (*paramapremāspada*).

17 A.D. translates by a plural, *JISOA IX*, 1941, p. 54: "Deities, their beauty and appeal are useful"; French version, *MCL*, 1993, p. 77: "Les divinités [...] sont utiles et les aimer est bénéfique".

18 A.D., *ms.* 1992: "by ethic"; French version, *MCL*, 1993, p. 77: "par la morale".

19 A.D., from the *JISOA IX,* p. 54, suppression of this sentence. In *ms.* 1992, addition of a sentence carrying an opposite meaning: "As a general rule, pleasure and love draw us closer to the divine". French version, *MCL*, 1993, p. 77: "En principe le plaisir et l'amour nous rapprochent du divin".

20 A.D., from the *JISOA IX,* p. 55, mixed this sentence with the following sentence, modifying the mood: "Undoubtedly bliss and love are everywhere, still the love for sensuous women who are also truly a part of God (*ātman*) but are spoiled by impure things, is called lust or passion, while the love which has divinity as its object is called devotion or faith."

21 Mistranslation A.D., ms. 1992: "auto-eroticism"; French version, *MCL*, 1993, p. 79: "cet auto-érotisme divin".

22 Mistranslation A.D., ms. 1992: "Thus realizing absolute sensual delight"; French version, *MCL*, 1993, p. 80: "la volupté totale".

23 The number sixteen is a symbol of fullness and perfection. The sixteenth digit of the moon is beyond the bright and the waxing cycles, and represents that fullness which is not related to this world: the whole perfection of this universe is a mere shadow compared to that perfection.

24 We tried to trace this half verse in the *Subhagodayastuti* of Gauḍapāda, but we could not find it.

25 Interpolation of A.D., *ms.* 1992, between commas: "Lalita, primordial sensual delight"; *MCL*, 1993, p. 80: "la volupté primordiale".

26 A.D., ms. 1992: "This dualism in the supreme being is symbolized by the phallus (*liṅga*) and the vagina (*yoni*)"; French version, *MCL*, 1993, p. 81: "symbolisé par le phallus et le vagin".

27 The *arghā* is the base on which the *śivaliṇga* is get, by which the offerings of water, milk, etc. of the devotees can flow away.

28 This concept is often expressed by the allegorical reference to the limping man seeing (*dṛk puruṣa*) all but unable to act; and the blind man/woman (*dṛśya prakṛti*) carriying the former on his/her shoulders, unable to see but walking and acting. The union of the two is capable to produce proper activities. See the *Sāṃkhyakārikā* 21.

29 Transl. Svāmī Gambhīrānanda, Advaita Ashrama Publisher, Kolkata, 2003, p. 569.

30 Here is mentioned the doctrine of *Vedānta* concerning the *abhinnanimittopādāna-kāraṇatva* of *brahman*, according to which the Absolute, in its qualified form, is the material by which He, Himself, produces this universe, as well as He is the consciousness that pervades it.

31 Interpolation, *MCL*, 1993, p. 83: "represente par un phallus, un *linga*".

32 Sentence not translated by AD from *JISOA IX*, p. 57; *MCL*, 1993, p. 83.

33 Here there is an allusion to the distinction between the sensorial potentialities and their seats.

34 Here, A.D. made a new part, separated by *** (*JISOA IX*, p. 59, ms. 1992).

35 The *śālagrama* is a fossil ammonite which is considered the aniconic way to worship Viṣṇu, as the *liṅga* is for Śiva.

36 A.D., *ms.* 1992: "Shiva's image in phallus shape"; French version, *MCL*, 1993, p. 86: "Le Linga de Mahadeva, l'image de Shiva sous la forme d'un phallus".

37 The sun is the universal eye of the sky because it illuminates all this world, destroying the darkness. The same function is satisfied by the individual eye which, grasping its objects, destroys the ignorance surrounding them. If the sun would not illuminate this world through its rays, then, the eye could never catch its own objects.

38 A.D., ms. 1992: "The *linga* erected in this *yoni* represents sensual delight"; French version, *MCL*, 1993, p. 87: "le *linga* dressé dans ce *yon*i représente la volupt".

39 Addition, A.D., *ms.* 1992: "its substance is sensual delight"; French version, *MCL*, 1993, p. 83: "sa substance est la volupté".

40 Addition of A.D., 1992: "Sensual delight is the substance of the supreme Being clothed with Nature"; French version, *MCL*, 1993, p. 83: "La volupté est la substance de l'Etre suprême enrobé dans la Nature". In the philosophical *milieu*, the Sanskrit term for the sexual pleasure is the word *ānanda*, but we have not to confuse this meaning limited to this particular context with the limitless bliss.

41 A.D., from *JISOA IX*, p. 60: "On pure *Brahma* rests all the elements of enjoyment which are: seing the beloved (*priya*), obtaining him (*moda*), union with him (*pramoda*) and resulting pleasure (*ānanda*)"; French version, *MCL*, 1993, p. 83: "C'est dans la vision du bien-aimé, dans l'effort pour le séduire et dans l'union avec lui qu'on atteint le bonheur absolu".

42 A.D., *JISOA IX*, p. 60: "erect"; French version, *MCL*, 1993, p. 88: "le réel linga dressé dans le yoni".

43 This sentence was omitted by A.D. from *JISOA IX*, p. 60; French version, *MCL*, 1993, p. 88.

44 For a valid discussion on the Supreme *Puruṣa* (*Puruṣottama*) see the fiftheenth chapter of the *Bhagavadgītā*.

45 Interpolation of A.D., *JISOA IX*, p. 60: "Śrī Kṛṣṇa, unable to copulate because he was alone"; French version, *MCL*, 1993, p. 88: "l'Etre suprême appelé Krishna, incapable d'accomplir l'acte d'amour".

46 Hiraṇyagarbha, the Golden Embryo, is associated in *Vedānta* with the essence presieding on the totality (*samaṣṭi*) of all the subtle bodies (*sūkṣmaśarīra*). In the subtle sphere dominates the universal mind (*samaṣṭi antaḥkaraṇa*), which, in its individual aspect is divided in four functions (*vṛtti*). Among these four functions the ascertaining one (*adhyavasāya*) is *buddhi*, *mahat*, the intellect, which the most pure, owing to the predominance of *sattva* in it.

47 Footnote of A.D., *JISOA IX*, p. 61: "In the microcosm (man) ten fingers" breadth represents the distance between the navel, the center of the manifested, and the heart, the centre of consciousness. Addition, ms. 1992: "Ten fingers' breadth is also the length by which a man's erect penis towers above his body, or which separates the universe from his creator"; French version, *MCL*, 1993, note p. 91: "La largeur de dix doigts représente également la longueur de laquelle le sexe dressé de l'homme dépasse du corps ou l'univers de son créateur".

48 If we refer to the condition of Śiva as unveiled, the purport of the word *śiva* is *nirguṇa brahman*, following the *Māṇḍūkya Upaniṣad* 7.

49 A.D., *JISOA IX*, p. 62: "when joined with Śiva *Prakṛti* becomes the flow of evolution (*vikāra*)"; French version, *MCL*, 1993, p. 89: "évolution".

50 Addition, A.D., *ms.* 1992: "in which the *liṅga* rises erect"; French version, *MCL*, 1993, p. 91: "duquel le Linga sort dressé".

51 Sentence omitted by AD.

52 See also *Śiva Mahāpurāṇa*, I.16.105-107, trans. by S. L. Nagar, Parimal Publications, Delhi, 2007, vol. I, p. 101. The differences with the mistranslation of these *ślokas* wrongly attributed to Svāmī Karpātrī by Daniélou are very important. Particularly, the wrong translation of the *śloka* 106: "One should worship the generator (*liṅgit*) in the 'organ of generation' (*liṅga*)". (A.D., *JISOA IX*, p. 65) can be found in several publications, by the responsibility of Daniélou, as a Svāmī Karpātrī's translation. See also without reference to Svāmī Karpātrī: " 'The Lord is the source of all enjoyment... For existence to be a perpetual joy, the follower must worship the phallus which is the god Shiva himself, the sun which gives birth to the world and upholds it. It is the symbol of the origin of all things. Shiva, the origin of all things, should be worshipped in the form of the phallus, through which the male principle is recognizable. The phallus is thus the symbol of the god.' (*Shiva Purana, Vidyeshvara Samhita,*1, chap 16, 103-106)." *Shiva and Dionysus*, Inner Traditions International, 1984, p. 56. Significantly, Daniélou omits the *śloka* 107 quoted here by Svāmī Karpātrī: "Liṅga is said to be the symbol of the union of Śiva and Śakti. The combined form of Śiva and Śakti is called *liṅga*."

53 Interpretation of 'the worship of the *liṅga*' by A.D. in his *Hindu Polytheism*: "It is through the union of sexes that new beings, new lives, come into existence [....] The shape of the organ which perform this ritual is, verily, a symbol —the visible form of the divine creator" (*Hindu Polytheism*, 1964, *The Myths and Gods of India*, 1991, pp. 226-227).

54 The first translation of this sentence by A.D. was: "It is called liṅga because through it one penetrates — knows — the supreme Śiva-principle" (JISOA IX, 1941, p. 65); in *ms.* 1992 this translation became: "It is called *liṅga* because through it, the supreme principle called Shiva is penetrated, raped"; French version, *M CL*, 1993, p. 97: "On le nomme Linga parce qu'á travers lui on pénètre — on viole — le Principe suprême appelé Shiva".

55 In the *Śiva Mahāpurāṇa,* Parimal Publications, New Delhi, 2003, see *Vid. Saṃ*, chapter 5, 'The Glory of Śiva-liṅga', p. 48-51.

56 Here there is a reference to the inference a posteriori (*śeṣavat anumāna*). In the inference the probans (*hetu*) is called also *liṅga*, literally 'sign', as through the sign, the symbol, we can know the symbolised (*liṅgita*).

57 Translation of A.D., *ms.* 1992: "God is represented by a phallus because he is the basis of all creation"; French version, *MCL*, 1993, p. 98: "Dieu est representé par un phallus parce qu'il est la base de toute création".

58 Mistranslation by A.D., *ms.* 1992: "In the Trinity, Shiva becomes the ruler of Darkness"; French version, *MCL*, 1993, p. 99: "Dans la Trinité, Shiva devient le souverain de l'obscurité, *Tamas*".

59 Addition of A.D., *ms.* 1992: "the disintegrating, obscuring tendency, who is also called Shiva"; French version, *MCL*, 1993, p. 100: "la tendance désintegrante, obscurcissante, qui est aussi appelée Shiva". After this sentence, A.D. makes a new paragraph.

60 After this word, A.D., ms. 1992, made a new part separated by [***]

61 These last four words, opposed to Danielou's idea of Śaivism, presented as 'ecstatic', were omitted by him from the *JISOA IX*, p. 68; *MCL*, 1993, p. 102: "Shiva tua d'abord la luxure et alors seulement il s'accoupla". The following sentence and *śloka* are also omitted in the French version.

62 A.D., *ms*. 1992: "erect in the triangular *yoni*"; French version, *MCL*, 1993, p. 103: "dressé dans le yoni triangulaire".

63 A.D., *ms.* 1992: "Brahman being the phallus-like dry tree"; *MCL*, 1993, p. 104: "brahman étant l'arbre sec, pareil à un phallus".

64 In the *JISOA IX*, p. 71, A.D. made here a new part to emphasize the next quotation.

65 One finds these *ślokas* also in the *Śiva Purāṇa, Vidyeśvara Saṃhitā* I.21.23-24, 26.

66 Interpolations and mistranslation of A.D. in his quotation of this passage, 1964: "Those who do not recognize the divine nature of the phallus, who do not measure the importance of the sex-ritual, who consider the act of love as low or contemptible or as a mere physical function, are bound to fail in their attempts at physical as well as spiritual achievement. To ignore the sacredness of the *liṅga* is dangerous, whereas through its worship the joy of life (*bhukti*) and the joy of liberation (*mukti*) are obtained (Karapātrī, '*Lingopasana rahasya*')" (*Hindu Polytheism*, 1964; *The Myths and Gods of India*, 1991, p. 227).

67 See also the transl. by S. L. Nagar, *Śiva Mahāpurāṇa*, Parimal Publications, New Delhi, 2007, vol. 1, p. 138-139. In Daniélou's publications, several translations of the sanskrit *ślokas* seemed to be made by Svāmī Karpātrī. In the Daniélou's first translation of these *ślokas*, there were discrete interpolations, as 'morality', 'prevails' or 'because': "He whose life is spent without worshipping the *liṅga* incurs great loss. After death he will not reach a better world. His mind also will become wicked. If on one side one puts charities, fasts, pilgrimages, sacrifices, morality and on the other the worship of the *liṅga*, the *liṅga* prevails because it gives enjoyment and salvation and removes adversity." (*JISOA IX*, pp. 71-72) Further, the '*liṅga*' became 'phallus', several mistranslations deeply modifying the meaning: "He who spends his life without honoring the phallus is verily unfortunate, sinful and ill-fated. If we put in balance the worship of the *liṅga* as against charities, fasts, pilgrimage, sacrifice, and virtue, it is the worship of the giver of pleasure and liberation, the remover of adversity that prevails." (*Śiva Purāṇa* 1.21.23-24, 26, quoted in Daniélou's *Hindu Polytheism*, 1964; *The Myths and Gods of India*, 1991, p. 227).

68 The *śivaliṅga* of the Kedāreśvara temple at Varanasi resembles petrified *kicharī*, mixed rice and pulse. Near this temple is the Karapātra *dhāma*, the place in which Svāmījī spent the last part of his life.

69 From the *JISOA IX*, p. 72-73 this sentence and the beginning of the following sentence were omitted by A.D, who didn't start a new paragraph here. French version, *MCL*, 1993, p. 106.

70 A.D., *JISOA IX*, p. 73, ms. 1992: "his phallus in his hand"; French version, *MCL*, 1993, p. 107: "tenait son sexe dans sa main".

71 A.D., *JISOA IX*, p. 73 and ms. 1992: "sexual organ"; French version, *MCL*, 1993, p. 107: "ton sexe".

72 *Śiva Mahapurāṇa*, *Koṭi Rudra Saṃhitā*, 12.17 S. L. Nagar edition, op. cit., vol II, p. 549.

73 *Aparādha*: offense, crime, sin. This sentence was omitted by A.D., *JISOA IX*, p. 73; ms. 1992, *MCL*, 1993, p. 107.

74 These three sentences were omitted by A.D., *JISOA IX*, p. 73; *MCL*, 1993, p. 108.

75 A.D., *JISOA IX*, p. 73: "Some theologians".

76 This sentence was also omitted from *JISOA IX*, p. 74, and in the French translation. *MCL*, 1993, p. 109.

77 *Śiva Mahāpurāṇa,* VII.12.3, transl. into English by S. L. Nagar, *op. cit.*, vol II, p. 548.

78 Daniélou omitted from the *JISOA IX*, p. 75 these three sentences concluding the original paragraph. See also *MCL*, 1993, p. 110.

79 Before this paragraph, A.D. made a new part (*JISOA IX*, p. 75).

80 See infra, p. 75 the note 125 on *arthavāda* in 'The refutation of Śakti'.

81 Kāmadeva is also called Anaṅga, because after being burnt by the third eye of Śiva, due to the praises of his wife Ratī, Śiva gave him a new form, a bodiless one.

82 This sentence and the five following *ślokas* were omitted by A.D., from the *JISOA IX*, p. 78.

83 These two sentences were omitted and never translated by A.D., from the *JISOA IX*, p. 78.

84 A.D., ms. 1992: "when he is inclined to creation, he becomes the phallus"; French version, *MCL*, 1993, p. 114: "C'est lui qui, quand il est enclin à la procréation, devient le phallus".

85 Transl. A.D., ms. 1992: "The same duality is found in instrument of knowledge, in which knowledge of the phallus-worship is a symbol"; French version, *MCL*, 1993, p. 115: "et là aussi la connaissance du culte du phallus a valeur de symbole".

86 Sentence omitted by A.D. from *JISOA IX*, p. 79.

87 Mistranslations of these *ślokas* in several Daniélou's publications: "Shiva said: 'I am not distinct from the phallus. The phallus is identical with me. It draws my faithful to me, and therefore must be worshipped. My well-beloved! Wherever there is an upright male organ, I myself am present, even if there is no other representation of me' (*Shiva Purana, Vidyeshvara Samhita* 1. chap 9. 43-44)." *Shiva and Dionysus*, Inner Traditions International, 1984, p. 56.

88 Interpretation of A.D., *JISOA IX*, p. 80: "Śiva is the 'possessor of the liṅga' (*liṅgī*)"; French version, *MCL*, 1993, p. 116: "Il est le 'possesseur du linga' (*lingi*)".

89 All the remaining part of the article starting from here was completely omitted by A.D., *JISOA IX*, p. 80, ms. 1992, *MCL*, 1993, p. 116, omitted all the end of the article.

90 *Pārthiva liṅgas* are earthly *liṅgas* made in clay and used in special occasional rites.

91 A *bāṇa liṅga* bestows the presence on Śiva even without rites of installation, see R.N. Bhatt, *Shaivism in the Light of Epics, Purāṇas and Āgamas*, Indica Books, 2008, p. 248.

92 Round stones from the bed of the *Nārmadā* river treated as natural *Śiva liṅgas.*

93 The invocation used in the ancestors oblations.

94 *"Aghorebhyo 'tha, ghorebhyo, ghoraghoratarebhyaḥ | Sarvaśarvebhyo namaste astu rudrarūpebhyaḥ ||"*, these *ślokas* are recited by the priests in every Śiva *pūjā*.

श्री भगवती-तत्त्व

THE PRINCIPLE OF THE GREAT GODDESS

श्रीभगवती-तत्त्व

अनन्तकोटिब्रह्माण्डात्मक प्रपञ्च की अधिष्ठानभूता सच्चिदानन्दरूप भगवती ही सम्पूर्ण विश्व को सत्ता, स्फूर्ति तथा सरसता प्रदान करती है। विश्व प्रपञ्च उन्हीं में उत्पन्न होता है, स्थित होता है, अन्त में उन्हीं में लीन हो जाता है। जैसे दर्पण में आकाशमण्डल, मेघमण्डल, सूर्य्य-चंद्रमण्डल, नक्षत्रमण्डल, भूधर, सागरादि प्रपञ्च प्रतीत होता है। दर्पण को स्पर्श करके देखा जाय, तो वास्तव में कुछ भी नहीं उपलब्ध होता, वैसे ही सदानन्दस्वरूप महाचिति भगवती में सम्पूर्ण विश्व भासित होता है। जैसे दर्पण के बिना प्रतिबिम्ब का भान नहीं होता, दर्पण के उपलम्भ में ही प्रतिबिम्ब का उपलम्भ होता है, वैसे ही अखण्ड, नित्य, निर्विकार महाचिति में ही, उसके अस्तित्व में ही, प्रमाता-प्रमाण-प्रमेयादि विश्व उपलब्ध होता है। भान न होने पर भास्य के उपलम्भ की आशा ही नहीं की जा सकती।

सामान्य रूप से तो यह बात सर्वमान्य है कि प्रमाणाधीन ही किसी भी प्रमेय की सिद्धि होती है, अतः सम्पूर्ण प्रमेय में प्रमाण कवलित ही उपलब्ध होता है। प्रमाता, प्रमाण एवं प्रमेय—ये अन्योन्य की अपेक्षा रखते हैं। प्रमाण का विषय होने से ही कोई वस्तु प्रमेय हो सकती है। प्रमेय को विषय करने वाली अन्तःकरण की वृत्ति प्रमाण कहला सकती है। प्रमेय-विषयक प्रमाण का आश्रय अन्तःकरणावच्छिन्न चैतन्य ही प्रमाता कहलाता है। प्रमात्राश्रित प्रमेयाकार वृत्ति को ही प्रमाण कहा जाता है। परन्तु इन सबकी उत्पत्ति, स्थिति, गति का भासक नित्य बोध आत्मा है। वही साक्षी एवं वही ब्रह्म कहलाता है। यद्यपि वह

THE PRINCIPLE OF THE GREAT GODDESS

Bhagavatī,[1] having the nature of Being, Knowledge and Bliss, is the substratum [2] of the universe which supports countless worlds, bestowing reality, vigour and 'juiciness' (*sarasatā*). This manifestation that we call 'the world' arises from Her and Her alone; it is located only within Her and, in the end, merges only into Her.[3] Just as in a mirror we can catch a glimpse of the vault of the sky, the clouds, the solar and lunar spheres, the stellar constellations, the ground and the oceans, and yet despite touching this mirror we cannot grasp any of these, similarly does the entire world appear within Bhagavatī, whose form is of eternal Bliss and Absolute Consciousness (*mahāciti*). Just[4] as we cannot see any reflection without a mirror, and just as the existence of a reflection presupposes the existence of a mirror, similarly is the world [summarized by triads] as the knower (*pramātā*), the means of knowledge (*pramāṇa*) and the knowable entity (*prameya*), only available within an indivisible, eternal, incorruptible Absolute Consciousness. We simply cannot hope for the existence of the thing to be known without the pre-existence of the knowledge.

Ordinarily, as it is universally accepted that any knowable thing can only be so established through some means of knowledge, that means of knowledge is therefore found to be included in the entire knowable entity. Knower, knowledge and the thing to be known all depend on each other. Only when something is a subject of examination can it be knowable. The modification of the internal organ (*antaḥkaraṇavṛtti*)[5] that makes a knowable thing a subject of enquiry can be called a means of knowledge. The knower is understood to be the consciousness limited by the internal organ (*antaḥkaraṇāvacchinnacaitanya*), that is, the seat of the cognition whose subject is the knowable entity. The knowable entity-shaped modification of the internal organ based on the knower is called knowledge. But it is the

स्त्री, पुमान् अथवा नपुंसक नहीं है, तथापि चिति-भगवती आदि स्त्रीवाचक शब्दों से, आत्मा-पुरुष आदि पुंबोधक शब्दों से, ब्रह्म-ज्ञान आदि नपुंसक शब्दों से व्यवहृत होता है । वस्तुतः स्त्री, पुमान्, नपुंसक इन सबसे पृथक् होने पर भी तादृक्-तादृक् शरीर सम्बन्ध से या वस्तु सम्बन्ध से वही अचिन्त्य, अव्यक्त, स्वप्रकाश सच्चिदानन्दस्वरूपा महाचिति भगवती ही आत्मा, पुरुष, ब्रह्म आदि शब्दों से ही व्यवहृत होती है ।

मायाशक्ति का आश्रयण करके वही त्रिपुरसुन्दरी, भुवनेश्वरी, विष्णु, शिव, कृष्ण, राम, गणपति, सूर्य आदि रूप में भी प्रकट होती है । स्थूल, सूक्ष्म, कारण, त्रिशरीर रूप त्रिपुर के भीतर रहने वाली सर्वसाक्षिणी चिति ही त्रिपुरसुन्दरी है । उसी मायाविशिष्ट तत्व के जैसे राम-कृष्णादि अन्यान्य अवतार होते हैं, वैसे ही महालक्ष्मी, महासरस्वती, महागौरी आदि अवतार होते हैं । यद्यपि श्रीभगवती नित्य ही है, तथापि देवताओं के कार्य के लिए वह समय-समय पर अनेक रूप में प्रकट होती है । वह जगन्मूर्ति भगवती नित्य ही है, उसी से चराचर प्रपञ्च व्याप्त है, तथापि उसकी उत्पत्ति अनेक प्रकार से होती है । देवताओं के कार्य के लिए जब वह प्रकट होती है, तब वह नित्य होने पर भी उत्पन्न हुई कही जाती है—

नित्यैव सा जगन्मूर्तिस्तया सर्वमिदं ततम् ।
तथापि तत्समुत्पत्तिर्बहुधा श्रूयतां मम ॥
देवानां कार्यसिद्ध्यर्थमाविर्भवति सा यदा ।
उत्पन्नेति तदा लोके सा नित्याप्यभिधीयते ॥

कुछ लोगों का कहना है कि "शास्त्रों में मायारूपा भगवती की ही उपासना कही गयी है, माया वेदान्त-सिद्धान्तानुसार मिथ्याभूत है,

eternally-aware Self (*ātman*) which is the illuminator of the origin, being and dynamics of all of these. It is He who is the witness; it is He alone who is called the Absolute (*brahman*). Although neither feminine nor masculine nor neuter, nevertheless consciousness (*cit*), Bhagavatī and the like are referred to in the feminine gender; [things like] *ātman* and *puruṣa*, in the masculine gender; and as *brahman*, *jñāna* (knowledge) are naturally used in the neuter gender. In fact, even though it is free from all gender, be it feminine, masculine or neuter, it is Bhagavatī who is the same supreme consciousness, beyond the scope of thought (*acintya*), beyond expression, self-illumined (*svaprakāśa*), whose nature of Being, Knowledge and Bliss (*saccidānanda*), due to the relation with a particular body or with an entity who gets expressed as '*ātman*', '*puruṣa*', '*brahman*' and so forth.

By taking recourse[6] to the power of illusion (*māyā*), the selfsame Tripurasundarī Bhuvaneśvarī also appears as Viṣṇu, Śiva, Kṛṣṇa, Rāma, Gaṇapati, Sūrya, and so on. Tripurasundarī is none other than the all-witnessing consciousness that resides inside the *tripura* ('the three cities'), the composite of the three bodies — the gross body (*sthūla*), the subtle body (*sūkṣma*) and the causal body (*kāraṇa*). Just as that reality determined by *māyā* has incarnations like Rāma, Kṛṣṇa, similarly does it also have incarnations like Mahālakṣmī, Mahāsarasvatī, Mahāgaurī, and the like. Even though Bhagavatī is eternal, She appears from time to time in various forms to fulfil tasks requested by the gods.

Of course,[7] this Bhagavatī with the form of the world (*jagan-mūrti*) is eternal, for She pervades the entire manifestation of rooted and mobile life forms; still, Her emergence takes place in various ways. Though She is ever-present, [yet] when She makes an appearance in order to favour the gods, She is then said to have arisen.

> She is eternal, the icon of the universe, by Her all this is pervaded,
> Still in many ways, may I hear about Her birth.

मुक्ति में उसकी अनुगति नहीं हो सकती, अतः भगवती की उपासना अश्रद्धेय है।'' 'तापनीय' में ऐसा स्पष्ट उल्लेख है कि नारसिंह माया ही सब प्रपञ्च की सृष्टि करती है, वही सबकी रक्षा करती है, वही सबका संहार करती है, उसी मायाशक्ति को जानना चाहिये। जो उसे जानता है, वह मृत्यु को तरता है, पाप्मा को तरता है, अमृतत्व एवं महती श्री को प्राप्त करता है—

माया वा एषा नारसिंही सर्वमिदं सृजति, सर्वमिदं रक्षति, सर्वमिदं संहरति, तस्मान्मायामेतां शक्तिं विद्याद् य एतां मायां शक्तिं वेद, स मृत्युं जयति, स पाप्मानं तरति, सोऽमृतत्वं गच्छति, महतीं श्रियमश्नुते।

आप वैष्णवीशक्ति अनन्तवीर्य्या एवं विश्व की बीजभूता माया हैं—

"**त्वं वैष्णवीशक्तिरनन्तवीर्य्या विश्वस्य बीजं परमासि माया।**"
इत्यादि वचनों से स्पष्ट मालूम पड़ता है कि मायारूपा ही भगवती है। उसी की उपासना का तत्र-तत्र स्थानों में विधान है। माया स्वयं जड़ा है इत्यादि-इत्यादि। परन्तु यह ठीक नहीं है, क्योंकि यह सब निम्नलिखित प्रमाणों से विरुद्ध है—

सर्वे वै देवा देवीमुपतस्थुः कासि त्वं महादेवी, साब्रवीदहं ब्रह्मरूपिणी, मत्तः प्रकृति पुरुषात्मकं जगत्। (देव्यथर्वशिर)

अर्थात् देवताओं ने देवी का उपस्थान करके उससे प्रश्न किया कि "आप कौन है?"

देवी ने कहा—"मैं ब्रह्म हूँ, मुझसे ही प्रकृति-पुरुषात्मक जगत् उत्पन्न होता है।"

> When She manifests to fulfil the deities, then She is said 'Born' in the world, though She is eternal.

Some people[8] opine that "in the Scriptures, only the worship of Bhagavatī in her *māyā* form has been prescribed. According to the principles of *Vedānta*, *māyā* is illusion; it cannot have prosecution in liberation (*mukti*),[9] therefore the worship of Bhagavatī is not worthy of reverence." It is clearly mentioned in the *Tāpanīya* [*Upaniṣad*] that it is *Nārasiṃhī māyā* alone who creates this whole [worldly] manifestation, She alone who protects everything and she alone who annihilates all; so, we ought to know this very *māyā* power. He who knows Her transcends death, impurity (*pāpmā*), obtains immortality and profound glory.

> She, the Nārasiṃhī *māyā* (illusion) manifests all this universe, all this She preserves and all this She annihilates, therefore this illusive power should be known. He who knows this illusive power conquers the death, crosses over the impurity, reaches immortality and obtains a great glory.

"You are the Potency of Viṣṇu, with infinite powers, the Cause of the universe, You are the Supreme Illusion." Such words clearly suggest that She who is of the form of *māyā* is none other than Bhagavatī, that it is Her worship alone that is enjoined in various places, that *māyā* is inert in Herself, and so on and so forth. But this is incorrect, because it is contrary to the following proofs.

In the *Devyatharvaśīrṣa* [1-2] [it is said]:

> Having come before Her, the gods [10] asked the Goddess: "Who are you oh Great Goddess?
> The Goddess replied: "I am of the nature of *brahman*; from Me and Me alone arises the world characterized by puruṣa and *prakṛti*.
>
> So in the opening of *brahman* he obtains Her, the aspect of the Supreme: She is Bhuvaneśvarī, beyond the fourth state.
> (*Bhuvaneśvarī Upaniṣad*)

अथ ह्येनां ब्रह्मरन्ध्रे ब्रह्मरूपिणीमाप्नोति ।
भुवनाधीश्वरी तुर्य्यातीता । (भुवनैश्वर्युपनिषद्)

स्वात्मैव ललिता । (भावनोपनिषद्)

इत्यादि वचनों से तुर्य्यातीत ब्रह्मात्मस्वरूपा ही भगवती है, यह स्पष्ट है। 'त्रिपुरातापनीय', 'सुन्दरीतापनी'यादि उपनिषदों में 'परोरजसे' इत्यादि गायत्री के चतुर्थ चरण से प्रतिपाद्य ब्रह्म के वाचकरूप से 'ह्रीं' बीज को बतलाया है । 'काली' 'तारोपनिषदों' में भी ब्रह्मरूपिणी भगवती की ही उपासना प्रतिपादित है ।

"अतः संसारनाशाय साक्षिणीमात्मरूपिणीमाराधयेत् परां शक्तिं प्रपञ्चोल्लासवर्जिताम् ।" (सूतसंहिता) । अर्थात् संसारनिवृत्ति के लिये प्रपञ्चस्फुरणशून्य, सर्वसाक्षिणी, आत्मरूपिणी, पराशक्ति की ही आराधना करनी चाहिये ।

परातु सच्चिदानन्दरूपिणी जगदम्बिका ।
सर्वाधिष्ठानरूपा स्याज्जगद्भ्रान्तिश्चिदात्मनि ॥ (स्कान्द)

अर्थात् सच्चिदानन्दरूपिणी पराजगदम्बिका ही विश्व की अधिष्ठानभूता है, उन्हीं चिदात्मस्वरूपा भगवती में ही जगत् की भ्रान्ति होती है ।

सर्ववेदान्तवेदेषु निश्चितं ब्रह्मवादिभिः ।
एकं सर्वगतं सूक्ष्मं कूटस्थमचलं ध्रुवम् ॥
योगिनस्तत्प्रपश्यन्ति महादेव्याः परं पदम् ।
परात्परतरं तत्वं शाश्वतं शिवमच्युतम् ॥
अनन्तं प्रकृतौ लीनं देव्यास्तत्परमं पदम् ।
शुभ्रं निरञ्जनं शुद्धं निर्गुणं दैन्यवर्जितम् ॥
आत्मोपलब्धिविषयं देव्यास्तत्परमं पदम् । (कूर्म पुराण)

Lalitā is one's own self [*Bhāvana Upaniṣad*]

According to sayings such as these, it is none other than Bhagavatī who is beyond *turīya* [11] and whose form is that of inner most Self, the *brahman*; this much is clear.

In the *Tripurātāpanīya,*[12] the *Sundaritāpanīya* and other *Upaniṣads,* the Absolute reality expounded through the fourth quarter of the *Gāyatrī mantra* has '*Hrīṁ*' as its seed.[13] In the *Kālī* and *Tārā Upaniṣads* as well, the worship of Bhagavatī as the very form of *brahman* has been enjoined. [Following the] *Sūtasaṃhitā*:

> To rid oneself of this *saṃsāra*, one should worship the Transcendental Power (*parāśakti*), devoid of the emission of the manifestation of the world, the all-witnessing One whose form is that of the ātman (*ātmārūpiṇī*).[14]

In the *Skānda* [*Purāṇa* it is said:]

> The Transcendental World-Mother (*parājagadambikā*) of the form of Being, Consciousness and Bliss alone, is the ground of the world; the illusion (*bhrānti*) of the Universe is based on the self-same Bhagavatī, whose nature is that of Knowledge (*cidātmārūpiṇī*).[15]

> [Written] in all the *Upaniṣads* and affirmed by the seers who speak about the absolute, it is one, pervasive, subtle, firm, immovable, unchangeable; the yogins contemplate that supreme abode of the Great Goddess, even superior to *prakṛti*, the reality, eternal, benevolent, imperishable, infinite; that supreme abode of the Goddess lay within in the nature, resplendent, without impurity, pure, unqualified, without misery; that supreme goal of the Goddess is the object of the realization of the Self. (*Kūrma Purāṇa*)[16]

Such statements have been used to declare that only the incorruptible, infinite, infallible, indecipherable, non-qualified Absolute is the actual form of Bhagavatī.

इत्यादि वचनों से निर्विकार, अनन्त, अच्युत, निरञ्जन, निर्गुण ब्रह्म ही को भगवती का वास्तविक स्वरूप बतलाया गया है। 'देवी भागवत' में भी कहा है कि—

निर्गुणा सगुणा चेति द्विधा प्रोक्ता मनीषिभिः।
सगुणा रागिभिः सेव्या निर्गुणा तु विरागिभिः॥

अर्थात् निर्गुणा-सगुणा दो प्रकार की भगवती है, रागिजनों को सगुणा सेव्या हैं, विरागियों को निर्गुणा सेव्या हैं। 'ब्रह्माण्डपुराण' के 'ललितोपाख्यान' में भी कहा है—

चितिस्तत्पदलक्ष्यार्था चिदेकरसरूपिणी।

अर्थात् चिदेकरसरूपिणी चिति ही तत्पद की लक्ष्यार्थस्वरूपा है।

कहा जा सकता है कि "फिर तो ब्रह्मस्वरूपताबोधक वचनों से भगवती के मायात्वबोधक वचनों का विरोध अवश्य होगा।" परन्तु ऐसा कहना उचित नहीं है, क्योंकि वेदान्त में माया को मिथ्या कहा गया है। मिथ्यापदार्थ अधिष्ठान में कल्पित होता है। अधिष्ठान सत्ता से अतिरिक्त कल्पित की सत्ता नहीं हुआ करती। माया में अधिष्ठान की ही सत्ता का प्रवेश रहता है, अतः माया स्वरूप की उपासना से भी सत्तास्वरूप ब्रह्म की ही उपासना होगी। इस आशय से मायास्वरूपत्वबोधक वचनों का भी कोई विरोध नहीं है। जैसे ब्रह्म की उपासना में भी केवल ब्रह्म की उपासना नहीं होती, किन्तु शक्तिविशिष्ट ही ब्रह्म की उपासना होती है, क्योंकि ब्रह्म से पृथक् होकर शक्ति नहीं रह सकती और केवल ब्रह्म की उपासना हो नहीं सकती, वैसे ही केवल माया की भी उपासना सम्भव नहीं हो सकती। केवल माया की स्थिति ही नहीं बन सकती, फिर उपासना तो दूर रही।

In[17] the *Devī Bhāgavata* [*Purāṇa*] it is said: "Bhagavatī has two forms: one is without attributes (*nirguṇā*), and the other with attributes (*saguṇā*). The latter is worthy of worship by those who relish the world of sensory experience; for those who have lost interest in such an existence, the former is worth serving."

Furthermore in[18] the *Lalitopākhyāna* of the *Brahmāṇḍa Purāṇa,* this is said: "The term '*tat*' (that) is the implied meaning of that form of Consciousness which has the nature of the nectar of upsurging knowledge."

It[19] can be argued that "therefore, in that case, the statements that call Her 'the form of the Absolute' would surely contradict the sentences that refer to Her as 'the essence of *māyā*'" — but it would be incorrect to say so. This is because, in *Vedānta*, *māyā* has been called illusion (*mithyā*).[20] An illusory substance is imagined to exist within its own ground; that which is imagined does not have any existence separate from the existence of its basis. What is inherent in *māyā* is the existential presence of its basis; therefore, by worshipping the nature of *māyā* we would necessarily be worshipping the *brahman*, which is of the nature of pure Being (*sattāsvarūpa*). By this logic there is no contradiction with statements that call Bhagavatī 'She-with-the-nature-of-*māyā*'. In[21] the worship of the Absolute, also, there is no worship of only 'the Absolute' (*brahman*), but is rather the worship of the Absolute associated with *śakti* (power) — for *śakti* cannot exist apart from the Absolute, and the worship of 'the Absolute' alone is not possible. Similarly, it is not possible to worship *māyā* alone. The presence of *māyā* alone is not possible [given its nature]; hence, worshipping it alone is out of the question.

Māyā exists only in association with the Absolute (*brahman*), which is its basis (*adhiṣṭhānabhūta*); hence, by even describing Bhagavatī as having the nature of *māyā*, one inevitably comes to prove Her supreme reality.

[It is said:] "Just as within fire resides heat, as within the sun are its rays, as inside the moon resides its tender lunar light, similarly inside Śiva resides His natural śakti." Thus we find Bhagavatī

अधिष्ठानभूत ब्रह्म से युक्त होकर ही माया रहती है, अतः भगवती की मायारूपता वर्णन करने पर भी फलतः ब्रह्मरूपता ही सिद्ध होती है।

पावकस्योष्णतेवेयमुष्णांशोरिव दीधितिः ।
चन्द्रस्य चन्द्रिकेवेयं शिवस्य सहजा ध्रुवा ॥

अर्थात् जैसे पावक में उष्णता रहती है, सूर्य्य में किरण रहती है, चन्द्रमा में चन्द्रिका रहती है, वैसे ही शिव में उसकी सहज शक्ति रहती है । इस तरह विश्वस्वरूपभूता शक्ति के रूप में भगवती का वर्णन मिलता है । जैसे अग्नि में होम करने पर भी अग्नि-शक्ति में होम समझा जाता है, वैसे ही अग्नि-शक्ति में होम करने से अग्नि में होम समझा जाता है । इसी तरह माया को भगवती कहने पर भी ब्रह्म को भगवती समझा जा सकता है, अतः ब्रह्म की ही उपासना समझनी चाहिये । जो वाक्य माया को मिथ्या प्रतिपादित करते हैं, उनमें तो केवल माया का ही ग्रहण होता है, क्योंकि ब्रह्म का मिथ्यात्व नहीं है, वह तो त्रिकालाबाध्य सत्स्वरूप अधिष्ठान है । उपास्य मायापदार्थान्तर्गत ब्रह्मांश मोक्षदशा में भी अनुस्यूत रहेगा, अतः मुक्ति में उपास्यस्वरूप का त्याग भी नहीं होगा ।

'अन्तर्यामि ब्राह्मण' में पृथ्वी से लेकर माया पर्य्यन्त सभी पदार्थों को चेतन सम्बन्ध से देवता बतलाया गया है । "**सर्वं खल्विदं ब्रह्म**" इस श्रुति के अनुसार भी सब कुछ ब्रह्म ही है ऐसा कहा गया है ।

'सूतसंहिता' में कहा है—

चिन्मात्राश्रयमायायाः शक्त्याकारो द्विजोत्तमाः ।
अनुप्रविष्टा या संविन्निर्विकल्पा स्वयंप्रभा ।
सदाकारा सदानन्दा संसारोच्छेदकारिणी ।
सशिवा परमा देवी शिवाभिन्ना शिवङ्करी ॥

described as the power (*śakti*) which embodies the nature of the universe. Just as when we give oblations to the fire it is believed that we are giving oblations to the power (*śakti*) of fire, similarly by giving oblations to the power of fire it is believed that one is giving oblations to fire. Like this, even by calling *māyā* 'Bhagavatī' one can believe Bhagavatī to be 'the Absolute'; hence, Her worship should be seen as the worship of the Absolute. The [22] statements that declare *māyā* to be illusion are talking only about *māyā*, because the Absolue is not illusory. [The Absolute] is unconstrained in the past, present or future; it is the locus of everything, in the very form of Being. Falling under the realm of *māyā*, that portion of the *brahman* which is an object of worship shall also remain valid in the state of liberation; therefore, upon liberation there shall be no abandonment of the form of the worshipped. In the part [of the text] called *antaryāmi* (internal controller) *Brāhmaṇa*,[23] every substance from the earth (*pṛthivī*) up to *māyā* has been said to be a deity, on the basis of its relationship with Consciousness. According to the saying *'indeed all this is brahman'* [*Chāndogya Upaniṣad* III.14.1], it has been also said that everything is nothing other than the Absolute.

In [24] the *Sūta Saṃhitā* it is said:

> O best among the twice born, *māyā* who is based on the Absolute knowledge has the nature of power,
> She is that Consciousness which permeates everywhere, without distinctions, self-illuminous,
> Always identical to Herself, eternal bliss, who eradicates the incessant death-birth cycle,
> Constantly auspicious, the supreme Goddess, benevolent, She is Śiva himself.

"Having the shape of the power of *māyā* [and being] dependent on *parabrahman*, being knowledge alone (*cinmātra*), the Supreme Goddess is of the form of Śiva and is inalienable from Śiva: self-luminous, without distinctions, always identical to Herself, eternally blissful, knowledge itself." Similarly, words like *māyā*, *śakti*, *kalā*

अर्थात् चिन्मात्र परब्रह्म के आश्रित रहनेवाली माया के शक्त्याकार में अनुप्रविष्ट स्वयंप्रभा, निर्विकल्पा, सदाकारा, सदानन्दा, संविद् ही शिवाभिन्न शिवस्वरूपा परमा देवी है अथवा भगवतीस्वरूपप्रतिपादक वाक्यों में जो माया, शक्ति, कला आदि शब्द हैं, वे सब लक्षणा से मायाविशिष्ट, कलाविशिष्ट ब्रह्म के बोधक समझने चाहिये। तथा च मायाविशिष्ट ब्रह्म ही 'भगवती' शब्द का अर्थ है।

वही बात शिव ने कही थी—

नाहं सुमुखि मायाया उपास्यत्वं ब्रुवे क्वचित्।
मायाधिष्ठानचैतन्यमुपास्यत्वेन कीर्तितम्।
मायाशक्त्यादिशब्दाश्च विशिष्टस्यैव लक्षकाः।
तस्मान्मायादिशब्दैस्तद्ब्रह्मैवोपास्यमुच्यते॥

यहाँ एक-एक पक्ष में केवल चैतन्य ही मायादि शब्दों से उपास्य कहा गया है, द्वितीय पक्ष में मायाविशिष्ट ब्रह्म मायादिशब्द से कहा गया है। साकार देवताविग्रह सर्वत्र ही शक्तिविशिष्ट ब्रह्मरूप से ही उपास्य होता है। भगवतीविग्रह में भी भाषण, दर्शन, अनुकम्पा आदि व्यवहार देखा ही जाता है, फिर उसमें जड़त्व की कल्पना किस तरह की जा सकती है।

विराट्, हिरण्यगर्भ, अव्याकृत, ब्रह्म, विष्णु रुद्रादिकों के स्वरूप में एक-एक गुणों की प्रधानता है, माया गुणत्रय का ही साम्यावस्था रूप है, वह केवल शुद्ध ब्रह्म के आश्रित है। मायाविशिष्ट, तुरीयब्रह्म ही भगवती की उपासना में ग्राह्य है, यह दिखलाने के लिये माया, प्रकृति आदि शब्दों से कहीं-कहीं भगवती को बोधित किया गया है।

'मैत्रायणी श्रुति' में कहा है—

(digit) and the like, occuring when the form of Bhagavatī is being described, should be understood as referring to the *brahman* in its *māyā*-specified and *kalā*-specified form. And the word 'Bhagavatī' means nothing other than the *brahman* in its form associated with *māyā*.

Śiva[25] [Himself] had expressed the same thought:

> · Oh Beautiful-faced One, sometimes I don't express the worship-worthiness of Māyā,
> But the [Absolute] consciousness who is the ground of *māyā* is proclamed as an object to be worshipped.
> The words as *māyā*, *śakti*, etc., are indeed indicators of the qualified [Principle],
> Therefore, through the term '*māyā*' and the likes, that *brahman* alone is said to be the Adorable One.

Herein, everywhere it is mentioned that Consciousness (*caitanya*) alone is worth worshipping with words like '*māyā*' and the like; in the second part, the *māyā*-associated *brahman* has been referred to with words like '*māyā*' and such. Every concrete image of God is worshipped as the Absolute in His form qualified by *śakti*. Even in an image (*vigraha*) of Bhagavatī, one encounters such behaviour as speech, visibility, [the gesture that bestows] grace and the like — how, then, could one imagine Her to be inert?

In[26] the forms of *virāṭ* (the macrocosmic consciousness), *hiraṇya-garbha* (the golden embryo), *avyakta* (the unmanifested), Brahmā (the Creator), Viṣṇu (the Preserver) and Rudra (the Destroyer), a single *guna* will predominate. *Māyā* is nothing but the state of equilibrium of the three *guṇa* (*sattva*, *rajas, tamas*); it is dependent only on the pure *brahman*. The *māyā*-qualified *brahman* of the *turīya* state[27] is available in the worship of Bhagavatī; to demonstrate this, here and there Bhagavatī has been addressed as *māyā*, *prakṛti,* and so on.

In the *Maitrāyanī Śruti* it is said:

> In the beginning there was only darkness; then, by [the agency of] another did the imbalance increase, and the expanding

तमो वा इदमेकमग्र आसीत् तत्परे तस्मात्परेणेरितं विषमत्वं प्रयात्येतद्वै रजः तद्रज एव स्वीरितं विषमत्वं प्रयात्येतद्वै सत्त्वम् ।

इन वचनों से स्पष्ट कहा गया है कि तीनों गुणों की साम्यावस्थारूपा प्रकृति परब्रह्म में रहती है, उसी के अंश सत्वादि गुण हैं, तत्तद्गुणों से विशिष्ट ब्रह्म जो अंशभूत है, मूलप्रकृति-उपलक्षित ब्रह्म शुद्ध तुरीयस्वरूप ही है । "**त्वं वैष्णवी शक्तिः**" इत्यादि स्थलों में ब्रह्मरूपिणी भगवती का ही शक्तिरूप से वर्णन किया गया है । उपासनास्थल के अतिरिक्त माया आदि शब्दों से भी कहीं-कहीं शक्ति का ग्रहण किया गया है अथवा यह समझना चाहिये कि जगत्कारण परब्रह्म माया-ब्रह्म उभयरूप है ।

कहीं मायोपसर्जन ब्रह्म की उपासना है । जहाँ ऐसा है, वहाँ शक्तिसहायभूता है—

तस्मात् सह तया देवं हृदि पश्यन्ति ये शिवम् ।
तेषां शाश्वतिकीशान्तिर्नेतरेषां कदाचन ॥ (शिव पु०)

कहीं पर ब्रह्मोपसर्जन माया की उपासना है । इसीलिये माया, प्रकृति आदि शब्दों से भगवती की उपासना का विधान मिलता है । यह पक्ष सर्वतन्त्रों को मान्य है ।

शिवेन सहितां देवीं भावयेद् भुवनेश्वरीम्
(भुवनेश्वरीपारिजात)

दोनों ही पक्ष में ब्रह्म का चिदंश ही उपासना में आता है । इसीलिये माया पर मुक्ति के अनन्वयी होने का या अश्रद्धेय होने का कोई भी दोष लागू नहीं होता ।

> tendency (*rajas*) proceeded. Situated as it was, that *rajas* became umbalanced, and so unfolded the upward tendency (*sattva*).

These words clearly state that the balanced state of the three *guṇa* that is *prakṛti* lies within the *parabrahman* (the Transcendant Universal Absolute); *sattva, rajas,* and *tamas* are nothing but its limbs, and in *brahman* qualified by one or another *guṇa* they are parts, [whereas] the *brahman* characterized by the primeval Nature (*mūla-prakṛti*) is pure and of the nature of the 'fourth': *turīya*. In places where Bhagavatī has been described with words like "You are the Power of Viṣṇu", Bhagavatī — who is essentially of the nature of the *brahman* — has been described in Her *śakti* form. In some places, '*śakti*' has been referred to with words like *māyā* and the like, even surpassing the context of worship; alternatively, we should see this to mean that the Worldly Cause, the Transcendant Absolute (*para-brahman*) is *māyā* and *brahman*, a double-faced aspect.

The [28] worship of *brahman* qualified by *māyā* (*māyopasarjana*) has been mentioned in some places. Wherever this is the case, she is the helper of Śakti:

> So, they see in their heart the auspicious deity with Her, of them and never of others is the eternal peace. (*Śiva Purāṇa*)

In other places, we find the worship of *māyā* to be inalienable from *brahman* (*brahmopasarjana māyā*). Hence, by words like *māyā*, *prakṛti* and such, we find the injunction of worshipping Bhagavatī. This aspect is accepted in every *tantra*.

> He should meditate on the Goddess Bhuvaneśvarī (the Lady of the Worlds) united with Śiva. (*Bhuvaneśvarī Pārijāta*)

Anyway, in both the sides, it is only the Supreme Being in its conscious part (*cidaṃśa*) that is worshipped. Therefore, *māyā* avoids the accusation of being unworthy of reverence, or of not being included in liberation.

Although [29] according to statements like "Indeed all is *brahman*" [*Chāndogya Upaniṣad* III.14.1] everything is only the Supreme

यद्यपि "**सर्वं खल्विदं ब्रह्म**" इत्यादि श्रुति के अनुसार सब कुछ चिन्मात्र ब्रह्म ही है, तथापि भक्तों के चित्तावलम्बन के लिये अनेक प्रकार के स्वरूपों का उपदेश किया गया है। मलिन, शुद्ध, शुद्धतर, शुद्धतम आदि उपाधियों का उपदेश किया गया है। जैसे पात्र, मणि, कृपाण, दर्पणादि में शुद्धि के तारतम्य से प्रतिबिम्बित-प्रतिफलन में तारतम्य होता है, वैसे ही उपाधियों के तारतम्य से ब्रह्म के प्रसाद, प्राकट्य में भी तारतम्य होता है। इसी अभिप्राय से विभूतियों को उत्कृष्टता, उत्कृष्टतरता आदि का व्यवहार शास्त्रों में प्रसिद्ध है। एक-एक गुणों की अपेक्षा गुणों की साम्यावस्था उत्कृष्ट है।

इसीलिये भगवती की उपासना परमोत्कृष्ट है। इसके अतिरिक्त ब्रह्म का प्रथम सम्बन्ध माया के ही साथ है। गुणों का सम्बन्ध माया द्वारा है। इसीलिये साम्यावस्था में ब्रह्म का अव्यवहित सम्बन्ध है। अतएव 'सूत संहिता' में कहा गया है—

परतत्वप्रकाशस्तु रुद्रस्यैव महत्तरः।

फिर भी ब्रह्मतत्व सर्वत्र ही समान है। इसीलिये सभी में परमकारणत्व का व्यपदेश सर्वत्र मिलता है। कामार्थी, मोक्षार्थी सभी के लिये भगवती की उपासना परमावश्यक है। वही ब्रह्मविद्या है, वही जगज्जननी है, उसी से सारा विश्व व्याप्त है, जो उसकी पूजा नहीं करता, उसके पुण्य को माता भस्म कर देती है—

यो न पूजयते नित्यं चण्डिकां भक्तवत्सलाम्।
भस्मीकृत्वास्य पुण्यानि निर्दहेत्तमपीश्वरी॥

Consciousness (*cinmātra*),[30] numerous forms have been taught for the sake of providing a basis for visualisations appropriate to the inclinations of its devotees. Forms such as 'sullied' (*malina*), 'pure' (*śuddha*), 'purer' (*śuddhatara*), 'purest' (*śuddhatama*) and so on have been preached. Just as there is reciprocal symmetry between an object and its reflection in accordance with the degree of 'purity' of the reflecting surface — as with various surfaces like a metal vessel, a gem, a sword's blade or a mirror — similarly, there is a different degree (*tāratamya*) of the manifestation (*prākaṭya*) of the graciousness (*prasāda*) of the Absolute, due to the different degrees of its various accidental conditions.[31] It is with this in mind that in the Scriptures divine powers are called 'excellent', 'more than excellent', and so on. As compared to an individual *guṇa*, the undifferentiated balanced state of the *guṇas* is a more excellent state.

This[32] is why the worship of Bhagavatī is most exalted. Besides, it is with *māyā* alone that the *brahman* has its first relationship. Its relation with the *guṇas* is via *māyā*; hence, in an undifferentiated state, the Absolute has a direct relation. Thus has it been said in the *Sūta Saṃhitā*:

> The light of the supreme reality of Rudra is greater.

In any event,[33] the essence of *brahman* is equal everywhere; so, in everything it is found to function as the supreme causal principle. The worship of Bhagavatī is absolutely necessary for everyone, be they pleasure-seekers (*kāmārtha*) or seekers of liberation (*mokṣārtha*). She alone is the science concerning the Absolute (*brahmavidyā*); She alone is the mother of the world (*jagajjananī*). She pervades the entire world; the mother turns to ash the merits (*puṇya*) of he who does not worship Her:

> He who does not worship constantly the fearsome Caṇḍikā, who loves the devotees,
> The Goddess, having reduced his merits to ash, burns him as well.

'देवी भागवत' के प्रथम ही मन्त्र में भगवती के सगुण-निर्गुण दोनों ही रूपों का संकेत इस प्रकार मिलता है—

सर्वचैतन्यरूपां तामाद्यां विद्याञ्च धीमहि ।
बुद्धिं या नः प्रचोदयात् ॥

अर्थात् वह भगवती सर्वचैतन्यरूपा अर्थात् सर्वात्मस्वरूपा है, सबका प्रत्यक्-चैतन्य आत्मस्वरूप ब्रह्म वही है, वह स्वतः सर्वोपाधि-निरपेक्ष तथा अखण्ड बोधस्वरूप आत्मा ही है । ब्रह्मविषयक शुद्धसत्वान्तर्मुख वृत्ति पर प्रतिबिम्बित होकर वही अनादि ब्रह्मविद्या है । एक ही शक्ति अन्तर्मुख होकर विद्यातत्वरूपिणी होती है, तदुपाधिक आत्मा 'तुरीय' कहलाता है । बहिर्मुख होकर वही 'अविद्या' कहलाती है, तदुपाधिक आत्मा 'प्राज्ञ' है । मायाशबल ब्रह्म ही ध्यान का विषय है, वही बुद्धिप्रेरक है । शाक्तागम मतानुयायियों की दृष्टि से अत्यन्त अन्तर्मुख होकर शक्ति शिवस्वरूप ही रहती है । वेदान्त दृष्टि से सर्वोपाधिविनिर्मुक्त स्वप्रकाश चिति ही रहती है । वही परब्रह्म, आत्मा आदि शब्दों से लक्षित होती है ।

शक्ति का खण्डन

भगवती का ही शक्तिस्वरूप से भी आराधन होता है । हर एक कार्य की उत्पादनानुकूल शक्ति उसके कारण में होती है । कार्य्य के अनन्त होने से वह शक्ति भी अनन्त है—

शक्तयः सर्वभावानामचिन्त्यज्ञानगोचराः ।

We [34] get a glimpse of both forms of Bhagavatī — one non-qualified and the other qualified — in the very first *mantra* of *Devī Bhāgavata* [*Purāṇa*]:

> You meditate upon that Consciousness of everything, the primeval wisdom itself. May She stimulate our intellect.

In other words, that Bhagavatī is of the form of universal Consciousness — that is, She is of the nature of everyone's soul. She alone is the internal Consciousness *brahman* that is the Self (*ātmasvarūpa-brahma*); She is nothing but the nature of the indivisible awareness (*akhaṇḍabodhasvarūpa*), and is suo moto free from every happening. She [35] being reflected (*pratibimbita*) upon the inward modification of the purified internal organ that has *brahman* as its object, She alone is the causeless [unborn] knowledge concerning *brahman* (*brahmavidyā*). It is this same power which is the essence of supreme wisdom (*vidyā-tattvarūpiṇī*) when introverted, and which is called '*turīya*' [in relation to] the limited Self. It is called ignorance (*avidyā*) when extroverted, and the Self bearing this limitation is called the causal individual consciousness (*prājña*). It is the *brahman* equipped with the power of *māyā* who is the object of meditation, for it is the inspirer of the intellect. According to followers of the *śākta* beliefs, when She is extremely introverted, Śakti keeps the form of Śiva. According to *Vedānta*, only the self-illuminated Consciousness remains free from every qualification. It is She that is implied through such words as *parabrahman* and *ātman*.

The refutation of Śakti * [36]

The Goddess is worshipped even in the form of Śakti (power). Power inheres within the material cause of every effect, leading to the production of the effect. Since the effects are innumerable, therefore their potentialities also are innumerable.

> Śakti is inherent in everything, are objects of cognition beyond the reach of imagination (*acintya*).[37]

---

* The next two sections are the most technical chapters of this book. The reader can consult the explanatory notes, or else reach directly '*Bhagavatī as māyā*' p. 203.

शक्ति के सम्बन्ध में तार्किकों का कहना है कि कोई प्रमाण न होने से स्वरूप सहकारिमेलन के अतिरिक्त 'शक्ति' नाम का कोई पदार्थ नहीं है। स्फोटादिरूप कार्य की अन्यथानुपपत्ति को शक्ति में प्रमाण नहीं कहा जा सकता, क्योंकि जब प्रतिबन्धकाभाव आदि सहकारी से सहकृत अग्न्यादि के स्वरूप से ही स्फोटादिरूप कर्मोपपत्ति हो जाती है, तब अतीन्द्रिय शक्ति की कल्पना करना व्यर्थ है। अभाव की अकारणता होने से प्रतिबन्धकाभाव को सहकारी मानना ठीक नहीं है, ऐसा भी नहीं कहा जा सकता, क्योंकि अभाव को कारण मानने में न तो अन्वय-व्यतिरेकित्व में कोई बाधा पड़ती है, न किसी अनिष्ट की प्रसक्ति ही होती है। भाव की तरह अभाव का भी कार्य से अन्वय-व्यतिरेक दृष्ट है और अभाव की प्रमिति में योग्य की अनुपलब्धि एवं विभ्रम में विवेकाग्रह की हेतुता भी स्पष्ट ही है।

यदि कहा जाय कि क्या प्रतिबन्धक का प्रागभाव कारण है या उसका प्रध्वंसाभाव, तो दोनों की कारणता नहीं बनती, क्योंकि उत्तम्भक को प्रतिबन्धक के पास ले जाने पर प्रतिबन्धक के रहने पर भी प्रागभाव के बिना ही कार्योत्पत्ति देखी जाती है, अतः प्रागभाव को कारण नहीं कहा जा सकता। एवञ्च प्रतिबन्धक की अनुदयदशा में भी अर्थात् उसका प्रागभाव रहने पर भी कार्योत्पत्ति होती है, अतः प्रध्वंसाभाव की

About this power the view of the logicians (*tārkika*) is the following, that is there is no proof to support this power [separate from the already recognized *padārthas*], therefore there is no such *śakti* as a separate category, for it is not different from the combination of the associate causes (*sahakāri melana*). It is not possible to indicate as a proof for the *śakti* the otherwise impossibility of explaining (*anyathā anupapatti* = *arthāpatti*)[38] of an effect like a crackling sound (*sphoṭādi*) and other such effects, because when the action of crackling [the burning] takes place through the fire helped by the auxiliary causes[39] like the absence of any obstructing element (*pratibandhakābhāva*), in that situation it is useless to imagine any power which is beyond the capacity of the senses (*atīndriya* = *anumeya*). This also cannot be said. It is not correct to consider as an auxiliary cause the absence of the obstructing entity, since an absence cannot be a cause;[40] in fact there is not a single problem in accepting absence (*abhāva*) as cause, on the basis of the positive and negative concomitance (*anvaya-vyatireka*),[41] as well there is also no occurrence of an undesirable effect (*aniṣṭaprasakti*).[42] As for the presence (*bhāva*), both positive and negative concomitances are seen; the same also happens for an absence and, in the cognition of the absence, the apprehension of something worthy to be perceived (*yogyānupalabdhi*)[43] is clear, as with the illusive appearance (*vibhrama*), the causality (*hetutā*) of the incapacity to distinguish (*vivekāgraha*)[44] is also clear.

If someone might ask [45] whether the prior-absence (*prāgabhāva*) of the obstructing agent (*pratibandhaka*) is a cause, or if such is instead the subsequent destruction of the obstructing agent (*pradhvaṃsābhāva*), then the answer is that neither is a cause, for when you take an *uttambhaka* [46] near the obstructing object, then, even though there is no prior absence of the obstructing agent (*pratibandhaka*), the effect nevertheless comes to be. Therefore a *prāgabhāva* cannot be said to be a cause. Also, when the obstructing agent is not present (*anudayadaśā* = *anupasthiti*) — that is, when its prior absence is there — even then the effect (*kārya*) takes place, so

भी कारणता नहीं कही जा सकती । परन्तु यह ठीक नहीं है, क्योंकि उत्तम्भक मणि, मंत्र आदि के अभाव से सहकृत ही प्रतिबन्धक वस्तुत: प्रतिबन्धक होता है, न कि केवल मणि आदि । अत: वहाँ प्रतिबन्धक से सहकृत की ही कारणता होने से उक्त दोष नहीं रह जाता । सर्वत्र प्रतिबन्धक-संसर्गाभावविशिष्ट की ही कारणता मानी गयी है, अत: अनियतहेतुकत्वदोष भी नहीं कहा जा सकता । अन्यथा अनुपलब्धि में भी उपलब्धि के प्रागभाव एवं प्रध्वंसाभाव के विकल्प से अभावप्रमिति की अनियतहेतुकता दुष्परिहार्य होगी ।

शक्तिपक्ष में भी अप्रतिबद्ध ही शक्ति को कारण मानने से अभावविकल्प से उत्पन्न दोष एवं उसका परिहार तुल्य है ।

प्रतिबन्धो विसामग्री तद्धेतुः प्रतिबन्धकः ।

इस कुसुमाञ्जलि के वचनानुसार सामग्री-वैकल्य प्रतिबन्ध है और उसका हेतु प्रतिबन्धक है । यहाँ प्रतिबन्धपक्ष प्रतिबन्धकाभाव के कारण होने और कारणापेक्ष ही प्रतिबन्धकाभाव के प्रतिबन्ध होने के कारण अन्योन्याश्रयग्रस्त होने से यदि कहा जाय कि प्रतिबन्ध का भाव में कारणता मानना ठीक नहीं है, तो यह अनुचित है, क्योंकि अभाव की कारणता मानकर ही कार्यानुदयमात्र ही से मन्त्रादि में कार्यप्रतिकूलता

the absence due to the subsequent destruction of the *pratibandhaka*, can also not be called a cause.[47] But this is false, because it is the lack of the stimulator gem (*uttambhaka maṇi*), *mantra*, and so on, which cooperates with the obstructing agent to become such, rather than the gem or the *mantra* alone.[48] Therefore, since in such a condition, causality (*kāraṇatā*) comes about due to cooperation (*sahakṛta* = *viśiṣṭa*) with the obstructing agent (*pratibandhaka)*; for this reason the above-mentionned flaw does not stand. The causality qualified by the related absence (*saṃsargābhava*) of the obstructing object [49] is universally accepted, therefore it cannot be said that this argument is flawed with the defect consisting in indetermination of the causal factor (*aniyatahetukatva doṣa*).[50] Otherwise, according to the options of the prior absence of the apprehension and its subsequent absence, also in the non-apprehension (*anupalabdhi*),[51] will it be impossible to avoid the flaw consisting in indetermination of the causal factor of the cognition of the absence.

Also, following the ones who consider the power of an effective (*apratibaddha* = *unobstructed*)[52] *śakti* to be a cause, the flaw which arises by the absence-option and the solution of this problem are the same as yours.

> The obstruction is the insufficiency of the cause-complex, and the obstructing object is its cause.
>
> [Udayanācārya, *Nyāyakusumāñjalī,* I.10b53]

According to this statement of *Nyāyakusumāñjalī*, the insufficiency of the cause-complex is an obstruction (*pratibandha*) and its cause is the obstructing agent (*pratibandhaka*). Here [54] on the side of the obstruction, being the cause, the absence of the obstructing agent and on the other side of the cause, being the obstruction of the absence of the obstructing agent, there is a reciprocal dependence (*anyo-nyāśraya*); therefore if it would be said that to admit the causality of the absence of *pratibandhaka* is not possible, to this we reply that it is not correct, because admitting the [*pratibandhaka*] *abhāva* as a cause, by only the mere lack of onset of the effect, in the *mantra* [and

का बोध होता है और मणि, मन्त्रादि में कार्य की प्रतिबन्धता का निर्धारण किये बिना ही मन्त्रादि के अभाव में अन्वय-व्यतिरेक ही से कारणता का निश्चय होता है। इसके अतिरिक्त यह भी विचारणीय है कि अन्योन्याश्रयत्व उत्पत्ति या ज्ञप्ति में हुआ करता है। यहाँ मन्त्र एवं तदभाव (प्रागभाव) की परस्परहेतुता न होने से अज्ञात भी मन्त्र तथा तदभाव की कार्य के प्रति प्रतिकूलता एवं कारणता होने से दोनों प्रकार का अन्योन्याश्रय नहीं है।

यदि कहा जाय कि कार्याभाव से मन्त्रादि कारणाभावरूप माने जाते हैं, अतएव मन्त्रादि का अभाव भी कारण माना जाता है। एवञ्च मन्त्र तथा तदभाव में रहने वाले प्रतिबन्धकत्व और कारणत्व के अन्योन्यनिमित्तक होने से उत्पत्ति या ज्ञप्ति में अन्योन्याश्रयता दुर्वार है, तो यह ठीक नहीं है, क्योंकि अभाव की कारणता का अवगम हुए बिना भी कार्याभावमात्र से मन्त्रादि की कार्यप्रतिकूलता का ज्ञान हो सकता है, अतएव तदभाव को कारणता का भी ज्ञान अन्वय-व्यतिरेक से ही सुकर है।

यदि कहा जाय कि मणि-मन्त्रादि के सान्निध्य असान्निध्य में, उभयथापि अग्न्यादि के रूप में कोई अन्तर नहीं पड़ता, फिर भी दाहादि का प्रतिबन्ध होता ही है, अतः यदि स्वरूपातिरिक्त शक्ति न मानें, तो प्रतिबन्ध असम्भव हो जायगा, इसलिये शक्ति माननी चाहिये, यह भी ठीक नहीं, क्योंकि प्रतिबन्धशब्द से बोधित होने वाला कार्य के प्रति औदासीन्य ही अग्न्यादि में विशेष रूप से उपलब्ध होता है। यदि ऐसा न मानें, तो शक्ति मानने पर भी प्रतिबन्ध का विवेक कठिन हो

so on], will be understood to be adverse to the result (*kāryapratikūlatā*) and through the positive and negative concomitance, the accertainment of the causality in the absence of *mantra* etc., would not determine the opposition towards the effect about the gem, *mantra* and the like.[55] More than this, another subject is worthy to be investigated; mutual dependence usually happens with regards to birth (*utpatti*) or cognition (*jñapti*).[56] Here, *mantra* and its absence [prior absence] because their reciprocal causality is not given and also because an unknown *mantra* and its absence, which are, the former, advers towards the effect, and the latter, cause of the same effect, both the types of reciprocal dependence are not present.[57]

If [58] it has been said that, from the absence of the effect, *mantra* and other are considered as absence of the cause, so also the absence of *mantra*, etc., can be considered a cause. So the obstructing capacity (*pratibandhakatva*) residing in *mantra* and the causality residing in the absence of *mantra*, being the reciprocal causes of each other (*anyonyanimittaka*),[59] the mutual dependence, be it by birth or by cognition, will be unavoidable. All this [say the *Naiyāyikas*] is not correct, because without also understanding the causality of an absence by the mere absence of the effect (*kāryābhāvamātra*), it is possible to recognize the negative influence towards [the production of] effect (*kāryapratikūlatā* = *pratibandhakatva*) of *mantra* and the like, so recognizing the causality of their (*mantrādi*) absence (*tadabhāva*) through positive and negative concomitance will be quite easy.[60]

If someone says:[61] "When the gem or a *mantra* are present (*saṃnidhya*) [or *asaṃnidhya*], in both the situations no modification occurs in the fire nature, although there is an obstruction to the burning and the like effects. Therefore, if we will not maintain a power other than the essential nature, the obstruction will become impossible, so we must accept *śakti*." This is not accurate, because we find particularly in the fire and other [causes] an indifference (*audāsīnya*)[62] towards the effects, that is showed by the word 'obstruction' (*pratibandha*). If we do not accept this, — even considering power — it will be difficult to discriminate the obstruction. We also cannot

जायेगा। शक्ति का नाश प्रतिबन्ध नहीं कहा जा सकता, अन्यथा प्रतिबन्ध हट जाने पर कार्याभाव की प्रसक्ति होगी। स्फोटरूप कार्य की उत्पत्ति के लिये वहाँ शक्त्यन्तर की उत्पत्ति मानना भी उचित नहीं है, क्योंकि उसके किसी कारण का वहाँ निरूपण नहीं किया जा सकता। अग्निसामग्री से वहाँ कार्योत्पत्ति नहीं कही जा सकती, क्योंकि वह तो नष्ट ही हो चुकी है। अशक्त अग्नि उत्पादक न होने से उस आश्रय-भूत अग्नि से भी कार्योत्पत्ति नहीं कही जा सकती। यदि उत्पादकत्व मानें, तो कार्य में भी वह वैसे ही विद्यमान होने से शक्ति को मानना निष्प्रयोजन है। यदि वह शक्त है, तो उस शक्ति को कार्य के विषय में भी मान लेने से काम चल जाता है। ऐसी स्थिति में कारणान्तर का निरूपण न होने से शक्त्यन्तर की उत्पत्ति नहीं मानी जा सकती। प्रतिबन्धाभाव को भी कारण नहीं कहा जा सकता, क्योंकि अभाव की कारणता अस्वीकृत है।

यदि अभाव को कारण माना जाय, तो उसी से स्फोटादि कार्यों की उत्पत्ति हो जायगी, फिर अतीन्द्रिय शक्ति की कल्पना से क्या लाभ ? एक शक्ति से दूसरी शक्ति का प्रतिबन्ध मानने से अनवस्था-प्रसङ्ग प्राप्त होगा, क्योंकि उसमें भी उक्त दूषण के परिहारार्थ शक्तिप्रतिबन्ध कहना पड़ेगा। अत: शक्ति के बिना भी कार्य के अन्यथापि उपपन्न हो जाने से अतीन्द्रिय शक्ति की कल्पना का कोई अवकाश नहीं है।

उपादानोपादेय भावरूप नियम की अनुपपत्ति भी शक्ति में प्रमाण नहीं कही जा सकती अर्थात् दुग्धादि जैसे दध्यादि का उपादान है, न कि तिलादि। एवञ्च तिलादि ही तैलादि का उपादान है, न कि दुग्धादि। ऐसा जो नियम है, उसकी शक्ति को बिना स्वीकार किये उपपत्ति न

consider the destruction of the power;[63] otherwise, when the obstruction will be removed, there will be no effect. Therefore it is also not correct to maintain another power (*śaktyantara*)[64] in order to produce the effect like the crackling sound and the like, because there we cannot properly identify anything else of that new *śakti*. In that situation, we cannot say that 'the emergence of the effect is due to the fire and the entire complex of causes' because that particular complex is already finished.[65] Being impotent, fire cannot generate [effects], so even if it is the base of it, it cannot produce any result.[66] If we accept the capacity to produce [the burning effect also in an impotent fire] (*utpādakatva* = *dāhakāryajanakatva*), so [the fire] also being equally present in effect, it would be useless (*niṣprayojana*) to believe in the theory of *śakti*.[67] Otherwise, if the fire is also capable (*śakta* = *samartha*) to burn [to generate the burning] without the *śakti*, our task can be fulfilled also considering that power in respect to the effect.[68] Faced with this situation, not identifying cause (*kāraṇāntara*), we cannot accept the creation of a new *śakti*. We also cannot accept the absence of the obstructing agent as cause, because the causality of *abhāva* is not accepted.[69]

If we accept absence as cause, then from it would be the production of effects like the crackling sound (*sphoṭa*) and others; in this condition what is the profit in considering *śakti*? Accepting the obstruction of a power by another one, there will be a regressus ad infinitum (*anavasthāprasaṃga*)[70] — because for the solution of the mentioned flaw we will have to accept the obstruction of the power. Therefore also without *śakti*, another way will be able to explain the effect, so, in conclusion, the acceptance of a power beyond the range of the senses finds no place.

If someone objects like this:[71] Also the impossibility in the invariable rule of the relation between material cause and effect (*upādānopādeyabhāva*) cannot be said to be a proof in respect to *śakti*. This is the sense: just as material cause of curd is milk and not sesame seeds, and the material cause of sesame oil, are sesame seeds, not milk. If we don't accept *śakti* there are inconsistencies [72] within

होने के कारण शक्ति मानना आवश्यक है— ऐसा नहीं जा सकता, क्योंकि शक्ति के बिना माने ही अनादिसिद्ध वृद्धव्यवहार से निर्णीत तत्तत्कार्यानुकूल स्वभाव की विशेषता से ही उपादानोपादेय-नियम की सिद्धि हो जाती है। यदि स्वभाव को नियामक न माना जाय तो शक्ति में भी नियम न रह सकेगा। "यह शक्ति यहीं क्यों है, अन्यत्र क्यों नहीं है", इसका समाधान स्वभावभेद के अतिरिक्त और क्या हो सकता है? अतः कहना होगा कि दोनों प्रकार की अर्थापत्तियों को उपर्युक्त रीति से शक्ति में प्रमाण नहीं कहा जा सकता।

यदि—

विमतं (अग्न्यादि) अजनकदशातो जनकदशायामतिशययोगि कारकत्वात् कुण्ठकुठारवत्।

इस अनुमान को शक्तिसाधक कहें, तो यह भी नहीं हो सकता, क्योंकि सहकारिसमवधान के अतिशय से ही सिद्ध-साधनता है।

यदि—

अग्निः अतीन्द्रियसामान्यवन्निष्क्रियाश्रयः, कारणत्वात् गुरुत्वाश्रयवत्।

इस अनुमान द्वारा शक्ति को सिद्ध करें, तो भी जो योगी को मानता है, उसके मत में किसी वस्तु के अतीन्द्रिय न होने से उक्त अनुमान में दिया हुआ 'अतीन्द्रिय' विशेषण सिद्ध नहीं होता, अतः

this rule, so we must accept her as a cause; so then we reply that this is not tenable, because also without accepting *śakti* the invariable rule (*niyama* = *vyāpti*) of the material cause and its effect is proved by the particularity of the essential nature (*svabhāva*)[73] capable of producing this or that effect (*tattatkāryānukūla*) as ascertained by the beginningless (*anādi*) behaviour of the elders (*vṛddhavyavahāra*). If we do not accept as instrumental the ascertaining (*niyama*) [of the cause-effect relation] of the essential nature (*svabhāva*),[74] so there also will be no rule in respect to *śakti*. "Why is this power like this? Why is it not elsewhere?" the solution to this questions cannot be other then the particular nature of an entity (*svabhāvabheda* = *svabhāvaviśeṣa*).[75] Therefore, in the previously explained mode, we must say that neither type of presumption (*arthāpatti*)[76] is sufficient proof for power.

[We infer like this:]

> The thing under discussion (*vimatam*)[77] [that is the fire, etc.] is endowed with some special property (*atiśayogin*) in the condition of producing the effect (*janakadaśāyām*) compared to the condition in which effect is not produced (*ajanakadaśātaḥ*)[78] because there it is as effective (*kārakatvāt* = *karotīti kārakam*) as a blunt axe.

We cannot consider this inference establishing the *śakti* (*śaktisādhaka*), because from the abundance of gathering (*samavadhāna* = *upasthiti* = *saṃnidhya*) of the auxiliary causes, will come the flaw that involve proving that which has already been proved (*siddhasādhanatā*).[79]

> The fire is endowed with a general attribute beyond the range of the senses (*atīndriyasāmānyavat*) and is the base of something without action (*niṣkriyāśraya*), because it is a cause, as is the basis of gravity.[80]

In this inference there is the effort to prove *śakti*, but for he who believes that for a *yogin* nothing remains beyond the range of the senses, for him the adjective given in the inference is useless; so,

वैसे विशेषण से गर्भित अनुमान से शक्ति की सिद्धि कैसे हो सकती है? यदि कहा जाय कि 'जैसे हमारा चक्षु, इन्द्रिय होने के कारण गुरुत्वजातिविषय नहीं है, वैसे ही योगी का चक्षु इन्द्रिय होने के कारण गुरुत्व- जातिविषय न होगा।' इस अनुमान से अतीन्द्रिय की सिद्धि करके पूर्वोक्त अतीन्द्रियसामान्यगर्भित अनुमान द्वारा शक्तिसिद्धि हो जायेगी, तो यह भी उचित नहीं, क्योंकि वहाँ यह शंका होगी कि ऐसा अनुमान करनेवाले की दृष्टि में योगीन्द्रिय प्रसिद्ध है या अप्रसिद्ध? यदि अप्रसिद्ध है, तो योगी को माननेवाले मीमांसक की दृष्टि में आश्रयासिद्धि होगी। यदि प्रसिद्ध है, तो धार्मिग्राहक प्रमाण का बाध होगा अर्थात् अस्मदादिकों के इन्द्रिय से विलक्षण योगीन्द्रिय को ग्रहण करता हुआ प्रमाण ऐन्द्रियक-अतीन्द्रियक साधारण ही उसका ग्रहण करायेगा, अत: उस प्रमाण से गुरुत्वजातिविषयत्वाभावरूप साध्य का बोध हो जायगा। यदि उस अतीन्द्रिय विशेषण को अस्मदादि के अभिप्राय से मानें, तो भी काम न चलेगा क्योंकि जब परमाणु को जानता हूँ, आकाश को जानता हूँ, ऐसा अनुव्यवसाय होता है, तब परमाणु और उसका ज्ञान मानसप्रत्यक्षरूप अनुव्यवसाय का विषय होता है।

इस तरह सभी वस्तु ऐन्द्रियकज्ञानविषय बन जाने से अस्मदादि की दृष्टि से भी अतीन्द्रियत्व अप्रसिद्ध ही रहता है और इस तरह पूर्वोक्त दोष ज्यों-का-त्यों रहने से उक्त अनुमान से शक्तिसिद्धि नहीं हो सकती। यदि उस अनुमान में, अनुव्यवसायातिरिक्त अस्मदादि ऐन्द्रियकबुद्धि के अगोचर होने के आशय से वह अतीन्द्रियत्वरूप विशेषण है, ऐसा

how can the selfsame inference which contains that adjective prove the power? If someone objects, just as my eye — being a sense organ — cannot make its object the general character of the gravity (*gurutvajātiviṣaya* = *gurutvāśraya*),[81] in the same way the eye of a *yogin*, being an *indiriya,* cannot have as an object the generic character of gravity. Having proved by this inference the fact to be beyond the range of the senses, thereafter there will be the [possibility of] proving *śakti* through the aforementioned inference containing the word 'general character beyond the senses'. To this we reply that is not possible because there will be such a doubt:[82] "According to that inference maker, are the sense organs of a *yogin* established or not? If not, then also on the side of the *Mīmāṃsakas* who do not admit the [omniscience of the] *yogins* there will be the flaw of the lack of establishment of the locus of inference (*āśrayāsiddhi*).[83] Otherwise, if it is established, there will be the opposition (*bādha*) of the means of proof capable of grasping that locus (*dhārmigrāhaka* = *pakṣa* = *yogīndriyagrāhaka*)." [84] This means: just as a means of knowledge (*pramāṇa*) in contact with the senses of the *yogin* who are different from ours, will make him grasp equally both what is sensory and supersensory as well, so too through that means of knowledge, the probandum (*sādhya*) is in the form of the absence of the possibility to be an object of [common] perception of the generic character of gravity.

If we consider the adjective 'beyond the range of the senses' meaning our senses, then also there will be no success, because when we have this kind of subsequent cognition (*anuvyavasāya*):[85] "I know the atom (*paramāṇu*)", "I know the ether", then the atom and its cognition will be an object of the subsequent cognition that has a form of mental perception (*mānasapratyakṣa*). So, in this way, all the things will become perceptible by sensorial cognition [86] and for us, as well, nothing will remain beyond the range of the senses. Therefore the previously applied flaw remaining as it is, the inference is not capable of establishing *śakti.* If someone would object that,[87] in this inference, the 'being out of the capacity of the senses' (*atīndriyatva*)

कहें, तो भी ठीक नहीं, क्योंकि अन्यप्रमाण से उपनीत विशेषणावगाहिविशिष्टज्ञान माननेवाले के मत में सभी पदार्थों की ऐन्द्रियकता सम्भव होने से पूर्वोक्त दोष ज्यों का त्यों रह जाता है अर्थात् जिनके मत में '**सुरभिचन्दनम्**' इत्यादि विशिष्ट ज्ञान प्रमाणान्तर घ्राण आदि से उपनीत गन्धादि को भी विषय कहते हैं, उनके मत में यत्किञ्चित् प्रत्यक्षार्थ विशेषण होने से सभी पदार्थ ऐन्द्रियकबुद्धिबाध्य हो सकते हैं, अतः अप्रसिद्ध विशेषणता उक्त अनुमान में तदवस्थ ही है।

यदि पूर्वोक्त—

> **अग्निः अतीन्द्रियसामान्यवन्निष्क्रियाश्रयः कारणत्वात् गुरुत्वाश्रयवत्।**

इस अनुमान में विशिष्टज्ञान एवं अनुव्यवसाय के अतिरिक्त अस्मदादि ऐन्द्रियकबुद्धि का अविषयत्व ही अतीन्द्रियत्व माना जाय, तो वहाँ फिर यह शंका हो सकती है कि इस अनुमान में 'आश्रय' पद से जो आधाराधेयभाव विवक्षित है, वह संयोगि रूप से विवक्षित है या समवायिरूप से? यदि संयोगिरूप से, तो गुरुत्वाश्रय के दृष्टान्त में साध्यवैकल्य होता है। यदि 'आश्रय' पद का अर्थ समवायी मानें, तो समवाय को न माननेवाले मीमांसकभाट्ट के मत में उक्त विशेषण ही अप्रसिद्ध होने से वह अनुमान नहीं बन सकेगा और वह्नि में स्थितिस्थापक संस्कारसिद्धि होने से सिद्धसाधनता भी होती है। यदि कहा जाय कि

with a sense of 'not being an object (*agocara*) of our sensory cognition', is other than the subsequent one (*anuvyavasāyātirikta),* this too cannot be maintained, because according to the doctrine which accepts the 'cognition qualified by the apprehension of the qualifier' (*viśeṣanāvagāhiviśiṣṭajñāna* = *jñānalakṣaṇapratyāsatti*) presented by another proof, the sensory perception (*aindriyakatā*) of everything being possible, the previously mentioned flaw remains unaltered.[88] This means that for him who follows the view according to which 'the sandal is fragrant' (*surabhi candanam*) and this kind of qualified cognition, makes for its object the odour presented by a different mean of knowledge other than the smelling organ, applying their theories, every object can be knowable through a sensorial cognition, being the qualifier of whatever, an directly perceivable object (*yatkiṃcit-pratyakṣārtha-viśeṣaṇa* = *yatkiṃcidvastu-pratyakṣaviṣayībhūta-padārtha-viśeṣaṇa*); so in the previous inference, the unestablishment of the adjective (*viśeṣaṇatā* = *atīndriyatva*) remains as it is.[89]

> The fire is endowed with a generic attribute beyond the range of the senses and is the base of something without action, since it is a cause, as is the basis of gravity.[90]

If in this said inference we consider the *atīṇdriyatva* to be different from the qualified knowledge and from the subsequent cognition (*anuvyavasāya),* as the absence of object (*aviṣayatva*) of our sensory cognition is different, then a doubt can arise. In this inference, is the relation of ground and the sustained object (*ādhārādheyabhāva*) implied by the term 'ground' (*āśraya*) a contact relation (*saṃyogin* = *saṃyogasambandhāśrita*) or an inherence relation (*samavāyin* = *samavāyasambandhāśrita*)[91]? If it is the former, then in the example of 'the ground of gravity' there will be the lack of the probandum (*sādhyavaikalya*).[92] If the latter one, for the *Mīmāṃsaka* followers of Kumārila Bhaṭṭa who do not accept inherence,[93] that same inference finds no room, being an unestablished (*aprasiddha*) qualifier (*viśeṣaṇa*). More than this, with fire being the proved impression (*saṃskāra*) of elasticity (*sthitisthāpaka*), we will again have the flaw

सिद्धिसाधनता और स्थितिस्थापक के अस्तित्व में कोई प्रमाण न होने से क्यों मानें? तो यह भी ठीक नहीं है, क्योंकि उसके अस्तित्व में

विमतः स्थितिस्थापकसंस्कारवान् रूपवत्त्वात्, कटवत् ।

यह अनुमान विद्यमान है । इस अनुमान को स्थितिस्थापककार्य-वत्त्वरूप उपाधि से दूषित भी नहीं कहा जा सकता, क्योंकि उपाधि की साध्यव्यापकता होने आवश्यक है, किन्तु उत्पन्न होते ही नष्ट हो गये कटादि में स्थितिस्थापकरूप कार्य का उपलम्भ न होने पर भी यहाँ तथाविध संस्कार का अभ्युपगम होने से साध्याव्याप्ति रहती है ।

अपि च जो मीमांसक अपने सिद्धान्तानुसार सिद्धसाधनता कह रहा है, उसको सैकड़ों अनुमानों से भी स्वसिद्धान्त से किस तरह प्रच्युत किया जा सकता है और कैसे उसके सिद्धसाधनता इस अभिधान को प्रत्युद्धृत किया जा सकता है? यदि इस प्रकार स्वसिद्धान्त के अनुरोध से सिद्धसाधनता माननेवाले की अनुमानों द्वारा तदीय सिद्धान्त से प्रच्युति अशक्य होने और सिद्धसाधनता के अपरिहार्य होने से स्वाभिप्रायसिद्ध्यर्थ पूर्वोक्त अनुमानगत "**अतीन्द्रियसामान्यवन्निष्क्रियाश्रय**" में "**स्थितिस्थापकेतर**" यह विशेषण जोड़कर दूषण का परिहार किया जाय, तो भी प्रभाकर के मत में—जो कि कर्म की अप्रत्यक्षता मानते हैं—कर्म से अर्थान्तरतापत्ति होगी, क्योंकि उनके मत में अप्रत्यक्ष एवं

of proving what is already proven (*siddhasādhana*).[94] If someone says that there is no proof for the existence of either *siddhasādhanatā* or of elasticity, is there therefore no meaning in accepting them?[95] We reply that that is not correct; in fact this inference (*anumāna)* is a proof of their existence.

> The entity under discussion (*vimataḥ*) is endowed with the impression called elasticity, because it possess colour, just as a straw-mat (*kaṭavat*).[96]

It is also not possible that this inference is contaminated by a conditional agent (*upādhi*), that is possessing an activity due to elasticity (*sthitisthāpakakāryavattva*), because the conditional agent must be pervader of the probandum (*sādhyavyāpaka*), but in the mats and the like destroyed just after they are made, we find no activity — like elasticity — so here, accepting this kind of impression, there will be the non-pervasion of the probandum (*sādhyāvyāpti*).[97]

Moreover, there is an effort — with many inferences — to topple the *Mīmāṃsaka* from his point of view, the one who objects to the *Naiyāyika*s on the basis of his doctrine, the flaw of proving what is already proven, as well as [the *Naiyāyika*s] rejecting (*pratyuddhṛta* = *nirākṛta*) the accusation of proving what is already proven (*siddhā-sādhanatā*).[98] While so following one's own point of view, and given that one shan't be toppled from one's own beliefs, [and with] the inferences of those who accept the *siddhāsādhanatā* [the *Naiyāyika*s], and given that this *siddhāsādhanatā* is unavoidable, if the solution to the flaw [of *siddhāsādhanatā*] will be found included in the previously given inference [in the *sādhya*]: 'the ground of an actionless entity endowed with a generic attribute that is beyond the range of the senses' (*atīndriyasāmānyavānniṣkiyāśraya*), [and if] in order to clarify the intended meaning [99] the adjective 'other than elasticity' (*sthitisthāpa-kāntara*) is given, then there will be the flaw of 'meaning expressed other than that which was intended' (*arthāntarāpatti*) in the action (*karman*) as according to Prabhākara.[100] In fact, Prabhākara considers action to be not directly perceptible, because in an action not direc-

निष्क्रिय कर्म में अतीन्द्रिय सामान्यवत्वादिरूप साध्य विद्यमान ही है। किन्तु यह ठीक नहीं है, फिर जो भी कादाचित्क होता है, वह स्वाश्रयातिशयपुरः सर देखा गया है, जैसे संयोग-विभागजन्य कार्य संयोग-विभागरूप स्वाश्रयातिशयपुरःसर होता है । इस व्याप्ति से कादाचित्क होने के कारण संयोग-विभाग में भी स्वाश्रयातिशयपुरःसरत्व का अनुमान किया जाता है । जो यह अतिशय है, वह कर्म है, ऐसा माननेवाले प्रभाकर के मत में कर्म से अर्थान्तरता होती ही है और वह्नि भी अतीन्द्रियसामान्यवन्निष्क्रियकर्माश्रय है ही । अनुमान का 'कारणत्वात्' यह हेतु शक्ति से अनेकान्त है । यदि कहा जाय कि नहीं, शक्ति भी साध्यवान् होने से उससे अनेकान्तता नहीं है, तो यह ठीक नहीं, क्योंकि शक्ति में भी यदि शक्त्यन्तर मानें, तो अनवस्था की प्रसक्ति होगी ।

यदि कहा जाय कि जनन-शक्तियुक्त ही अर्थात् शक्तिमान् ही यहाँ कारणत्वेन विवक्षित है, अतः शक्ति में अनेकान्तिकता नहीं है, तो यह कथन भी उपयुक्त नहीं है, क्योंकि विशेषणीभूत शक्ति के बिना सिद्ध हुए शक्ति-युक्ततारूप कारणत्व ही सिद्ध नहीं हो सकता । यदि प्रमाणान्तर से विशेषणीभूत शक्ति की सिद्धि करना हो, तो फिर इसके लिये इतने प्रपञ्च की क्या आवश्यकता थी? साथ ही गुण आदि में अनेकान्तता भी आती है । जैसे कि-द्रव्य, गुण और कर्म में ही

tly perceptible, and actionless, we find the probandum to be the possessor of a general attribute beyond the range of the senses. But all this is also incorrect,[101] because every occasional happening (*kādacitka*) is preceded by a special property [excellence] related to its own ground (*svāśrayātiśayapuraḥsara*), just as an action produced by union or separation (*saṃyoga-vibhāgajanya*) is proceeded by a special property of its own ground that can be an union or a separation.[102]

Thanks to this invariable concomitance being an occasional happening, it is possible to infer within [both] union and separation necessity to be preceeded by a certain special property in their own grounds.

This special property (*atiśaya*),[103] is action (*karma*), and for a follower of this theory like Prabhākara, there is a different meaning than the desired one (*arthāntara)* in this action. The fire is the ground of the action without action, endowed with a generic attribute beyond sense perception. The probans (*hetu*) of this inference, 'since it is a cause', has an inconsistent relation to *śakti* (*anekānta* = *vyabhicārin*).[104] If [the *Mīmāṃsakas*] say that the probans is not fallacious because the power also is endowed with the probandum (*sādhyavān*),[105] the answer will be no. In fact, it is also in power that, if we accept another power, it will result in a regressus ad infinitum (*anavasthā*).

*Mīmāṃsaka*s may object that he who is endowed with the power of generation (*janana-śakti yukta*), being the possessor of *śakti,* is here intended (*vivakṣita*) as a cause (*kāraṇatvena*); therefore in the power there is not found the flaw of the [inconsistent] fallacious relation (*anaikāntikatā*).[106] This statement is also false, for without proving power as a qualification, it is not really possible to establish one causality in the form of the ownership of *śakti* (*śaktiyuktatārūpa*).[107]

If we must establish *śakti* as a qualification through another means of knowledge, then what would be the need of such an extension?[108] Furthermore, there is a fallacious relation (*anaikāntikatā*) in the

सामान्य रहता है । वहाँ निष्क्रियत्वरूप विशेषण होने से यद्यपि द्रव्याश्रयत्व नहीं आता, क्योंकि सावयव होने के कारण आश्रित द्रव्य सक्रिय है, तथापि गुण और कर्म, इन दोनों की अन्यतराश्रयता तो होगी ही और वे दोनों भी द्रव्यलक्षण या द्रव्यत्व व्याप्त हैं, अतः गुणादि में भी द्रव्यत्व की प्रसक्ति होगी ही । ऐसा न हो, इसलिये वहाँ तद्रहितत्व कहना पड़ेगा । तथा च उसमें कारणत्व होने से वह अनैकान्तिक है अर्थात् गुणादि में यथोक्त शक्त्याश्रयत्व उपपन्न नहीं होता ।

यदि उपर्युक्त अनुमान को त्याग कर शक्तिसिद्ध्यर्थ "**विवादाध्यासितः स्फोटः उभयवादिसम्प्रतिपन्नस्फोट-कारणातिरिक्तकारणाजन्यः कार्यत्वात् घटवत्**" ऐसे अनुमानान्तर को स्वीकार करें, तो यह भी ठीक नहीं है, क्योंकि प्रतिवादी से विप्रतिपन्न होने के कारण उभय-वादिसम्प्रतिपन्न कारण से अतिरिक्त कारण तो प्रतिबन्धकाभाव होता है, अतः उससे अर्थान्तरता होती है, क्योंकि प्रतिवादि द्वारा असम्प्रतिपन्न प्रतिबन्धकाभावरूप कारण से सिद्धिसाधन होता है ।

यदि कहा जाय कि वहाँ भावजन्यत्वरूप विशेषण के न होने से अर्थान्तरता नहीं है, तो यह भी नहीं कहा जा सकता, क्योंकि भावजन्यरूप

qualities and the like.[109] In fact, the generic attribute resides in the substances, in the qualities (*guṇa*) and in actions (*karman*).[110] There we also find the adjective 'absense of action' and, although the ground-ness of the substance (*dravyāśrayatva*) does not come — due to being endowed with parts (*sāvayava*) — a substance with a base is also endowed with action (*sakriya*); despite that quality and action, surely there will be the 'ground-ness' of one of the two (*anyatarāśrayatā*) both of them are also dependent on substance (*dravyalakṣaṇa*) or pervaded (*vyāpta*) by substantiality (*dravyatva*), so also in quality and the like we will start to find substantiality.[111]

In order to avoid this, it will be necessary to state 'the deprivation of that' (*tadrahitatva*). Therefore, there is a causality which is being fallaciously related, meaning that the so-called 'ground-ness' of *śakti* (*śaktyāśrayatā*) shall not be found in [such categories as] quality, or the like.

If the *Mīmāṃsakas*, having abandoned the previous inference, would accept the other in order to prove the existence of *śakti*, [they would argue as such] 'the object of debate (*vivādādhyāsitaḥ*) being a crackling noise (*sphoṭaḥ* = *pakṣa*), it would be not produced by a cause different from that of the crackling sound accepted by either of these debators (*ubhayavādi-sampratipanna-sphoṭa-kāraṇātirikta-kāraṇa-ajanyaḥ* [112] = *sādhya*) as it is an effect (*kāryatvāt* = *hetu*) just as is a pitcher (*ghaṭavat* = *dṛṣṭānta*)'; this too is not correct.[113] This is because, being debated by the opponents (*prativādin* = *Mīmāṃsaka*) the cause other than the cause accepted by both opponents (*ubhaya-vādisaṃpratipanna kāraṇa*) is the absence of the obstructing agent (*pratibandhakābhāva*),[114] so through that inference there will be the flaw of [expressing] a different meaning than that which was desired (*arthāntaratā)*, because there is also the proof of what is already proven, the absence of the obstructing agent as a cause, which is not accepted by the debator.

If the *Mīmāṃsakas* would join [to the probandum of the inference] the adjective 'production by a positive entity' (*bhāva-janyatva* = *bhāvakāraṇajanyatva*), then the flaw of the meaning

विशेषण होने पर भी ईश्वर से सिद्धिसाधनता होगी, क्योंकि शक्तिवादी मीमांसक ईश्वर को स्वीकार नहीं करता। इस तरह यद्यपि सहजशक्ति में न तो अर्थापत्ति और न अनुमान ही प्रमाण हो सकता है, तथापि आधेय शक्ति में "**व्रीहीन् प्रोक्षति, यूपं तक्षति, अग्नीनादधीत**" इत्यादि आगम प्रमाण होने से तद्बलात् सहजशक्ति की भी सिद्धि हो सकती है। "**ब्रीहीन् प्रोक्षति**" इत्यादि वाक्यों में '**ब्रीहीन्**' इस द्वितीया श्रुति से—"**ग्रामं गच्छति**" इत्यादि वाक्यों में जैसे '**ग्रामम्**' इस द्वितीयाश्रुति से ग्राम की कर्मता अवगत होती है, वैसे ही व्रीहि आदि की कर्मता ज्ञात होने से यह निश्चित होता है कि उन ब्रीह्यादिकों में प्रोक्षणादिजन्य कोई अतिशय है, क्योंकि वहाँ कोई अन्य दृष्ट फल दिखलायी नहीं पड़ता। शक्तिवादी उसी अतिशय को शक्ति मानते हैं। किन्तु संस्कार-संज्ञक चेतनगत अदृष्ट का अचेतन व्रीहि आदि में समवाय नहीं हो सकता, अर्थात्, आत्मगुण अदृष्ट अनात्मभूत व्रीह्यादि में नहीं हो सकता। कदाचित् यह कहा जाय कि '**व्रीहीन्**' इस द्वितीयाश्रुति से एक तो व्रीहि की संस्कार्यता बोधित होती है, दूसरे 'व्रीहि प्रोक्षण से संस्कृत हुए' ऐसी प्रसिद्धि भी है, अत: व्रीहिगत संस्कार को चेतनगत मानना विरुद्ध है, परन्तु यह ठीक नहीं है, क्योंकि घटविषय ज्ञान से उत्पन्न संस्कार जैसे घटविषयक होने से, न कि घटाधार होने से घटसंस्कार कहा जाता है, वैसे यहाँ भी व्रीहिप्रोक्षणादि

different than the desired one (*arthāntaratā)* shall not be found,[115] but this statement is also not tenable. In fact, if we also accept the adjective 'produced by a positive entity', the proving of what is already proved (*siddhasādhana*) will still remain, since the *Mīmāṃsakas*, who accept *śakti*, do not accept *Īśvara*, the Lord.[116]

In this way, even if neither presumption (*arthāpatti*) nor inference can be said to be proven about the innate power (*sahajaśakti-janmajātaśakti*), nevertheless there remains the proof of the textual authority (*āgama*) concerning the sustained *śakti* (*ādheyaśakti*),[117] such as "he sprinkles the grains", "he builds the sacrificial pole", "he arranges the fires" [118] [according to the rules], (*vidhivat*) and so on, by their force [119] we can establish as well the innate *śakti*. In sentences like, "he sprinkles the grains", and the like, by this accusative expression (*dvitīyā śruti*)[120] 'the grains' (*vrīhīn*) are known for their object-ness (*karmatā*), just as in sentences like "he goes to the village" (*grāmam*); this word is accusative, so the object-ness of the village is understood.[121] Therefore, it is ascertained that in the grains and the like comes a special property produced by the sprinkling, since we cannot see any other visible result (*dṛṣṭa phala*). He who maintains the power (*śaktivādin*) says that this special property (*atiśaya*) is *śakti*.

Anyway,[122] the so-called impression, the invisible power (*adṛṣṭa*) related to a sentient being, cannot inhere in an insentient one.[123] Or, better the quality pertinent to the individual self like *adṛṣṭa* cannot be present in the grains and the like which are not the [sentient] individual self. If someone would make this objection, about 'the grains' (*vrīhi*), then by this accusative word, first understood would be that the grains are worthy to be purified (*saṃskāryatā*),[124] and second, there also being a recognized expression, "the grains are purified by sprinkling",[125] it is therefore contradictory to consider the purification of the grains to be related to a sentient being. Then we say that this is also wrong, because just as the impression produced by the cognition of the pitcher has the same pitcher as its object, it is not called the impression of the pitcher, for its base is the pitcher.[126] In the same way is the purification awakened by the sprinkling of the

से उद्भूत संस्कार की भी व्रीहिविषयक प्रोक्षणादि क्रिया से उत्पन्न होने मात्र से तदीयत्व-प्रतीति की उपपत्ति हो सकती है, अतः द्वितीयाश्रुति या प्रसिद्धि व्रीह्यादिगत शक्ति की साधिका न होने से कहना होगा कि शक्ति की कल्पना में कोई भी प्रमाण नहीं है। अतएव लीलावतीकार ने भी कहा है कि विवादाध्यासित अग्न्यादि निजरूपमात्र से सम्बद्ध अतीन्द्रियसापेक्ष नहीं है, क्योंकि प्रमाण द्वारा वैसा उपलभ्यमान नहीं होता। प्रमाण से जो जैसा उपलब्ध नहीं होता, वह वैसा नहीं होता, जैसे नील पीतरूप में उपलब्ध न होने से पीत नहीं होता। इससे सिद्ध होता है कि शक्ति का साधक कोई प्रमाण नहीं है।

शक्ति समर्थन

परन्तु यह कहना उचित नहीं है, क्योंकि शक्ति के अस्तित्व में—

परास्य शक्तिर्विविधा सर्गाद्या भावशक्तयः।
इतिश्रुतिस्मृतिमिताशक्तिः केन निवार्यते॥

न तस्य कार्यं करणं च विद्यते न तत्समश्चाभ्यधिकश्च विद्यते।
परास्य शक्तिर्विविधैष श्रूयते स्वाभाविकी ज्ञानबलक्रिया च॥

ते ध्यानयोगानुगता अपश्यन्देवात्मशक्तिं स्वगुणैर्निगूढ़ाम्।

य एकोऽवर्णो बहुधा शक्तियोगात्।

शक्तयः सर्वभावानामचिन्त्यज्ञानगोचराः।
यतोऽतो ब्रह्मणस्तास्तु सर्गाद्या भावशक्तयः॥

सर्वज्ञता तृप्तिरनादिबोधः स्वतन्त्रता नित्यमलुप्तशक्तिः।
अचिन्त्यशक्तिश्च विभोर्विधिज्ञाः षडाहुरङ्गानि महेश्वरस्य॥

grains, being produced only by the action of sprinkling which has the grains as object; your cognition being tenable, so neither the accusative word, nor the recognized expression pertaining to the grains, can prove *śakti*, so we will have to say that there is no evidence to maintain the existence of *śakti* [as a separate category].

This is also why the author of the *Nyāyalīlāvatī* [Śrī Vallabhācārya] says that the object of the debate, the fire, is only related with its own nature (*nijarūpamātra se sambaddha* = *svasambaddha*) and does not need anything beyond the sensory range,[127] because it is not supported by any evidence. What is not confirmed is proven to not be, just as we do not find the colour yellow in blue, because it is not yellow. All this having been ascertained, there is therefore not one single proof to establish *śakti*.

The confirmation of Śakti

But we can say that all this is not tenable, because there are innumerable passages in the *Veda* (*śruti*) and the *smṛti* [supporting] the existence of *śakti*:

1) "There is the supreme Śakti of Him as well as innumerable [others supporting] creation and the like, who are powers of existence. How is it possible to negate this śakti proved by *śruti* and *smṛti*?"

2) "For Him there is neither effect nor instrument, nor is there any like Him or to Him any superior. But this is heard about His supreme polyformed power, the natural knowledge, strength and activity." [*Śvetāśvatara Upaniṣad* VI.8]

3) "Who, following the discipline of meditation, saw the power in the essence of the deity, hidden by his qualities?" [*Śvet. Up.* I.3]

4) "Who is without colour, [appearing] in many ways through the union with His power?" [*Śvetāśvatara Upaniṣad* IV.1]

5) "The powers inherent in all things are the objects of cognition beyond the reach of imagination; so, because the powers of existence, creation and the like all arose from *brahman*."

6) "The sages knowing the rules say that there are six parts of the pervading Great Lord: omniscience (*sarvajñatā*), fulfilment (*tṛpti*),

इत्यादि सैकड़ों श्रुति-स्मृतियों से गीयमान शक्ति का अपह्नव किस तरह किया जा सकता है? उक्त वचनों में कार्य-कारणादि सहकारियों के निरासपूर्वक शक्ति का प्रतिपादन है, अत: यह नहीं कहा जा सकता कि ये वचन स्वरूप सहकारिमात्र के प्रतिपादन है। शक्ति की स्वरूपमात्रता भी नहीं हो सकती, क्योंकि वहाँ '**परा अस्य**' इत्यादि षष्ठ्यन्त पद से स्वरूपातिरिक्तता का प्रतिपादन किया गया है। "**अस्य शक्ति-र्विविधाः**", "**तास्तु शक्तयः**" इत्यादि वचनों से उस शक्ति की अनेकता भी श्रुत होने से उसे एकरूप ब्रह्म भी कहना ठीक नहीं है। उपक्रम, उपसंहार आदि लिङ्ग से ईश्वरस्वरूप की निश्चायिका होने से उक्त श्रुति-स्मृतियों को अर्थवाद भी नहीं कहा जा सकता। साथ ही नैयायिक आदिकों ने भी इन वचनों को ईश्वर-स्वरूपपरक माना है, अत: उन्हें अर्थवाद बतलाना उचित नहीं है। फिर भी यदि किन्हीं तार्किकम्मन्य को शक्ति के अस्तित्व में उक्त आगम वचनों से ही सन्तोष न होकर वे अर्थापत्ति और अनुमान की ही अपेक्षा रखते हों, तो उनको अग्रिम अर्थापत्ति और अनुमान से भी सन्तुष्ट किया जा सकता है।

पीछे स्फोटादि कार्य की अन्यथानुपपत्ति से प्रथम अर्थापत्ति को दिखलाया ही जा चुका है। यदि उस सम्बन्ध में यह कहा जाय कि वहाँ पर भी यह कहा गया था कि प्रतिबन्धक के अभाव में सहकृत ही अग्निस्वरूप से कार्य की उत्पत्ति होने से अन्यथा भी उपपत्ति होती है और प्रागभाव प्रध्वंसाभावादि विकल्प से अभाव की अकारणता भी नहीं कही जा सकती; क्योंकि अप्रतिबद्ध ही शक्ति में भी कारणता बन सकने से उसमें भी उक्त प्रसङ्ग समान ही है। परन्तु, उस पर यह

beginningless comprehension (*anādibodha*), independence (*svatantratā*), eternally-present power (*aluptaśakti*) and incomprehensible power (*acintyaśakti*)."

So, how can it be possible to negate Her?

In these statements, there is the description of power accompanied by the refutation of such auxiliaries as effects, causes and the like; therefore, we cannot affirm that they present a mere auxiliary as the essential nature. It also cannot be that mere being is the essential nature (*svarūpamātratā*) of the *śruti*, since in these passages 'His supreme' and the like, as the word ends in the genitive (*ṣaṣṭhyanta*), what is demonstrated is a difference from this essential nature (*svarūpātiriktatā*) [of *śakti*].[128] Moreover, through 'His power, innumerable', 'but those powers' and other such phrases, also heard is the multiplicity of that *śakti*, so we cannot affirm that it is only the unique *brahman*. Thanks to the six means of ascertaining the sense of a passage of *śruti* (*tātparyaliṅga*),[129] like 'beginning' and 'conclusion' and the like, She being the giver of confirmation of the nature of the Lord, we cannot consider those *śruti* and *smṛti* statements as laudative passages.[130] Furthermore, the *Nyāya* followers and others also accept those phrases as descriptive of the Lord's essential nature, so it is not proper to consider them to be only laudative passages. But if someone who considers himself a logician shall not be satisfied by these textual statements, and needs only presumption and inference; so, we will fulfil his desire with the following presumptions and inferences.

Previously, through the otherwise impossibility of explaining, the first presumption (*arthāpatti*) has been shown. If someone would say something about it, such as "there also it was said that, being the production of the effect out of the essential nature of fire favoured by the absence of the obstructing agent, there is an alternative consistency, and by the option of the prior absence and that subsequent, the non-causality of absence cannot be substantiated". This is also because an unobstructed (*apratibaddha*) power can be a cause; in it there will be something like the aforementioned flaw. Anyhow, we can only repeat

कहना है कि क्या इस प्रकार का यह एक प्रतिकूल तर्कमात्र है कि यदि प्रतिबन्धकाभाव कारण न हो तो शक्ति भी कारण न होगी अथवा शक्ति कारण है, अतः प्रतिबन्धकाभाव भी कारण है, इस तरह विपर्यय में पर्यवसान होने से अभाव का कारणत्व सिद्ध किया जा रहा है ?

पहली बात नहीं कही जा सकती, क्योंकि केवल तर्क से उपालम्भ नहीं किया जा सकता, उसका विपर्यय में भी पर्यवसान होना चाहिये, अन्यथा वह तर्काभास हो जाता है और ऐसे तर्काभास द्वारा प्रतिपक्ष का निराकरण नहीं किया जा सकता।

दूसरी बात भी सङ्गत नहीं है, क्योंकि जो शक्ति का अङ्गीकार नहीं करता, वह उक्त रीति से प्रतिबन्धकाभाव में कारणता दिखलाते हुए विपर्यय में पर्यवसान कैसे कर सकता है ?

तर्क दो प्रकार का होता है-एक स्वपक्ष-साधकानुकूल और दूसरा प्रतिपक्षदूषक। पहले में विपर्यय पर्यवसान की अपेक्षा हुआ करती है, अन्यथा साधनानुकूलत्व सिद्ध नहीं होता। दूसरे में उसकी अपेक्षा नहीं होती, वहाँ परमतासिद्ध व्याप्ति से ही परपक्ष की अनिष्ट सिद्धि की जा सकती है। यहाँ भी यही स्थिति मान कर यदि यह कहा जाय कि परासिद्ध शक्ति से परपक्ष का अनिष्टसाधन किया जा रहा है, तो यह भी ठीक नहीं, क्योंकि जो ऐसा मानता है कि प्रमित में अर्थात् अधिकरण में प्रमित प्रतियोगिक ही निषेध होता है, न कि अप्रमितप्रतियोगिक, वह— "यदि प्रतिबन्धकाभाव कारण न हो, तो शक्ति भी कारण न होगी, इस तरह शक्ति की कारणता का निषेध नहीं कर सकता—क्योंकि शक्ति और उसकी कारणता, दोनों अप्रमित है।"

here such an opposite reasoning (*pratikūlatarka*), that is, if the absence of the obstructing agent would not be a cause, so *śakti* too cannot be such; otherwise, *śakti* being a cause, the absence of the obstructing agent (*pratibandhākābhāva*) is [also] a cause.[131]

Then we say, is it really possible to establish the causality of absence without concluding that the opponent's view bears a contradiction?

The first statement [132] cannot be said, since we cannot understand anything through mere reasoning. Reasoning must be pointed towards finding some incontrovertible inconsistency in the opponent's view; otherwise, there will only be the semblance of reasoning, and this is not capable of nullifying the opinion of one's opponent.

The second statement is not logically tenable, because for one who does not accept *śakti* after being shown the causality of the absence of the obstructing agent (*pratibandhaka*) in that manner, how can anyone demonstrate the problem of the inconsistency of the opponent's view?

The reasoning (*tarka*) is of two types. One corroborates one's own arguments (*svapakṣa-sādhakānukūla*), the other vitiates the arguments of the opponent (*pratipakṣa dūṣaka*).[133] In the first it is necessary to conclude with the opposite statement of the opponent, otherwise the favourable corroboration shall not be established.[134] In the second case, this is not needed, because through the invariable concomitance not accepted by the opponent there (*paramatāsiddha* = *svamatasiddha*), an undesired result for the opponents is proved.[135]

If this situation is now accepted as well, then through the *śakti* disestablished in *Nyāya* (*parāsiddha*) the opponent's view will be nullified; but this is also not correct. Since it is accepted that something is cognized (*pramita*), that means within a base (*adhikaraṇa*), the confutation (*niṣedha*) regards the object substantiated in the cognized [base] (*pramitapratiyogika*), not what is not grasped on that ground. The *Naiyāyikas* cannot neglect in this manner the causality of *śakti* by saying "if the absence of obstructing agent (*pratibandhaka*) is not a cause, then the *śakti* also cannot be a cause"; in fact, neither *śakti*

यदि उन्हें प्रमित कहें, तो स्वरूप से उनका निषेध नहीं किया जा सकता ।

तात्पर्य यह हुआ कि भले ही यहाँ तर्क का भी पर्यवसान विपर्यय में न हो, पर शक्तिकारणत्व का निषेध ही नहीं सिद्ध किया जा सकता । फिर भी जल्पकथा छोड़कर यदि सुहृद्भाव से कोई यह पूछे कि प्रतिबन्धभाव यदि कारण न हो, तो प्रतिबन्ध रहने पर भी शक्ति कार्य को क्यों न उत्पन्न करेगी? तो इसका उत्तर यह है कि शक्तिवादी के मतानुसार प्रतिबन्धक वह कहा जाता है, जो पुष्कल कारण रहते हुए भी कार्योत्पत्ति का विरोधी हो । अत: यह नहीं कहा जा सकता कि सामग्रीवैकल्य से कार्य का उदय नहीं हुआ, अपितु यही कहना होगा कि विरोधी रहने से ही कार्योदय नहीं हुआ ।

लोकसिद्धि विरुद्ध होने से सामग्रीवैकल्य को ही प्रतिबन्ध नहीं कहा जा सकता । कोई भी लौकिक पुरुष भूमि, वायु, जल एवं तेज के संसर्ग से विरहित कोठी में भरे हुए बीजों को या तुरी, वेमा, कुविन्द आदि से विरहित पेटी में रखे हुए तन्तुओं को प्रतिबद्ध नहीं समझता । सामग्रीराहित्यमात्र को यदि प्रतिबन्ध कहा जाय, तो समस्त कारणों को केवल प्रतिबन्धभाव में ही उपक्षीणता हो जाने से यह इस कारण है, यह प्रतिबन्धाभाव है इस तरह परीक्षकों के विभक्तरूप से दोनों का विशेषावधारण ही न होना चाहिये । अभाव को कारण न मानने पर कार्य के साथ अन्वय-व्यतिरेक विरोध होगा, यह कथन भी असङ्गत होगा, क्योंकि अन्वय-व्यतिरेक कार्य-कारण-भाव के विषय होने से प्रतिबन्धकाभाव अन्यथासिद्ध है ।

nor its causality are cognised,[136] for otherwise they would be considered to be cognized and hence they could not be isolated from their nature.[137]

The meaning is that, even if there is nothing leading to the contradiction of one's opponent's view, nevertheless it is impossible to refute the causality of *śakti*. Anyhow, if we leave for a while the mode of debate (*jalpakathā*),[138] and if someone would kindly ask "if the absence of an obstructing agent [139] is not a cause, why does not *śakti* produce an effect when there is an obstruction?" The answer will be that the *Śaktivādins* consider as an obstructing agent that which is opposite to the production of an effect, even if all the causal complex (*puṣkalakāraṇa* = *kāraṇasāmagrī*) is present.[140] "Hence, it is impossible to affirm that an effect does not arise due to the insufficiency of the causal complex (*sāmagrīvaikalya*), yet it is better to say that then a hostile entity is present, then [to say that] the effect does not take place."

As it is opposed to the common belief (*lokaprasiddhiviruddha*), we cannot consider the insufficiency of the causal complex as an obstruction.[141] No ordinary person considers as obstructed the seeds in a container, free from the contact with earth, wind, water and fire, nor does he so consider threads locked in a box, free [from contact with] brush (*turī*), loom (*vemā*) or weaver (*kuvinda*). If the mere insufficiency of the causal complex (*sāmagrīrāhitya* = *sāmagrīvaikalya*) is an obstruction, then every cause would just vanish in the absence of opposition,[142] and such a deliniation of the difference between the two separated entities by the examiners, like "this is the cause" and "this is the absence of obstruction" would not be possible.

Also, this assertion is illogical; if the absence is not accepted as cause, there will be an opposition of the concomitance, positive and negative, with the effect. The inconsistency is given because, if the concomitance, positive and negative, is about the cause-effect relation here,[143] the absence of the obstructing agent will result in superfluity (*anyathāsiddha*).

यहाँ यदि यह कहा जाय तो फिर अनुपलब्धि भी अभाव के उपलम्भ की हेतु नहीं हो सकती, क्योंकि विरोधिनीभावोपलब्धि का अभाव होने से उनके अन्वयव्यतिरेक को भी अन्यथासिद्ध कहना सहज है, तो यह भी उचित नहीं है, क्योंकि वहाँ कारणान्तर न होने अगत्या अनन्यथासिद्ध अनुपलब्धि को कारण मानना पड़ा है, किन्तु यहाँ ऐसी बात नहीं है। यहाँ उसके बिना अभावोपलम्भ के कारण का निरूपण नहीं किया जा सकता।

इन्द्रिय को ही यदि अभावोपलम्भ का कारण कहें, तो भी ठीक नहीं, क्योंकि उसके अभाव से सन्निकर्ष न होगा। वहाँ संयोग तथा समवाय का अभाव होने और सम्बन्धान्तरगर्भ ही विशेषण-विशेष्यभाव के प्रत्यक्षाङ्ग होने से वहाँ अभाव प्रत्यक्षगम्य नहीं, अपितु अनुपलब्धिगम्य ही है। अन्यथा 'पर्वतो वह्निमान्' यहाँ संयुक्त विशेषण होने के कारण अग्नि का भी प्रत्यक्षत्व होने लगेगा।

यदि यह कहा जाय कि असम्बद्ध ही अभाव इन्द्रिग्राह्य हो, तो क्या हानि है, क्योंकि उसकी प्रतीति इन्द्रियान्वय-व्यतिरेक की अनुविधायिनी होने से अपरोक्ष है और इसके अतिरिक्त दूसरी गति भी नहीं है, तो यह कहना भी उचित नहीं है, क्योंकि अयोगि प्रत्यक्ष की प्रमिति में इन्द्रियों से सम्बद्ध अर्थग्राहकत्व-नियम का निराकरण नहीं किया जा सकता और अभाव की प्रतीति का अपरोक्षत्व सिद्ध न होने से इन्द्रियान्वय और व्यतिरेक अधिकरण के ग्रहणमात्र में उपक्षीण हो जाने से अन्यथासिद्ध भी हो जाते हैं। इसपर यह कहा जा सकता है कि नहीं, अन्वयव्यतिरेक की अधिकरण के ग्रहणमात्र में उपक्षीणता कहना ठीक नहीं है, क्योंकि

It is also wrong to affirm [144] "so also the means of non-apprehension (*anupalabdhi*) cannot be the cause of grasping the absence, for, there being not the opposite (*virodhinī*) apprehension of the presence (*bhāvopalabdhi*),[145] it would be natural to also classify as superfluous its positive-negative concomitance."

This affirmation is wrong because, no other cause being present, with no alternative (*agatyā*), the absolutely necessary (*ananyathā-siddha*) non-apprehension must be accepted to be the cause.[146] However, the case in question is different.[147] Here, without her [*śakti*], we cannot identify the cause of the perception of the absence.

If one affirms that the senses are the causes for the perception of absence, this is contradicted, for without them it is not possible to make contact with the object (*saṃnikarṣa*).[148] There, neither contact nor inference is found, and being the relationship of qualifier-qualified, connected with other relations, a part of perception, there [then] the absence is knowable not through direct perception, but rather through non-apprehension.[149] Otherwise, [given the statement] 'the mountain has fire' which presents a united qualifier (*saṃyukta viśeṣaṇa*), the fire too shall become directly perceptible.[150]

A *Naiyāyika* might ask, "Since only an unrelated (*asambaddha*) absence is graspable by the senses, then please tell me what is the problem? Because its cognition is direct, closely following (*anu-vidhāyinī*) the concomitance, positive and negative, with the senses. Beyond this, there is no other solution." Answering this,[151] we shall say that this is not correct because in the cognition arising from the direct perception of an ordinary man (*ayogin pratyakṣa*), it is impossible to cancel the rule of the possibility to grasp only an object connected with the senses. Moreover, the direct cognition of an absence is not established, so the positive-negative concomitance (*anvaya-vyatireka*) with the senses, being limited to the perception of the ground, will be recognized as superfluous. On this, the *Naiyāyikas* might object, "This cannot be; it is not correct to state that the vanishing of the positive and negative concomitances (*anvaya-vyatireka*) only [in reference to] the perception of the ground. In fact,

अभाव को इन्द्रियग्राह्य न माना जायगा, तो अन्ध द्वारा त्वगादि से घटादिरूप अधिकरण के गृहीत होने पर उसको रूपाभाव की प्रतीति मान लेना पड़ेगा, क्योंकि अधिकरण तो उस अन्ध से गृहीत ही है ।

यदि कहें कि चक्षुरिन्द्रिय के न होने से वहाँ अन्ध को रूपाभाव का प्रत्यक्ष न होगा, तो यह भी ठीक नहीं, क्योंकि इन्द्रिय अभाव का ग्राहक है ही नहीं, अतएव यह कहा जाय कि अन्ध को प्रतियोगी ग्राहक इन्द्रिय न होने से ही रूपाभाव की प्रतीति न होगी । तथा च अभाव की ऐन्द्रियकत्वसिद्धि हो जाती है । परन्तु यह ठीक नहीं है, क्योंकि फिर अभाव को प्रतियोगिग्राहक इन्द्रियग्राह्य माननेवाले के मत में भी अनन्ध को भी असन्निहित मेरु आदि में घट एवं उसके रूपादि के अभाव की चाक्षुषता क्यों न होगी? यदि कहा जाय कि वहाँ प्रतियोगी के चाक्षुष होने पर भी अधिकरण के चाक्षुष न होने से रूपाभाव का चाक्षुषत्व नहीं होता, तो इधर से भी कहा जा सकता है कि इसीलिये त्वगिन्द्रिय से गृहीत घटादि में अन्ध को रूपाभाव की प्रतीति नहीं होती, क्योंकि प्रतियोगिग्राहक इन्द्रिय द्वारा घटादि रूप अधिकरण का वहाँ ग्रहण नहीं होता ।

यदि कहा जाय कि तब तो घ्राणेन्द्रिय के अगोचर कुसुमादि या चक्षुरिन्द्रियग्राह्य वायु में गन्ध या रूप के अभाव का प्रत्यक्ष न होगा, तो इसपर यही कहना होगा कि भले न हो, वहाँ वायु आदि में रूपादि का अभाव चाक्षुष न होने पर भी उनमें रूपाभाव ज्ञानरूप व्यवहार में कोई बाधा नहीं पड़ती ।

षष्ठ प्रमाणवादियों के यहाँ सर्वत्र यह नियम नहीं है कि अभाव अनुपलब्धिगम्य ही है, क्योंकि व्यापकाभाव से व्याप्त के अभाव को

if the absence will not be considered perceptible by the senses, then we will have to admit that even a blind man, having grasped one pitcher or another, will by touch be able to know the absence of colour in it, since he has grasped its basis (*adhikaraṇa*)."

Furthermore, [the *Naiyāyikas* might say], "it is incorrect to reply that there the blind man would not have a direct perception of the lack of colour, because his sight is absent. In fact, the senses cannot grasp absence, so it would be appropriate to say that the blind man, being deprived of the sense capable of catching the counterpositive (*pratiyogin* = *rūpa*), [that is, the colour], in such a context the absence of colour would not be cognized, and therefore the possibility of sensual knowledge of *abhāva* is established."

However, none of these considerations are correct, since according to the theory of 'who accepts the absence as graspable by the senses, wherein [the senses] grasp the counterpositive' (*pratiyogi-grāhaka-indriya-grāhya*) as well,[152] would not a non-blind man (*anandha*) also be able to directly see the absence of the colour and the like of a pitcher on mount Meru, rather than right before him?[153] If the *Naiyāyikas* answer that "there, even if the counterpositive (*pratiyogin* = *rūpa*) is seen, yet the ground is not seen directly, there is therefore no direct sight of the absence of colour." We [*Mīmāṃsakas*] can say from our side that a blind man cannot know the absence of colour (*rūpābhāva*) in a pitcher or the like via the senses, and is only able to grasp the counterpositive [of that absence].[154]

If it would be said that "in the flower or the like, which is not an object (*agocara*) of the sense of smell (*ghrāṇendriya*), and the wind, not visible by eye, there would not be the direct perception of the absence of the smell,[155] and the like", then the reply to this would be "Well, this isn't so, for even if in the wind and the like the absence of *rūpa* is not visible; anyhow, no obstruction is found there in the absence of colour: that is common knowledge".[156]

The *Bhāṭṭa-Mīmāṃsakas* accept the not universally held sixth means of knowledge (*anupalabdhi*), the rule [saying] that absence is graspable only by non-apprehension, since [such are] considered

और कारणाभाव से कार्याभाव को अनुमेय मान लिया गया है अर्थात् यदि वक्ष्यमाण तत्तत् भट्टपादादि वृद्धों की सम्मति से अभाव का प्रमाणान्तरगम्यता भी है, तो योग्यानुपलब्धिगम्यस्थल में ही प्रति-योगिग्राहक द्वारा अधिकरण के ग्रहण का नियम है, क्योंकि अभाव की उपलब्धि का व्यापकीभूत जो अनुपलब्धि आदि कारण है, उसके अतिरिक्त इन्द्रियादिरूप कारण की पुष्कलता ही योग्यता है और इन्द्रिय उसका अन्त:पाती होने के कारण उसके अभाव में भी योग्यता न बनेगी ।

जहाँ प्रमाणान्तरगम्यता होती है, वहाँ उसके बिना भी अभाव का ग्रहण हो सकता है, जैसे व्यापकाभाव से व्याप्याभाव का अनुमान । इस विषय में भट्टपाद लिखते हैं कि अग्नि और धूमरूप भाव के नियम्यत्व-नियन्तृत्व जैसे माने जाते हैं, वे ही नियम्यत्व और नियन्तृत्व अग्नि-धूम सम्बन्धी अभाव के विपरीत प्रतीत होते हैं । भावावस्था में धूम नियन्ता और अग्नि नियम्य होता है और अभाव में इसके विपरीत स्थिति होती है अर्थात् तब धूमाभाव नियम्य और अग्नि का अभाव नियन्ता होता है—

नियम्यत्वनियन्तृत्वे भावयोर्यादृशी मते ।
विपरीते प्रतीयेते त एव तदभावयोः ॥

objects of inference, and that from the absence of the pervader (*vyāpakābhāva*) [arises] the absence of the pervaded and from the absence of cause [arises] the absence of effect; this means that, by the accord with the elders who are the followers of *Bhāṭṭa Mīmāṃsā*, if there is the possibility to grasp the absence by another means of knowledge (*pramāṇa*)[157] then where we have a non-apprehension of something that should be worthy of perception there is present the rule of the cognition of the ground *(adhikaraṇa)* by the cognizer of the counterpositive. In fact, [it is] a cause being non-apprehension, which is the pervader of the apprehension of an absence.[158] In addition to this non-apprehension, we see that the totality of causes, like *indriya* and the like, is worthy [to be perveived]; moreover, the sense falls into the middle, and there will not be any worthiness (*yogyatā*) with regards to the absence.[159]

Where there is the possibility of grasping through another mean of knowledge (*pramāṇāntaragamyatā*) [than *anupalabdhi*], then also without it (*anupalabdhi*) the *abhāva* can be grasped, just as the absence of the pervaded (*vyāpyābhāva*) is inferred through the absence of the pervader (*vyāpakābhāva*). On this matter, Kumārila Bhaṭṭa and his followers write that, just as fire and smoke are considered respectively to be pervader (*niyamyatva*) and pervaded (*niyantṛtva*) when they are present (*bhāva* = *anvaya*), the same fire-smoke, pervader-pervaded relations are considered in the exact opposite way in their absence (*abhāva* = *vyatireka*). When they are present, smoke is the pervaded (*niyantā* = *vyāpya*), and fire the pervader (*niyamya* = *vyāpaka*). When they are absent, we have an opposite situation, that is, the absence of smoke (*dhūmābhāva*) is the pervader (*niyamya*) and the absence of fire is the pervaded (*niyantā*).[160]

> Just as the 'pervading-ness' (*niyamyatva*) and the 'pervaded-ness' (*niyantṛtva*) are considered between two objects at hand, both are conceived exactly oppositely when the two objects are absent.

कारणाभाव से कार्याभाव के अनुमान विषय में श्रीमण्डन मिश्र ने, ब्रह्मसिद्धि में बतलाया है कि हेतु के अभाव से फलाभाव का नियम होने से दोषाभाव से विपर्ययाभाव का अनुमान किया जा सकता है—

विपर्ययाभावस्तु युक्तोऽनुमातुं हेत्वभावे फलाभाव इति ।

अतएव स्थलविशेष में अनन्यथासिद्ध अन्वय-व्यतिरेकबल से अनुपलब्धि की अभाव प्रतीति में कारणता निश्चित होती है । प्रकृत में स्वपुष्कल कारण से कार्योत्पत्ति हो सकती है, तब प्रतिबन्धकाभाव को कारण मानना आवश्यक नहीं है और इस मत में अन्योन्याश्रता का वारण करना भी कठिन होगा । यद्यपि मण्यादि की कार्यप्रतिकूलता का निश्चय अन्वय-व्यतिरेक से हो सकता है, तथापि विसामग्रीरूपता लक्षणप्रतिबन्धत्व तदीय अभाव की सामग्री के अन्तर्भाव विज्ञान के सापेक्ष है, क्योंकि, विसामग्री प्रतिबन्ध है, यह मान्य है ।

अत: प्रतिबन्धत्व और सामग्रीत्व का ज्ञान परस्पर सापेक्ष होने से अन्योन्याश्रयता दुर्निवार होगी, अर्थात् वैसामग्र्य ही प्रतिबन्ध है और प्रतिबन्धाभाव रूप कारण, वैकल्य ही वैसामग्र्य है । ऐसी स्थिति में मणि आदि के वैसामग्र्यरूप प्रतिबन्धत्व का ज्ञान मन्त्रादि सम्बन्धी अभाव सामग्री के अन्तर्भाव ज्ञान सापेक्ष है और मन्त्रादि के अभाव का सामग्र्यन्तर्भाव ज्ञान, मणि आदि के प्रतिबन्धत्व ज्ञान के अधीन है,

Concerning the inference of the absence of effect (*kāryābhāva*) through the absence of cause (*kāraṇābhāva*), Maṇḍana Miśra wrote in his *Brahmasiddhi* that according to the rule of the absence of result, due to the absence of cause, we can also infer the absence of erroneous knowledge (*viparyayābhāva-yathārthajñāna*) by the absence of any flaw:[161]

> It is correct to infer the absence of erroneous knowledge, on the same basis of the absence of the cause yielding no result.

Hence, in a particular situation, by strength of the necessary *anvaya* and *vyatireka* we ascertain the causality of non-apprehension in the matter of condition of the absence. In our context, by all our causes, the effect can be produced; therefore, there is no necessity to consider the absence of the obstructing agent as a cause.[162] Moreover, it will be very difficult in this theory to avoid reciprocal dependence.[163] Even if the ascertainment of the adversity towards the effect of the gem and others is possible through *anvaya* and *vyatireka*, still the obstruction (*pratibandhatva*) that has the form of the insufficiency of the causal complex (*visāmagrīrūpatālakṣaṇa*) depends on the knowledge of inclusion of the causal complex of absence of effect (*tadīya* = *kārya*), since it is established that the obstruction is the insufficiency of the causal complex (*visāmagrī* = *sāmagrīvaikalya*).

So, the knowledge of the obstruction and of the causal complex are mutually dependent, therefore reciprocal dependence is unavoidable. The insufficiency of the causal complex is obstruction and the cause, as the absence of obstruction, is the insufficiency of the causal complex, its weakness. In this situation, the knowledge of the obstruction that is the insufficiency of the causes due to a gem or what have you is dependent on the knowledge of the inclusion of the causal complex of the absence related to *mantra* or whatever.[164] On the other side, the knowledge of the inclusion of the causal complex of the absence of *mantra* or what have you depends on the knowledge related to the obstructive nature of the gem or whatever

क्योंकि प्रतिबन्धाभाव रूप, कारण वैकल्य से वैसामग्र्य का उपपादन होगा, अतएव अन्योन्याश्रयता सुतरां सिद्ध है ।

यदि कहा जाय कि मण्यादि के विसामग्रीत्व का ज्ञान भले ही मण्याद्यभाव सम्बन्धी सामग्री के अन्तर्भाव ज्ञान के सापेक्ष रहे, पर वह्निस्वरूप की तरह अन्वय व्यतिरेक से ही मण्यादि के अभाव की सामग्र्यन्तर्भाव सम्बन्धी अवगति हो सकती है, अत: अन्योन्याश्रयता न होगी, तो यह ठीक नहीं, क्योंकि वहाँ यह शङ्का होगी कि क्या प्रत्येक मण्याद्यभाव अन्वय-व्यतिरेक द्वारा कारणरूप से निश्चित किये जाते हैं या प्रतिबन्धाभावरूप उपाधि से क्रीड़ीकृत होकर? पहली बात हो नहीं सकती, क्योंकि मण्याद्यभाव अनन्त है, उनके उपसङ्ग्राहक के बिना प्रत्येक के अन्वय-व्यतिरेक का निश्चय सौ वर्षों में भी नहीं किया जा सकता । दूसरा पक्ष मानें, तो विसामग्रीरूप प्रतिबन्धज्ञान के अधीन प्रतिबन्धाभावत्वरूप उपाधि का ज्ञान हुए बिना मण्याद्यभाव सम्बन्धी सामग्र्यन्तर्भाव का ज्ञान होना कठिन है, अत: अन्योन्याश्रयता का निराकरण फिर भी बना ही रहेगा, इसलिये द्वितीय पक्ष भी अस्वीकार्य है ।

शक्ति पक्ष में प्रतिबन्ध की जो असम्भवता पीछे कही गयी, वह भी ठीक नहीं है, अन्यथा शक्ति को न माननेवालों को भी कारणों के कार्यौदासीन्य को ही प्रतिबन्ध मान लेना पड़ेगा, क्योंकि वैसामग्र्यरूप प्रतिबन्ध का तो उपर्युक्त अन्योन्याश्रय दोषरूप रीति से खण्डन किया ही जा चुका है । अत: प्रतिबन्धाभाव के कारण न बनने से

it is.[165] There will be the establishment of the insufficiency of the causal complex through the weakness of the cause, the absence of obstruction.

The mutual dependence is clearly proven.

If it be said that [166] even if knowledge of the causal complex-insufficiency is dependent on the knowledge of the inclusion of the causal complex related to the absence of the gem or what have you, then in any event just as the essential nature of fire [is proved] through the positive concomitance (*anvaya*) and the negative one (*vyatireka*), there can be the comprehension related to the inclusion of the causal-complex of the absence of the gem or whatever. Hence, there will not be any mutual dependence. This statement is also false, for there will be this doubt: "Maybe every absence of the gem or whatever is ascertained as a cause through positive and negative concomitance (*anvaya-vyatireka*),[167] or maybe is being classified collectively with a name like 'absence of the obstructing agent'?" [168]

The first option cannot be accepted, because the absences of gems and the like are innumerable and without something presenting them collectively (*upasaṃgrāhaka*), it will be impossible even in one hundred years to establish their positive and negative concomitance (*anvaya-vyatireka*).[169] If we consider the second option, then without the knowledge of what passes under the collective name 'absence of an obstructing agent', dependant on the knowledge of the obstruction whose shape is that of the causal complex insufficiency, it will be really difficult to know the inclusion of the causal complex (*sāmagrī*) related to the absence (*abhāva*) of the man or whoever.[170]

Therefore, it will not be possible to conceal the mutual dependence, so the second is also unworthy to be accepted.

The impossibility previously attributed to the side of *śakti* is also false, otherwise whoever does not accept *śakti* will be forced to accept as obstruction the disinterest towards producing effect of the causes,[171] since we have already refuted the obstruction in the form of the causal complex insufficiency giving the mutual dependence flaw. Hence, if the absence of obstruction is not a cause, it is

कार्यार्थापत्ति की, बिना शक्ति को स्वीकृत किये, अन्यथा उपपत्ति हो ही नहीं सकती ।

शक्ति का स्वीकार किये बिना उपादानोपादेयभाव-नियम की उपपत्ति नहीं हो सकती, अतः उसे भी शक्ति में प्रमाण मानना ही चाहिये । वहाँ स्वभावभेद से ही उपपत्ति करके जो पहले अन्यथा उपपत्ति कही गयी थी, उसका अभिप्राय क्या है? क्या शक्तिवादी को भी अन्ततोगत्वा जब स्वभाव की शरण लेनी ही पड़ती है, तब अच्छा है कि पहले से ही स्वभाव मान लिया जाय, यह, अथवा स्वभावातिरिक्त शक्ति में प्रमाण का न होना । यदि प्रथम पक्ष तो वैसा मानने से सर्वत्र स्वभाववाद का पाद-प्रसार होने से सामान्य, समवाय एवं विशेष आदि का भी पराकरण प्रसक्त हो जायगा । अनवस्था भय से जैसे सत्ता सत्तान्तर माने बिना ही स्वभाव-विशेषवश सद्व्यवहार हेतुत्व मान लिया जाता है, वैसे ही अन्यत्र द्रव्यादि में भी स्वभाव विशेष से सद्व्यवहार उत्पन्न हो जाने से सत्तासामान्य का अपलाप हो जायगा । इसी तरह—

समवायवान् अयं घटः ।

यहाँ अनवस्था भय से जैसे समवायान्तर माने बिना ही समवाय की घट के प्रति विशेषणता मान ली जाती है, वैसे ही "**शुक्लः पटः, चलति चैलाञ्चलम्**" यहाँ भी गुण-कर्म में स्वभाव-भेद से ही विशेषण-विशेष्य भाव होकर समवाय का अपलाप हो जायगा । इसी प्रकार जैसे

not possibly an otherwise applicability (*anyathā upapatti*) of the presumption of the effect (*kāryārthapatti*) without accepting power (*śakti*).[172]

Without accepting *śakti*, there would not be any logical applicability of the rule of the relation between the material cause and the effect, hence this can be accepted as a proof of *śakti*.[173] However, the otherwise applicability there has previously been applied to the applicability of the particular proper essential nature (*svabhāvabheda*); what does this means?[174] If the *Śaktivādins* must, in the end, take refuge in the essential nature, then it would have been better to have accepted it previously. The other option is the non-acceptance of a proof regarding a *śakti* different from the essential nature. If we accept the first alternative, the theory of the essential nature (*svabhāvavāda*) will spread everywhere and we will have to face the cancellation of categories like generality, inherence, particularity and the like.[175] Then, out of fear of the regressus ad infinitum (*anavasthā*) the causality (*hetutva*) of the practical way of [establishing something as] existent (*sadvyavahāra*) due to one's essential nature is accepted as well without any consideration regarding the existence (*sattā*) of another existence (*sattāntara*). In the same way, in other situations as well for the substances and the like, there will be the cancellation of the general attribute 'existence' accepting the possibility of the common behaviour 'to be' from the particular essential nature.

In the same way: [176]

> This pitcher is endowed with inherence.

Just as here, out of fear of a regressus ad infinitum (*anavasthā*), it is accepted that the 'qualifier-ness' (*viśeṣaṇatā*) of the inherence (*samavāya*) towards the pitcher, even not accepting any other inherence, similarly as well in statements such as 'the white cloth', 'the fringe of the white cloth moves' there will be a cancellation of the inherence in quality and action, since the relation of qualifier-qualified is performed by their particular *svabhāva*. In the same

अन्त्यविशेषों में स्वभाववशात् परस्पर व्यावृत्ति मानी जाती है, क्योंकि विशेषों में विशेषान्तर मानने से उनकी भी, अनुगतरूपवत्ता से रूपादि की तरह, एक तो अन्त्यविशेषत्व की हानि होगी और दूसरे, अनवस्थाप्रसक्त होगी । अगत्या किन्हीं विशेषों को निर्विशेष मानने पर उन्हीं को अन्त्यविशेष मानना पड़ता है, वैसे ही नित्य द्रव्यों को भी स्वभाववशात् व्यावृत्तिबुद्धिजनकत्व होने से अन्त्यविशेष का अपलाप हो जायगा ।

इसी तरह कालादि का भी अपलाप-प्रसक्त होगा । अत: स्वभावाश्रयण से काम नहीं चल सकता । यदि स्वभावातिरिक्त शक्ति में कहीं भी प्रमाण नहीं है, यह कहा जाय, तो यह भी ठीक नहीं है । यदि कहा जाय कि जहाँ प्रमाण है, वहाँ-वहाँ वस्त्वन्तराधीन ही प्रमाण-व्यवहार हुआ करता है और जहाँ वह नहीं है, वहाँ उसके स्वभाव-भेद से ही व्यवहार होता है, ऐसी व्यवस्था है, तो यहाँ भी प्रमाण होने से ही स्वरूप से अतिरिक्त शक्ति का अङ्गीकार कर लेना चाहिये, ऐसी स्थिति में स्वभाववाद का अवलम्बन अनावश्यक है ।

इस तरह अर्थापत्ति के अतिरिक्त-

वह्निः अद्विष्ठातीन्द्रीयस्थितिस्थापकेतरभावाश्रयः गुणवत्वात् घटवत् ।

यह अनुमान भी शक्ति के अस्तित्व में प्रमाण है । ईश्वर माननेवालों के मत में अतीन्द्रियता सिद्ध नहीं है, यह भी कहना ठीक नहीं, क्योंकि अतीन्द्रिय शब्द का अर्थ है प्रमाणान्तर से उपनीत विशेषण के अतिरिक्त

manner, in the ultimate differentiating particuliarity (*antyaviśeṣa*), a reciprocal differentiation by nature is accepted, because accepting another particularity within the particularities, there will be from one side the harm of the theory of the ultimate differentiating particularity, and on the other a regressus ad infinitum as to colour and the like, with their possibility to be endowed with a subsequent colour (*anugatarūpavattā*). So, without any other escape, accepting some particularity as free from particularity, we could consider them 'ultimate differentiating particularities'. Similarly as well for the eternal substances, in fact being out of their own essential nature, have the capacity to generate a differentiating cognition, therefore there will be the cancellation of the ultimate differentiating particularity (*antyaviśeṣa*).[177]

So too shall there be the cancellation of time and the like,[178] therefore we cannot be satisfied by taking refuge in mere essential nature.

If this too could be affirmed, that there is no evidence anywhere regarding a *śakti* different from the essential nature (*svabhāva)*, we would reply that this is not correct.[179] Furthermore, it would be said that where there is proof, there is often also the behaviour of the means of knowledge depending on another entity. Where there is no evidence, the common use is possible through the particular essential nature: this is the regulated organization.[180] But we shall say that here too there is evidence, so we must accept a *śakti* other than *svabhāva*, hence to take the support of this theory of *svabhāva* is meaningless.[181]

In this way, with this presumption, we also have the following inference to prove the existence of *śakti*:

> Fire is the ground of a positive entity which does not dwell in two entites,[182] beyond the range of the senses, different from elasticity, since it possesses qualities, just like a pitcher.

"According to those who accept the existence of the Lord, existence beyond the senses is not established." This statement is also false, for the meaning of the word '*atīndriya*', 'beyond sensual

और अनुव्यवसाय के अतिरिक्त अस्मदादि प्रत्यक्ष का अविषय होना। वह अतीन्द्रियत्व गुरुत्वादि और भावनादि में प्रसिद्ध होने से प्रशस्तपाद ने कहा है कि गुरुत्व, धर्माधर्म और भावना अतीन्द्रिय है—

गुरुत्वधर्माधर्मभावना अतीन्द्रियाः।

यहाँ भावना पद स्थितिस्थापक का भी उपलक्षण है। प्रश्न हो सकता है कि यहाँ आश्रय शब्द से आधार मात्र विवक्षित है या उसका समवायित्व? वह्नि कदाचित् परमाणु या वायु का आधार होकर सिद्धसाधनता होने से प्रथम पक्ष नहीं माना जा सकता। दूसरी बात भी नहीं कही जा सकती, क्योंकि समवाय न माननेवाले भाट्ट के मत में विशेषण अप्रसिद्ध हो जायगा। परन्तु ऐसा नहीं कहा जा सकता, क्योंकि समवाय न मानते हुए भी स्वीय रूपादि के समान अयुतसिद्ध होने के कारण अग्नि की विशिष्ट धर्माधारता ही आश्रय शब्द का अर्थ है। अतीन्द्रिय कर्माश्रय होने से मीमांसक की अर्थान्तरता कहना भी ठीक नहीं, क्योंकि प्रभाकर की तरह शक्ति माननेवाले भाट्ट और वेदान्ती भी कर्म की अतीन्द्रियता नहीं मानते। विपक्ष में वह्निस्वरूप ही कारण होने से प्रतिबन्ध के अभाव की कारणता का पहले ही निराकरण किया जा चुका है, अतः मन्त्रादि के रहने पर समान रूप से कार्य-जननप्रसङ्ग बाधक है। यह भी कहना ठीक नहीं कि एवंविध धर्माश्रय होने से गुण-कर्मादि भी द्रव्य कहे जायेंगे, क्योंकि वे गुण के अधिकरण नहीं हैं। यदि कहा जाय कि एतादृश धर्माश्रय होने से गुणाधिकरण भी हो जाय, तो यह ठीक नहीं, क्योंकि इसका विपर्यय में पर्यवसान नहीं होता।

perception', is other than the qualifier presented by another means of knowledge, not being an object of our perception, which is not the subsequent one (*anuvyavasāya*).[183] This kind of *atīndriyatva* is also established in gravity and in impressions like one's inner feeling (*bhāvanā*), as Praśastapāda [184] also stated:

> Gravity, righteousness and unrighteousness and inner feelings are beyond the sensual range.

The term '*bhāvanā*' is an indicator of elasticity as well.[185] Here, there can be the question: "With the word 'ground' (*āśraya*) is only implied a basis, or its inherence?" [186] The first option cannot be accepted, because there will be the flaw of proving what was already proved, fire being sometimes the basis of the atom or of the wind.[187] The other option is also incorrect; in fact, for the followers of the *Bhāṭṭa Mīmāṃsā*, who do not accept inherence,[188] the qualification (*viśeṣaṇa* = *samavāyitva*) will be established.[189] But both these statements are false, since even without accepting inherence, the right meaning of the word 'ground' is the being of the qualified basis of an attribute, for fire; in fact, it does not exist in separation like its own colour and so forth. Moreover, it is not possible to attest to the *arthāntaratā* of the *Mīmāṃsakas* [190] out of being beyond sensory perception of the ground of action, because the followers of *Vedānta* and of the *Mīmāṃsā* of Kumārila Bhaṭṭa do not accept the *atīndriyatva* of the action as does Prabhākara. From the other point of view [the *Naiyāyikas* one], where the cause is *svabhāva*, we have already denied the causality of the absence of obstruction, so then like the presence of the *mantras* and what have you, the impediment comes from the production of the effect.[191]

It is also wrong to affirm that qualities and actions shall be called substances, they being grounds of such-and-such an attribute. In fact, they [*guṇakarmādi*] are not the basis for qualities.[192] If someone were to object that, being the ground of that kind of attribute, it can also be the basis for the quality, we would reply that it is because its conclusion does not touch any real inconsistency.[193]

यदि कहा जाय कि जो गुण का अधिकरण नहीं है, वह एवंविध धर्म का अधिकरण नहीं होता, ऐसा प्रतिवादिसम्मत उदाहरण होने से उक्त प्रसङ्ग का विपर्यय में पर्यवसान हो जायगा, क्योंकि शक्ति के अतिरिक्त सभी पक्ष कोटि में निक्षिप्त हैं। इस तरह प्रथम अनुमान का समर्थन किया गया।

अब यदि दूसरे अनुमान के सम्बन्ध में कहा जाय कि वेदान्ती ईश्वर को मानते हैं, इसलिये उभय वादिसम्मत होने के कारण तदतिरिक्त न होने से ईश्वर अर्थान्तर न हो, पर ईश्वर न माननेवाले मीमांसकों को तो ईश्वर से अर्थान्तरता होती है, तो यह ठीक नहीं, क्योंकि जन्यभाव से जन्य ऐसा दूसरा विशेषण देकर भाट्ट के मत में अर्थान्तर का परिहार किया जा सकता है। यदि कहा जाय कि ऐसी स्थिति में नित्य पदार्थों में शक्ति का समर्थन न किया जा सकेगा, तो यह भी उचित नहीं, क्योंकि अनित्य पदार्थों में शक्ति सिद्ध हो जाने पर उसी दृष्टान्त से नित्य पदार्थों में भी शक्ति की सिद्धि हो सकती है। शक्ति एक ही नहीं, अपितु प्रत्येक पदार्थ में भिन्न-भिन्न है। जैसे कि अवयवावयवि में अनित्य होने पर भी जल, तेज आदि के परमाणुओं में रूप जैसे नित्य है, वैसे ही नित्य-अनित्य रूप से शक्ति भी दो प्रकार की मानने में कोई आपत्ति नहीं है। आधेय शक्ति को भी अप्रमाण नहीं कहा जा सकता, क्योंकि '**व्रीहीन् प्रोक्षति**' इत्यादि द्वितीया श्रुतियों से व्रीहि आदि में अतीन्द्रिय शक्ति का अस्तित्व सिद्ध होता है।

चेतन धर्म अदृष्ट का अचेतन व्रीहि आदि में रहना सम्भव न होने से व्रीह्यादिविषयकक्रियाजन्यमात्र होने से ही तदीयत्व की प्रतिपत्ति हो सकती है, अतः वहाँ द्वितीया श्रुति गौण है, ऐसा जो कहा गया था,

If someone would say that what is not the basis of the quality cannot be the ground of such a characteristic (*evaṃvidhadharma* = *śakti*),[194] this being an example accepted by the contendent [*Naiyāyikas*], there would be a conclusion of real contrariness to the said context, because what is other than *śakti* is deposited into all the loci (*pakṣa koṭi*) of the inference. In this manner, the first inference is supported.

About the second inference, if it would be said that the followers of *Vedānta* [so] consider the Lord, therefore as it is accepted by both opponents and being no different from Him, the Lord would not be a different purpose [than that which was wished for] (*arthāntara*), but for he who does not accept *Īśvara*, like the *Mīmāṃsakas*, then there will be in Him an *arthāntaratā*.[195] However, these statements are all false, according to the point of view of Kumārila Bhaṭṭa, since it is possible to avoid the *arthāntara* flaw by giving another adjective [to the probandum], such as 'born from a born existent entity' (*janyabhāva se janya* = *janyabhāvajanya*). If the *Naiyāyikas* still object that to do so would not confim *śakti* among the eternal entities, then this too would be improper. In fact, just as *śakti* is established in the non-eternal entities, using the same example, we can prove *śakti* is not merely one, but is different in every thing.[196] For example, even if it is non-eternal in part and in all (*avayavāvayavin*),[197] just as within the atoms of water and fire and the like color is eternal, similarly there is no difficulty in accepting two kinds of *śakti*, colour also being eternal and non-eternal.[198] Also, we cannot consider the based power (*ādheyaśakti*) as non-established (*apramāṇa*),[199] since through accusative expressions like "he sprinkles the grains", with regard to the grain, the existence of a *śakti* beyond the range of the senses is proved.

The invisible power like *adṛṣṭa* is an attribute of a conscious entity, so its presence in an unconscious one like grains or what have you is impossible, being merely produced by an action whose object are grains and such; such a comprehension is possible, so there the accusative expression is secondary (*gauṇa*). This objection is also

वह भी ठीक नहीं, क्योंकि धर्माधर्मरूप अदृष्ट से अतिरिक्त ही कोई एक अतिशय मान्य है, जो तण्डुल, पिष्ट, पुरोडाशादि परम्परा से प्रधानापूर्व उत्पन्न करता है। इसे न माने, अर्थात् व्रीह्यादि स्वरूप से ही यदि उस प्रधानापूर्व को उत्पन्न कर सकते, तो प्रोक्षणादि विधान व्यर्थ हो जायगा। दृष्ट फल न दिखलायी पडने पर अदृष्ट फल की कल्पना करनी पड़ती है और मुख्य अर्थ सम्भव होने पर लक्षणा करनेका अवकाश नहीं रहता।

इस प्रकार लीलावतीकार के दिये हुए दूषण का भी निराकरण किया गया। शक्ति के अस्तित्व में उपर्युक्त रीति से आगम, अर्थापत्ति और अनुमानरूप प्रमाणों का संक्षिप्त दिग्दर्शन करने से यह नहीं कहा जा सकता कि किसी प्रमाण से शक्ति सिद्ध नहीं होती।

मायारूपिणी भगवती

माया रूप में भी उसी भगवती के ही एक स्वरूप का वर्णन होता है।

मायान्तु प्रकृतिं विद्यान्मायिनन्तु महेश्वरम्।

अर्थात् माया को ही विश्व की प्रकृति समझना चाहिये और मायाविशिष्ट ब्रह्म को ही परमेश्वर समझना चहिये। उसी का अन्यत्र 'अजा' शब्द से निरूपण किया गया है—

अजामेकां लोहितशुक्लकृष्णां बह्वीः प्रजाः सृजमानां सरूपाः।
अजो ह्येको जुषमाणोऽनुशेते जहात्येनां भुक्तभोगामजोऽन्यः॥

not tenable, since it is also acceptable [to have] a special property (*atiśaya*) different from *aḍṛṣṭa*, which is shaped like righteousness and unrighteousness (*dharmādharmarūpa*),[200] which indirectly produce the new principal invisible resultants of the sacrificial act (*pradhānāpūrva*), through the grain, the powder, the sacrificial cakes, and so on.[201] If we do not accept this — or, better, if we can produce that principal *apūrva* only through the essential nature of the grains or whatever it is — the injunction regarding the sprinkling will be useless. We must, in fact, imagine an invisible result (*adṛṣṭaphala*) if no visible result is seen;[202] moreover, if the direct meaning is acceptable, there is no need to use the implication (*lakṣaṇā*).[203]

In this way, the flaws found by the author of the *Nyāyalīlāvatī* have been confuted. Hence, having briefly shown in the preceding manner the existence of *śakti* through a survey of evidences like scriptural testimony, presumption and inference, the position according to which *śakti* is not established by the correct means of knowledge is absolutely untenable.

Bhagavatī as *māyā*

The[204] same Bhagavatī is described also in another form, as *māyā*.

> *Prakṛti* should be known as *māyā*, and the Great Lord as the possessor of *māyā*. [*Śvetāśvatara Upaniṣad* IV.10].

One should consider *māyā* to be the Nature (*prakṛti*) of the world and *māyā*-qualified *brahman* to be the Supreme God (*parameśvara*). It is she who has elsewhere been called 'the Unborn' or the 'Ewe' (*ajā*):

> One billy goat (*aja* = the unborn *jīva*) follows behind one red, white and black coloured nanny goat (*ajā* = unborn *prakṛti*), who gives birth to many offsprings like her; another billy goat, having enjoyed [her as well], leaves her.
>
> [*Śvetāśvatara Upaniṣad* IV.5]

Just as a goat of variegated colour, such as red, white and black, gives birth to many children of her colour, similarly does Nature

अर्थात् जैसे कोई लोहित-शुक्लकृष्ण रङ्ग की कबरी बकरी अपने समान ही बहुत बच्चों को उत्पन्न करती है, वैसे ही सत्व, रज, तम तीनों गुणोंवाली प्रकृति भी अपने समान ही त्रिगुण महदादि प्रपञ्च का निर्माण करती है। आवरणात्मक होने से उसका तमोगुण ही कृष्णरूप है, प्रकाशात्मक होने से सत्वगुण ही शुक्ल रङ्ग है, रञ्जनात्मक होने से रजोगुण ही लोहित रङ्ग है। जैसे कबरे बच्चों वाली कबरी बकरी का उपभोग करते हुए कोई बकरे उसका अनुगमन करते हैं, कोई उससे भोग प्राप्त कर विरक्त होकर उसे त्याग देते हैं, वैसे ही कोई जीव महदादि प्रपञ्चवती त्रिगुणा प्रकृति का उपभोग करते हुए उसका अनुगमन करते हैं, कोई उससे भोगापवर्ग प्राप्त करके उसको त्याग देते हैं। यह अजा भी माया ही है। ईश्वर को कोई भी कार्य्य करने के लिये प्रकृति की अपेक्षा होती है।

प्रकृतिं स्वामवष्टभ्य सम्भवाम्यात्ममायया।

अर्थात् ईश्वर अपनी प्रकृति का ही सहारा लेकर अवतीर्ण होते हैं। ईश्वर की अध्यक्षता में प्रकृति ही चराचर प्रपञ्च का निर्माण करती है—

मयाध्यक्षेण प्रकृतिः सूयते सचराचरम्।

भगवान स्वयं कहते हैं कि प्रकृति मेरी योनि है, उसी में मैं गर्भाधान करके विश्व का निर्माण करता हूँ—

मम योनिर्महद् ब्रह्म तस्मिन्गर्भं दधाम्यहम्।
सम्भवः सर्वभूतानां ततो भवति भारत॥

सम्पूर्ण प्राणियों में जो मूर्तियाँ उत्पन्न होती हैं, उन सबकी प्रकृति ही जननी है और मैं बीज प्रदान करने वाला पिता हूँ—

comprised by the three qualities of *sattva*, *rajas* and *tamas* produces the vast universe starting with the universal intellect (*mahattattva*) and the other elements like her, made up by the three *guṇas*. Since by nature it obscures, it is black just like its *tamoguṇa*; it is radiant, hence it is as white as its *sattvaguṇa;* since *rajas* adds 'colour' by nature, it is red. Just [205] as some billy goat follows such a multi-coloured nanny, some — after having enjoyed her and having grown disinterested — abandon her; similarly, some living beings enjoy the threefold nature constituted by the display of *mahat* and other elements and follow it, but some renounce it after having obtained enjoyment and liberation (*bhogāpavarga*). This unborn she-goat-nature is *māyā*. The Lord (*īśvara*) needs *māyā* to perform any task.

> Keeping my own *prakṛti* under control, I project forth again and again. [*Bhagavad Gītā*, IX.8][206]

The Lord descends only by taking recourse to His own nature. It is Nature (*prakṛti*) that creates this manifest world under the command of God.

> Under Me as the supervisor, *prakṛti* produces [the world] of moving and immobile things. [*Bhagavad Gītā*, IX.10]

The Lord Himself says that "*Prakṛti* is my *yoni*; I create the world by seeding its womb."

> My womb is the great sustainer. In that I place the seed.
> From that, O scion of the Bhārata dynasty, occurs the birth of all things. [*Bhagavad Gītā*, XIV.3]

> It is Nature who is the mother of all those who arise among all living beings, and I am the father who provides the seed.
> O son of Kunti, for whatsoever forms are born from all the wombs,
> Their great sustainer is the womb; I am the father who deposits the seed. [*Bhagavad Gītā*, XIV.4]

सर्वयोनिषु कौन्तेय मूर्त्तयः सम्भवन्ति याः ।
तासां ब्रह्म महद्योनिरहं बीजप्रदः पिता ॥

गुणमयी प्रकृति का अतिक्रमण बहुत ही कठिन है । अधिष्ठान ब्रह्म के साक्षात्कार से ही उसका अतिक्रमण हो सकता है, अन्यथा नहीं—

दैवी ह्येषा गुणमयी मम माया दुरत्यया ।

भूतप्रकृति को बाधित करके ही परप्राप्ति होती है—

भूतप्रकृतिमोक्षञ्च ये विदुर्यान्ति ते परम् ।

कहीं-कहीं अविद्या को 'क्षर' और विद्या को 'अमृत' कहा है—

क्षरन्त्वविद्याऽमृतं तु विद्या विद्याऽविद्ये ईशते यस्तु सोऽन्यः ।

पुराणों में जो सृष्टि में परमा है, वही प्रकृति है ऐसा प्रकृति का अर्थ किया गया है—

प्रकष्टवाचकः प्रश्च कृतिश्च सृष्टिवाचकः ।
सृष्टौ या परमा देवी प्रकृतिः सा प्रकीर्तिता ॥

चतुष्कपर्दा युवतिः सुपेशा घृतप्रतीका वयुनानि वस्ते ।
सत्या सुपर्णा वृषणा निषेदतुर्यत्र देवा दधिरे भागधेयम् ।

इस मन्त्र में उसी भगवती के अविद्यारूप का वर्णन है । माया स्थूल,सूक्ष्म, कारण और समाधि इन चार रूपों में प्रकट होती है, युवती रहती है, सुपेशा, सुन्दर रूपवाली, घृत के समान प्रतीत होती है, ज्ञानों को ढँकने वाली है, जीव-ईश्वर दोनों ही उससे सम्बन्ध रखते हैं ।

It is extremely difficult to transcend this *guṇa*-qualified Nature. It is only upon realizing her ground, the Supreme *brahman*, that one can transcend her, and not otherwise:

> This divine *māyā* of Mine which is constituted by the *guṇas* is difficult to surpass. [*Bhagavad Gītā,* VII.14]

Only[207] after having sublated the nature of the elements can someone attain *para* (that which is beyond perception and cognition):

> They who knew the elemental nature and liberation, they go to the supreme.

In some places, *avidyā* (ignorance) has been called '*kṣara*' (that which gets dissipated) and *vidyā* (true knowledge) has been called '*amṛta*' (immortal):

> Ignorance is perishable and knowledge is immortal;
> But who masters over *vidyā* and *avidyā*, he is another.

In the *Purāṇa*s, [it is said that] that *prakṛti* is in creation is *paramā,* supreme:

> '*Pra*' express superiority and '*kṛti*' denotes the manifestation. Within [the realm] of manifestation, the supreme Goddess is extolled as *prakṛti.*[208]

> Endowed with four conditions, young, with a lovely form, whose symbol is clarified butter, she veils the right cognitions. Within her, where the deities receive their part of the oblations, sit two mighty birds. [*Ṛg Veda* X.114.3][209]

This *mantra* describes the same Bhagavatī as *avidyā* (ignorance). *Māyā* appears in four forms: gross (*sthūla*), subtle (*sūkṣma*), causal (*kāraṇa*) and *samādhi.* She forever remains a young woman; she is *supeśā* (with a lovely figure) and beautiful; she looks like *ghī* (clarified butter); she veils knowledge, and both *jīva* (the individual soul) and *Īśvara* (God) are related to her.

तम आसीत्तमसा गूढमग्रेऽप्रकेतं सलिलं सर्वमा इदम् ।
तुच्छ्येनाभ्वपिहितं यदासीत्तपसस्तन्महिना जायतैकम् ॥

इस वचन से भी एक तत्वावरक तम के अस्तित्व का पता लगता है ।

सा च ब्रह्मस्वरूपा च नित्या सा च सनातनी ।
यथात्मा च तथा शक्तिर्यथाग्नौ दाहिका स्थिता ॥
अतएव च योगीन्द्रैः स्त्रीपुम्भेदो न मन्यते ॥

सर्वं ब्रह्ममयं जगत् ।

अहमेवासपूर्वन्तु नान्यत्किञ्चिन्नगाधिप ।
तदात्मरूपं चित्संवित्परब्रह्मैकनामकम् ॥

आसीदिदं तमोभूतमज्ञातमलक्षणम् ।
अप्रतर्क्यमनिर्देश्यं प्रसुप्तमिव सर्वतः ॥

आदि वचनों से भी उसी तत्व की सिद्धि होती है ।

माया और अविद्या

माया को ही कहीं-कहीं अविद्या और अज्ञान शब्द से भी कहा गया है । यहाँ अज्ञान ज्ञान का अभावरूप नहीं, किन्तु ज्ञाननिवर्त्त्य, भावरूप, अनिर्वचनीय पदार्थ ही है । तभी उसमें आवरण हेतुता बन सकती है । "**अज्ञानेनावृतं ज्ञानम्**" इस वचन में अज्ञान को ब्रह्मस्वरूप ज्ञान का आवरक कहा गया है । यह तभी बन सकता है जब अज्ञान भी भावरूप हो, क्योंकि असत्व किसी का आवरक नहीं हो सकता ।

> There was darkness covered by darkness in the beginning; all this [world] was indistinguishable water;
> That empty united [world] which was covered by a mere nothing, was produced through the power of austerity. [*Ṛg Veda* X.129.3]

This statement also indicates the presence of *tamas,* which conceals reality (*tattva*).

> She is *brahman* itself, constant, eternal.
> Just as the burning power is situated within the fire, so in the Self is Śakti.
> Therefore the best among the yogins do not consider any difference to exist between man and woman.[210]

> All this universe is sustained by *brahman.*[211]

> Before I was alone, O king of the mountains, [there was] nothing else;
> Then, Self, consciousness, knowledge, supreme *brahman* all are but names of mine.[212]

> This darkness was unknowable without characteristics.
> Unthinkable,without any desire, from every side [did it seem that] I slept.[213]

These words also prove the existence of that very element (*tattva*).

Māyā and *avidyā*

In [214] some places *māyā* has been called *avidyā* and *ajñāna* (ignorance or false knowledge). Here *ajñāna* is not the absence of *jñāna* (knowledge) but is rather an entity removable by knowledge; [it is both] existent (*bhāva*) and indescribable.[215] Only due to these qualities can it can be the cause of concealment. "Knowledge is covered by ignorance"— by this statement it has been said that *ajñāna* is the concealer (*āvaraka*) of *jñāna*, which is *brahman* itself. This can only come about if *ajñāna* is also an existent entity, because *asattva* (non-existence) cannot conceal anything.

जैसे अज्ञान को आवरक कहा गया है, वैसे ही माया को भी आवरक कहा गया है—

नाहं प्रकाशः सर्वस्य योगमायासमावृतः ।

मैं अर्थात् अस्मत्पदलक्ष्य परब्रह्म योगमाया से आवृत है, इसीलिये स्वप्रकाश होने पर भी उसे लोग नहीं जानते । "**अहमज्ञः**", "**मामहं न जानामि**" इस रूप से अज्ञान का प्रत्यक्ष अनुभव होता है । "**त्वामहं न जानामि**" इस रूप से भी अज्ञान का अनुभव होता है । यदि अज्ञान, ज्ञानाभाव ही हो, तब तो उसका ऐसा अनुभव ही न बन सकेगा, क्योंकि अभाव के ग्रहण में अनुयोगी-प्रतियोगी दोनों के ग्रहण की अपेक्षा होती है । जैसे घट और भूतल के ज्ञान के बिना भूतलनिष्ठ घटाभाव का ज्ञान नहीं हो सकता, वैसे ही आत्मा और ज्ञानरूप अनुयोगी-प्रतियोगी के ज्ञान के बिना ज्ञानाभाव का बोध भी न हो सकेगा ।

यदि अनुयोगी-प्रतियोगी का ज्ञान स्वीकार न किया जाय, तो भी ज्ञानाभाव का ज्ञान नहीं हो सकता और यदि स्वीकार कर लिया जाय, तो भी ज्ञानाभाव का बोध नहीं हो सकता, क्योंकि जैसे भूतल में एक भी घट होने पर घटाभाव नहीं कहा जा सकता, वैसे ही एक भी ज्ञान रहे, तो ज्ञानाभाव का अनुभव नहीं कहा जा सकता । परन्तु जब भावरूप अज्ञान मानते हैं, तब तो साक्षी से उसका बोध हो जाता है । फिर अनुयोगी-प्रतियोगी के ग्रहणाग्रहण का कोई भी विकल्प नहीं उठता, क्योंकि भावरूप अज्ञान साक्षी के द्वारा प्रकाशित हो सकता है । यद्यपि भावरूप अज्ञान के प्रत्यक्ष में भी विशेषण या निरूपकरूप से घटादि विषय का भान होना आवश्यक होता है, फिर उसके भी ज्ञान रहने पर उसका अज्ञान नहीं कहा जा सकता और उसके ज्ञान न रहने से विशेषण ज्ञान के बिना विशिष्ट अज्ञान का अनुभव भी नहीं हो

Just as *ajñāna* has been called a covering, so too has *māyā* also been called a concealment:

> I am covered by the *yogamāyā*, so I am not the Light of all.

'I' — or better, the supreme principle (*parabrahman*), the implied meaning of the term 'I' — is covered by *māyā*; hence, even if it is self-luminous (*svaprakāśa*), people do not know it. "I am ignorant", "I do not know myself": in this way we experience *ajñāna* directly. We also experience *ajñāna* as "I do not know you". If *ajñāna* be merely the lack of *jñāna*, then we cannot experience it in this way because, in grasping an absence (*abhāva*), we will have to accept the idea of both *anuyogin* [the base upon which something is absent] and *pratiyogin* [the thing whose absence is presented — that is, the absent thing]. Just [216] as without the knowledge of a 'pot' or of 'clay' we cannot be aware of the absence of a clay pot, similarly without an awareness of the base (*anuyogin*) and the counter-positive (*pratiyogin*) that are knowledge and self (*ātman*), we will not be able to experience the absence of knowledge (*jñāna*).[217]

Even if we do not accept the knowledge of *pratiyogin* and the *anuyogin*, we still cannot experience the lack of knowledge. Even if we accept this idea, still we cannot experience the lack of knowledge, for just as if there is even a single clay pot surviving in the world, we cannot say that there is a non-presence of a clay pot; similarly, if even one fact remains, then we cannot claim to experience the absence of knowledge. But if we believe *ajñāna* to be an existent category, we can be aware of it through the witness (*sākṣin*). Then no alternative arises, such as whether or not one grasps the absence-base or the counter-positive, because the existent *ajñāna* can be illuminated by the *sākṣin*. Although even when *ajñāna* is perceived it is necessary [to recognize] the cognition of objects [like pots] as the representation or as the qualifier of that [ignorance], when this knowledge is present still we cannot say that we have *ajñāna* of it; if we have no knowledge of it, then in the absence of the knowledge of the qualifier we will not be able to experience the qualified *ajñāna*. Furthermore, if we are

सकेगा, तथापि साक्षी से द्वारा ही अज्ञान और उसके विशेषण घटादि का भी भान होने से किसी भी दोष की प्रसक्ति नहीं होती। ज्ञानरूप से सर्ववस्तु साक्षिभास्य होती है, यह निगमान्तविदों का सिद्धान्त है—

ज्ञानतया अज्ञानतया वा सर्वं वस्तु साक्षिभास्यम्।

"**घट ज्ञातः**" यहाँ जैसे ज्ञान का विषय होकर साक्षी द्वारा घट भासित होता है वैसे ही '**घटो न ज्ञायते**' यहाँ भी अज्ञान के विषयरूप से घट साक्षीरूप से भासित होता है। योगनिद्रा, जड़शक्ति, अचित्, अज्ञान, अविद्या, माया, प्रकृति इत्यादि सभी शब्द एक ही अर्थ के बोधक हैं "**परास्य शक्तिर्विविधैव श्रूयते**" (परमात्मा की पराशक्ति विविध प्रकार की सुनी जाती है) इत्यादि स्थलों की शक्ति भी तद्रूप ही है।

शक्ति की अन्तरङ्गता-बहिरङ्गता

कुछ लोग इस शक्ति को अन्तरङ्गा और माया, प्रकृति आदि को बहिरङ्गा शक्ति कहते हैं। भगवल्लोक, भगवद्विग्रहादि में अन्तरङ्ग दिव्य शक्ति का उपयोग मानते हैं। जगन्निर्माण में माया, अविद्यादि बहिरङ्ग शक्ति का उपयोग मानते हैं। कुल लोग अचित् को प्राकृत-अप्राकृत भेद से दो प्रकार का मानते हैं। प्राकृत अचित् से जगत् की और अप्राकृत अचित् से भगवल्लोकादि की रचना मानते हैं। कुछ लोग जगन्निर्माण अथवा लीलामय के लीलोपयोगी पदार्थों की सृष्टि के लिये भगवत्स्वरूपभूत ही अघटितघटनापटीयान् भगवदीयस्वात्मवैभव स्वीकार करते हैं। वही परमात्मा अविकृत-परिणाम द्वारा सर्वरूप में व्यक्त होता है। जैसे कल्पवृक्ष, चिन्तामणि, कामधेनु आदि से तत्तत् अभीष्ट पदार्थ की सृष्टि होने पर भी वे निर्विकार रहते हैं, वैसे ही परमात्मा से भी विविध विश्व बनने पर भी परमेश्वर निर्विकार ही रहता है। विचार

aware of *ajñāna* and of its objects like pots and so on only through the witness, then no fault at all accrues by doing so. There is a doctrine of the followers of *Vedānta* according to which everything is illumined by the *sākṣī* through knowledge:

> In [218] the form of knowledge, or in the form of ignorance, every thing is illumined by the Witness.

"The pot is known" — here, just as the pot is perceived through the witness [due to it] being an object of knowledge, similarly in "The pot has not been known" the pot is also perceived as the subject of ignorance (*ajñāna*) via the witness. *Yoganidrā*, *jaḍaśakti* (insentient power), *acit* (insentient matter), *ajñāna*, *avidyā*, *māyā*, *prakṛti*, and so on — all these words denote the same meaning. "His supreme power is described in many ways", "it is heard that the *parāśakti* of *paramātman* is of various types"; the *śakti* concerning these references is also similar.

The internality-externality of *śakti*[219]

Some people say that this *śakti* is internal (*antaraṅgatā*) and *māyā*, *prakṛti* and the like are external *śakti* (*bahiraṅgatā*). It is believed that the internal, divine *śakti* plays an important role in relation to the world and forms [and everything else] of the Lord, and such things as *māyā* and *avidyā* — external *śakti* aspects — take part in the manifestation of the world. For[220] the production of the universe, or for the creation of things useful for the divine play of what has the nature of the divine game, some [people] accept the Lord's inherent glory — capable of causing to be that which never was — to be of the same nature as that of the Lord. It is the selfsame *paramātman* who becomes expressed as everything via *avikṛtapariṇāma* (a mutation). Just as the wish-fulfilling tree (*kalpavṛkṣa*), the wish-fulfilling gem (*cintāmaṇi*) and the wish-fulfilling cow (*kāmadhenu*) create a desired object but themselves remain unchanged, similarly are various worlds made from the *paramātman,* who nevertheless remains unchanged. Once one ponders whether one should consider this majestic nature (*svātmavaibhava*) to be the nature of the Lord (*bhagavatsvarūpa*), then

करने से मालूम होगा कि यह स्वात्मवैभव यदि भगवत्स्वरूप ही है, तब तो फिर पृथक् नाम-रूप कल्पना की अपेक्षा नहीं हो सकता। तब कृत्स्नप्रसक्ति, निरवयवत्वव्याकोपादि शंकाओं का समाधान भी न हो सकेगा। सम्पूर्ण ब्रह्म यदि प्रपञ्च बन जायगा, तब तो मुक्तोपास्य ब्रह्म अवशिष्ट न रहेगा। यदि एकदेशेन ब्रह्म विश्व बनेगा, तब तो सावयवत्व, विकारित्व आदि दोष अनिवार्य ही होंगे। कल्पवृक्षादिकों की विलक्षण शक्ति की महिमा से ही तादृक् विलक्षण कार्य्यकारिता सिद्ध होती है।

माया की अनिर्वचनीयता

इस तरह स्वात्मवैभव अथवा अचित् किंवा अन्तरङ्गा शक्ति यदि अधिष्ठान से पृथक् होकर सत् है, तब तो श्रुति सिद्धान्त बाधित होगा। यदि अत्यन्त असत् है तो कार्य्यकारिता न बन सकेगी। विरुद्ध होने से सदसद्रूपता भी नहीं कही जा सकती। फिर तो पारिशेष्यात् अनिर्वचनीय मानना होगा। इस तरह अवान्तर चाहे कितने भी भेद मान लिये जायँ, परन्तु अनिर्वचनीयत्वेन रूपेण उन सबकी एकता ही है।

देवदत्तनिष्ठप्रमा तन्निष्ठप्रमाप्रागभावातिरिक्तानादिप्रध्वंसिनी प्रमात्वात्, यज्ञदत्तनिष्ठप्रमावत्।

अर्थात् देवदत्तनिष्ठ प्रमा अपने प्रमा के प्रागभाव से अतिरिक्त किसी अनादि की प्रध्वंसिनी है, प्रागभाव से अतिरिक्त अनादि भावरूप अज्ञान ही हो सकता है, इस अनुमान से भी अनादि अज्ञान सिद्ध होता है। इसी को '**तम आसीत्**' इत्यादि श्रुतियों में तमोरूप भी माना गया है। इस तम को कण्ठतः अनिर्वचनीय कहा गया है—

one cannot imagine a different *nāma-rūpa* [to distinguish one from the other], and then we will not be able to resolve such doubts as [those regarding the] entire connection [applicability] or the contradiction with the absence of parts, or what have you. If the entire *brahman* became the manifestation (*prapañca*), then there would be no *brahman* left to worship in order to get liberation. If by one part (*ekadeśena*) *brahman* would become the world, then such flaws as having parts (*sāvayavatva*), derangement (*vikāritva*) and the like would also become inevitable. Such a particular agency towards the effects (*kāryakaritā*) is proved only by the wonder of the particular power of the *kalpavṛkṣa* and the like.

The indescribability of *māyā*

If this *svātmavaibhava,* or *acit*, or the internal *śakti* would truly be separate from its substratum, then the principle of the *Vedas* would be invalidated. If it is absolutely non-existent, then it would be incapable of being an efficient cause for anything. Due to this conflict, her existent-non-existent nature cannot be affirmed. Then the conclusion will be that we would have to call it 'indescribable'. Thus, regardless of how many secondary variants it is believed [to comprise], all of these forms are one by their indescribability.

> The real knowledge of Devadatta is the destroyer of something beginningless other than the [mere] prior absence of his own right knowledge, because it is a right knowledge, as is the right knowledge of Yajñadatta.

The true knowledge resting within Devadatta is the destroyer of something without origin that is different from the prior-absence (*prāgabhāva*) of his own true knowledge, and only ignorance (*ajñāna*) can be an originless and positive entity different from *prāgabhāva*. By this inference, also, originless *ajñāna* is proved. This is what is considered to be the embodied *tamas* in such statements of the *śruti*s as "There was darkness". This *tamas* has been said to be indescribable:

"**नासदासीन्नो सदासीत्तम एवासीत्**" (न सत् था, न असत् था, किन्तु तम ही था) यह सदसद्विलक्षणता ही अनिर्वचनीयता है । "**अनृतेन हि प्रत्यूढाम्**", इत्यादि वचनों से तो इस आवरक तम को प्रत्यक्ष ही अनृत कहा है ।

ज्ञानेन तु तदज्ञानं येषां नाशितमात्मनः ।

मायामेतां तरन्ति ते ।

इत्यादि वचनों से माया, अज्ञान आदिकों की निवर्त्त्यता कहने से ही अनिवर्चनीयता का बोधन होता है । सत् की शक्तिरूप होने से भी इसकी अनिर्वचनीयता बोधित होती है, क्योंकि जैसे वह्नि की शक्ति वह्निरूप नहीं होती, किन्तु वह्नि से विलक्षण होती है, वैसे ही सत् की शक्ति सद्रूप न होकर सत् से विलक्षण ही होती है । वह सद्विलक्षणता भी अनिर्वचनीयता है । इस प्रकार माया की अनिर्वचनीयता ही सिद्ध होती है ।

तान्त्रिक दृष्टि में शक्ति

तन्त्रों के अनुसार प्रकाश ही शिव और विमर्श ही शक्ति है । संहार में शिव का प्राधान्य रहता है, सृष्टि में शक्ति का प्राधान्य रहता है । प्रभा में इदमंशग्राह्य होता है, अहमंश ग्राहक होता है । माना यह जाता है कि भीतर वर्तमान पदार्थों का ही बाह्यरूप में अवभास होता है—

वर्त्तमानावभासानां भावानामवभासनम् ।
अन्तःस्थितवतामेव घटते बहिरात्मना ॥

प्रकृति में ही सूक्ष्मरूप से सब वस्तु स्थित हैं । परम शिव और शक्ति दोनों ही श्लिष्ट होकर रहते हैं । निःस्पन्द परम शिवतत्व और निषेधात्मक तत्व ही शक्तितत्व है ।

"Neither being (*sat*), nor not-being (*asat*) was there; there was only darkness (*tamas*)" [*Ṛgveda* X.129.1]. This difference from being and not being (*sadasadvilakṣaṇatā*) is the indescribability. Statements like "It is enveloped by falsity" and the like declare that this veiling *tamas* is the directly perceivable falsity (*anṛta*).

> But those who have destroyed that ignorance through the realization of the Self.
>
> They cross over that illusion.

These and similar verses, explaining the possibility to annihilate such things as *māyā* and ignorance, denote indescribability. [The fact that it is] the *śakti* of *sat* also denotes its indescribability, because just as the power of fire is not the fire itself but is rather distinct from it, similarly the *śakti* of *sat* is not of the nature of *sat* but is rather distinct from it. That distinction from *sat* is indescribability; thus, what is proved is the indescribability of *māyā*.

Śakti in the *tāntrika* view

According to the *Tantras*, Śiva is light and Śakti is reflection (*vimarśa*). Śiva is predominant in annihilation and Śakti in manifestation. In light the grasped object is the part pertaining to 'that' (*idamaṃśa*), and the perceived is the part pertaining to the 'I' (*ahamaṃśa*). It is believed that we see outside what lies inside us:

> The appearance of the objects, that are only appearances present in the interior by [the agency of] *ātman* [in the sense of internal organ, *antaḥkarana*], is organized externally.

All objects are present within *prakṛti* in their subtle form. Paramaśiva and Śakti dwell in a perpetual embrace; the *śivatattva* is motionless (*niṣpanda*), and the *śaktitattva* is apophatic (*niṣedhātmaka*).

> There was the meaning, the essentially knowing, one and changeless.

आसीज्ज्ञानमयो ह्यर्थः एकमेवाविकल्पितः ।

अर्थात् ज्ञान और अर्थ दोनों ही अविकल्पित होकर एक में रहते हैं, तब साम्यावस्था समझी जाती है ।

प्रकृति की सत्ता

ज्ञानस्वरूप पुरुष की सत्ता पारमार्थिक है, अर्थरूप प्रकृति की सत्ता अवास्तविक है । उसकी अविद्यमानता का वर्णन बहुत स्थानों में मिलता है ।

अर्थे ह्यविद्यमानेऽपि संसृतिर्न निवर्त्तते ।
ध्यायतो विषयानस्य स्वप्नेऽनर्थागमो यथा ॥

अर्थ के न रहने पर भी संसृति की निवृत्ति नहीं होती, जैसे स्वप्न में अर्थ न रहने पर भी वह भासमान होता है, वही स्थिति अर्थ की है । विशेषतः माया का यही लक्षण श्रीमद्भागवत में किया गया है कि जिसके कारण कोई वस्तु न होने पर भी प्रतीत हो, वस्तु होती हुई भी न प्रतीत हो, वही माया है, जैसे स्वाप्निक प्रपञ्च, शुक्तिरूप्य, रज्जुसर्पादि पदार्थ न होने पर भी भासमान होते हैं, तम-राहु आकाश में विद्यमान रहने पर भी नहीं भासित होते—

ऋतेऽर्थं यत्प्रतीयेत न प्रतीयेत चात्मनि ।
तद्विद्यादात्मनो मायां यथा भासो यथा तमः ॥

भगवती और माया का वैलक्षण्य

शक्ति शब्द से जैसे अचित् प्रकृति के अतिरिक्त पराप्रकृति, जीव आदि का भी ग्रहण होता है, वैसे ही भगवती शब्द से शुद्ध निर्गुण

In other words, knowledge and meaning, being both changeless (*avikalpita*), remain as one; this is understood to be the state of equilibrium (*sāmyāvasthā*).

The existence of *prakṛti*

The level of existence of the essentially knowing (*jñānasvarūpa*) *puruṣa* is the absolute one, and the level of being of *prakṛti* — of the nature of the object (*artharūpa*) — is unreal. In numerous places we can find descriptions of Her [in the form of the] absence [of an object].

> Even if the object is not present, the movement does not cease,
> Just as [happens] in the dream to who projects the objects, even if the object is not [present].

Even in the absence of the object, there is no cessation of restless motion (*saṃsṛti*), Just as objects appear within dreams, despite their actual non-presence, so it is with the object [of waking reality]. This[221] is the characteristic of *māyā* notably described in the *Śrīmad-bhāgavata*; *māyā* is [therein said to be] that which makes cognisable a non-existent object, or an existent one knowable — [as in the well known examples of] a dream world, [of perceiving] silver within the mother-of-pearl (*śuktirūpya*) or a snake instead of a rope, even if they are not, they appear to be; conversely, darkness and Rāhu ('the Northern Node') are not perceived, though they are present in the sky.

> What appears, even without the object, and what is not grasped by itself,
> All this should be known as the māyā of the Self, similar to light and darkness.[222]

The distinction between Bhagavatī and *māyā*

Just as through the word '*śakti*' there is the grasping of the supreme *prakṛti* other than the insentient one of the individual soul, similarly does, the word '*bhagavatī*' also evoke the pure *cit-śakti*,

चिच्छक्ति का भी बोध होता है। इसीलिये उपासकों की उपास्यशक्ति या भगवती को केवल प्रकृति या माया न समझना चाहिये, किन्तु सच्चिदानन्दात्मिका भगवती ही उपास्य होती है।

रात्रिरूपिणी

रात्रिसूक्त रात्रिदेवता का प्रतिपादन करता है। रात्रिदेवता दो हैं, एक जीवन-सम्बन्धिनी, दूसरी ईश्वरसम्बन्धिनी। प्रथम का अनुभव सभी लोग करते हैं, जिसके सम्बन्ध से प्रतिदिन समस्त व्यवहार लुप्त हुआ करता है। ईश्वररात्रि वह है, जिसमें ईश्वर का व्यवहार भी लुप्त होता है, उसी को महाप्रलय कालस्वरूप कहा जाता है। उस समय दूसरी कोई भी वस्तु नहीं रहती, केवल मायाशबलित ब्रह्म ही रहता है, उसे ही अव्यक्त भी कहा जाता है।

ब्रह्ममायात्मिका रात्रिः परमेशलयात्मिका।
तदधिष्ठातृदेवी तु भुवनेशी प्रकीर्तिता॥ (देवी पुराण)

ब्रह्ममायात्मिका रात्रि की अधिष्ठात्री देवता ही भगवती भुवनेश्वरी है। "**रात्री व्यख्यदायती पुरुत्रा देव्यक्षभिः विश्वा**" इत्यादि का सारांश यह है कि "सर्वकारणभूता चिच्छक्ति भगवती पूर्वकल्पीय अनन्त जीवों के अपरिपक्व अतएव फलानभिमुख सत्-असत् कर्मों को देखकर फल प्रदान का समय न होने से ऐश्वरप्रपञ्च को अपने में ही प्रलीन कर लेती है। पश्चात् वही रात्रिरूपा चिच्छक्ति फलप्रदान का समय आने पर महदादि द्वारा प्रपञ्च का निर्माण करके असाङ्कर्येण तत्तत्प्राणियों के कर्मों को देखती है।" फिर उन कर्मों का फल प्रदान करती है। इससे रात्रिरूपा भगवती की सर्वज्ञता स्पष्ट है। वह अमर्त्त्या

free from any attribute. Hence we should not consider the worship-worthy Bhagavatī — or '*śakti*' — to be 'mere' *prakṛti* or *māyā*; rather, who is venerable is [none other than] Bhagavatī whose essence is Being, Consciousness, and Bliss (*saccidānandātmikā*).

She whose form is the Night (Rātrirūpiṇī)

The[223] *Rātrisūkta* describes the deity of the Night (*rātridevatā*). There are two deities of the night, one related to living beings, the other to *īśvara*. The first is experienced by everyone; from Her contact, all the daily social conventions (*vyavahāra*) disappear (*lupta*). The 'night of God' (*īśvararātri*) is when the activities of God are themselves made to disappear; this is what is called the Great Dissolution (*mahāpralaya*), the intrinsic form of [the all-consuming] time (*kālasvarūpa*). At that point, not one single thing remains, only *brahman* qualified by *māyā* (*māyāśabalita*). This is also called *avyakta* ('the unmanifest').

> The Night has the nature of the māyā of *brahman*; Her substance [is evidenced by] the dissolution of *parameśvara*.
> Her presiding divinity is extolled as Bhuvaneśī. (*Devī Purāṇa*)

Bhagavatī Bhuvaneśvarī is the patron goddess of this Night [which is] given its substance by the *māyā* of *brahman* (*brahmamāyā*). Such statements as "In the night, she annihilated all the world before Her" means, in essence, that "Bhagavatī, who is the power of Consciousness (*cit-śakti*) and the cause of everything (*sarvakāraṇabhūtā*), having seen the unripe and fructifying deeds — both virtuous and evil — of countless individual souls since the previous aeon (*pūrvakalpīya*) and, seeing that there is insufficient time to give them the fruit [deserved from these deeds], merges the manifestation of *īśvara* (*īśvaraprapañca*) into Herself. Later, when the time comes to give the fruit [of those actions], the same *rātrirūpa cit-śakti* ('the power of Consciousness of the form of the night') creates the manifest world and, without any mistaken cross-over mixture (*asaṃkaryeṇa*), She witnesses the actions of living beings and grants them the fruit

देवी अन्तरिक्षोपलक्षित समस्त विश्व को अपने स्वरूप से पूरित कर देती है । नीची वस्तु लता-गुल्मादि और उच्छ्रित वृक्षादि को भी अधिष्ठान चैतन्य से पूरित कर देती है और वही परा चिद्रूपा देवी स्वाकार-वृत्तिप्रतिबिम्बितस्वरूप चैतन्य ज्योति से तम उपलक्षित सम्पूर्ण प्रपञ्च को बाधित कर देती है । आती हुई देवनशील रात्रि चिच्छक्ति प्रकाशस्वरूपा उषा (प्रात:काल) को अर्थात् अविद्या की आवरण शक्ति को तिरस्कृत करती है ।

यद्यपि रात्रि द्वारा प्रकाशस्वरूपा उषा का निराकरण असम्भव मालूम पड़ता है, तथापि यहाँ चिद्रूपा रात्रि ही परम प्रकाशरूपा है, तदपेक्षया सन्ध्या या उषा अन्धकाररूप ही है । जैसे सूर्य के प्रकट होने पर सन्ध्या मिट जाती है, वैसे ही चिच्छक्ति के स्वीकार वृत्ति पर प्रतिबिम्बित होने पर अविद्या की आवरण शक्ति मिट जाती है । आवरण शक्ति के दग्ध बीज हो जाने पर प्रारब्ध क्षय के अनन्तर मूलाज्ञानरूप तम सर्वथा नष्ट हो जाता है । दोनों शक्तियों के नष्ट हो जाने पर मूलाज्ञान का भी अवशेष नहीं रहता । वह रात्रिदेवता पराचिच्छक्ति हम सब पर प्रसन्न रहे, जिसकी प्राप्ति में हम सब सुखस्वरूप में वैसे स्थित होते हैं, जैसे अपने घोंसले में पक्षी रात्रिवास करता है । ग्राम के आसपास सभी लोग तथा गवाश्वादि, पक्षी तथा भिन्न प्रयोजन से चलनेवाले पथिक एवं श्येन आदि उस रात्रि में प्रविष्ट होकर सुख से स्थित होते हैं । दिन के सञ्चार से भ्रान्त प्राणियों को यह रात्रि ही सुख पहुँचाती है, उस समय सब लोग विश्राम करने लगते हैं । सारांश यह है कि जो प्राणी भुवनेश्वरी के नाम तक से भी परिचित नहीं हैं, वे भी करुणामयी परा चिच्छक्ति अम्बा की करुणा से ही उसके अङ्क में जाकर सुख से उसी तरह सोते हैं, जिस तरह मूढ़ बालक माता की करुणा से स्वस्थ सोते हैं । ऐसी करुणामयी यह चिच्छक्ति है । हे

of their respective deeds." This makes clear the omniscience of this goddess whose essence is that of the Night (*rātrirūpā*). That immortal Goddess, with Her essence fills the entire world, implied by the term middle space (*antarīkṣa*). She fills the ground with Consciousness [infusing everything, from the] lowly, like creepers and undergrowth, to tall trees and the like; the same transcendent goddess, whose essence is consciousness, sublates the entire universe whose metaphor is the darkness by the light of the essential Consciousness reflected upon the mental modification that has Her own form. Having arrived, the god-intoxicating (*devanaśīla*) night of *cit-śakti* disdains Uṣā (Dawn), the veiling *śakti* of unsteady ignorance (*avidyā*).

Although it would seem impossible that night can eradicate that dawn which is of the nature of light, *rātri* of the form of Consciousness is yet the ultimate form of light; comparatively, dusk (*saṃdhyā*) and dawn are darkness. Just as [dawn] is obliterated at the appearance of the sun, similarly is the veiling power of *avidyā* annihilated upon being reflected onto that mental modification whose shape is the selfsame *cit-śakti*. When the seed of the veiling power is burned away, one's *prārabdha* [224] dissipates; at this point *tamas*, the beginingless root of ignorance, is completely destroyed. When both these powers are destroyed, no trace of the root ignorance shall remain. Be [225] pleased with all of us, O Deity of the Night (*rātridevatā*), O absolute power of Consciousness; when we attain You, we shall all be [well] situated within the bliss as is a bird at night, asleep inside his nest. Everybody in a village, cows, birds and travellers moving with different purposes, jackals and so on, all rest happily once they enter that night. It is the night that brings pleasure to living beings that have wandered about during the day's transit; all find rest at that time. In short, even those beings unfamiliar with the mere name 'Bhuvaneśvarī' also sleep happily in Her lap, only out of Her compassion, in the same way as unaware children sleep a healthy sleep, out of the compassion of their mother. This *cit-śakti* is so very replete with compassion.

ऊर्म्ये! रात्रिदेवी! चिच्छक्ते! आप परम दयामयी हैं, अतः हमारे कृत्यों की ओर न देखकर हिंसा करनेवाले मारक पापरूप वृक (भेड़िया) और नानावासनारूपी वृकी को हमसे पृथक् कर दो और चित्त-वित्त के अपहारक कामादि दोषों को भी हमसे हटा दो और हमारे लिये आप सुखेन तरणी और क्षेमकरी हो। सम्पूर्ण वस्तुओं में फैला हुआ कृष्णवर्ण स्पष्ट अज्ञान हमको घेरे हुए है। हे उषोदेवते! आप ऋण के समान उस अज्ञान को दूर कर दो। जैसे अपने स्तोताओं का ऋण आप दूर करती हैं, वैसे ही हमारे अज्ञान को दूर करें। हे रात्रि देवते! चिच्छक्ते! कामधेनु के समान सर्वाभीष्टदायिनी आपको प्राप्त करके स्तुति-जपादि से अभिमुख करता हूँ। आप प्रकाशरूप परमात्मा की पुत्री हैं।'' परमात्मा से ही अन्यत्र चैतन्य शक्ति की अभिव्यक्ति होती है, इस विवक्षा से भगवती को दिवोदुहिता कहा गया है।

चण्डी

एक दृष्टि से भगवती को परब्रह्म की महिषी कहा जाता है—

त्वमसि परब्रह्ममहिषी।

उसी दृष्टि से उनका नाम 'चण्डिका' है। ''**चण्डभानुः चण्डवातः**'' इत्यादि स्थानों में इयत्तानवच्छिन्न असाधारणगुणशाली वस्तु में 'चण्ड' शब्द का प्रयोग होता है। देश-काल वस्तु परिच्छेदशून्य वस्तु परमात्मा ही है। भानु, वात आदि का विशेषण होने से वह सङ्कुचित वृत्ति हो जाता है। 'चडि कोपे' धातु से 'चण्ड' शब्द की निष्पत्ति है।

"O Night! O Goddess of the night! Oh You who are the power of awareness! You are supremely merciful; so, ignoring our deeds, please keep from us the violent, murderous wolf of sin and the wolf-bitch of our manifold cravings, and also please drive back our inclination to be overtaken by such flaws as lust; please, be She who makes us cross-over easily (*sukhena taraṇī*); please also be more peace-confering. The [226] obscure, but clear ignorance that is spread out in everything has surrounded us. O Goddess of the dawn! Cancel that ignorance, as You would a debt. Just as You cancel the debts of those who sing Your praise, similarly remove our *ajñāna*. O Goddess of the Night! O *cit-śakti*! I have obtained You who grant every desire, like the wish-fulfilling cow (*kāmadhenu*); by chanting Your hymns and repeating Your *mantra*, I make You turn towards me. You are the daughter of *paramātman*, who is of the nature of light (*prakāśarūpa*)." The expression of the power of Consciousness is somewhere other than in the *paramātman*. Due to this, Bhagavatī is said to be the daughter of the day (*divo-duhitā*).

The Fearsome (Caṇḍī)

From one point of view, Bhagavatī is said to be the queen of *parabrahman*:

> You [227] are the Queen of the Supreme *brahman*.
>
> [*Saundaryalaharī* 97]

From [228] this perspective, Her name is Caṇḍikā. In statements like '*dreadful sun* [*and*] *dreadful wind*', the word '*caṇḍa*' denotes that which is endowed with the extraordinary quality of an unbroken range (*iyattānavacchinna*). The Supreme *ātman* is that real entity absolutely free from the limitations of space, time and absolutely any [other] characteristic. When it is qualified [with a term like] 'sun', 'air' or the like, it acquires a constrained function. The word '*caṇḍa*' comes from the root (*dhātu*) '*caṇḍi kope*' [which means: to become angry].

कस्य बिभ्यति देवाश्च कृतरोषस्य संयुगे।

किसको रोष उत्पन्न होने से देवताओं को भी डर होता है?

प्रसादो निष्फलो यस्य कोपोऽपि च निरर्थकः ।
न तं भर्तारमिच्छन्ति षण्ढं पतिमिव प्रजाः ॥

अर्थात् जिसका क्रोध और प्रसाद निष्फल होता है, उसे प्रजा उसी तरह स्वामी नहीं मानती, जिस तरह षण्ढ पुरुषों को स्त्रियाँ पति नहीं बनातीं। इसीलिये सफल उग्र क्रोध या उग्र क्रोधवाला पुरुष भी 'चण्ड' कहलाता है । महाभयजनक कोप ही चण्ड कहा जाता है और वह भयजनक कोप परमेश्वर का नहीं है। "**नमस्ते रुद्रमन्यवे**" इस वचन में रुद्र के मन्यु-कोप को प्रणाम किया गया है । संसार में चण्ड से ही सब डरते हैं । स्पष्ट है कि जिसका दण्ड प्रबल होता है, उसी का शासन चलता है। सर्व-संहारक से सब डरते हैं, सर्वसंहारक मृत्यु से भी सब डरते हैं मृत्यु भी चण्ड है ।

भीषास्माद्वातः पवते भीषोदेति सूर्य्यः ।
भीषास्मादग्निश्चेन्द्रश्च मृत्युर्धावति पञ्चमः ॥

अर्थात् परमेश्वर के डर से वायु चलता है, भय से सूर्य्य उदित होता है, भय से अग्नि और इन्द्र भी अपना-अपना काम करते हैं । सर्वभय कारण मृत्यु भी जिससे डरता है, वही भगवान् परमात्मा है । उसको मृत्यु का भी मृत्यु, काल का भी काल या महाकाल किंवा चण्ड कहा जा सकता है, वही सर्वसंहारक है । उससे भिन्न सब संहार्य्य कोटि में आ जाता है । उत्पादक, पालक ब्रह्मा, विष्णु आदि उसके स्वरूप ही हैं, इसलिये वे भी असंहार्य्य हैं । यदि भिन्न होते तो अवश्य संहार्य्य होते, अन्यथा इसीको एकोनसर्वसंहारक कहना पड़ेगा । इसीलिये जिसका विश्व, वही उसका उत्पादक, वही पालक और वही संहारक है ।

[She is the one][229] of whose anger in battle the gods are also afraid. [*Vālmīki Rāmāyaṇa*, I.1.4.]

He whose happiness is fruitless, he whose anger is meaningless, He is not desired by his subjects to be their Lord, just as no woman desires an impotent husband.

That is to say, he whose anger and pleasure are inconsequential cannot be considered by his subjects to be their Lord, just as women don't marry impotent men. Therefore only one having a fruitful fury, or a man whose anger is intense, can be called '*caṇḍa*'. The anger that produces extreme fear is called *caṇḍa*; *Parameśvara* does not fear that anger. In the saying "I salute the wrath of Rudra" [*Yajurveda*], obeiscience to dreadful anger of Rudra [is expressed]. Everyone in *saṃsāra* fears this *caṇḍa*. It is clear that he who can punish (*daṇḍa*), rules. Everyone fears that which destroys everything; everyone fears that death which kills everything. Death is also *caṇḍa*.

Out of his fear wind (Pavana) blows, out of his fear rises the sun (Sūrya).
By the fear of him, Agni and Indra, and Death as the fifth, run.
[*Taittirīya Upaniṣad*, I.8.1.]

Out [230] of fear of *parameśvara* does the wind blow, does the sun rise and do both Agni and Indra do their respective tasks. The one feared even by Death, the source of all fear, is God, *param-ātman*. He can be called the death of Death, the Time of even the [all-consuming] Time (*kāla*), or Mahākāla — otherwise known as *caṇḍa*. He is all-annihilating. Everything different from Him goes into the category of 'destructible'. As the Creator and Preserver — Brahmā and Viṣṇu — are also of His own nature (*svarūpa*), so they are also indestructible. If they had been distinct [from Him], then surely they would have been destructible; otherwise we have to call Him the 'the all-but-one Destroyer'. As such, He who rules the world is also its creator, He is its preserver and He alone is the annihilator.

एकेश्वरवाद सर्वत्र मान्य है ही, उसी को महद्भय वज्ररूप भी कहा गया है। "**महद्भयं वज्रमुद्यतम्**" जैसे उद्यत वज्र के डर से भृत्य लोग तत्परता से काम करते हैं, वैसे ही परमात्मा के डर से सूर्य्य, इन्द्र, चन्द्र आदि सावधानी से अपने-अपने कार्य में संलग्न होते हैं। उसी चण्ड की स्वरूपभूता शक्ति पत्नी चण्डिका है। जैसे परमेश्वर के ही घोर रूप से पृथक् शान्त रूप भी है "**घोरान्या शिवान्या**" वैसे ही भगवती के भी उग्र और शान्त दोनों ही रूप हैं। कुछ लोगों का कहना है कि एक ही परब्रह्म माया से धर्मी और धर्म दो रूप में प्रकट होता है। सृष्टि के आरम्भ में जो "**तदैक्षत बहुस्यां प्रजायेय**", "**सोऽकामयत**", "**तत्तपोऽकुरुत**" इत्यादि से ज्ञान, इच्छा और क्रिया का श्रवण है, यही तीनों ब्रह्म के धर्म हैं। यह सब धर्मीरूप ब्रह्म से अभिन्न ही हैं, क्योंकि श्रुति ने ही इन्हें स्वाभाविकी कहा है। "**स्वाभाविकी ज्ञानबलक्रिया च।**" यहाँ 'बल' से इच्छा का ग्रहण समझना चहिये। इस धर्म को ही शक्ति कहा जाता है। तथा च समष्टि ज्ञानेच्छाक्रियारूप ब्रह्मधर्मरूपा शक्ति ही चण्डी है, यही महाकाली, महालक्ष्मी, महासरस्वती है। कार्यवशात् इसी का अनेक रूप में प्राकट्य होता है। वस्तुतस्तु उसी चण्डरूप परमात्मा में ही पुंस्त्व, स्त्रीत्व भक्तभावना के अनुसार है। पुंस्त्वविवक्षा से वही महारुद्र आदि शब्दों से, स्त्रीत्व-विवक्षा से वही चण्डी, दुर्गा आदि शब्दों से व्यवहृत होता है।

नवार्ण मन्त्रार्थ

नवार्णमन्त्र का भी अभिप्राय यही है। 'डामरतन्त्र' में उसका अर्थ इस प्रकार बतलाया गया है—

Monotheism (*ekeśvaravāda*) is universally accepted;[231] that [One] is said to [be He who has] the "greatly terrifying nature of the [Adamantine] Thunderbolt" (*mahadbhaya vajrarūpa*) [*Kaṭha Upaniṣad* II.3.2.]: as servants work with alacrity out of fear of a raised stick, similarly the Sun, Indra, the Moon and the others do their respective tasks diligently, out of fear of *paramātman*. Caṇḍa's wife, Śakti, is Caṇḍikā, his essential nature (*svarūpabhūtā*). Just as *Parameśvara* has a peaceful (*śānta*) form distinct from His fierce (*ghora*) form — "*ghoranya śivānya*" [*Aitareya Āranyaka* III.33.] — similarly does Bhagavatī also have forms both fierce and tranquil. Some people say that it is the same *parabrahman* who appears both as quality (*dharma*) and qualified (*dharmin*), due to *Māyā*. The knowledge, volition and action (*jñāna, icchā aur kriyā*) that are heard of as being present at the beginning of creation in such passages as "Then he thought: may I become many, may I create offspring" [*Taittitrīya Upaniṣad* II.6.1], "He desired", "He performed austerities", and the like, these are the three characteristics (*dharma*) of *brahman*. These are inalienable from *brahman* as the *dharmin* (the bearer of *dharma*), because *śruti* has called them *svābhāvikī*: "Natural knowledge, strength and action" [*Śvetāsvatara Upaniṣad* VI.8]. Here we should believe '*bala*' to mean '*icchā*'. It is this *dharma* that is called *śakti*. And it is this *śakti*, whose nature is of the totality (*samaṣṭi*) of knowledge, volition and action (*jñānecchākriyārūpa*), who is the *dharma* of *brahman*, it is this very *śakti* who is Caṇḍī, as well as Mahākālī, Mahālakṣmī and Mahāsārasvatī. It is She who appears in various guises, according to the task at hand. Actually, a devotee sees masculinity or feminity in the same *paramātman*, who is *caṇḍa* in form, according to his tendency. As masculine, it is given such names as 'Mahārudra', and as feminine it is called by such names as Caṇḍī and Durgā.

The meaning of the *mantra* of nine letters

The [232] meaning of the nine-lettered *mantra* (*navārṇamantra*) has been explained thus in the *Ḍāmara Tantra*:

निर्धूतनिखिलध्वान्ते नित्यमुक्ते परात्परे ।
अखण्डब्रह्मविद्यायै चित्सदानन्दरूपिणि ।
अनुसन्दध्महे नित्यं वयं त्वां हृदयाम्बुजे ।

अर्थात् हे निर्धूतनिखिलध्वान्ते! हे नित्यमुक्ते! हे परात्परतरे! चित्सदानन्दरूपिणि मां! मैं अखण्ड ब्रह्मविद्या के लिये आपका अपने हृदय-कमल में अनुसन्धान करता हूँ ।

'ऐं' इस वाग्बीज से चित्स्वरूपा सरस्वती बोधित होती हैं, क्योंकि ज्ञान से ही अज्ञान की निवृत्ति होती है । महावाक्यजन्य परब्रह्माकारवृत्ति पर प्रतिबिम्बित होकर वही चिद्रूपा भगवती अज्ञान को मिटाती है । 'ह्रीं' इस मायाबीज से सद्रूपा महालक्ष्मी विवक्षित हैं । त्रिकालाबाध्य वस्तु ही नित्य है । कल्पित आकाशादि प्रपञ्च के अपवाद का अधिष्ठान होने से सद्रूपा भगवती ही नित्यमुक्ता हैं ।

'क्लीं' इस कामबीज से परमानन्दस्वरूपा महाकाली विवक्षित है, सर्वानुभव-संवेद्य आनन्द ही परम पुरुषार्थ है । "**आत्मनस्तु कामाय सर्वं प्रियं भवति**" इस श्रुति से सिद्ध है कि सब कुछ आत्मा के लिये ही प्रिय होता है, इसलिये आत्मस्वरूपा आनन्द ही शेषी है, तदितर सब शेष है । मानुषानन्द से लेकर गन्धर्व, देवगन्धर्व, अजानजदेव, श्रौतदेव, इन्द्र, बृहस्पति, प्रजापति, ब्रह्मान्त उत्तरोत्तरशतगुणित आनन्द

> O You, who are cleansed from every darkness, who are eternally liberated, beyond the Supreme, O you whose intimate nature is Consciousness, Being and Bliss, for the knowledge of the indivisible *brahman*, we meditate ceaselessly upon on You, in the lotus of the heart.

That is to say, "O source of the Universal Sound (*nirdhūta-nikhiladhvānte*)! O Eternally Free! O She who is beyond even the Beyond! O Mother, of the form of Being, Bliss and Awareness! I seek You in my lotus-like heart for the knowledge of the indestructible *brahman* (*akhaṇḍabrahmavidyā*)."

Sarasvatī,[233] who is of the nature of Consciousness, is known by the seed-syllable '*AIṀ*' because only knowledge brings an end to ignorance. [Being] reflected as the mental modification (*vṛtti*) whose shape is of the Supreme *brahman*, that has arisen from the great saying (*parabrahmākāravṛtti*),[234] it is She, Bhagavatī, whose nature is Consciousness (*cidrūpā*), who destroys ignorance. '*HRĪṀ*', the seed [syllable] of *māyā*, denotes Mahālakṣhmī, whose nature is Being (*sadrūpā*). Only that essential entity which is not limited to the three temporalities [of past, present and future] (*trikālābādhya*) is eternal. Because *sat*-natured Bhagavatī is the ground on which the imagined extension of ether and other telements are sublated, She is eternally free.

Mahākālī[235] is she who is indicated by '*KLĪṀ*', the seed [syllable] of desire (*kāmabījā*). Her nature is the Ultimate Bliss (*param-ānandasvarūpā*); this very bliss, perceptible within every cognition, is the supreme goal: *ātman*. "But it is for the desire of *ātman* that everything is dear": [*Bṛhadāraṇyaka Upaniṣad* II.4.5][236] this statement from *śruti* establishes that everything is pleasurable to the *ātman*; therefore, bliss, of the nature of the *ātman*, alone is *śeṣin* (the entire), compared to which all else is *śeṣa* (the rest). Comparatively, the bliss [experienced by] humans, *gandharvas*, *devagandharva*s, *ajānaja-deva*s (divine beings born and unborn), *śrautadevas* (the gods of the *Veda*), Indra (the king of the gods), Bṛhaspati (the divine *guru*),

जिसका बिन्दुमात्र है, वह परमातिशायी ब्रह्मरूप आनन्द कहा गया है। वही परात्पर आनन्द महाकालीरूप है। "**चामुण्डायै**" शब्द से मोक्षकारणीभूत निर्विकल्पक ब्रह्माकार वृत्ति विवक्षित है। वियदादिरूप चमू को जो नष्ट करके आत्मरूप कर लेती है, वही 'चामुण्डा' ब्रह्मविद्या है। अधिदैव के मूलाज्ञान और तूलाज्ञानरूप चण्ड-मुण्ड को वश में करनेवाली भगवती भी चामुण्डा कही गयी है—

यस्माच्चण्डञ्च मुण्डञ्च गृहीत्वा त्वमुपागता।
चामुण्डेति ततो लोके ख्याता देवि भविष्यसि॥

'विच्चे' में 'वित्', 'च', 'इ' ये तीन पद क्रमेण चित्, सत्, आनन्द के वाचक हैं। 'वित्' का ज्ञान अर्थ स्पष्ट ही है, 'च' नपुंसकलिङ्ग 'सत्' का बोधक है, 'इ' आनन्दब्रह्ममहिषी का बोधक है। इसका सारांश यही है कि हे चित्-सत्-परमानन्दरूपे! निर्धूतनिखिलध्वान्ते! नित्यमुक्ते! परात्परे महासरस्वति! महालक्ष्मि! महाकालि! हम आपके तत्वज्ञान को प्राप्त करने के लिये आपका हृदयकमल में ध्यान करते हैं।

प्रथम चरित्र

'दुर्गासप्तशती' में यह स्पष्ट बतलाया गया है कि भगवती की कृपा से ही सम्यक् तत्त्व ज्ञान प्राप्त होता है। ज्ञान की प्रशंसा सर्वत्र है, ज्ञान के होने से अज्ञान, मोहादि मिट जाते हैं। ज्ञान सम्पादन के लिये ही श्रवणादि किये जाते हैं। जप, तप, यज्ञादि सबका परम

Prajāpati (the father of all), and finally Brahmā have been said to be respectively one hundred times greater than that of the one previous — yet all this is but a drop compared to that Bliss which is the nature of the Absolute (*brahmarūpa*).[237] That [238] transcendental bliss is the characteristic of Mahākālī. The word 'to Cāmuṇḍā' denotes the mental tendency of the shape of the changeless of the *brahman* which is the cause of liberation. Having destroyed and assimilated the calamity [which arose in the shape] of an army, she is the knowledge of *brahman* (*brahmavidyā*) named Cāmuṇḍā. Cāmuṇḍā is also said to be that Bhagavatī who controls Caṇḍa, whose nature is of the universal primeval ignorance (*mūlājñāna*)[239] of the highest divinities (*adhidaiva*), and Muṇḍa, whose nature is of the relative individual ignorance (*tūlājñānarūpa*).

> Because having seized Caṇḍa and Muṇḍa you arrived, so, O Goddess,
> In the world you will be famous as Cāmuṇḍa.
> [*Durgāsaptaśatī* VII.27]

In '*vicce*' [one finds, in a compounded form] the three [phonemes] '*vit*' '*ca*' and '*i*'; they represent respectively Consciousness (*cit*), Being (*sat*) and Bliss (*ānanda*). The meaning of '*vit*' is quite clear, it is knowledge; the neuter-gendered '*ca*' represents '*sat*', essence; '*i*' denotes the queen-consort who is Absolute Bliss (*ānandabrahma-mahiṣī*). In brief this passage means: "O You, whose nature is of Consciousness, Being and the Ultimate Bliss! O You who are free from every obscurity (*nirdhūtanikhiladhvānte*)! O Eternally Liberated! O Supreme Sarasvatī! O Great Lakṣmī! O Great Kālī! We meditate upon You in our lotus heart in order to attain knowledge of reality.

The first deed [240]

In the *Durgāsaptaśatī* it has been clearly said that one attains complete *tattvajñāna* only by the grace of Bhagavatī. *Jñāna* is praised everywhere; through *jñāna*, one's *ajñāna*, delusions and the like (*mohādi*) are annulled. One listens to the master's teachings (*śravaṇa*)

उपयोग ज्ञान में ही है। परन्तु वह ज्ञान साधारण ज्ञान नहीं है, क्योंकि शब्दादि विषयों का ज्ञान तो प्राणिमात्र को होता है। उलूकादि दिन में अन्धे होते हैं, रात्रि में नहीं; कोकादि रात्रि में अन्धे होते हैं, दिन में नहीं। लता, जलजन्तु आदि दिन-रात समान रूप से अन्धे ही रहते हैं।

राक्षस, मार्जार, तुरगादि दिन-रात समान चाक्षुष ज्ञानवाले होते हैं और सबकी अपेक्षा मनुष्यों में अधिक ज्ञान होता है, परन्तु अज्ञान उनमें भी होता है। पशु, पक्षी आदि सभी बहुत ज्ञानवाले होते हैं। व्यवहारज्ञान मनुष्यों जैसा ही पशु-पक्षियों में भी दिखायी देता है। पक्षीगण स्वयं भूखे रहकर भी इतस्ततः से कणों को लाकर अपने बच्चों के मुँह में छोड़ते हैं। मनुष्य भी प्रत्युपकार की आशा से बच्चों के भरण-पोषण में तल्लीन रहते हैं, यह सब ज्ञान सामान्य ज्ञान है। इनसे संसार के मूलभूत अज्ञान की निवृत्ति नहीं होती। यही महामाया का प्रभाव है, जिससे सर्वाधिष्ठान, स्वप्रकाश परब्रह्म का बोध नहीं होता। वही उपनिषज्ज्ञाननिष्ठ वशिष्ठ, भरत, विश्वामित्रादिकों के भी चित्त को बलात् मोहित कर देती है। वही चराचर प्रपञ्च का निर्माण करती है, वही प्रसन्न होकर मुक्ति प्रदान करती है, विद्यारूपा होकर वही मुक्तिप्रदा है, अविद्यारूप से वही संसारबन्ध का हेतु है, वही भगवान् विष्णु की योगनिद्रा कहलाती है। जिस समय भगवान् शेष पर कल्पान्त में विराजमान थे, उस समय कूर्मपृष्ठ पर जल में विलीन होने के कारण पृथ्वी नवनीत के समान कोमल हो गयी। सृष्टिकाल में यह प्राणियों को किस तरह धारण कर सकेगी, यह सोचकर भगवती ने विष्णु को अपनी योगनिद्रा शक्ति से प्रसुप्त करके अपने वामहस्त की कनिष्ठिका के

and the like in order to acquire *jñāna*. Be it by reciting *japa*, doing penance, or performing ritual sacrifice or anything else (*yajñādi*), all of this finds its highest utility in attaining *jñāna*. But this *jñāna* is no ordinary knowledge, for all living beings have knowledge of perceptible objects like sounds, and the like. Owls [241] and similar [beasts] are blind in the daytime, but not at night; cuckoos and their ilk (*kokādi*) are blind at night but not in the daytime. Vines, aquatic animals and other such creatures are as blind in the daytime as they are as night.

Demons, cats, horses and other similar beings, have eyes that can see equally well by day and night. Humans possess more knowledge than all these, yet even they have *ajñāna*. Birds and animals all possess a great deal of knowledge. Birds and beasts also exhibit behavioural knowledge akin to humans. Birds [242] themselves go hungry, but feed their chicks grains collected from all over the place. Humans [243] also dillegently raise their children in the hope of getting the same care from them when they grow old. All [244] this is ordinary knowledge. This knowledge does not eradicate the *ajñāna* that is at the very core (*mūlabhūta*) of this worldly existence. This is the influence of *mahāmāyā*, due to which one remains unaware of the *parabrahman*, the light of one's own self, the substratum of everything. This *mahāmāya* forcibly (*balāt*) enthralls the minds of even [those great sages] who remain firmly established in the wisdom of the *Upaniṣads*, like Vasiṣṭha, Bharata and Viśvāmitra.[245] It is She who makes manifest the universe, moving and unmoving (*carācara prapañca*). When pleased (*prasanna*), it is She who grants liberation. Being of the nature of *vidyā*, She bestows this liberation, and [yet] out of her nature of *avidyā* is She who is the cause of worldly ties (*saṃsārabandha*). She is the one who is called *yoganidrā* of Lord Viṣṇu [between cosmic aeons]. At the end of one *kalpa* [cosmic aeon], when the Lord was resplendent (*virājamāna*) upon [the serpent] Śeṣa, the earth had grown as soft as fresh butter (*navanīta*) from being immersed in water on the back of the [Great] turtle's shell. "At the time of the [next] creation, how shall this earth support [the weight]

नखाग्र भाग से कर्णमल निकालकर उसी से मधु नामक दैत्य को और दक्षिण कर्णस्थ मल से कैटभ को बनाया। उत्पन्न होकर वे दोनों दैत्य पहले कीट के समान ही प्रतीत हुए, पश्चात् महाबलवान् हो गये। वरदान देकर देवी के अन्तर्हित होने पर विष्णु की नाभि से उत्पन्न कमल में उन दोनों ने ब्रह्मा को देखा। ब्रह्मा को देखकर उन्होंने कहा—

"हम तुम्हें मारेंगे। अगर तुम जीना चाहते हो, तो विष्णु को जगाओ।"

यह सुनकर ब्रह्मा ने जगत्प्रसूयोगनिद्रा की अनेक स्तुतियों से प्रार्थना की। भगवती ने प्रसन्न होकर ब्रह्मा से वरदान माँगने को कहा। ब्रह्मा ने भगवान् का जागना और दोनों असुरों को मोह होना माँगा। माता ने विष्णु को जगा दिया। विष्णु से उन दैत्यों का पाँच हजार वर्ष तक घोर युद्ध हुआ। महाप्रमत्त उन दैत्यों ने महामाया से मोहित होकर विष्णु से वर माँगने को कहा।

विष्णु ने कहा—

"तुम दोनों हमारे वध्य हो, हम यही वर माँगते हैं।"

उन्होंने कहा—

"अच्छा, जहाँ सलिल से व्याप्त पृथ्वी न हो, वहाँ हमें मारो।"

विष्णु ने अपने जघन प्रदेश पर उनका शिर रखकर चक्र से उन्हें मार दिया, पश्चात् उन्हीं के मेद का विलेपन कर पृथ्वी को दृढ़ किया गया, इसीलिये पृथ्वी को 'मेदिनी' भी कहा जाता है। इस तरह भगवती ही अनेक रूप में प्रकट होकर जगत् को धारण करती है। यही सृष्टि, स्थिति, संहार करती है, यही योगनिद्रा होकर विष्णु को विश्राम देती है, यही स्वाहारूप से देवताओं को. स्वधारूप से पितरों को, वषट्काररूप से श्रौतदेवताओं को तृप्त करती है। यही उदात्तादि स्वरों और सुधारूप से विराजमान होती है। ह्रस्व, दीर्घ, प्लुतरूप में

of the living?" Thinking these thoughts, Bhagavatī put Viṣṇu to sleep, using Her *yoganidrā śakti*. Using the nail of the little finger of Her left hand, from Her ear She extracted some filth, from which She created the demon named Madhu; from the filth of Her right ear She created the demon Kaiṭabha. Upon being created, at first the two demons appeared as [small as] insects, but later grew extremely strong. The Goddess granted them a boon and then disappeared. The two saw Brahmā seated on the lotus which arose from the navel of Viṣṇu. Upon seeing Brahmā, they said, "We'll kill you — if you want to live, then wake up Viṣṇu."

Hearing this, Brahmā sang numerous hymns of praise to *yoganidrā*, the Mother of the World (*jagatprasūyoganidrā*). Bhagavatī was pleased, and she offered a boon to Brahmā. Brahmā asked that Viṣṇu should wake, and that the two demons fall into delusion (*moha*). The Mother woke Viṣṇu. For five thousand years, Viṣṇu engaged those demons in a fierce battle. Deluded by *mahāmāyā*, those completely intoxicated demons offered a boon to Viṣṇu.

Viṣṇu asked: "That the two of you be killed by me: this is all the boon I request."

They replied: "Wherever the earth is not covered with water, you can kill us there. Be it so?"

Viṣṇu put their heads on his thigh and killed them with his discus (*cakra*). Thereafter, he made the earth firm (*dṛḍha*) by churning the fat (*meda*) of the demons into it; for this, the earth is also known as '*medinī*'. In [246] this way, [it is shown how] Bhagavatī appears in a multitude of forms to support this world. She is the one who creates, nurtures and destroys. She is the one who gives rest to Viṣṇu by becoming His yogic sleep (*yoganidrā*). She is the one who satiates the gods in Her form of *svāhā*, the anscestors with her nature of *svadhā*,[247] and the gods of the *Veda* (*śrautadevatā*) in Her form of *vaṣaṭkāra*. She[248] is the one present as the sharp-toned (*udātta*) sounds; She is resplendent as the divine nectar (*sudhārūpa*). Within Her nature of the syllables, She is resplendent in the short vowels (*hrasva*), in the longs vowels (*dīrgha*), in the prolungated vowels (*plutarūpa*) —

किंवा अ, उ, म् रूप में यही अक्षररूपा भगवती विराजमान होती है। अ, उ, म् इन तीनों वर्णों एवं तद्वाच्य विश्व, तैजस, प्राज्ञ आदि के रूपों में भी वही भगवती स्थित है। वाच्य-वाचक के अधिष्ठानरूप अर्धमात्रास्वरूप से भी भगवती ही विराजमान है।

अकारश्च तथोकारो मकारश्चाक्षरत्रयम्।
एता एव त्रयो मात्रा सत्वराजसतामसाः॥
निर्गुणा योगिगम्याऽन्या चार्धमात्रात्र संस्थिता।

(दत्तात्रेयसंहिता)

प्रथम मात्रा व्यक्त है, द्वितीय मात्रा अव्यक्त है, तृतीय मात्रा चिच्छक्ति है, अर्द्धमात्रा परमपद है, वही कूटस्थ सर्वाधिष्ठान है, सर्वरूप से भगवती ही विराजमान है। सन्ध्या, सावित्री तथा जगज्जननी मूलप्रकृति रूप से भी माता की ही स्थिति है। सृष्टिकाल में वही सृष्टिरूप में, पालनकाल में स्थितिरूप से तथा अन्त में संहृतिरूप से भगवती ही व्यक्त होती है। वही महाविद्या अर्थात् तत्वमस्यादि महावाक्यों से व्यक्त ब्रह्मविद्यारूपा है वही देहात्मबुद्धिरूपा माया भी है, सर्वार्थावधारणरूपा मेधा, महास्मृतिरूपा भी वही है, उसी से अतीत अनेक कल्पों का स्मरण तथा तदनुकूल सृष्टि-निर्माण सम्भव होता है,

as well as within the form of the letters '*A*', '*U*', '*M*'. It is Bhagavatī who is established as the '*A*', '*U*', and '*M*' as well as their directly-expressed entities like the condition of consciousness of the *jīva* in waking state (*viśva*), in dream state (*taijasa*) and during deep sleep (*prājña*). It is Bhagavatī who is replendent as the nature of [both] that which is described and as the one who describes (*vācya-vācaka*), appearing in her form as the half-letter (*ardhamātrā*) [that is, the nasalized semi-silent '*Ṃ*' which follows the three letters of '*AUṀ*'].

> The '*A*', the '*U*' and '*M*', these are the three letters.
> These three quantities represent *sattva*, *rajas* and *tamas*,
> But the half-quantity who dwells here is another, unqualified,
> graspable only by yogins. (*Dattātreya Saṃhitā*)

The first letter (*mātrā*) represents the manifest (*vyakta*), the second letter, the unmanifest (*avyakta*), and the third, the power of awareness (*cit-śakti*). The half-letter represents the ultimate abode (*paramapada*) [that is, liberation]. This is the inamovable substratum of everything (*sarvādhiṣṭhāna*) — this is[249] [actually] Bhagavatī, who is present in every form. It is the Mother of the World who is the twilight (*saṃdhyā*), who is Sāvitrī, [the *śakti* of the sun] and as the primordial, root Nature (*mūlaprakṛti*). At the time of creation (*sṛṣṭi-kāla*), Her nature is of creation (*sṛṣṭirūpa*); at the time of nurturing [the world], it is She whose nature is preservation (*sthiti*); in the end, it is this Bhagavatī who manifests as annihilation (*saṃhṛtirūpa*). She is the *mahāvidyā* — that is, [it is She] who is expressed by such great sayings as 'You are That' and the like, and as such Her nature is thereby of the ultimate knowledge (*brahmavidyārūpā*).[250] She is also *māyā* when present as the cognition that the self is the body. She is also the intellect able to catch every meaning (*sarvārthāvadhāraṇa-rūpā*); Her nature is of the supreme memory (*mahāsmṛtirūpā*) — for example, from Her comes the memory of the various cosmic aeons (*kalpa*s), and thereby makes possible the [next] manifestation (*sṛṣṭi-nirmāṇa*) according to those memories. She is the great delusion (*mahāmoha*), the goddess whose nature is the pleasures and rewards

ग्राम्यसुखभोगैषणारूप महामोह भी वही है, महादेवी इन्द्रादि देवशक्ति, हिरण्याक्ष प्रभृति असुरों की शक्तिरूपा भी वही हैं।

सत्वादि गुणत्रय विभाविनी मूल प्रकृति, वही कालरात्रि, मरणरात्रि या शिवरात्रिरूपा है और वही महारात्रि अर्थात् प्रलयरात्रि भी है, मोहरात्रि भी भगवती है। कृष्णजन्माष्टमी को अवतीर्ण होकर भगवती ही कंसादि को मोहित करके कृष्ण को नन्दगृह पहुँचाने में सहायक हुई है। वही श्री, वही ईश्वरी, वही लज्जा, वही बोधलक्षणा बुद्धि है। पुष्टि, तुष्टि, शान्ति, क्षान्ति भी वही है। खड्ग, शूल, गदा, चक्र, शंख, चाप, बाण, भुशुण्डी, परिघ आदि आयुधों को धारण करनेवाली महाघोरा है, वही परमप्रशान्तरूपा भी है, वही सौम्यतरा एवं अशेष सौम्यों से भी अति सुन्दरी है अथवा भक्तों के लिये सौम्या और दैत्यों के लिये अत्यन्त असौम्या अर्थात् क्रूरतरा है। सब आह्लादहेतुओं से अत्यन्त सुन्दरी है, ब्रह्मादि सम्पूर्ण देवताओं से वही परमोत्कृष्टा है। परा, पश्यन्ती, मध्यमा, वैखरी के मध्य में परावाक्स्वरूपा वही है। वस्तुतस्तु संसार में सत्-असत्, कार्य-कारण, चेतन-अचेतन, जहाँ भी, जो भी कोई वस्तु है, उन सबकी जो शक्ति है, वह भगवती ही है—

यच्च किञ्चित्क्वचिद्वस्तु सदसद्वाखिलात्मिके।
तस्य सर्वस्य या शक्तिः सा त्वं किं स्तूयसे तदा॥

जो परमेश्वर महाशक्ति द्वारा ही जगत् का उत्पादन, पालन, संहरण करता है, जब स्वयं वही भगवती की योगनिद्रा के वश होते हैं, तब फिर कौन भगवती के गुणों का वर्णन कर सकता है? विष्णु आदि भी शक्ति की महिमा से ही देहवान् होते हैं। अनन्तानन्तशक्तियों

of mundane life (*grāmyasukhabhogaiṣaṇārūpā*). She is the Great Goddess who is the divine power of such gods as Indra; hers is the power of such demons as Hiraṇyākṣa, as well.

She is the root nature who makes manifest the *sattva* and the other *guṇas*, [She is] the [infinite and terrifying] night of time (*kāla-rātri*); She the night of death (*maraṇarātri*), or the night of Śiva (*śivarātri*), and [indeed], She the great night (*mahārātri*), the night of universal dissolution (*pralayarātri*) as well as the night of delusion, *moharātri* [that is, the night on which Kṛṣṇa was born, *janmāṣṭamī*]. She was helpful when Kṛṣṇa had come to the house of Nanda, She incarnated on the day of Kṛṣṇa's birth, bringing Kaṃsa and his minions under Her spell. She is Śrī (prosperity), Īśvarī (Goddess), Lajjā ('the Shy'), Buddhi (intellect) whose nature is *bodha* (knowledge). She[251] is *puṣṭi* (health and well-being) and *tuṣṭi* (satisfaction), *śānti* (calm) and *kṣānti* (patience). She is the fierce one (*mahāghorā*) who bears weapons such as a sword, a trident, a club, a discus (*cakra*), a conch shell, a bridle, an arrow, *bhuśuṇḍi*, an iron bar (*parigha*) and the like; She also has supremely tranquil form. She is more mild than mildness itself and even more beautiful than any other gentle creature; She is *saumyā* (the mild-one) for Her devotees, and for demons, *asaumyā* — extremely cruel. She is more beautiful than any cause of merriment; She is supreme among all the gods, including Brahmā. Having the nature of the Absolute Sound (*parāvāksvarūpā*), She is at the core of *parā*, *paśyanti*, *madhyamā* and *vaikharī*.[252] Whatever there is (*vastutastu*) in this world — be it true or false (*sat-asat*), an effect or its cause, conscious or unconscious — its *śakti* is Bhagavatī.

> O Goddess, who neither is nor is not, You are the power of everything, whatever and wherever it may be — so, how can you be 'bestowed'? [*Durgasaptaśatī* I.42b, I.43a]

The Supreme Lord — who [himself] creates, nurtures and destroys the world through His great power (*mahāśakti*) — even He comes under the spell of Bhagavatī in Her form as *yoganidrā*; who, then, can describe the character (*guṇa*) of Bhagavatī? Even gods like

से सम्पन्न आनन्दप्रधाना भगवती महाकाली रूप से 'सप्तशती' के प्रथम चरित्र में वर्णित है ।

मध्यम चरित्र

किसी समय वही महालक्ष्मी के रूप में प्रकट होती है । कभी पूरे सौ वर्ष तक देवताओं और असुरों का भयानक संग्राम चल रहा था । असुरों का राजा महिषासुर और देवताओं का इन्द्र था । महिषासुर सब देवताओं को जीतकर स्वयं इन्द्र हो गया । देवता लोग पराजित होकर ब्रह्मा को लेकर शिव और विष्णु के पास गये और विस्तार से महिषासुर की विजय और देवताओं की पराजय बतलायी । देवताओं की बात सुनकर मधुसूदन और शङ्कर दोनों ने कोप किया और उनके मुख से एक महातेज प्रकट हुआ । ब्रह्मा के भी मुख से वैसा ही तेज निकला । इन्द्र, वरुणादि देवताओं के भी देह से दिव्य तेज प्रकट हुआ ।

इस तरह सब देवताओं के देह से निकलकर वही महातेज पर्वत के समान दिखलायी पड़ने लगा और उसकी ज्वाला से दिशाएँ-विदिशाएँ सब व्याप्त हो गयीं । वही अतुल तेज एकत्रित होकर एक स्त्री के रूप में परिणत हो गया । उस तेज की दिव्यदीप्ति तीनों लोक में फैल गयी । समस्त देवताओं के तेज से उस तेज के अन्यान्य अङ्ग उत्पन्न हुए । समस्त देवताओं की तेजोराशि से अद्भुत भगवती को देखकर सब प्रसन्न हुए । सब देवों ने विभिन्न आयुध तथा आभूषण उसे प्रदान किया । सबने माता का सम्मान किया । मां प्रसन्न होकर सिंहनाद करने लगीं । उसके घोर नाद से सम्पूर्ण नभ पूर्ण हो गया और उसकी प्रतिध्वनि से सब लोक क्षुब्ध हो गये और समुद्र काँप उठे । देवता प्रसन्नता से जय-जय रव करने लगे, मुनि लोग स्तुति करने लगे ।

ऐसी स्थिति देखकर असुर लोग अस्त्र-शस्त्र लेकर युद्ध के लिये

Viṣṇu are embodied only through the greatness of Śakti. Imbued with endless powers and predominantly blissful, Bhagavatī has been described in Her form of Mahākālī in the first chapter of the [*Durgā*] *Saptaśatī*.

The second deed[253]

Once, She appeared as Mahālakṣmī. There was a period when a terrible century-long battle took place between the gods and the demons. Mahiṣāsura was the king of the demons and Indra was the king of the gods. Mahiṣāsura vanquished every god, and himself became Indra. The defeated gods took Brahmā with them to see Śiva and Viṣṇu; in great detail, they they told them the story of Mahiṣāsura's victory and the gods' defeat. On hearing the account of the gods, both Śiva and Viṣṇu grew furious, and from their mouths a great *tejas* (vibrant, radiant energy) appeared; a similar *tejas* also emerged from the mouth of Brahmā. Divine *tejas* emanated from the bodies of such gods as Indra and Varuṇa as well.

Thus, the [accumulating] *tejas* emanating from the bodies of all the gods began to seem like a mountain of radiance, and its flames burst forth in all the ten directions. That incomparable *tejas* became concentrated; it assumed the form of a woman. The resplendent light of that energy spread through the three worlds. From the divine energy arose various bodily limbs, composed of light. All the gods were elated upon seeing a marvelous goddess appear from the mountain of light. The gods all presented Her with various weapons and ornaments. They all honoured the Mother. The Mother, pleased, became to roar like a lion. All the heavens were filled by her roar, and every realm of existence trembled from to its echo, and the oceans shook. The gods worshipped Her out of joy, and the sages began to sing hymns of praise.

Seeing this, the demons took up their weapons and readied themselves for battle. Mahiṣāsura, surrounded by [his] horde of demons, saw standing [before him] a Goddess, filling the three worlds with her great radience, humbling the earth under Her feet, etching

तत्पर हो गये। अनेक असुरों से समावृत महिषासुर ने देखा कि तीनों लोकों को अपने महातेज से व्याप्त करके पादाक्रमण से पृथ्वी को विनत करती हुई, अपने किरीट से नभोमण्डल को खचित करती हुई, धनुष के टङ्कार से पाताल तक को क्षुब्ध करनेवाली सहस्त्रों भुजाओं से दिशाओं को व्याप्त करके देवी स्थित है। बस फिर क्या था? असुरों ने युद्ध प्रारम्भ कर दिया। भयानक संग्राम हुऔ। गिरे हुए हस्ति, अश्व, रथ एवं असुरों से वह भूमि अगम्य हो गयी। शोणित की भयानक नदी बहने लगी। अन्त में बड़े-बड़े अस्त्र-शस्त्र, शक्ति आदि के प्रयोग हुए। बहुतों को अस्त्र से, बहुतों को हुङ्कारमात्र से भगवती नष्ट कर देती थी। देवी के सिंह ने विचित्र युद्ध करके चामर प्रभृति दैत्यों को मारा। बहुत दैत्यों के मारे जाने पर स्वयं महिषासुर ने महिषरूप से अद्‌भुत पराक्रम दिखलाया। चण्डिका ने उसे पाश से बाँधा, तो वह सिंह हो गया। जब तक सिंह का सिर काटने का चण्डिका प्रयत्न करती है, तब तक वह खड्‌गपाणि पुरुष हो गया। जब तक पुरुष पर अम्बा प्रहार करती, तब तक वह गज हो गया। गज होकर सिंह को शुण्डा से आकृष्ट करने लगा। देवी ने तलवार से शुण्डा काट दी। पश्चात् वह फिर महिष बनकर त्रैलोक्य को त्रस्त करने लगा। अन्त में देवी ने उछलकर उसके ऊपर आरूढ़ होकर उसे चरण से आक्रान्त कर शूल से ताड़न किया। इतने में वह महिष के मुख से अर्धनिष्क्रान्त असुर के रूप में लड़ने लगा। अन्त में अम्बा ने विशाल खड्‌ग से उसका सिर काट दिया। असुरसैन्य में हाहाकार मच गया। देवतागण बड़े प्रसन्न हुए। देवताओं ने वहीं श्रद्धा से नम्र होकर इस तरह स्तुति की— "हे मां! आप जगदात्म शक्ति हैं, आपसे सम्पूर्ण विश्व व्याप्त है, आप सब देवताओं की शक्ति समूह मूर्ति हैं। आपके प्रभाव को विष्णु, ब्रह्मा तथा हर भी नहीं कह सकते, फिर और की तो बात ही क्या? आप ही सुकृतियों के घरों में लक्ष्मी तथा पापियों के घर में दरिद्रा रूप से रहती

the sky with Her crown and churning even the hell-worlds with the snapping of Her bowstring, Her thousands of arms extending everywhere. And then what happened? The demons went to war. A terrible fight took place, the earth became impassible due to the fallen elephants, horses, chariots and demons. A terrible river of blood began to flow. In the end, gigantic weapons and missiles (*astra-śastra*) were used by Śakti and Her enemies. Bhagavatī destroyed many demons with her missiles, and many others with her terrifying war stream. The Goddess's lion waged its own war, and killed the demon Cāmara. When many demons were killed, Mahiṣāsura showed himself to be valourous, (fighting) in the form of a buffalo. When Caṇḍikā (the Furious One) lassoed him, he turned into a lion. Before Caṇḍikā could behead this lion, he changed into a sword-wielding man. Before Ambā could strike a blow at this man, he turned into an elephant; he then began to draw the [Goddess's] lion towards himself with his trunk — which the Goddess cut off with her sword. Then, again he assumed the form of a buffalo, and in this guise afflicted the three worlds. [Seeing this,] the Goddess sprang upon him and, standing upon him, pressing him down with Her foot, She wounded him with Her trident. Then, in the form of a demon half-emerged out of the mouth of the buffalo, he began to fight Her. In the end, Ambā beheaded him with her immense sword. A shout of terror swept through the demon army, and the gods were elated. The gods bowed to Her right there with reverence and sang her praise like so: "O Mother! You are the power and the essence of this world (*jagadātma śakti*). You fill the whole world. You are the very embodiment of the collective *śakti* of all the gods. Even Viṣṇu, Brahmā and Hara (Śiva) cannot describe Your glory, so then what to say about anyone else? For those who do good deeds, You dwell in their homes as Lakṣmī, and as Daridrā (the goddess of poverty) in the homes of sinners. You are the wisdom in the hearts of the wise, and the shyness of respectable women. You are the unknowable, unmanifested (*avyākṛtākhyā*) nature (*prakṛti*); You are She who satisfies [everyone, such as] the gods [when] You appear as *svāhā*, and the ancestors as

हैं। कृतबुद्धियों के हृदय में सुबुद्धि एवं कुलांगनाओं की लज्जा भी आप ही हैं, आप ही अव्याकृताख्या प्रकृति हैं, आप ही स्वाहा, स्वधारूप से देव, पितर आदि को तृप्त करती हैं। मोक्षार्थी यति लोग भी ब्रह्मविद्यारूप से आपका ही सेवन करते हैं। विश्व को अभ्युदय-निःश्रेयस प्राप्त कराने के लिये आप ही वेदत्रयी के रूप में प्रकट होती हैं। विष्णु के हृदय में महालक्ष्मी रूप से, शशिमौलि के यहाँ गौरीरूप से आप ही प्रतिष्ठित हैं।'' बहुत स्तुति करके देवताओं ने देवी से अनेक वर की प्रार्थना की। माता 'तथास्तु' कहकर अन्तर्हित हो गयी।

उत्तरचरित्र

इस तरह जब शुम्भ और निशुम्भ ने पराक्रम से इन्द्र से त्रैलोक्य छीन लिया; यज्ञ भाग भी स्वयं लेना प्रारम्भ कर दिया; सूर्य, चन्द्र तथा कुबेर, वरुण का पद स्वयं ले लिया, तब सब देवता पराजित और भ्रष्टराज्य होकर अपराजिता भगवती का स्मरण करने लगे। माता ने वरदान दिया है कि आपत्ति में जब भी आप लोग हमारा स्मरण करेंगे, मैं तत्क्षण आप सबकी आपत्तियों को दूर करूँगी, यह सोचकर सब देव हिमाचल पर जाकर विष्णुमाया की स्तुति करने लगे। वहाँ उन्होंने देवी, महादेवी, शिवा, प्रकृति, भद्रा, रौद्रा, नित्या, गौरी, धात्री, ज्योत्स्ना, इन्दुरूपिणी, सुखा, कल्याणी, वृद्धि, सिद्धि, नैर्ऋति, शर्वाणी, दुर्गा, दुर्गपारा, सारा, सर्वकारिणी, ख्याति, कृष्णा, धूम्रा, अतिसौम्या, अतिरौद्रा, जगत्प्रतिष्ठा, कृति, विष्णुमाया, चेतना, बुद्धि, निद्रा, क्षुधा, छाया, शक्ति, तृष्णा, क्षान्ति, जाति, लज्जा, शान्ति, श्रद्धा, कान्ति, लक्ष्मी, वृत्ति, स्मृति, दया, तुष्टि माता, भ्रान्ति, व्याप्ति, चितिरूप से भगवती को प्रणाम किया। निर्गुणा, सगुणा तथा सगुणा में भी

svadhā. You alone are She to whom bow those who seek liberation, as the Absolute knowledge (*brahmavidyā*). You are She who manifests as the three *Vedas*, so as to uplift and nurture the world. You are established as Mahālakṣmī in the heart of Viṣṇu and as Gaurī with Śaśimauli (Śiva)." Having sung Her praise, the gods requested many boons from the Goddess. The Mother said "So be it", and disappeared.[254]

The last deed [255]

A similar [story[256] is told], wherein Śumbha and Niśumbha took away the three worlds from Indra and appropriated the gods' share [of offerings] from the fire sacrifices; they took for themselves the offices of the Sun and Moon, of Kubera (the treasurer of the Gods) and of Varuṇa (the God of oceans); then, defeated and evicted from their kingdom, the gods all remembered Bhagavatī. They thought to themselves: "The Mother has given us the boon that, whenever we remember Her in a time of crisis, She shall instantly remove all our misfortunes." With this in mind, the gods all went to Himācala (the Himālaya) and began to sing praise to Viṣṇumāyā. There [257] they bowed to Bhagavatī in all Her forms: as Devī (the Goddess), Mahādevi (Great Goddess), Śivā (the *śakti* of Śiva), Prakṛti (Nature), Bhadrā (the Good), Raudrā (the *śakti* of Rudra), Nityā (the Eternal), Gauri (the Fair-complexioned) Dhatrī (the Sustainer), Jyotsnā (the Luminous), Indurūpiṇī (She of the Nature of the Moon), Suklā (the White), Kalyāṇī (Giver of Welfare), Vṛddhi (Increaser), Siddhi (Accomplished), Nairṛti (the presiding deity of the South-West), Śarvāṇī (the consort of the Archer Śiva), Durgā (the Unassailable), Durgapārā, Sārā (Essence), Sarvakariṇī (the Doer of Everything), Vyāpti (the All-pervading), Khyāti (Fame), Kṛṣṇā (the Black; the *śakti* of Kṛṣṇa), Dhūmrā (the Smoke coloured), Atisaumyā (Extremely Peaceful), Atiraudrā (Extremely Dreadful), Jagatpratiṣṭhā (the Substratum of the World), Kṛti (Effort), Viṣṇumāyā (the illusive power of Viṣṇu), Cetanā (Consciousness), Buddhi (Intelligence), Nidrā (Sleep), Kṣudhā (the Hungry), Chāyā (the Shadow), Śakti

सात्विकी, राजसी, तामसी भेद से सब शक्तियाँ भगवती में ही अन्तर्भूत हो जाती हैं। देवता स्तुति कर ही रहे थे कि हिमाद्रि-कन्या पार्वती जाह्नवी में स्नान करने आयीं । देवताओं से उन्होंने प्रश्न किया कि "आप किस देवता की स्तुति कर रहे हैं ?" देवताओं का उत्तर देना ही था कि तब तक पार्वती के ही शरीर से प्रकट होकर शिवा भगवती ने पार्वती से कहा कि "शुम्भ से निराकृत होकर ये सब हमारी ही स्तुति कर रहे हैं ।" पार्वती के शरीर-कोश से निकली हुई अम्बिका लोक में 'कौशिकी' नाम से प्रसिद्ध हुईं । कौशिकी के निकलने पर पार्वती कृष्णवर्ण की हो गयीं । तभी से वह 'कालिका' कहलाने लगीं । परमरूपवती कौशिकी अम्बिका को कभी शुम्भ-निशुम्भ के सेवक चण्ड-मुण्ड ने देखा और जाकर अपने स्वामी से उसके रूप की प्रशंसा की और उसे स्वाधीन बनाने की सलाह दी । शुम्भ-निशुम्भ ने दूत भेजकर कहलाया कि "हमारी आज्ञा सर्वत्र अप्रतिहत है, संसार के सब रत्न, ऐरावत, उच्चैःश्रवा आदि हमारे पास हैं, तुम भी स्त्रीरत्न हो, हम रत्नभुक् हैं, अतः तुम भी हमारे पास आओ, हमारे पास आने से तुम्हें परमैश्वर्य्य प्राप्त होगा ।"

भगवती ने गम्भीर स्मित के साथ कहा—

"ठीक है, परन्तु मेरी प्रतिज्ञा है कि जो मुझे संग्राम में जीत लेगा, मेरा दर्प दूर करेगा, मेरे समान बलवान् होगा, वही मेरा भर्त्ता होगा । अतः शुम्भ या निशुम्भ कोई भी आकर मुझे जीतकर पाणिग्रहण कर ले"—

यो मां जयति संग्रामे यो मे दर्पं व्यपोहति ।
यो मे प्रतिबलो लोके स मे भर्त्ता भविष्यति ॥
तदागच्छतु शुम्भोऽत्र निशुम्भो वा महासुरः ।
मां जित्वा किं चिरेणात्र पाणिं गृह्णातु मे लघु ॥

(the Power) Tṛṣṇā (Thirst), Kṣānti (Patience), Jāti (Birth), Lajjā (Shame), Śānti (Peace) Śraddhā (Reverence), Kānti (Lustry), Lakṣmī (Fortune), Vṛtti (Function), Smṛti (Memory), Dayā (Compassion), Tuṣṭī (Contentment), Mātā (Mother), Bhrānti (Error), Vyāpti (All-pervading) and Citirūpa (of the Nature of Knowledge). All the powers merged into Bhagavatī as Sātvikī, in Her *nirguṇa* form (without attributes) as Rājasī in Her *saguṇa* form (with attributes), and Tāmasī [also] in Her *saguṇa* form. The [258] gods were still busy praying when Pārvatī, the daughter of Himādri (the Himālayas), came to bathe in Jāhnavī (Gaṅgā). She asked the gods: "Of which divinity do you sing praise?" The gods were just about to answer when the Bhagavatī Śivā appeared out of the body of Pārvatī and told Her, "Having been humiliated by Śumbha, these (gods) are all singing our praise." Ambikā, [then] emerging from the body of Pārvatī, became famous throughout the world as 'Kauśikī.' When Kauśikī came out, the complexion of Pārvatī grew darker; She then began to be called 'Kālikā'. [Some time thereafter,][259] [two] servants of Śumbha and Niśumbha called Caṇḍa and Muṇḍa saw the supremely beautiful Kauśikī Ambikā; they went to their masters, praised Her beauty and advised them to bring Her under their domination. Śumbha and Niśumbha sent a messenger to Her, with the message that "Everywhere, we reign supreme. Every precious jewel of the world is ours: Airāvata (the elephant of Indra), Uccaiḥśravā (the divine horse) and their ilk. You, too, are a jewel among women — and we are connoisseurs of jewels! — so, You must also come to us. By our side, You shall have the greatest authority (*paramaiśvaryya*)."

With an unfathomable smile, Bhagavatī said: "I am ready [to come]. But I have taken a vow that only he will be my husband who will defeat Me in battle, who will be as strong as I am and who will humble my pride. So, let either Śumbha or Niśumbha come, and he can marry Me — after defeating Me."

"Who conquers Me in battle and vanishes my pride,
Who will be strong as Me, in this world he will be my husband."

दूत ने बहुत कुछ समझाया, परन्तु देवी ने कहा— "क्या करूँ, मेरी ऐसी प्रतिज्ञा ही है।" दूत ने जाकर सब बात सुना दी। इसपर धूम्रलोचन भेजा गया, घोर युद्ध के बाद वह मारा गया। उसके पश्चात् शुम्भ ने चण्ड-मुण्ड को भेजा। महासंग्राम हुआ, अम्बिका ने जब कोप किया, तब उसके ललाट से करालवदना कालिका प्रकट हुई। उसने असुरों के बल (सैन्य) को भक्षण करना आरम्भ कर दिया। उसने बड़े-बडे गज, तुरङ्ग, रथ, योद्धाओं को मुँह में डालकर चबाना आरम्भ कर दिया। सर्वनाश होते देखकर चण्ड आया और अनेक चक्रों से काली को आच्छादित कर दिया। देवी के मुँह में वे चक्र लीन हो गये। महातलवार से देवी ने चण्ड का सिर काट डाला। इसके बाद मुण्ड लड़ने आया। उसकी भी वही गति हुई। चण्ड-मुण्ड दोनों का सिर लेकर काली ने आकर कौशिकी को दिया। कौशिकी ने चण्ड-मुण्ड का सिर लाने के कारण काली का 'चामुण्डा' नामकरण किया। चण्ड-मुण्ड का वध सुनकर शुम्भ ने अपनी सब सेना को आज्ञा दी। महामहाकुल से भयानक-भयानक दैत्य आये, भयंकर युद्ध होने लगा। देवी ने धनुष के टङ्कार से धरणी और गगन को पूरित कर दिया। सिंहनाद भी सर्वत्र फैल गया, महाकाली ने भी मुख फैलाकर भीषण नाद किया। उस नाद को सुनकर दैत्यसेना ने चारों ओर से देवी को घेर लिया। इसी समय दैत्यों के नाश और देवताओं के अभ्युदय के लिये ब्रह्मा, शिव, विष्णु, इन्द्र आदि देवताओं के शरीरों से उनकी शक्तियाँ उसी-उसी रूप में प्रकट होकर देवी की सहायता के लिये आयीं। उन शक्तियों से परिवृत होकर भगवान् रुद्र आये और चण्डिका से कहा कि "हमारी प्रसन्नता के लिये शीघ्र ही इन दैत्यों को मारो।" यह सुनते ही देवी के शरीर से एक अतिभीषण शक्ति प्रकट हुई और उसने रुद्र से कहा—

"आप हमारे दूत बनकर जाओ और शुम्भ-निशुम्भ से कहो कि

> So would come here the great *asura* Śumbha or Niśumbha, having conquered Me;
> There is no matter of delay, immediately he would take my hand. [*Durgāsaptaśatī* V.120-121]

The messenger tried his best to reason with Her, but the Goddess said: "What to do — my vow is such." The messenger returned and reported everything; [the two demons] then sent Dhūmralocana, who was killed after a fierce battle. Thereafter, Śumbha sent Caṇḍa and Muṇḍa.[260] A great battle ensued; Ambikā grew enraged, and from Her forehead appeared the fang-mawed (*karālavadanā*) Kālikā, who began to devour the demonic forces. She put into Her mouth many huge elephants, horses, chariots and warriors, and began to chew them. Witnessing this complete destruction, Caṇḍa came and blanketed Kālī with a multitude of (razor-sharp) discus weapons (*cakra*); [even these] discuses fell into Kālī's mouth. With Her great sword Kālī cut off the heads of [both] Caṇḍa and Muṇḍa and brought them over to Kauśikī. Kauśikī then named Kālī 'Cāmuṇḍā', for bringing the heads of Caṇḍa and Muṇḍa. Upon hearing of the slaughter of Caṇḍa and Muṇḍa, Śumbha ordered his entire army to march. Terrifying demons of great lineages came, and a terrible battle began. The Goddess filled heavens and earth with the 'twang' of Her bowstring. The roar of Her lion also spread everywhere, and Kālī too opened Her mouth and let loose a horrifying cry. Hearing that roar, the demon army encircled the Goddess on all sides. Just then, emerging from the bodies of such gods as Brahmā, Śiva, Viṣṇu and Indra came their respective *śaktis*, in bodies reflecting their own, coming forth to assist the Goddess, in order to destroy the demons and support the gods. Lord Rudra came and said to Caṇḍikā, surrounded by these *śakti*s: "For our pleasure, please quickly slay these demons."

Hearing this, an extremely terrifying *śakti* emanated from the body of the Goddess and said to Rudra: "Be our messenger; go and tell Śumbha and Niśumbha: 'Deliver the three worlds to Indra, allow

त्रैलोक्य इन्द्र को दे दो, देवता हविभुक् हों और तुम लोग यदि जीना चाहते हो, तो पाताल चले जाओ। यदि बल के घमण्ड से लड़ना चाहते हो, तो आओ, तुम्हारे मांस से हमारे श्रृगाल तृप्त हों।'' देवी ने शिव को दूत बनाया, अत: उसका नाम 'शिवदूती' प्रसिद्ध हुआ। दैत्य शिव के द्वारा देवी का सन्देश सुनकर क्रुद्ध होकर वहाँ आये, जहाँ देवी स्थित थी और अस्त्र-शस्त्र से देवी के ऊपर खूब प्रहार किया। देवी ने लीलामात्र से सबको नष्ट कर डाला। कौशिकी के आगे-आगे काली शूल और खट्वाङ्ग से शत्रुओं को नष्ट करती चलती थी। ब्रह्माणी, माहेश्वरी, वैष्णवी, कौमारी, ऐन्द्री आदि अपने शस्त्रास्त्रों से सहस्रों दैत्यों को मारती थीं। असुरों का संहार करती हुए नाद से दिशाओं को पूर्ण कर रही थी। जब मातृगणों से पीडित होकर असुर भाग चले, तब रक्तबीज नाम का एक महान् असुर आया। रक्तबीज के शरीर से जितने बिन्दु रक्त भूमि पर गिरते थे, उतनी ही संख्या में वैसे ही रक्तबीज उत्पन्न होते थे। वह रक्तबीज गदा लेकर इन्द्रशक्ति से युद्ध करने लगा। उससे महाभयंकर संग्राम हुआ। असंख्य रक्तबीज से संसार व्याप्त हो गया। देवी ने अपनी जिह्वा भूमि पर फैला दी और सब रक्त पान करने लगी। अन्त में वह दैत्य क्षीणरक्त होकर मर गया।

फिर शुम्भ-निशुम्भ का भी देवी से घोर युद्ध हुआ। महायुद्ध के बाद निशुम्भ मारा गया। उस समय शुम्भ ने आकर देवी से डाँटकर कहा—

"हे दुर्गे ! तू घमण्ड न कर, दूसरों का बल लेकर तू लड़ती है।''

इस पर देवी ने कहा—

"इस जगत में मैं ही एक हूँ, दूसरा कोई नहीं। देख, ये सब मेरी विभूति हैं, मुझमें प्रविष्ट हो रही हैं।''

यह कहते ही ब्रह्माणी प्रमुखा देवी उसमें लीन हो गयीं, वह अकेली रह गयी—

the gods to partake in the *havi* (oblations to fire) (as is fitting), and if you wish to continue to live, then go to *pātāla* (the netherworld). If, in the arrogance born of strength, you wish to fight, then come — and may our jackals be satisfied with your flesh'." The Goddess made Śiva Her messenger, hence She became celebrated as 'Śivadūtī' ('She who made Śiva Her messenger'). Upon hearing from Śiva the message of the Goddess, the demons grew enraged and approached Her, and with their weapons struck many blows at the Goddess. The Goddess destroyed them all with Her *līlā* alone. Kālī preceeded Kauśikī and, with a trident and the wooden leg of a cot, destroyed every enemy in Her path. The (*śakti*s) including Brahmāṇī, Maheśvarī, Vaiṣṇavī, Kaumārī and Aindrī killed thousands of demons with their weapons and missiles; slaughtering the demons, they filled every direction with their roars. The demon horde having taken flight, afflicted at the hands of the Divine Mothers (*mātṛkā*), a great demon named Raktabīja then came. As many drops of blood would fall to the ground from the body of Raktabīja, that many identical Raktabījas would rise. Raktabīja began to battle Indraśakti with a club. They fought a terrible duel, and the world was filled with countless Raktabījas. The Goddess spread Her tongue upon the ground and drank all the [demon's fallen] blood. In the end, his blood drained away (*kṣīṇarakta*), and that demon died.[261]

Śumbha and Niśumbha[262] then also attacked the Goddess fiercely. Niśumbha was killed after a great duel; Śumbha then mocked the Goddess, saying: "O Durgā! Don't be so proud; You fight borrowing the strength of others."

To this the Goddess replied: "There is no one else in this world but Me. Look, these are all my manifestations; see them come into Me."

The moment She said this, all the prominent goddesses like Brahmāṇī merged completely into Her, leaving Her all alone:

> In this world I am alone, there is no other separate from Me.
> Look, O wicked, my potencies merged into Me alone.

एकैवाहं जगत्यत्र द्वितीया का ममापरा ।
पश्यैता दुष्ट मय्येव विशन्त्यो मद्विभूतयः ॥
ततः समस्तास्ता देव्यो ब्रह्माणी प्रमुखा लयम् ।
तस्या देव्यास्तनौ जग्मुरेकैवासीत्तदाम्बिका ॥

देवी ने कहा— "मैं ही अपनी विभूति से अनेक रूपों में स्थित थी । अब उन सबका उपसंहार करके अकेली ही संग्राम में स्थित हूँ । तू सावधान स्थिर हो ।"

अनन्तर देवी और शुम्भ का देवताओं के समक्ष महाघोर युद्ध हुआ । बड़े-बड़े दिव्यातिदिव्य शस्त्रास्त्रों का प्रयोग हुआ । कभी गगन में, कभी भू पर महान् आश्चर्यकर युद्ध हुआ । उस महासंग्राम के बाद भगवती ने उसके हृदय को विशाल शूल से विदीर्ण कर भूमि पर मार गिराया । देवता तथा ऋषियों ने देवी की इस प्रकार स्तुति की ।

देवताओं ने कहा—

"हे मातः ! आप प्रपन्न प्राणियों की आर्त्ति दूर करनेवाली हैं, आप अखिल ब्रह्माण्ड की माता हैं, आप ही चराचर विश्व की ईश्वरी हैं, आप ही पृथ्वीरूप में स्थित होकर सबकी आधारभूत हैं, जलरूप से भी स्थित होकर सम्पूर्ण विश्व का आप्यायन करती हैं, आप अनन्त वीर्य्यवाली वैष्णवी शक्ति हैं, आप ही विश्व की बीजभूता माया है, सम्पूर्ण विश्व आपसे ही मोहित है, प्रसन्न होकर आप ही मुक्ति की हेतु बन जाती हैं, संसार की समस्त विद्याएँ आपकी ही अंश हैं, समस्त स्त्रियाँ भी आपकी ही अंश हैं, एक आपसे ही सारा विश्व पूरित है, फिर आपकी क्या स्तुति की जाय? स्तुति साधन परा, अपरा वाक् भी तो आप ही हैं, स्पष्टोच्चरित वाक् 'वैखरी' है, स्मृतिगोचर वाक् 'मध्यमा' है, अर्थ की द्योतिका 'पश्यन्ती' है, ब्रह्म ही 'परा' वाक् है—

> Then all those goddesses, among whom Brahmāṇī was foremost,
> Merged in the body of that Goddess, so Ambikā remained alone.
> [*Durgā Saptaśatī* X.5-6]

The Goddess said: "Out of my power of manifestation, it was I [alone] who was present in such a multitude of forms. Now, having withdrawn every one of them, I stand alone, ready for battle. Steady yourself, and take care."

Thereafter, before the gods ensued a fierce battle between the Goddess and Śumbha; divine weapons, huge and powerful, were brought to bear. A great and astonishing battle took place, sometimes in the heavens, sometimes on the earth. After a fierce struggle, with a huge trident did Bhagavatī pierce the heart of Śumbha, causing him to fall to the ground, dead. Thereafter, for this did the gods and *ṛṣis* all praised the Goddess.

The gods proclaimed: "O Mother! You are She who removes the suffering from afflicted living beings. You are the Mother of the entire universe (*brahmāṇḍa*). You are sovereign (*īśvarī*) of this world, [presiding over both] the moving and the immobile. In Your manifestation as Earth (*pṛthvīrūpa*), You alone are the substratum for everything; also, You slake [the thirst of] the entire world in Your form of Water. You are the *śakti* of Viṣṇu, She of endless strength; You alone are the *māyā*, the seed of this world. The whole world is captivated by You alone. It is You who, when pleased, brings about liberation; all the knowledge of this world is but one of Your parts, and every woman is also Your limb. Only by You is the whole world made complete; how can [anyone] possibly sing Your praise? Indeed, You[263] alone are the *parā* and *aparā vāk*, the [sole] means of [uttering] praise: articulated speech is '*vaikharī*', the speech that remains in the mind is '*madhyamā*', the significance of meaning is '*paśyantī*' and the Absolute (*brahman*) is the transcendant word ('*parā*' *vāk*):

> *Vaikharī* is the manifestation of the sound, *madhyamā* is its being object of memory,

वैखरी शब्द-निष्पत्तिर्मध्यमा स्मृतिगोचरा ।
द्योतिकार्थस्य पश्यन्ती सूक्ष्मा ब्रह्मैव केवलम् ॥

स्थान, करण, प्रयत्न तथा वर्णविभागशून्य, स्वयंप्रकाश ज्योति 'परा' वाक् है । सूक्ष्म बीज से उत्पन्न अंकुर के समान किञ्चित् विकसित शक्ति ही 'पश्यन्ती' है । अन्तःसङ्कल्परूपा वाक् 'मध्यमा' है, व्यक्त वर्णादिरूप 'वैखरी' है । 'स्वर्ग-मुक्तिदायिनी आप ही हैं । बुद्धिरूप से पुरुषार्थप्रदा, कालरूप से परिणामप्रदायिनी, अवसान समय में कालरात्रिरूप से आप ही विराजती हैं । सर्वमङ्गलदायिनी, सर्वार्थसाधिका, शरणागत-वत्सला, सृष्ट्यादिकारिणी, सनातनी, गुणाश्रया, गुणमयी, शरणागत-दीनार्त-परित्राण-परायणा, आर्तिहरा, ब्रह्माणी, माहेश्वरी, कौमारी, वैष्णवी, वाराही, चामुण्डा, लक्ष्मी, लज्जा, विद्या, श्रद्धा, पुष्टि, स्वधा, महारात्रि, महाविद्या, मेधा, ध्रुवा, सरस्वती, वरा, भूति, वाभ्रवि (राजसी), तामसी, नियन्त्री आप ही हैं । कहाँ तक कहा जाय, आप ही सर्व-स्वरूपा हैं, आप ही सर्वशक्तिसमन्विता हैं । आप और आपके आयुध हमें सब भीति से बचायें । आप सर्वानर्थनिवारिणी, सर्वाभीष्टदायिनी हैं, सर्वस्तुत्या हैं । आपके आश्रितों को विपत्ति नहीं आती, आपके अश्रित दूसरों के आश्रय होते हैं । आप विश्वेश्वरी, विश्वपालिनी एवं विश्वरूपा हैं, विश्वेशवन्द्या हैं । जो आपको प्रणाम करते हैं, वे विश्व के आश्रय बनते हैं ।"

देवी ने प्रसन्न होकर वर माँगने को कहा । देवताओं ने यह वर माँगा कि "अखिलेश्वरी ! आप सर्वदा त्रैलोक्य की सर्वबाधाओं का प्रशमन करें और समय-समय पर इसी तरह असुरों का संहार करें ।"

देवी ने कहा— "यह शुम्भ-निशुम्भ आदि दैत्य फिर अट्ठाईसवीं

> *paśyanti* is the illuminating power of the meaning, and sūkṣ ma (*parā*) is only the selfsame *brahman*.

'*Parā*' speech is the self-illuminated light, devoid of location, action, effort or alphabetical division. '*Paśyantī*' is the somewhat developed *śakti*, akin to a germinated subtle seed. The speech in the form of [one's] internal resolve (*antaḥsaṃkalparūpā*) is '*madhyamā*' speech, and speech expressed in such ways as letters (*varṇādirūpā*) is called '*vaikharī*'. "You[264] grant [both] heaven and liberation. In Your appearance as the intellect, You bestow the goals of human existence (*puruṣārtha*); in the form of time, You grant results (*pariṇāmapradāyanī*); at the time of ending (*avasāna*), it is You who is present as the night of time (*kālarātri*). You are the giver of all welfare and the fulfiller of every wish; [You are] motherly towards those who seek refuge in You, the original cause of creation, the Eternal (*sanātanī*); [You are] the refuge of every attribute, replete with *guṇas*; [You] are eager to alleviate the suffering of those oppressed and humble people who seek refuge in You, the remover of anguish; [You are] Brahmāṇī, Maheśvarī, Kaumārī, Vaiṣṇavī, Vārāhī, Cāmuṇḍā, Lakṣmī, Lajjā, Vidyā (Knowledge), Śraddhā (Reverence), Tuṣṭi (Robustness), Svadhā, Mahārātri, Mahāvidyā (The Great Knowledge), Medhā (intelligence), Dhruvā (the Fixed), Sarasvatī, Varā (Boon-giver), Bhūti, Vābhravi (Rājasī), Tāmasī, and Niyantā (the Controller). How much one can say about You: You are the essential nature of everything (*sarvasvarūpā*); You are fully endowed with every power (*sarvaśaktisamanvitā*). You and Your weapons deliver us from every terror. You eradicate every unthinkable calamity; You grant every wish; You are venerated by all. No calamity befalls those who seek refuge in You, [and] those to whom You have granted refuge [themselves also] give shelter to others. You are the queen of the world (*viśveśvarī*), the preserver of the world (*viśvapālinī*), the form of the world (*viśvarūpā*), the Goddess praiseworthy by the Lord of the entire world (*viśveśavandyā*); those who revere You, give shelter to the (whole) world." The Goddess

चतुर्यगी में उत्पन्न होंगे, वहाँ भी नन्द गोप के गृह में यशोदा से उत्पन्न हो विन्ध्यवासिनीरूप से मैं उनका संहार करूँगी। उसी रूप से वैप्रचित्त दानवों को मारकर उनका भक्षण करूँगी। दन्तों के रक्त होने से उस समय मेरा 'रक्तदन्तिका' नाम प्रसिद्ध होगा। पुनश्च शतवार्षिकी अनावृष्टि होने पर 'शताक्षी' रूप से प्रकट होकर मुनियों पर अनुग्रह करूँगी। अपने देह से उद्भूत प्राणधारक शाकों द्वारा लोक का रक्षण करूँगी, इसीलिये मेरा 'शाकम्भरी', नाम होगा। उसी अवतार में दुर्गम दैत्य को मारने से मेरा 'दुर्गा' भी नाम पड़ेगा। भीमरूप धारण करके हिमाचल के राक्षसों को भक्षण करूँगी, तब मेरा 'भीमा' नाम पड़ेगा। भ्रमररूप धारण कर अरुणासुर को मारने से मेरा 'भ्रामरी' नाम होगा। इस तरह जब-जब दानवों की बाधा फैलेगी, तब-तब मैं अवतार लेकर धर्म और देवताओं के शत्रुओं का क्षय करूँगी। जो इन स्तुतियों से मेरा स्तवन और श्रद्धा-भक्ति से पूजन करेगा, उसकी सब विपत्तियों को दूर कर सर्वाभीष्ट सम्पादन करूँगी।" 'सप्तशती' के चरित्रों से विविध शिक्षाएँ मिलती हैं।

मधु-कैटभ बड़े बलवान् थे, परन्तु बुद्धि-बल से विष्णु ने उनका वध किया, इससे यह स्पष्ट हो गया कि पशु-बल पर सर्वदा बौद्ध-बल की विजय होती है। महिषासुर के वध में देवताओं के सङ्ग से उद्भूत तेज:समूह से भगवती का आविर्भाव हुआ। तृतीय चरित्र से यह भी व्यक्त होता है कि एक शक्ति अग्रसर होने पर सभी शक्तियाँ उस कार्य में लग जाती हैं, इत्यादि-इत्यादि बहुत-सी शिक्षाएँ प्राप्त होती हैं।

'देवीसूक्त' में भगवती का स्वरूप

'देवीसूक्त' से विदित होता है कि साक्षात् परब्रह्म ही देवी आदि नामों से प्रख्यात है।

was pleased, and told them to ask for a boon. The gods requested the following boon: "O Queen of Everything (*akhileśvarī*)! Please forever keep under Your control every obstacle in the three worlds, and from time to time, please slay demons [like You have done today]." The Goddess replied: "Śumbha and Niśumbha will again be born in the 28th four-*yuga* cycle; then as Vindhyavāsinī shall I slay them, having taken my birth in the home of the cowherd Nanda from his wife Yaśodhā. In that form shall I slaughter and eat demons like Vaipracitta. At that time shall I be well-known with the name 'Raktadantikā' ('Whose teeth are red with blood'). Furthermore, during the century-long drought, I shall appear as 'Śatākṣī' and bestow grace upon the *munis*. By feeding the beings of the world with the vegetation sprouting from my body, I shall save their lives; hence, my name will be 'Śākambharī'; in that incarnation, after killing the demon Durgama, I shall gain the epithet 'Durgā'. Assuming a huge incarnation, I shall eat the demons of the Himālayas, and my title will then be 'Bhīmā'. From killing the demon Aruṇa by taking the form of a bumblebee, I shall come to be called 'Bhrāmarī'. In this way, whenever demon-spawned problems arise shall I incarnate and lay waste to the enemies of *dharma*, and of the gods. He who sings these hymns in praise of Me, and who worships Me with reverence and devotion, I shall remove all his misfortunes and fulfill his every wish." From [265] these sections of the *Saptaśatī*, we can draw several teachings. Madhu and Kaiṭabha were very strong but Viṣṇu slew them using the power of intelligence; clearly, the power of intelligence will always defeat brute strength. Bhagavatī came into being from the collective *tejas* of the gods in order to slay Mahiṣāsura. The third *caritra* also shows that if one *śakti* leads [towards a goal], then every *śakti* will [similarly help towards the completion] of that work; there is much learning of this sort to be obtained [from these tales].

The form of Bhagavatī in the *Devīsūkta* [266]

From [267] the *Devīsūkta* we learn that the different names of the Goddess reflect the Absolute Reality (*parabrahman*).

स्वयं देवी कहती है—

अहं रुद्रेभिर्वसुभिश्चराम्यहमादित्यैरुतविश्वदेवैः ॥

अर्थात् मैं ही रुद्र, वसु, आदित्यादि रूप से विहरण करती हूँ। इन्द्र, अग्नि एवं अश्विनीकुमारों को मैं ही धारण करती हूँ। सोम, त्वष्टा, पूषा, भग आदि को भी मैं ही धारण करती हूँ। देवताओं को हवि प्रदान करनेवाले यजमान को फल-प्रदान भी मैं ही करती हूँ।

अहं राष्ट्री सङ्गमनी वसूनां चिकितुषी प्रथमा यज्ञियानाम्।
तां मा देवा व्यदधुः पुरुत्रांभूरिस्थात्रा भूर्या वेशयन्तीम् ॥

अर्थात् सब जगत् की ईश्वरी, धन प्राप्त करानेवाली, तत्वज्ञानिनी एवं यज्ञार्हों में मैं ही मुख्य हूँ। मैं ही प्रपंच रूप से स्थित हूँ। अतएव, देवताओं ने अनेक स्थानों में अनेक रूप से मेरा ही विधान किया है, विश्वरूप से मैं ही स्थित हूँ। जहाँ भी, जो भी किया जाता है, सब मेरी ही तत्र-तत्र, तेन-तेन रूपेण सम्पत्ति है। खाना, देखना, प्राणन करना, श्वासोच्छ्वासादि व्यापार करना सब मेरी ही शक्ति से सम्भव है। जो मुझ अन्तर्य्यामिणीको नहीं जानते, वे उपक्षीण हो जाते हैं। हे विश्रुत ! श्रद्धायुक्त होकर सुनो, यह ब्रह्मवस्तु तुम्हें बतला रही हूँ—

मया सोऽन्नमत्ति यो विपश्यति यः प्राणिति य ईं शृणोत्युक्तम्।
अमन्तवो मां त उपक्षियन्ति श्रुधि श्रुत श्रद्धिवं ते वदामि ॥

मैं ही देवमनुष्यसेवित ब्रह्म का उपदेश करती हूँ। मैं ही जिसको चाहती हूँ, उग्र-अधिक-बनाती हूँ। ब्रह्मा (स्त्रष्टा), ऋषि (ज्ञानवान्) तथा शोभनप्रज्ञ बनाती हूँ। त्रिपुर विजय के समय हिंसक, ब्रह्मद्विट्

The Goddess herself says:

> I wander with the Rudras, the Vasus, I am with the Āditya and Viśvadevas. [*Devīsūkta* 1]

That is, "'I' alone abide as Rudra, Vasu, Āditya etcetera". Is it I who assumes the forms of Indra, Agni and the [two] Aśvinīkumāras (the physicians of the gods). I also support such [personages] as Soma and Tvaṣṭā, Pūṣā and Bhaga. For the worshipper who provides *havi* (sacrificial offerings) to the gods, it is I who bestows the fruit of [this] action:

> I am the ruler of the universe, I am the gatherer of the wealth, I am the understanding, I am the first among those who are worthy of sacrifice.
> Variously the deities who live in many places, enjoined that who is Me, who is present in many crated things as the manifestation, who is penetrated [in the living beings]. [*Devīsūkta* 3]

"I am the queen of the whole world; I am the provider of wealth, I am pre-eminent in the fire-sacrifice and knowledgeable about reality (*tattvajñāna*); I am the manifest world itself (*prapañcarūpa*). For this, in numerous places and in numerous ways have the gods set down the rules of my worship; my nature is that of the universe (*viśvarūpa*). Wherever it is, whatever it is, it is Mine." Eating, seeing, living, inhaling and exhaling, every action is only possible through my *śakti* alone. They grow weak, those who do not know Me to be inside everyone. O Viśruta! Listen with faith — I tell you this absolute truth (*brahmavastu*):

> O you Suta listen with faith what I say. Through Me he eats, he sees,
> He breathes, now he listens to what is said. They who don't believe in Me, vanish. [*Devīsūkta* 4]

I alone preach the Absolute, [which is] served by gods and human alike. Who I like, I make him extreme (*ugra*) — that is, great (*adhika*).

असुर के लिये रुद्र के धनुष को मैं ही विस्तृत करती हूँ, स्तोता जनों के सुखार्थ मैं ही शत्रुओं से संग्राम करती हूँ, मैं ही परमात्मा के सर्वोपरि स्वरूप में आकाश को बनाती हूँ।जैसे तन्तु में पट होता है, वैसे ही आकाशादि कार्य्य जगत् परमात्मा ही से उत्पन्न होता है। समुद्र (**समुद्रवन्ति प्राणिनोऽस्मादिति समुद्रः परमात्मा**) परमात्मा में जो व्याप्त बुद्धिवृत्तिरूप आप् हैं, उनके भीतर, बाहर, मध्य में फैला हुआ जो अनन्त चैतन्य है, वही मुझ भगवती का विश्वकारणभूत रूप है। अतएव मैं समस्त प्राणियों में व्याप्त होकर स्थित हूँ। कारणभूत मायामय निज देह से द्युलोकादि को स्पर्श कर मैं स्थित हूँ। अथवा भूलोक के ऊपर पितर अर्थात् आकाश की मैं रचना करती हूँ।

समुद्र में जल के भीतर मेरे कारणभूत अम्मय ऋषि हैं, उन्हीं महर्षि की पुत्री होकर मैं देवीसूक्त का दर्शन करती हूँ। अथवा समुद्र अर्थात् अन्तरिक्ष में अपने अर्थात् अम्मय देवशरीरों में मेरा कारणभूत ब्रह्म चैतन्य रहता है, अतः मैं कारणभूत होकर सर्वत्र व्याप्त हूँ। मैं ही सम्पूर्ण भूतों और सभी कार्यों का आरम्भ करती हूँ। जैसे वात बिना अन्य प्रेरणा के ही स्वयं कार्य करता है, वैसे ही परशक्तिरूपा मैं स्वेच्छा से ही सब काम करती हूँ। आकाश और पृथ्वी से पर मैं हूँ। असङ्ग, उदासीन ब्रह्मचैतन्यरूपा मैं हूँ।

भगवती की विविध विभूतियाँ

सर्वप्रपञ्च एवं अवतारों की मूलभूता प्रथमा महालक्ष्मी हैं। तीनों गुणों की साम्यावस्थारूपा त्रिगुणा वही भगवती परमेश्वरी है। वह लक्ष्य-अलक्ष्य दो रूप की है। मायारूप लक्ष्य है, ब्रह्मरूप अलक्ष्य

I give birth to Brahmā (the creator), the *ṛṣis* (possessors of knowledge) and Śobhanaprajña (He of distinguished knowledge). At the time of [Śiva's] victory over Tripura, it is I who stretches the bow of Rudra to kill the rampaging (*brahmadvit*) demon. I battle foes to please those who sing my praise. As a fabric is woven out of threads, so do I weave the ether and the other elements out of *paramātman*. As water (*āp*) pervades the ocean, so does the nature of the modification of the intellect (*buddhivṛttirūpa*) pervades the ocean of the Supreme Self (*paramātman*)[268] ("From whom the living beings run forth together, that is the sea, the Supreme Self") — inside it, outside it, in between it; such is my nature, Bhagavatī, the cause of this world. Thus am I established, pervasive in every living being. I am established in contact with worlds such as the skys (*dyulokā*) with my own body, which is *māyā* substantiated (*māyāmaya*), itself the cause (*kāraṇabhūta*). In addition, I created the abode of the ancestors, above [this] world of being — that is, in the heavens.

Within the waters of the ocean is the *ṛṣi* Ammaya, the cause of My occurrence; having becoming the daughter of that *maharṣi*, I see the *Devīsūkta*.[269] Or, in the cosmos — in other words, in the ocean — abides the cause for My being, the Absolute Consciousness — that is, the divine body of Ammaya. Therefore, being the cause of everything, I pervade everywhere. It is I who impels every reality, every action. Just as air acts of its own accord, without any stimulus, similarly do I, as transcendental power, perform everything out of My own self-will. I am beyond [both] heaven and earth. As Absolute Consciousness (*brahmacaitanyarūpa*), I am completely detached and indifferent.

The various manifestations of the potency of Bhagavatī

Mahālakṣmī[270] is the root essence of every [divine] descent (*avatāra*) and the whole manifested world. Bhagavatī is the supreme Goddess; She is the threefold *guṇa*-natured being, the undifferentiated state of these three *guṇas*. She has both a visible (*lakṣya*) and an invisible (*alakṣya*) form. Her form as *māyā* is *lakṣya*; Her form as

है । माया शबल ब्रह्मरूपा भगवती ही त्रिगुणा परमेश्वरी है । जैसे घटादि कार्य में कारणभूत-मृत्तिका व्याप्त है, वैसे ही सम्पूर्ण विश्व में वह व्याप्त है । हरेक पदार्थ में अस्ति, भाति, प्रिय यह तीन ब्रह्म के और नाम, रूप यह दो माया के रूप हैं । उपर्युक्त सूक्ष्मरूप के अतिरिक्त उपासकों के अनुग्रहार्थ भगवती के अवतारस्वरूप स्थूलरूप भी प्रकट होते हैं । दक्षिण भागके नीचे के हाथ में पान-पात्र, ऊपर के हाथ में गदा, वामभाग के ऊपर के हाथ में खेटक, नीचे के हाथ में श्रीफल तथा नाग, लिङ्ग एवं योनि को सिर में धारण किये हुए, तप्त काञ्चन के समान दिव्य वर्णवाली, तप्त ज्ञानशक्ति खेटक है, तुर्यावृत्ति (समाधि) पानपात्र है, लिङ्ग पुरुषतत्व है, योनि प्रकृति तत्व है, नाग काल है । मातुलिङ्ग (फल) ग्रहण से भगवती यह सूचित करती है कि मैं ही सर्वकर्म फलदात्री हूँ । गदा धारण से क्रियास्वरूप विक्षेपशक्ति और खेट धारण से ज्ञान-शक्ति का अधिष्ठात्रीत्व ही बोधित किया गया है । नाग, लिङ्ग, योनिधारण से यह सूचित किया गया है कि प्रकृति, पुरुष और काल तीनों का अधिष्ठान परब्रह्मरूपा मैं ही हूँ । 'ह्रीं' बीज का अभिप्राय भी यही है । यही भुवनेश्वरी है । सूक्तरूप भुवनेश्वरी और महालक्ष्मी दोनों एक ही है । तथापि पाश, अंकुश, अभय, वरादि आयुध धारण में भेद हैं ।

भगवती और सृष्टि

प्राणियों के परिपक्व कर्मों का भोग द्वारा क्षय हो जाने पर प्रलय होता है । उस समय सब प्रपञ्च माया के ही उदर में लीन रहता है । माया भी स्वप्रतिष्ठ निर्गुण ब्रह्म में लीन रहती है । "**अव्यक्तं पुरुषे**

the Absolute is *alakṣya*. Bhagavatī,[271] although of the nature of Absolute reality, it is [also] precisely that *māyā*-empowered form of three *guṇa*. Just as the material cause of clay pervades the effect — a pot, or what have you — similarly does She pervades the whole world. Every[272] substance contains three aspects of the Absolute (*brahman*) — existence (*asti*), knowledge (*bhāti*) and bliss (*priya*) — and two forms of *māyā*, name (*nāma*) and form (*rūpa*). Besides these subtle forms, as for the sake of Her devotees Bhagavatī also appears descending (*avatāra*) in Her gross manifestations. Her[273] bottom right hand holds a box containing a betel leaf, Her upper right hand holds a club, Her upper left hand holds a shield (*kheṭaka*), and Her bottom left holds a coconut (*śrīphala*) and a cobra; She bears the *liṅga* and the *yoni* on Her head, and has a complexion like burnished gold. Her shield represents the power of *jñāna*, the betel leaf box symbolizes the state of *turīya* — [which is to say,] *samādhi*; the *liṅga* represents the essence, *puruṣa*, the *yoni* is the basic nature-substance (*prakṛtitattva*), and the cobra is time (*kāla*). Possessing the sweet lime fruit (*mātuluṅga*), Bhagavatī says that "I alone grant the outcome of every action." It is said that the club represents the potentiality to emitt the universe, which has the nature of action;[274] the shield indicates that She is the presiding principle of the knowledge power (*jñānaśakti*). Through the [symbolism of the] cobra, *liṅga* and *yoni*, She says: "Be it *prakṛti*, *puruṣa* or time itself, it is Me alone, the Supreme *brahman* itself who is the substratum of these three." The[275] seed [syllable] '*HRĪṂ*' also means the same thing. She is Bhuvaneśvarī. Mahālakṣmī and Bhuvaneśvarī are one and the same, manifesting as the *Veda* (*sūktarūpa*). However, they differ in respect to the weapons they bear, like the lasso, goading iron, and the like, and in the display of such *mudrā*s as *abhaya* (dispelling fear) or *vara* (granting wishes).

Bhagavatī and creation

When[276] the mature *karman* of living beings dissipates though their enjoying the rewards of their actions, [the cosmic] dissolution occurs. At that time, the whole world (*prapañca*) is subsumed within

ब्रह्मन् निर्गुणे सम्प्रलीयते ।'' विष्णुपुराण के इन वचनों से अव्यक्त का भी ब्रह्म में लय स्मृत है । अव्यक्त का माया ही अर्थ है, प्राणियों के कर्म-फल-भोग का जब समय आता है, तब चिदात्मिका भगवती में सिसृक्षा (सृष्टि की इच्छा) उत्पन्न होती है । माया की उसी अवस्था को विचिकीर्षा आदि शब्दों से कहा जाता है । कर्म परिपाक का विनश्यद् अवस्थावाला प्रागभाव ही विचिकीर्षा है । यद्यपि गुणसाम्य दशा में कर्म परिपाकादि के अनुकूल कोई भी व्यापार नहीं होते, अत: साम्यावस्था भङ्ग का क्या कारण है यह जानना बहुत कठिन है, तथापि जैसे निद्रा के अव्यवहित प्राक्काल के प्रबोधानुकूल दृढ़ सङ्कल्प की महिमा से ही नियत समय पर निद्रा भङ्ग होती है, वैसे ही प्रलय के अव्यवहित प्राक्कालिक ईश्वरीय सङ्कल्प से ही नियत समय पर जाता है । विभाग को न प्राप्त हुआ यह बिन्दु ही 'अव्यक्त' कहलाता है ।

यह माया की ही अवस्था है, अत: यह माया पदवाच्य होता है । यद्यपि यह महदादि के समान तत्वान्तर रूप से उत्पन्न नहीं होता, अतएव, माया ही है, तथापि माया की एक विशिष्टाकार से उत्पत्ति हुई है, अत: "**तस्मादव्यक्तमुत्पन्नं त्रिविधं द्विजसत्तमम्**" इत्यादि वचनों से इसकी उत्पत्ति भी कही गयी है । केवल ब्रह्म में कारणता नहीं बन सकती, अतएव उसे भी सूक्ष्मावस्था विशिष्ट माया से मुक्त ब्रह्म में ही कारणता समझना चाहिये । बीज और अंकुर के बीच की उच्छूनावस्था को ही, जिसमें बीज, धरणि, अनिल, जल के सम्पर्क से क्लिन्न होकर कुछ फूलता है, अव्यक्तावस्था समझनी चाहिये । गुणसाम्य बीजावस्था है, वही शुद्ध माया है । बीज का अंकुरित

the womb of *māyā,* and *māyā* herself remains immersed in the self-supported Absolute without attribute.

> O *brahman*, the unmanifested is merged in the unqualified essence.

According to these words of the *Viṣṇu Purāṇa*, even the inexpressed remains immersed in the Absolute (*brahman*). *Avyakta* (unmanifested) also means *māyā*. When the time comes for living beings to experience the consequences of their actions, then within Bhagavatī — whose essence is of Consciousness (*cidātmikā*) — arises the desire to create. That state of *māyā* is called by such names as *vicikīrṣā* (extreme desire to create). *Vicikīrṣā* is the condition of the prior absence (*prāgbhāva*) which is immediately precedent to the destruction of the mature *karman*. Nothing that inclines the *karmans* to ripen occurs [of its own accord] when the three *guṇas* are in an undifferentiated state; it is difficult to understand what is it that disturbs this balanced state — yet just as one wakes from sleep at one's own proper time out of a firm resolve, similarly does the period of dissolution (*pralaya*) depart, at a certain time, out of God's intention. This point in time, indistinguishable from [the moment] before or after it, is what is called 'the inexpressable' (*avyakta*).

Since this is a condition (*avasthā*) of *māyā*, it is the direct meaning of the term '*māyā*'(*māyāpadavācya*). Although it does not arise from a derivative form, as do such elements like *mahat* ('Universal Intellect'), it is nevertheless *māyā*; as *māyā* has arisen with one particular form (*viśiṣṭākāra*), therefore do such sayings as "Therefore the threefold unmanifested is born best among the twice-born" say that *māyā* has also come into being. Only *brahman* is without cause; therefore one should consider the eternally-free Absolute to be the cause of the state of the subtle (*sūkṣmāvasthā*) *māyā*. Between seed and sprout exists a transitory period, when the seed swells a little, in contact with earth, air, and water: this is symbolic of *avyaktāvasthā* (the unmanifested state). The seed-like state is the undifferentiated state of the three *guṇas*; it is pure *māyā*. The seed's germination is the

होना कार्यावस्था है। स्पष्ट ईक्षण और अहंकार आदि ही महत्तत्व, अहन्तत्व आदि है। व्यष्टि जगत् में समझ सकते हैं कि निद्रावस्था बीजावस्था है, निद्रा का प्रबोधोन्मुख होना अव्यक्तावस्था है, विकल्पविशेषरहित प्रबोध महत्तत्व की अवस्था है, अहंकार का उल्लेख होना ही अहंतत्व की अवस्था है, तदनन्तर स्थूल कार्यादि सम्पत्ति होती है। अन्तर्मुख अव्यक्त की 'तुरीय' संज्ञा है, बहिर्मुख अव्यक्त की 'कारण देह' संज्ञा है। बहिर्मुख अव्यक्त से सूक्ष्म-स्थूल देह की उत्पत्ति होती है, इसी में सम्पूर्ण विश्व आ जाता है। समष्टि-व्यष्टि स्थूल देह और ज्ञानेन्द्रिय तथा अन्तःकरण के अधिपति सरस्वती सहित ब्रह्मा हैं। कियाशक्त्यात्मक लिङ्गदेह के अधिपति लक्ष्मीसहित विष्णु हैं। कारणदेह के अधिपति गौरीसहित रुद्र हैं। तुरीयदेह की अभिमानिनी भुवनेश्वरी और महालक्ष्मी हैं।

मूर्तिरहस्य

प्रथम महालक्ष्मी भगवती ने सम्पूर्ण जगत् को अधिष्ठाता से रहित देखकर केवल तमोगुण रूप उपाधि का आश्रय लेकर बड़ा सुन्दर एक दूसरा रूप धारण किया। साम्यावस्थाभिमानिनी महालक्ष्मी हैं। किञ्चिच्चालित सदृश तमोगुणविशिष्ट अव्यक्त में अभिमान करके उसी ने महाकालीरूप धारण कर लिया। यद्यपि वह मूल देवी से अभिन्न ही है, तथापि रूप में भेद है। कज्जल के समान नीलवर्ण वाली, सुन्दर दंष्ट्रा से युक्त मनोहर आननवाली, विशाल लोचन, सूक्ष्म कटिवाली वह देवी खड्ग, पात्र, शिरःखेट को धारण किये कबन्ध, हार और मुण्ड की माला अथवा शव शिरों की माला पहने थी। उस महाकाली ने महालक्ष्मी से कहा कि—

state of effect (*kāryāvasthā*). In it, such elements [of existence] (*tattva*) as *mahat* ('the Great', the universal intellect) and *ahaṃ* ('I', the subject) are clearly [both] the primeval volition distinct and the sense of 'I'. In the individual's universe, we can consider the sleeping state to be the seed state of creation, one's arousal from sleep to be the unmanifested state (*avyakta*), the wakeful state deprived of particular changes as the universal intellect, the declaration of 'I' as the state of *ahaṃtattva*, followed by the grosser effects. When turned inward, the unmanifested is called '*turīya*'; when turned outwards, it becomes the causal body (*kāraṇadeha*). Also from the extroverted *avyakta* arise the subtle (*sūkṣma*) and gross (*sthūla*) bodies, and from these the whole universe comes into being. In association with Sarasvatī, Brahmā is the overlord of both the [gross] universal [macrocosmos] (*samaṣṭi*) and the individual [microcosmos] (*vyaṣṭi*), along with the sense organs (*jñānendriya*) and the inner faculty (*antaḥkaraṇa*). Viṣ ṇu, with Lakṣmī, is the governor of the subtle body, ripened by the potency of action; Rudra, with Gaurī, is the ruler of the causal body. Mahālakṣmī and Bhuvaneśvarī rule the *turīyadeha* (that 'body' which exists 'beyond these three').

The secret of icons

Initially,[277] when She saw that the world was without a controller, having taken only the support of the quality of *tamas*, the Goddess Mahālakṣmī took another, very beautiful form [distinct from the one She already wore]. Mahālakṣmī is the presiding principle of the condition of the balance (*sāmyāvasthābhimāninī*). Identified with the unmanifest qualified by *tamas*, seeming to move very slighty, She adopted the form of Mahākālī. Although this one is not different from the primeval Goddess (*mūladevī*), they nevertheless differ in appearance. She [Mahākālī] is blue like kohl, arrayed with beautiful sharp teeth, with a lovely face and large eyes; slim-waisted, she carries sword, a box, a [severed] head and a shield; she wears a skirt of made of arms and a necklace of skulls or corpses' heads. Mahākālī said to Mahālakṣmī:

"मेरे लिये नाम और कर्म बतलाओ ।"

महालक्ष्मी ने ब्रह्मादिमोहिका होने से 'महामाया', उन सबका संख्यान और संहार करने से 'महाकाली' और सर्वविध भक्षण की इच्छावाली होने से 'क्षुधा', योग की अधिष्ठात्री 'योगनिद्रा', भक्तकृत भक्ति की इच्छावाली होने से 'तृष्णा' महापराक्रमी होने से 'एक वीरा' इत्यादि नाम और नामानुरूप ही कर्म बतलाये गये हैं । अनन्तर महालक्ष्मी ने अतिशुद्ध सत्व के द्वारा चन्द्रप्रभा के समान अति सुन्दर और रूप धारण किया । अक्षमाला, अंकुश, वीणा, पुस्तक धारण किये हुए वह बड़ी सुन्दरी देवी प्रकट हुई । उसके लिये भी महाविद्या, महावाणी, भारती, वाक्, सरस्वती, आर्या, ब्राह्मी, कामधेनु, बीजगर्भा, धनेश्वरी नाम और नामानुरूप ही कर्म बतलाये गये हैं । महालक्ष्मी स्वयं ही साम्यावस्था की अभिमानिनी होते हुए रजोगुण की भी अभिमानिनी हुई, अतएव महालक्ष्मी का रक्त-रूप वर्णन मिलता है । अन्त में महालक्ष्मी ने महाकाली और महासरस्वती से कहा कि—

"आप दोनों अपने अनुरूप स्त्रीपुरुषरूप मिथुन उत्पन्न करो ।"

ऐसा कहकर स्वयं महालक्ष्मी ने निर्मल ज्ञानमय कमल पर विराजमान एक स्त्री, एक पुरुष मिथुन बनाया । ब्रह्मा, धाता आदि पुरुष के नाम तथा श्री, पद्मा, कमला, लक्ष्मी आदि स्त्री के नाम हुए । महाकाली ने भी एक मिथुन बनाया, उसमें नीलकण्ठ, रक्तबाहु, श्वेताङ्ग, चन्द्रशेखर पुरुष हुआ और शुक्ल वर्ण की ही सुन्दरी स्त्री हुई । पुरुष के रुद्र, शङ्कर, स्थाणु, कपर्दी, त्रिलोचन नाम हुए । स्त्री के त्रयी, विद्या, कामधेनु, भाषा,अक्षरा, स्वरा आदि नाम हुए । सरस्वती से भी उत्पन्न मिथुन में विष्णु, हृषीकेश, वासुदेव, जनार्दन पुरुष के और उमा, गौरी, सती, चण्डी, सुन्दरी, सुभगा, शिवा स्त्री के नाम हुए । इस तरह बिना पुरुष के ही युवतियाँ ही पुरुष बन गयीं ।

Give Me a name, and tell Me what is My task.

Mahālakṣmī addressed Me as 'Mahāmāyā' because She enthralls even the Absolute , 'Mahākālī' because She destroys everything, 'Kṣudhā' because She wishes to devour everything, 'Tṛṣṇā' for Her thirst for all knowledge, 'Yoganidrā' because She is the regent of *yoga*, 'Tṛṣṇā' because of Her intense desire for the devotion of devotees, and 'Eka Vīrā' because She is extremely valiant; Her tasks were described, as appropriate to Her [various names and] forms. Thereafter, Mahālakṣmī adopted [another] most beautiful guise of the purest *sattva*, as beautiful as a moonbeam. This beautiful Goddess appeared carrying a rosary of *rudrākṣa* beads, an iron goad, a *vīṇā* and a book. She was also given names, like Mahāvidyā (Great Knowledge), Mahāvāṇī (Great Speech), Bhāratī, Vāk (Word), Sarasvatī, Āryyā (Noble One), Brāhmī, Kāmadhenu, Bījagarbhā (Womb of the seeds) and Dhaneśvarī (Goddess of wealth), and [was assigned] corresponding functions. Though She is the overlord of the undifferentiated state of the three *guṇa*, Mahālakṣmī became identified with the *rajas guṇa*; for this is She described as being ruddy in color. Finally, Mahālakṣmī said to Mahākālī and Mahāsarasvatī:

> Both of You: manifest a paired couple, male and female, as appropriate to Your nature.

Saying this, Mahālakṣmī Herself manifested a couple, a woman and a man sitting atop a perfect lotus, replete with knowledge (*jñānamaya*). The man came to be known by such names as Brahmā and Dhātā, and the woman such names as Śrī, Padmā, Kamalā and Lakṣmī. Mahākālī also made a couple: a man named Nīlakaṇṭha, Raktabāhu, Śvetāṅga, Candraśekhara and the like, and an extremely beautiful, fair-complexioned woman. The man came to be known as Rudra, Śaṅkara, Sthāṇu, Kapardī, Trilocana and the woman Trayī, Vidyā, Kāmadhenu, Bhāṣā, Akṣarā, Svarā, and so on. From the couple arising from Sarasvatī, Viṣṇu, Hṛṣīkeśa, Vāsudeva and Janārdana [278] became the names of the male, and Umā, Gaurī, Satī, Caṇḍī, Sundarī,

साधारण लोग इसे असम्भव समझते हैं, परन्तु अचिन्त्य मायाशक्ति की महिमा जाननेवालों के लिये यह असम्भव नहीं । महालक्ष्मी ने ब्रह्मा का सरस्वती से, रुद्रा का गौरी से, वासुदेव का लक्ष्मी से विवाह कर दिया । ब्रह्मा ने सरस्वती के साथ ब्रह्माण्ड बनाया, रुद्र ने गौरी के साथ संहार का काम किया और विष्णु ने लक्ष्मी के साथ पालन किया । ब्रह्म दृष्टि से चैतन्यरूपा सरस्वती, सत्तारूपा लक्ष्मी, आनन्दरूपा काली हैं, अतः चैतन्य का अभिव्यञ्जक सत्व, सत्ताव्यञ्जक रज और आनन्दव्यञ्जक तम है । सुषुप्ति में तम की बहुलता से आनन्दमय की व्यक्ति होती है । आनन्दभोक्ता सत्व का पर्यवसान तमोरूपा निद्रा में होता है, इसलिये रुद्र में तम का व्यवहार होता है । सत्ताव्यञ्जक रज का पर्यवसान सत्वात्मक ज्ञान में होता है, इसलिये विष्णु को सत्व कहा है । चैतन्यव्यञ्जक रज अपने रूप में रहता है, इसलिये ब्रह्मा में कहा जाता है । इतिहास की दृष्टि से पहले उत्पत्ति, फिर स्थिति, फिर संहार होता है । साधना में संहार, पालन और उत्पादन यह क्रम मान्य होता है । स्थितिकाल में भी उन्नति के लिये तीनों शक्तियों की अपेक्षा है । दोषों का संहार, रक्षणीय गुणों का पालन और फिर अविद्यमान गुणादिकों का उत्पादन अभीष्ट होता है । रोगों का नाश, प्राणों का रक्षण और बल का उत्पादन यह शिव, विष्णु एवं ब्रह्मा का काम है । वैसे यह सब-के-सब विशुद्ध सत्वमय हैं, इसलिये शैवपुराणों में शिव को भी सत्वमय कहा गया है । शैव, वैष्णव, शाक्त सबके यहाँ अपने इष्टदेव को ही मूलतत्व माना जाता है । मूलतत्व में ही पूर्ण सर्वज्ञता आदि की विवक्षा से सत्वमय कहा जाता है । गुणकृत आवरण एवं तत्प्रभाव से रहित होने के कारण उसे ही निर्गुण भी कहा जाता है ।

Subhagā and Śivā[279] became the names of the woman. In this way, even without men, the young women became male.

This is considered impossible by ordinary people; it is not thought impossible by those who know the greatness of the inconceivable power of *māyā*. Mahālakṣmī married Brahmā to Sarasvatī, Rudra to Gaurī and Vāsudeva to Lakṣmī. Brahmā and Sarasvatī toil at creating the world; Viṣṇu and Lakṣmī nurture it, and Rudra and Gauri destroy it. From an absolute point of view, Sarasvatī is of the nature of Consciousness, Lakṣmī, of the nature of Reality or Being (*sattā*) and the identity of Kālī is of Bliss (*ānanda*); therefore, *sattva* denotes Consciousness, *rajas,* Being or Reality, and *tamas* denotes Bliss. In the state of sleep, bliss finds its expression with the predominance of *tamas*. The Bliss-savouring reality (*sattva*) falls into a sleep characterised by *tamas*; that is why *tamas* is the dynamic principle of Rudra. *Rajas*, denoting existence (*sattāvyaṃjaka*), falls into the *sattva*-characterised knowledge (*jñāna*), hence Viṣṇu is called *sattva*. Consciousness-denoting *rajas* (*caitanyavyañjaka*) retains its form, hence Brahmā is said to possess it. From a secular, historical viewpoint, first comes creation, then preservation, and then annihilation. [When] on spiritual path (*sādhanā*), the accepted sequence is of destruction, preservation and production. [However,] even during the preservation [phase], all the three powers are required. The annihilation of flaws, the preservation of qualities worth keeping, and the creation of qualities not yet present: [these functions are all] desirable. Destroying affliction, protecting life and building strength: these are the respective functions of Śiva, Viṣṇu and Brahmā. Of[280] course, all three are characterized purely with *sattva*; that is why in Śaivite *Purāṇas* even Śiva is known as being replete with *sattva* (*sattvamaya*). *Śaivas*, *vaiṣṇavas* and *śāktas* all consider their respective chosen deity (*iṣṭadeva*) to be the original principle. When the original principle is defined as 'complete omniscience', then it is said to be of a *sāttvika* nature. Since it is devoid of the camouflage represented by the three *guṇa* and is thereby free from their effect, it is then also called *nirguṇa* (non-qualified).

जिस तरह मेघादि सूर्य के आवरक होते हैं, उपनेत्रादि नहीं, उसी तरह अस्वच्छ उपाधि सच्चिदानन्द की आवरक होती है, स्वच्छ नहीं। इसीलिये शिव की शक्ति काली से संहार होता है। केवल प्रकाश सृष्टि नहीं हो सकती, इसीलिये सरस्वती को रज के अधिष्ठाता ब्रह्मा का सहारा लेना पडता है। रज से कार्य बनता चलता है, परन्तु यदि उसमें टिकाव न हो, तो पालन नहीं बन सकता, अतः कार्य को टिकाऊ या स्थिर करने के लिये लक्ष्मी को तमोऽधिष्ठाता विष्णु की अपेक्षा होती है। तम के प्राबल्य में अत्यन्त रुकावट होने पर पालन न होकर संहार होता है। परन्तु संहार में भी किसका, कब, कितने दिन तक संहार हो, इसके ज्ञान के लिये सत्व की अपेक्षा है, इसीलिये काली शिव का सहारा लेती है। अन्यथा ब्रह्मा को रज, रुद्र को तम और विष्णु को सत्व का अधिष्ठाता कहा जाता है। ब्रह्मा का रङ्ग तो उनके गुण रज के अनुसार रक्त है, परन्तु शिव, विष्णु में यह नहीं घटता। सत्वगुण के अनुसार शिव शुक्ल और तम के अनुसार विष्णु कृष्ण हैं।

कुछ लोग कहते हैं कि शिव, विष्णु के परस्पर ध्यान से रूप में परिवर्तन हो गया। स्थिर रखना तम का कार्य है, अतः पालक में तम का परमापेक्ष है। अन्यत्र संहार होने से रुद्र में तम, पालक होने से विष्णु को सत्वमय कहा गया है, कहीं निराकार और अव्यक्त को आकाशादि के समान श्याम रङ्ग का व्यञ्जक माना जाता है, परन्तु त्रिदेवियों की रूपव्यवस्था तो सर्वथा गुणों के अनुसार है। त्रिदेवों में उत्पादक, पालक संहारक को क्रमेण राजस, सात्विक, तामस कहा है। इन गुणों के वश होने से जीव बद्ध होता है। उपर्युक्त त्रिदेव एवं त्रिदेवियाँ गुणों के वश नहीं किन्तु गुणों की नियन्त्री हैं, अतः वे स्वतन्त्र हैं। इसके अतिरिक्त एक विशेषता और है, वह यह कि गुणों का विमर्शवैचित्र्य होने से एक गुण के भीतर भी सब गुणों का अस्तित्व होता है।

Just as clouds veil the sun and not the eyes, similarly is *saccidānanda* veiled by an accidental attribute (*upādhi*), and not by a clean one. That is why annihilation takes place at the hands of Śiva's power, Kālī. Creation cannot only be light; that is why Sarasvatī has to take the help of Brahmā, the supervisor of *rajas*. Actions are performed through *rajas*, but preservation is impossible if they cannot last; hence, to give duration and stability to activity, Lakṣmī needs the help of Viṣṇu, the guardian of *tamas*. *Tamas* creates obstacles when is too strong, and destruction happens, instead of preservation. But even for annihilation we need *sattva* to know whom or what to annihilate, when to do it and for how long; hence, Kālī takes the help of Śiva. Otherwise, Brahmā is called the supervisor of *rajas*, Viṣṇu of *sattva* and Rudra of *tamas*. Brahmā is ruddy in color according to his *rajas guṇa*, but this is not so in the case of Viṣṇu or Śiva. Śiva is white from the *sattva guṇa*; Viṣṇu is dark, in accordance with his *tamas guṇa*.

Some people say that Śiva and Viṣṇu altered their appearances due to meditating upon each other. It is the function of *tamas* to keep things stable; hence, *tamas* is absolutely needed in a Preserver. Elsewhere, *tamas* is said to be within Rudra because of his task of destruction, and Viṣṇu has been said to be of a *sattva* nature due to his being the Preserver. In some places, the formless and unmanifested is believed to be dark as space (*ākāśādi*); [irregardless,] the schemata of the appearances of the three goddesses is in total accord with their respective *guṇa*. Among the three [male] gods, the Creator has been said to be (of) *rājas*, the Preserver is said to be *sātvika* [of the *sattva guṇa*], and the Destroyer, *tāmas*. So long as a living being remains under the control of these three *guṇa*, it remains bound. [However,] the three goddesses and the male trinity are not controlled by their respective *guṇa*; in fact, they are their controllers, and so are independent. Besides all this, there is one more special aspect [to consider]: that is the wonderful reciprocation through which within each of the *guṇa* is found in the other two as well.

जैसे तामसी प्रकृति जगत् का उपादान है, फिर भी उसके भीतर राजस और सात्विक अन्त:करणादि होते हैं, तमोलेशानुविद्ध, सत्वप्रधाना अविद्या में भी तमोरज आदि के तारतम्य से उत्कर्षापकर्ष होता है, वैसे ही विशुद्ध सत्वप्रधाना विद्या या माया में भी सात्विक, राजस, तामस भेद होते हैं । उसी भेद में ब्रह्मा, विष्णु आदि बनते हैं । यह ईश्वरकोटि है, इनकी उपाधि माया है, वह विशुद्ध सत्वप्रधाना होती है, फिर भी उत्पादक में रज, पालक में सत्व और संहारक में तम का अंश रहता है । पूर्वोक्त रीति से भगवती के महाकाली, महालक्ष्मी और महासरस्वती ये तीन रूप-प्रधान हैं । उपनिषदों में प्रकृति को "**लोहित-शुक्ल-कृष्ण**" कहा गया है, क्योंकि उसमें रज:, सत्व और तम यह तीन गुण होते हैं । किसी भी कार्य का सम्पादन करने के लिये हलचल, प्रकाश और अवष्टम्भ अर्थात् रुकावट इन तीनों की अपेक्षा हुआ करती है । इनमें से एक के बिना कोई भी कार्य सम्पन्न नहीं होता, इसीलिये सृष्टि को त्रिगुणात्मिका कहा जाता है । प्रकाश सत्व है, हलचल रज और अवष्टम्भ तम है । रज रक्त है, सत्व शुक्ल है, तम कृष्ण है । केवल निर्विकार, कूटस्थ, चैतन्य कुछ कर नहीं सकता, गुण योग से ही कार्य हो सकता है, अतएव गुणों का आश्रयण करने से ही त्रिदेवी एवं त्रिदेव भी तीन रङ्ग के ही हैं । शङ्कर-सरस्वती ये दोनों भाई-बहन शुक्ल रूप के हैं । ब्रह्मा-लक्ष्मी दोनों भाई-बहन रक्त वर्ण के हैं । विष्णु-गौरी ये दोनों भाई-बहन कृष्ण रङ्ग के हैं । भाई-बहन ही प्राय: एक रङ्ग के होते हैं, पति-पत्नी के एक रङ्ग होने का नियम नहीं होता । इसीलिये शिव-गौरी, विष्णु-लक्ष्मी, ब्रह्मा-सरस्वती ये दम्पती एक रङ्ग के नहीं हैं । गौरी की सरस्वती ननन्दा है, स्वयं उसकी भ्रातृजाया (भावज) है, सरस्वती लक्ष्मी की भावज है, लक्ष्मी उसकी ननद है, लक्ष्मी गौरी की ननद है । इसीलिये शिव, विष्णु, ब्रह्मा में भी श्यालक एवं भगिनीपति का सम्बन्ध है । सृष्टि

For example, the *tamas*-dominated nature (*prakṛti*) is the material cause of the world, yet within it exist inner faculties both *rājasika* and *sāttvika*. Also, in the predominantly *sattva*-natured *avidyā*, we find it rising and falling in harmony with the increase or decrease of *tamas* and *rajas*, because *avidyā* is followed with an iota of *tamas*; similarly, we also find the divisions of *sāttvika*, *rājasika* and *tāmasika* in the purest *sattva*-dominant *vidyā* or *māyā*. [Divinities like] Brahmā and Viṣṇu are born from these very distinctions. This is the condition of the Lord whose accidental attribute is *māyā*; in her the purest *sattva* predominates — yet in the Creator is present [a portion of] *rajas*, in the Preserver [a portion of] *sattva*, and the Destroyer [a portion of] *tamas*. As it had been said before, Mahākālī, Mahālakṣmī and Mahāsarasvatī are the three main forms of Bhagavatī. In the *Upaniṣads*, *prakṛti* has been described as '*lohita-śukla-kṛṣṇa*', or 'red white and black', because it comprises the three *guṇa* — *rajas*, *sattva* and *tamas*. To perform any action we need vibration (*halacala*), light (*prakāśa*) and limitation (*avaṣṭambha*). No activity can take place if even one of them is missing; that is why creation is known as 'that whose nature comprises the three attributes' (*triguṇātmikā*). Light is *sattva*, activity is *rajas*, limitation is *tamas*.[281] *Rajas* is red, *sattva* is white and *tamas* is black. The incorruptible, transcendental (*kūṭastha*) Consciousness alone cannot do anything; in union with *guṇa*, anything can happen. Hence, because of their presiding over in the three *guṇa*, the three goddesses have three colours, as do the three gods. Ṣaṇkara and Sarasvatī are brother and sister, and are white. Brahmā and Lakṣmī are brother and sister, and are red-coloured. The siblings Viṣṇu and Gaurī are black. Siblings are usually of the same complexion; there is no rule that a husband and wife must have the same complexion.[282] That is why the couples Śiva and Gaurī, Viṣṇu and Lakṣmī, and Brahmā and Sarasvatī are not of the same hue. Sarasvatī is the sister-in-law of Gaurī and Lakṣmī, and vice-versa. Similarly, Śiva, Viṣṇu and Brahmā are also all mutually inter-related. Creation needs both activity and the power of knowledge (*jñānaśakti*). Only the motion bestowed by *rajas* and the knowledge-power of *sattva*

में हलचल और ज्ञानशक्ति दोनों की अपेक्षा होती है । रज की हलचल और सत्व की ज्ञानशक्ति ही सृष्टि कर सकती है, इसीलिये ब्रह्मा की पत्नी सरस्वती से सृष्टि होती है । तम की रुकावट से और रज की हलचल से पालन होता है, अतएव विष्णुपत्नि लक्ष्मी से पालन होता है । सत्व के प्रकाश एवं तम के अवष्टम्भ से संहार होता है अतः शिवपत्नि गौरी से संहार होता है । सर्वसत्वमय भगवती साकार होकर अनेक नामोंवाली होती है, निराकाररूप से तो किसी का भी शब्द से वाच्य नहीं है ।

ज्ञानानां चिन्मयातीता शून्यानां शून्यरूपिणी ।
यस्याः परतरं नास्ति सैषा दुर्गा प्रकीर्तिता ॥
यतो वाचो निवर्तन्ते अप्राप्यमनसा सह ।

त्रिगुणा तामसी महाकाली है, वही हरि की योगनिद्रा है, उसकी विष्णु को जगाने के लिये ब्रह्मा ने स्तुति की है । वह दशमुख, दशभुज, दशचरण और तैंतीस विशाल नेत्रवाली है । यद्यपि शत्रुओं को उसका रूप बड़ा ही भयावना लगता है, तथापि भक्तों के लिये तो वह रूप सौभाग्य और कान्ति की एकमात्र प्रतिष्ठा है । खड्ग, बाण, गदा, शूल, चक्र, पाश, भुशुण्डि, परिघ, कार्मुक और सद्यःकृत्त शिर उसके हाथ में है । इसकी विधिपूर्वक पूजा करने से साधक चराचर विश्व को स्वाधीन कर लेता है । जो देवी सर्वदेव शरीरों से उत्पन्न हुई वह महालक्ष्मी है । यद्यपि वह सहस्र भुज या अनन्त भुजावाली है, तथापि साधक अष्टादशभुजा रूप से उसको पूजते हैं । उसका मुख शिव-समुद्भूत तेज से बना है, अतः श्वेत है । भुजा विष्णु के अंश से हुई है, अतः नील है । स्तनमण्डल सौम्यांश से बने हैं, अतः सुश्वेत हैं । कटि इन्द्रांश से हुई है, अतः रक्त है । चरण ब्रह्मांशजन्य होने रक्त, जङ्घा और ऊरु वरुणांश-जन्य हैं अतः नील हैं । सुचित्रजघना,

can bring about creation; for this, creation comes about through Brahmā's wife Sarasvatī. The nurturing [of existence] occurs through obstructions from *tamas* and the activity of *rajas*; hence, Viṣṇu's wife Lakṣmī nurtures. Destruction occurs by the light of *sattva* and the limitations supplied by *tamas*; so, Śiva's wife Gaurī annihilates. Comprising pure *sattva*, Bhagavatī assumes numerous names when she becomes manifest ('with-forms', *sākāra*); the formless (*nirākāra*) is not describable by any word.

> She is transcendent, the knowledge natural within all the cognition; among the voids She has the form of the voidness,
> She is exalted as Durgā, the unreachable, nothing is beyond Her.
> Words are unable to grasp Her, [and so] withraw from Her, together with the mind.[283]

Mahākālī[284] is *tāmasī* [of *tamas*], yet [comprises] all three *guṇa*; She is the *yoganidrā* of Viṣṇu, and Brahmā sang Her praise to wake him. She is ten-faced and ten-armed, with ten feet and thirty-three huge eyes. Although Her form appears very terrifying to Her enemies, for Her devotees She is the sole established source of beauty, good fortune and lustre. She[285] carries in Her hands a sword, an arrow, a club, a trident, a discus, a lasso, a goad (*bhuśuṇḍi*), an iron bar (*parigha*), a bow and a freshly-severed head. If we properly worship Her in the prescribed manner, we succeed in bringing under our control the entire world of moving and motionless life forms. Mahālakṣmī[286] is that goddess who arose from the bodies of all the [other] gods. Although She is thousand-armed, or infinitely-armed, aspirants (*sādhaka*) nevertheless worship Her in Her eighteen-armed form. Her face was made from the resplendence emanated from Śiva; hence, it is white. Her arms arose from a portion of Viṣṇu, hence they are blue. Her breasts are made from a part of the moon; hence they are most pleasantly white. Her waist is from a portion of Indra, and hence it is red. Her feet produced from a part of Brahmā are red, Her thighs and belly, being part of Varuṇa, are blue. The hidden part is beautiful

चित्र माल्य और अम्बर को धारण किये हैं । दाहिने वाम भाग के नीचे के क्रम से उसके निम्नलिखित आयुध हैं-अक्षमाला, कमल, बाण, असि, कुलिश, गदा, चक्र, परशु, त्रिशूल, शंख, घण्टा, पाश, दण्ड, चर्म, चाप, पानपात्र और कमण्डलु । इस महालक्ष्मी के पूजन से सर्वलोकाधिपत्य मिलता है । सरस्वती आठ भुजा की हैं । बाण, मुशल, शूल, चक्र, शंख, घण्टा, लांगल और कार्मुक उसके आयुध हैं । इनकी उपासना से सर्वज्ञता मिलती है ।

दशमहाविद्या

महाकाली

पूर्वोक्त भगवती के ही दश भेद और होते हैं । इसमें प्रथम महाकाली है । महाकाली प्रलयकाल से सम्बद्ध रहती है, अतएव वह कृष्णवर्ण की है । वह शव पर इसलिये आरूढ़ है कि शक्तिविहीन मृत विश्व के ऊपर विराजमान है । शत्रुसंहारक की शक्ति भयावह होती है, इसलिये काली मूर्ति भी भयावह है । शत्रुसंहार के बाद योद्धा का अट्टहास भीषणता के लिये होता है इसीलिये महाकाली हँसती रहती है । निर्बल के आक्रमण को विफल कर उसकी दुर्बलता पर हँसा जाता है, उसी तरह निर्बल विश्व के घमण्ड को चूर कर भगवती हँसती हैं । पूर्ण वस्तु को चतुरस्त्र कहा जाता है, इसीलिये पूर्णतत्व चार भुजा से प्रकट हुआ करता है । इसी से माँ काली की चार भुजाएँ हैं । वह स्वयं निर्भय है, उसका आक्रमण आश्रयण करनेवाले निर्भय होते हैं, इसीलिये भगवती ने अभय मुद्रा धारण की है । सांसारिक सुख क्षणभंगुर है, परमसुख भगवती ही है, जीवित विश्व का एवं मृत विश्व का भी आधार वही है । मृतप्राणियों का भी एकमात्र सहारा है, यही द्योतन करने के लिये देवी ने मुण्डमाला

multicoloured, so Her garland and the dress that She wears are multicoloured. The following are the weapons and other objects She carries, starting from Her bottom right hand: a *rudrākṣa* rosary, a lotus, an arrow, a sword, a thunderbolt (*kuliśa*), a club, a discus, an axe, a trident, a conch shell, a bell, a lasso, a scepter, a leather hide, a bridle, a betel leaf box and a *kamaṇḍala* (the water vessel carried by a *sādhu*). One gets overlordship of all the worlds through the worship of this Mahalakṣmī. Sarasvatī has eight arms; her weapons are the arrow, a mace, a trident, a discus, a conchshell, a bell, a plough (*lāṅgala*) and a bow. By worshipping Her, we gain omniscience.

The ten Mahāvidyās [287]

Mahākalī [288]

The aforementioned Bhagavatī has ten more aspects, of which Mahākalī is the first. She is of black complexion, as She is associated with the time of dissolution (*pralayakāla*). She has Her foot upon a corpse to symbolize that She sits astride a powerless, dead world. The power of a destroyer of enemies tends to be frightening; this is why the image of Kālī image is also terrifying. The loud laughter of a warrior after having annihilated a foe is meant to augment the feeling of terror — that's why Kālī keeps laughing. It is customary to laugh at the weakness of an inferior opponent; after having rebuffed his attack, Bhagavatī also laughs, having ground the arrogance of a weak world into the dust. Since a complete object is said to be fourfold, four arms are said to represent completeness or perfection; for this, Kālī has four arms. She Herself is fearless, and those who take shelter in Her become fearless as well; for this, She displays the *abhaya* ('be fearless') hand-pose (*mudrā*). Pleasures (*sukha*) of this world are momentary; only Bhagavatī is the supreme pleasure (*paramasukha*). She alone is the substratum of both the world of the living, and of the dead. She is the only shelter for the deceased; to indicate this, the Goddess wears a necklace of skulls. Only this world is the veil of Bhagavatī, who is of the nature of the Absolute; at [the time of]

पहनी है। विश्व ही ब्रह्मरूपा भगवती का आवरण है, प्रलय में सबके लीन होने पर भगवती नग्न ही रहती हैं। सारे विश्व के श्मशान के तरने पर उस तमोमयी का विकास होता है, इसीलिये वह श्मशानवासिनी है—

शवारूढां महाभीमां घोरदंष्ट्रां हसन्मुखीम्।
चतुर्भुजां खड्गमुण्डवराभयकरां शिवाम्॥
मुण्डमालाधरां देवीं ललज्जिह्वां दिगम्बराम्।
एवं सञ्चिन्तयेत् कालीं श्मशानालयवासिनीम्॥

(शाक्तप्रमोद–कालीतन्त्र)

तारा

हिरण्यगर्भावस्था में कुछ प्रकाश होता है, प्रलयरूपी कालरात्रि में ताराओं के समान सूक्ष्म जगत् के ज्ञान एवं तत्साधनों का प्राकट्य होता है, उसी हिरण्यगर्भ की शक्ति 'तारा' है। सूर्य कोटि भी हिरण्यगर्भ कहा जाता है, सूर्य रुद्र भी कहे जाते हैं। इनका शान्त और घोर दो रूप होता है। हिरण्यगर्भ पहले क्षुधा से उग्र था जब उसे अन्न मिलने लगा, तब शान्त हुआ। उसी उग्र हिरण्यगर्भ की शक्ति उग्रतारा है।

प्रत्यालीढपदार्पिताङ्घ्रिशवहृद्घोराट्टहासापरा
खड्गेन्दीवरकर्त्रिखर्परभुजा हुङ्कारबीजोद्भवा।
खर्वानीलविशालपिङ्गलजटाजूटैकनागैर्युता
जाड्यं न्यस्य कपालकर्तृजगतां हन्त्युग्रतारास्वयम्॥

क्षुधातुर हिरण्यगर्भ भी संहारक होता है, अत: उसकी शक्ति तारा भी संहारिणी है। उसने चारों हाथों में जहरीले सर्प लिये हैं। सर्प भी

dissolution (*pralaya*), because everything merges into Her, She remains naked. When the entire world crosses over the cremation grounds, then She who comprises *tamas*[289] blooms (*vikāsa*); hence, She is the dweller of the cremation grounds:[290]

> In this way Kālī, the dweller in the annihilation of the cremation ground, should be meditated upon:
> Seated in a corpse, extremely frightening, with dreadful teeth and smiling face, is four-armed
> Each holding a sword, a severed head, the *mudrās* which bestow boons and remove fear,
> Auspicious, She wears a garland of skulls; the Goddess, Her tongue dangling, dressed by the space directions.
> (*Śāktapramoda, Kālītantra*)

Tārā[291]

When the universe is in the [almost undifferentiated] state of *Hiraṇyagarbha* ('the Golden Embryo'), there is some light; in that black night of dissolution, subtle worlds of knowledge and their instruments (*tatsādhana*) appear like stars.[292] The *śakti* of that Hiraṇyagarbha is Tārā. The sun is also called Hiraṇyagarbha, as well as Rudra. He has two forms: one peaceful, one fierce. Hiraṇyagarbha was at first angry out of hunger, but when it began to be fed, it grew quiet. The power of that furious Hiraṇyagarbha is Ugratārā ('angry Tārā').

> Standing on the chest of a corpse with Her left foot extended ahead, the Supreme whose laugh is fearful and true,
> With Her arms she holds a sword, a blue lotus, a dagger and a half skull as begging bowl.
> She who is born from the *huṃkāra* sound; whose enormous matted billions of yellow locks are adorned with snakes;
> Having spread the dark [inert obscurity], the selfsame Ugratārā destroys the threefold universe in Her bowl.
> (*Śāktapramoda, Tārātantra*)

संहार का सूचक है। वह भी शव पर प्रतिष्ठित है। मुण्ड और 'खप्पर' से यह सूचित होता है कि वह भयानक होकर खप्पर द्वारा विश्व का रसपान करती है। उसकी जहरीली रश्मियों की भयानकता दिखलाने के लिये जटाजूट नाग का वर्णन है।

प्रकृतिः पुरुषं स्पृष्ट्वा प्रकृतित्वं समुज्झति।
तदन्तस्त्वेकतां गत्वा नदीरूपमिवार्णवे॥

पुरुष का स्पर्श करते ही प्रकृतित्व को छोड़कर पुरुष के साथ इस तरह मिल जाती है, जैसे नदी समुद्र में मिल जाती है।

अतस्त्वामाराध्यां हरिहरविरिञ्चादिभिरपि।
प्रणन्तुं स्तोतुं वा कथमकृतपुण्यः प्रभवति॥

हरि, हर, विरञ्चि प्रभृतियों से परमपूज्य अम्बा को प्रणाम या उनका स्तवन किसी अकृतपुण्य प्राणी द्वारा नहीं हो सकता। भगवती की पूजा जैन-बौद्धों में भी होती रही है, विशेषतः तारा की पूजा का रहस्य बुद्ध ही जानते थे। तारा ही द्वितीया रूप से प्रसिद्ध है, सुतारा रूप से वही जैनों में भी पूज्य है, अक्षोभ्य ही वहाँ अवलोकितेश्वर रूप में प्रसिद्ध हैं।

क्षोभादिरहितो यस्मात् पीतं हालाहलं विषम्।
अतएव महेशानि अक्षोभ्यः परिकीर्तितः॥
तेन सार्धं महामाया तारिणी रमते सदा।

हलाहल विष पीने पर भी जो क्षोभरहित रहे वही शिव अक्षोभ्य हैं, उनके साथ रमण करनेवाली तारा है।

As the hungry Hiraṇyagarbha is destructive, its power — Tārā — is also a destroyer. She carries a venomous snake in each of Her four hands; the snake is a symbol of annihilation, as well. She also stands upon a corpse. The skull and skull-bowl that She carries indicate that She has become terrible, and drinks the juice [that is, the vital essence] of the world from Her skull-bowl. The serpents entwined through Her dreadlocks show the poisonousness of Her rays of terror.

> Having made contact with the *puruṣa*, *prakṛti* completely abandons her identity (being *prakṛti*) [*prakṛtitva*],
> And then merges completely in the *puruṣa* as a river merges into the ocean.[293]

Just as She has touched the *puruṣa*, She leaves Her being nature and unite Herself with *puruṣa* in such a way as a river merges in the ocean.

> So how can one without merit bow [to you] or even exalt through hymns,
> You, who are worthy to be praised by Viṣṇu, Śiva and Brahmā.[294] [*Saundaryalaharī* 1]

No living being who has not acquired religious merit (*puṇya*) can [even] bow before or sing praise to the Mother, who is supremely venerable by such [gods as] Śiva, Viṣṇu and Brahmā.[295] The Jainas and the Buddhists have also always worshipped Bhagavatī (Tārā); the Buddhists in particular knew the secret of how to worship Tārā. Tārā is well-known as the second [of the *Mahāvidyās*]; Jainas worship Her as Sutārā, and Akṣobhya (the non-shakable) is famous as the form of Avalokiteśvara.

> O great Goddess, even having drunk the halāhalā poison
> He is without agitation, therefore is exalted as Akṣobhya.
> With Him, the great Māyā, Tārinī, always enjoys.

He who remains free from venom, despite drinking the deadly poison[296] — that one is Śiva, the unshakable (*akṣobhya*); Tārā is She who enjoys with Him.[297]

मदीयाराधनाचारं बौद्धरूपी जर्नादनः ।
एक एव विजानाति नान्यः कश्चन तत्त्वतः ॥

(ललितोपाख्याने)

तारा की ही उक्ति है कि बौद्धाचार से ही उनका पूजन श्रेष्ठ है । तारिणी शक्तियों से विशिष्ट महाशक्ति तारा है ।

सीते वन्दामहे त्वार्वाची सुभगे भव यथा नः सुभगा ससि यथा न सुफला ससि । (तै० आ० ६ ।६ ।२)

जनकस्य राज्ञः सद्मनि सीतोत्पन्ना सा सर्वपरानन्द-मूर्त्तिर्गायन्ति मुनयोऽपि देवाश्च ।

अनन्या राघवेणाहं भास्करेण यथा प्रभा ।

ऐश्वर्यावचनः शक्तिः सा पराक्रम एव च ।
तत्स्वरूपा तयोर्दात्री सा शक्तिः परिकीर्तिता ॥

षोडशी

प्रशान्त हिरण्यगर्भ या सूर्य शिव है, उनकी शक्ति 'षोडशी' है । इनकी विग्रहमूर्ति पञ्चवक्त्र है । चारों दिशाओं एवं ऊर्ध्वदिशा के अभिमुख होने से उन्हें पञ्चवक्त्र कहते हैं । तत्पुरुष, सद्योजात, वामदेव, अघोर और ईशान यही इनके प्रसिद्ध नाम हैं । पूर्वा, पश्चिमा, उत्तरा, दक्षिणा, ऊर्ध्वदिक् के हरित, रक्त, धूम्र, नील, पीतरङ्ग के मुख हैं । दश हाथों में अभय, टङ्क, शूल, वज्र, पाश, खड्ग, अंकुश, घण्टा, नाग और अग्नि लिये हैं ।

यह बोधरूप है—

> The conduct for my worship is the Buddhist way.
> Only one, Janardana, knows (it) properly, no any other.
> (*Lalitopākhyana*)

Tārā Herself said that She is best worshipped through the Buddhist method. Tārā is that *mahāśakti* who is (most) particularly equipped with the powers that cross over (*tāriṇī*).[298]

> O dark one, we celebrate You; O young one, be for us; O beautiful one, [You are] as charming as the sleep, for You are as fruitful as sleep. (*Taittirīya Āraṇyaka.* VI.6.2)

> In the abode of the king Janaka was born Sītā, who is the icon of the complete, supreme bliss: so extoll the saints and the deities.

> I am not different from Rāma, just as the light [is one with] the sun.

> That power is an indicator of sovereignity and is [found] within courage; she is also of that same essential nature and it is She who grants them both, and it thereby praised as Śakti.

Ṣoḍaśī

The pacified Hiraṇyagarbha, [who we also know as the] Sun, is Śiva;[299] His *śakti* is Ṣoḍaśi. His image is five-faced; He is called five-faced because He faces all four directions as well as upwards. His famous names include Tatpuruṣa, Sadyojāta, Vāmadeva, Aghora and Īśāna. The eastern, western, northern, southern and upward-looking faces are, respectively, green, red, smoky (grey), blue and yellow. In His ten hands He holds or displays the *abhaya mudrā,* a small sword (*taṅka*), a trident, a thunderbolt, a lasso, a sword, an iron goad, a bell, a cobra and a flame.

This is how He should be known:

मुक्तापीतपयोदमुक्तिकजपावर्णैर्मुखैः पञ्चभि-
स्त्र्यक्षैरञ्चितमीशमिन्दुमुकुटं पूर्णेन्दुकोटिप्रभम् ।
शूलं टङ्ककृपाणवज्रदहनान् नागेन्द्रपाशाङ्कुशान् ।
पाशं भीतिहरं दधानममिता वाग्भ्यो ज्वलाङ्गं भजे ॥

इसमें षोडशकलाओं का पूर्णरूप से विकास है, अतएव यह भी 'षोडशी' कहा जाता है । इस पञ्चवक्त्र की शक्ति षोडशी है ।

इसका ध्यान इस प्रकार है—

बालार्कमण्डलाभासां चतुर्बाहुं त्रिलोचनाम् ।
पाशाङ्कुशशरांश्चापं धारयन्तीं शिवां भजे ॥ (षोडशीतन्त्र)

बालार्कमण्डल के समान आभावाली, सूर्य, सोम, अग्नि इन तीन नेत्रोंवाली, चतुर्भुज, पाश, अंकुश, चाप और शर को धारण किये हैं ।

भुवनेश्वरी

वृद्धिगत विश्व का अधिष्ठाता त्र्यम्बक है, उसकी शक्ति भुवनेश्वरी है । उसका स्वरूप बतलाते हुए शास्त्र कहते हैं—

उद्यद्दिनद्युतिमिन्दुकिरीटां तुङ्गकुचां नयनत्रययुक्ताम् ।
स्मेरमुखीं वरदाङ्कुशपाशाभीतिकरां प्रभजे भुवनेशीम् ॥

सोमात्मक अमृत से विश्व का आप्यायन होता है, इसीलिये भगवती ने अपने किरीट में चन्द्रमा को स्थान दे रखा है । त्रिभुवन का भरण-पोषण भगवती ही करती है । उसी का संकेत करमुद्रा से है । कृपादृष्टि की सूचना उसके स्मेर (मृदुहार) से है । शासनशक्ति का सूचक अंकुश-पाश आदि से है ।

> I adore the handsome Lord with three eyes, five faces, smoky, yellow, blue, green and red coloured, who has the moon as His crest-jewel, of the lustre of millions of full moons,
>
> Bearing in His hand a Trident, a small sword, a knife, the thunderbolt, and a flame, the Lord of the snakes, a lasso and an iron goad, the noose and mudrā that dispels fear, with a burning [uncovered by words].

Since the sixteen divisions (*kalās*) (of the moon, etc.) are fully developed within Him, He is also known as 'Ṣoḍaśī'. The *śakti* of this five-faced God is (also) known as 'Ṣoḍaśī'.

> I bow down to the auspicious one, She who glows with the splendour of the newly-risen sun;
> Her three eyes (are the Sun, Moon and Fire), and with four arms She bears a lasso, an iron goad, a bit and an arrow. (*Ṣoḍaśī Tantra*)

Bhuvaneśvarī[300]

Tryambaka[301] ('The Three-eyed') is the ruler of the [new] world on its way to growth and expansion; His power is Bhuvaneśvarī.

The Scriptures (*śāstras*) describe Her form as follows:

> I ceaselessly adore the Goddess of the Worlds, resplendent like the risen sun, whose crest-jewel is the Moon, with prominent breasts, endowed with three eyes, with a smiling face, whose hands shows the boon-giving *mudrā*, an iron goad, a noose and the *mudrā* that dispels fear.

The world becomes inundated with nectar dripping from the Moon; for this, Bhagavatī gives a place in Her crown to the Moon. She nurtures and feeds the three worlds; this is shown by Her *mudrā*. Her sweet smile tells the world of Her grace-bestowing glance; holding a goad and a lasso, She shows Her power to rule.[302]

छिन्नमस्ता

विपरिणममान जगत् का अधिपति चेतन कबन्ध है, उसकी शक्ति 'छिन्नमस्ता' है । विश्व का उपचय-अपचय तो हर समय ही होता रहता है, परन्तु जब ह्रास की मात्रा कम और विकास या आगम की मात्रा ज्यादा रहती है, तब भुवनेश्वरी का प्राकट्य होता है । जब निर्गम अधिक और आगम कम हो जाता है, तब छिन्नमस्ता का प्राधान्य होता है । उसका ध्यान यह है—

प्रत्यालीढपदां सदैव दधतीं छिन्नं शिरः कर्त्रिकाम् ,
दिग्वस्त्रां स्वकबन्धशोणितसुधाधारां पिबन्तीं मुदाम् ।
नागाबद्धशिरोमणिं त्रिनयनां हृद्युत्पलालङ्कृतां,
रत्यासक्तमनोभवोपरिदृढां ध्यायेज्जवासन्निभाम् ॥
दक्षे चातिसिताविमुक्तचिकुरां कर्त्रीं तथा खर्परं,
हस्ताभ्यां दधतीं रजोगुणभुवां नाम्नाऽपि सावर्णिनीम् ।
देव्याश्छिन्नकबन्धतः पतदसृग्धारां पिबन्तीं मुदा,
नागाबद्धशिरोमणिर्मनुविदा ध्येया सदा सा सुरैः ॥
प्रत्यालीढपदा कबन्धविगलद्रक्तं पिबन्तीं मुदा,
सैषा या प्रलये समस्तभुवनं भोक्तुं क्षमा तामसी ।

(छिन्नमस्ता तन्त्र)

छिन्नमस्ता भगवती छिन्नशीर्ष और कर्तरी एवं खप्पर को लिये हुए स्वयं दिगम्बर रहती हैं । कबन्ध-शोणित की धारा को पीती रहती, कटे हुए शिर में नागाबद्ध मणि विराजमान है और नील नयन हैं, हृदय में उत्पल की माला है, रत्यासक्त मनोभाव के ऊपर विराजमान रहती है ।

Chinnamastā

Cetana Kabandha (the Conscious trunck) is the overlord of the continuously changing world (*vipariṇamāna*); His *śakti* is 'Chinnamastā'. The world always waxes and wanes (*upacaya-apacaya*), but when development and growth exceed decline and dissipation, then Bhuvaneśvarī appears on the scene. When the outflow (*nirgama*) exceeds the influx (*āgama*), Chinnamastā is dominant. She should be visualized like so:

> She should be always visualized with Her left foot forward, holding a severed head and scissors, naked, happily drinking the flow of blood like amṛta flowing from Her beheaded body, with Her head-jewel wrapped by a snake, with three eyes, with Her breasts adorned by blue lotuses, firmly standing on the god of Love united with Rati (Lust), shining like the china rose.
>
> She must be always visualized by the deities as married, with Her two right hands holding scissors and a begging bowl, with extremely black scattered hair, identical to Her rajas-given name, happily drinking the flow of the blood falling from the severed body of the Goddess, with Her head jewelset in a serpent, knower of the mankind.[303]
>
> With Her left foot forward, sensuously drinking the blood flowing from the body, She is the obscure one, able to withraw the whole world into dissolution. (*Chinnamastātantra*)

Chinnamastā stands naked, carrying Her [own] severed head, scissors and a skull-bowl in Her hands. She drinks the flow of blood gushing from Her torso; Her severed head bears a gem surrounded by a cobra. She is blue-eyed. She wears a lotus garland on Her chest, and stands atop of the god of Love united with Rati (*ratyāsakta manobhāva*).

त्रिपुरभैरवी

क्षीयमान विश्व का अधिष्ठाता दक्षिणामूर्ति कालभैरव है, उसकी शक्ति 'भैरवी' है । उसका ध्यान यह है—

उद्यद्भानुसहस्त्रकान्तिमरुणक्षौमां शिरोमालिकां
रक्तालिप्तपयोधरां जपवटीं विद्यामभीतिं वरम् ।
हस्ताब्जैर्दधतीं त्रिनेत्रविलसद्वक्त्रारविन्दश्रियं
देवीं बद्धहिमांशुरत्नमुकुटां वन्दे समन्दस्मिताम् ॥

(भैरवीतन्त्र)

उदित होते हुए सहस्त्रों सूर्य के समान अरुणकान्तिवाली, क्षौमाम्बर को धारण किये एवं मुण्डमाला पहने हैं । रक्त से उसके पयोधर लिप्त हैं, तीन नेत्र एवं हिमांशुबद्ध मुकुट को धारण किये तथा हाथ में जपवटी, विद्या, वर एवं अभयमुद्रा को धारण किये रहती हैं ।

धूमावती

विश्व की अमाङ्गल्यपूर्ण अवस्था की अधिष्ठात्रीशक्ति 'धूमावती' है । यह विधवा समझी जाती है, अतएव यहाँ पुरुष का वर्णन नहीं है । यहाँ पुरुष अव्यक्त है, चैतन्य, बोध आदि अत्यन्त तिरोहित होते हैं ।

इसका ध्यान यह है—

विवर्णा चञ्चला दुष्टा दीर्घा च मलिनाम्बरा ।
विमुक्तकुन्तला वै सा विधवा विरलद्विजा ॥
काकध्वजरथारूढा विलम्बितपयोधरा ।
शूर्पहस्तातिरूक्षाक्षा धूतहस्ता वरानना ॥
प्रवृद्धघोणा तु भृशं कुटिला कुटिलेक्षणा ।
क्षुत्पिपासार्दिता नित्यं भयदा कलहास्पदा ॥

Tripurābhairavī

Dakṣiṇāmūrti ('facing southwards') Kālabhairava is the overlord of the world in decline, and his *śakti* is 'Bhairavī'. This is how She is visualized:

> I adore the Goddess who has the lustre of thousands of risen suns, with a red linen dress and a garland of skulls, whose breasts are smeared with blood, with Her lotus-like hands holding a rosary, the *mudrā* which grants knowledge, freedom for fear and boons, the glory of Her lotus-like face blossoming out of Her three eyes, who wears as a diadem the moon, with a smiling face. (*Bhairavītantra*)

[She] has the ruddy glow of thousands of rising suns, and She wears a linen dress and a necklace of skulls. Her breasts are smeared with blood. She has three eyes and wears a moon-adorned crown. Her hands display a rosary for *mantra* recitation, a book (*vidyā*), and the *mudrā*s (known as) *vara* and *abhaya*.

Dhūmāvatī

Dhūmāvatī is the presiding deity of the condition of all what is inauspicious in the world. She is thought to be a widow; for this, there is no male deity described here [as being associated with Her]. Here the male deity is [the] unexpressed (*avyakta*), and Consciousness and understanding are extremely withdrawn.

Her visualization is as follows:

> She is of an unhealthy complexion; She is wicked-minded [and] malicious,
> Wearing a long, dirty dress, Her hair loose; snaggle-toothed,
> She keeps the appearance of a widow, [and] stands in a chariot that has a crow on its pennant;
> Her breasts are long [and pendulous]; Her nose is [extremely] long, and Her eyes are very cold and cruel;
> Her hands a-tremble, they hold a winnowing basket; Her

विवर्णा, चञ्चला, दुष्टा एवं दीर्घ तथा मलिन अम्बरवाली, खुले केशोंवाली, विरलदन्तवाली, विधवारूप में रहनेवाली, काकध्वजवाले रथ पर आरूढ़, लम्बे पयोधरवाली, हाथ में शूर्प लिये हुए, अत्यन्त रूक्ष नेत्रवाली, कम्पित हस्त, लम्बी नासिका, कुटिल स्वभाव, कुटिल नेत्रयुक्त, क्षुधा-पिपासा से पीड़ित, सदा भयप्रद और कलह का निवास-रूपिणी है ।

बगला

व्यष्टि में शत्रुसंजिहीर्षा, समष्टि में परमेश्वर की संहारेच्छा की अधिष्ठात्री शक्ति 'बगला' है । इसका ध्यान यह है—

जिह्वाग्रमादाय करेण देवीं वामेन शत्रून्परिपीडयन्तीम् ।
गदाभिघातेन च दक्षिणेन पीताम्बराढ्यां द्विभुजां नमामि ॥

अर्थात् शत्रु के हृदय पर आरूढ़, वामहस्त से शत्रुजिह्वा को खींचकर दक्षिण हस्त से गदाप्रहार करनेवाली, पीतवस्त्र धारण की हुई बगला है ।

मध्ये सुधाब्धिमणिमण्डपरत्नवेदी सिंहासनोपरिगतां परिपीतवर्णाम् ।
पीताम्बराभरणमाल्यविभूषिताङ्गीं देवीं नमामि धृतमुद्गर-रवैरिजिह्वाम् ॥

अर्थात् सुधासमुद्र के मध्यस्थित मणिमय मण्डप में रत्नमयी वेदी है, उसपर रत्नमय सिंहासन है । उस पर विराजमान पीतवर्णवाली और पीतवर्ण के ही वस्त्राभूषण, माल्य से सुशोभित अङ्गवाली भगवती बगला है, जिसके एक हाथ में शत्रु की जिह्वा और दूसरे में मुद्गर है ।

> temperament wicked, Her gaze wicked, She suffers from hunger and thirst;
> Always terrifying, [She is the] very abode of fractiousness [falsehood].[304]

Bagalā[305]

Bagalā is the *śakti* who at the universal level represents *parameśvara*'s desire to annihilate; at the individual level, She is the condition of a person's urge to vanquish their enemies. Her visualization is thus:

> Wearing a yellow dress, with two arms and standing upon the enemy's chest, Bagalā is She who, pulling the enemy's tongue with Her left hand, strikes with a club in Her right.[306]

> In the middle of the Ocean of Divine Nectar, within a pavillion decorated with many precious stones, there is a ritual altar adorned with jewels; upon the altar there stands a gem-studded throne, and upon it sits Bhagavatī Bagalā, wearing yellow clothes and with a yellow complexion, bearing yellow ornaments and a yellow garland. In one of Her hands [she grasps] the tongue of the enemy; Her other hand wields a mace.[307]

Mātaṅgī

Mataṅga is a name of Śiva, and His *śakti* is Mātaṅgī. This is how She should be visualized:

> I meditate on Mātaṅgī, the giver of delight, the provoker, who bestows desired objects,
> Dark, whose garland is the bright digit of the moon, who has three lotus-like eyes, seated on a throne made of precious stones,
> Bestower of desired objects to the devotee, whose pair of lotus feet are served by the hosts of deities,

मातङ्गी

मतङ्ग शिव का नाम है, उसकी शक्ति मातङ्गी है । उसका ध्यान इस प्रकार है—

श्यामां शुभ्रांशुमालां त्रिनयनकमलां रत्नसिंहासनस्थां
भक्ताभीष्टप्रदात्रीं सुरनिकरकरासेव्यकञ्जाङ्घ्रियुग्माम् ।
नीलाम्भोजांशुकान्तिं निशिचरनिकरारण्यदावाग्निरूपां
पाशं खड्गं चतुर्भिर्वरकमलकरैः खेटकञ्चाङ्कुशञ्च
मातङ्गीमावहन्तीमभिमतफलदां मोदिनीं चिन्तयामि ॥

(पञ्चचरणात्मकं पद्यम्)

अर्थात् श्यामवर्णा चन्द्रमा को मस्तक पर धारण किये हुए, तीन नेत्रोंवाली, रत्नमयसिंहासन पर विराजमान, नीलकमल के समान कान्तिवाली,राक्षसरूप अरण्य को दहन करने में दावानलरूपा, चार भुजाओं में पाश, खड्ग, खेटक और अंकुशवाली, भक्तों को अभीष्ट फल प्रदान करने वाली, असुरों को मोहित करने वाली मातङ्गी है ।

कमला

सदाशिव पुरुष की शक्ति कमला है । उसका ध्यान इस प्रकार है—

कान्त्या काञ्चनसन्निभां हिमगिरिप्रख्यैश्चतुर्भिर्गजैः
हस्तोत्क्षिप्तहिरणमयामृतघटैरासिच्यमानां श्रियम् ।
बिभ्राणां वरमब्जयुग्ममभयं हस्तैः किरीटोज्ज्वलां
क्षौमाबद्धनितम्बबिम्बवलितां वन्देऽरविन्दस्थिताम् ॥

अर्थात् सुवर्णतुल्य कान्तिमती, हिमालय के सदृश श्वेतवर्णवाले चार गजों के द्वारा शुण्ड से गृहीत सुवर्णकलशों से स्नापित, चार

> Whose brightness is that of the filaments of the blue lotus, whose lustre is like a forest fire, [if the] forest be a host of demons,
> She whose four lotus hands hold a noose, a sword, a shield and an iron goad.

In a poetic stanza in five feet is said, "[She is] dark-complexioned, [and] bears the Moon upon Her forehead; three-eyed, She sits on a gem-studded throne and is of the hue of the blue lotus; [She is] a veritable 'forest fire' when it comes to burning 'forests' of [countless hordes of] demons (*rākṣasa*), Her four hands holding a lasso, a sword, a shield and a goading iron; She grants Her devotees' wishes, and She enthralls the demons (*asuras*); She is Mātaṅgī."

Kamalā

Kamalā is the *śakti* of the male principle named Sadāśiva. She should be meditated upon thus:

> Bathed by water (pouring) from golden pitchers held by the trunks of four Himālaya-like white elephants, Kamalā is of a golden complexion, making the *vara* [boon-giving *mudrā* with one hand], *abhaya* [fearlessness *mudrā* with another hand] and with two lotuses in Her remaining hands, [She] wears a radiant crown and linen clothes.[308]

The Goddess Lalitā[309] ('the Most Beautiful') is one's own soul, the very Self of the world. *Vimarśa* (reflective awareness) is red-coloured. When the Absolute Self (*svātman*) is devoid of any attribute, then it is Māhāvāmeśvara ('The Great Leftward God'). Standing (*virājamāna*) upon His body, the *mahāśakti* named Kāmeśvarī[310] ('the Queen of Desire') is that very Self (*svātman*), eternally blissful and full of qualification.

> If Śiva is together with His power, then He is able to rule; otherwise that deity is not even able to vibrate.
> [*Saundaryalaharī* 1]

भुजाओं में वर, अभय और कमलद्वय धारण किये हुए तथा उज्वल किरीट धारण किये हुए और क्षौमवस्त्र से आवृत कमला है ।

स्वात्मा ही विश्वात्मिका ललिता है । विमर्श रक्तवर्ण है । उपाधिशून्य स्वात्मा महावामेश्वर है । उसके अङ्क में विराजमान सदानन्दरूप उपाधिपूर्ण स्वात्मा ही महाशक्ति कामेश्वरी है । "**शिवः शक्त्या युक्तो यदि भवति शक्तः प्रभवितुं, न चेदेवं देवो न खलु कुशलः स्पन्दितुमपि ।**" निर्गुण पुरुषरूप शिव कामेश्वरी से युक्त होकर विश्वनिर्माणादि कार्यों में सफल हो सकता है, उसके बिना कूटस्थ देव टस से मस नहीं हो सकता । ब्रह्मा, विष्णु, रुद्र, ईश्वर और सदाशिव इन्हीं की शक्तिराहित्य विवक्षा से महाप्रेत संज्ञा है । इनमें प्रथम चार में कामेशी के पलङ्ग के पाँवों की कल्पना है, सदाशिव में फलक की कल्पना है, निर्विशेष ब्रह्म के आश्रित श्रीकामेश्वरी के श्रीहस्त में पाश, अंकुश, इक्षु, धनुष और बाण हैं । राग ही पाश है, द्वेष ही अंकुश है, मन ही इक्षु-धनुष है, शब्दादि विषम पुष्पबाण हैं । कहीं इच्छाशक्ति को ही पाश, ज्ञान को ही अंकुश, क्रियाशक्ति को ही धनुष-बाण माना गया है—

इच्छाशक्तिमयं पाशमङ्कुशं ज्ञानरूपिणम् ।
क्रियाशक्तिमये बाणधनुषीर्दधदुज्ज्वलम् ॥

पूजारहस्य

नामरूपात्मक जगत् में सच्चिदानन्द की भावना ही अम्बा को पाद्यसमर्पण है । सूक्ष्मजगत् में ब्रह्मभावना ही अर्घ्यसमर्पण है । भावनाओं में ब्रह्मभावना ही आचमन है । सर्वत्र सत्वादिगुणों में चिदानन्दभावना ही स्नान है । चिद्रूपा कामेश्वरी में वृत्यविषयता का

Only when [that] non-qualified (*nirguṇa*) male principle (*puruṣa*) [called] Śiva becomes joined (*yukta*) with Kāmeśvarī can He be successful in tasks like creating the world or whatever; without Her, the transcendental God cannot budge in the slightest. Brahmā, Viṣṇu, Rudra, Iśvara and Sadāśiva are said to be [mere] ghosts (*mahāpreta*) when they are without *śakti*.[311] The first four of these are visualized as the legs of [the Goddess] Kāmeśī's bed, and Sadaśiva is thought to the bed-frame (*phalaka*); Śrī Kāmeśvarī, supported by the undifferenciated (*nirviśeṣa*) *brahman*, bears in Her auspicious hands a lasso, a goading iron, some sugarcane, a bow and an arrow. The lasso is nothing but desire (*rāga*), the goading iron is animosity and spite (*dveṣa*), the bow made of sugarcane is the mind (*mana*), and words, speech and the like are the delicate flower-tipped arrows. In some places, it is said that the lasso is the *icchāśakti*, the goad is the *jñāna* [*śakti*], the bow and arrow, his *kriyāśakti.*

> Substaining the splendid noose which is made by the power of volition, the iron goad of the nature of knowledge, and the arrow and bow which are of the power of action.

The secret of *pūjā* [312]

To feel the presence of *saccidānanda* in this world of names and forms truly is to [perform the ritual of] washing the feet of Ambā (the mother). Feeling the presence of the Absolute in the subtle world is to [perform the ritual of] offering the water [to the goddess]. Feeling the presence of the Absolute in every feeling is to [perform the purifying ritual of] sipping water from the right hand (*ācamana*). Feeling of *cidānanda* in every *guṇa* — *sāttvika* as well as the others [*rajas* and *tamas*] — this is the ritual bath. Meditating upon the state of imperceptibility (*vṛttyaviṣayatā*) in Kameśvarī, whose nature is of Consciousness, this is wiping [dry the body of the deity]. Feeling the presence of *nirañjanatva* (the state free from blemish), *ajaratva* (the state free from old age), *aśokatva* (the state free from grief), *amṛtatva* (the state free from death) and the like, these are the offering

चिन्तन करना ही प्रोञ्छन है । निरञ्जनत्व, अजरत्व, अशोकत्व, अमृतत्व आदि की भावना ही विविध आभूषणों का अर्पण है । स्वशरीर-घटक पार्थिवप्रपञ्च में चिन्मात्रभावना ही गन्धसमर्पण है । आकाश में चिन्मात्रत्व की भावना करना पुष्पसमर्पण है । वायु की चिन्मात्रभावना धूपसमर्पण है । तेज में चिन्मात्रत्व की भावना दीपसमर्पण है । अमृतत्वभावना नैवेद्यार्पण है । विश्व में सच्चिदानन्दभावना ही ताम्बूल समर्पण है । वाणियों का ब्रह्म में उपसंहार ही स्तुति है । वृत्तिविषय के जड़त्व का निराकरण ही आरार्त्तिक्य है । वृत्तियों को ब्रह्म में लय करना ही प्रणाम है ।

पुरुषरूपिणी

'देव्यथर्वशीर्ष' में देवी ने स्वयं को ब्रह्मरूपिणी कहा है और यह भी कहा है कि प्रकृतिपुरुषात्मक जगत् मुझ से आविर्भूत होता है—

> **अहं ब्रह्मस्वरूपिणी मत्तः प्रकृतिपुरुषात्मकं जगत्**
> **शून्यञ्चाशून्यञ्च ॥**

एतावता जो कहते हैं कि प्रकृतिरूपिणी ही देवी है, उनका यह कहना ठीक नहीं । अपनी सर्वात्मता को दिखलाते हुए अपने को ही आनन्द, अनानन्द, विज्ञान, अविज्ञान, ब्रह्म, अब्रह्म सब कुछ बतलाया है । अन्त में कहा है कि मैं ही सब जगत् हूँ— "**अहमखिलं जगत् ।**" वेद-अवेद, विद्या-अविद्या, अजा-अनजा सब कुछ भगवती ही है ।

of various ornaments. Merely [using] one's mind (*cinmātra*), to feel the presence of the five constituent elements [ether, air, fire, water, earth] within one's own physical body, this is the offering of [various] fragrant gifts. Perceiving Consciousness within the ether is to offer flowers. Perceiving air is to offer incense. Perceiving fire is to offer the lamp. Perceiving the element of immortality (*amṛtatva*) is to offer food (*naivedya*). Feeling the presence of *saccidānanda* in the world is to offer a betel leaf. To withdraw every kind of speech into the Absolute is to sing the praise [of Bhagavatī] (*stuti*). To eliminate the unconscious state of the object of the mental (*jaḍatva*) — [this] is the real *āratī* [of the Goddess]. [Finally,] to respectfully greet (*praṇāma*) [the deity] is nothing but merging one's mental modifications into the Absolute.

She of the male form (Puruṣarūpiṇī) [313]

In the *Devyatharvaśīrṣa*, the Goddess has called Herself Brahmarūpiṇī — 'She whose nature is of the (absolute) *brahman*'— and has also said that 'this world whose essence is [the union of the male and female principles, namely] *puruṣa* and *prakṛti* (*prakṛtipuruṣ ātmaka*) originates from Me':

> I am the nature of *brahman*; from Me [arises] this universe of the nature of essence and substance, from Me proceeds the void and what is not void. [*Devyatharvaśīrṣa* 2]

Hence, they are wrong, those who say that She who is of the form of Nature (*prakṛtirūpiṇī*) is the Goddess. Showing the universality of Her spirit, She has called Herself bliss (*ānanda*) and its opposite (*anānanda*), scientific knowledge (*vijñāna*) and its absence or opposite (*avijñāna*), the Absolute (*brahman*) and its opposite (*abrahman*): everything. In *ajā* She has said that "I alone am all the world, *ahamakhilaṃ jagat*". [Be it] *Veda* or its absence (*veda-aveda*), knowledge or ignorance (*vidyā-avidyā)*, the unborn or the not-unborn (*ajā-anajā*), everything is Bhagavatī.

कालरात्रिं ब्रह्मस्तुतां वैष्णवीं स्कन्दमातरम् ।
सरस्वतीमदितिं दक्षदुहितरं नमामः पावनां शिवाम् ॥

इस मन्त्र से भगवती के प्रसिद्ध अनेक रूपों का वर्णन करके उसे ही "**एषात्मशक्तिः, एषा विश्वमोहिनी**" इत्यादि वचनों से आत्मशक्तिरूप भी कहा है । यहाँ आत्मशक्ति का आत्मरूपाशक्ति भी अर्थ किया जाता है । तभी "**य एवं वेद, स शोकं तरति**" इस वचन से इसके वेदन में शोकोपलक्षित संसार का तरण कहा गया है । आगे चलकर कहा है— "**यस्याः स्वरूपं ब्रह्मादयो न जानन्ति तस्मादुच्यते अज्ञेया, यस्या अन्तो न लभ्यते तस्मादुच्यते अनन्ता..... एकैव सर्वत्र वेद्यते तस्मादुच्यते भगवती अज्ञेया ।**" अनन्ता, एका, अनेका सब कुछ है ।

आचार्य भगवान् शङ्कर ने भी भगवती के सगुण-निर्गुण दोनों ही रूपों को बड़े सुन्दर शब्दों में कहा है— "हे देवि! आपके निमेष-उन्मेष से जगत् की उत्पत्ति और प्रलय होता है । सन्त लोग कहते हैं कि आपके निमेष से जगत् का प्रलय हो जाता है, इसीलिये मालूम पड़ता है कि आप जगद्रक्षण के लिये ही निर्निमेषा नयनों से भक्तों को देखती हैं—

निमेषोन्मेषाभ्यां प्रलयमुदयं यादि जगती
तवेत्याहुः सन्तो धरणिधरराजन्यतनये ।
त्वदुन्मेषाज्जातं जगदिदमशेषं प्रलयतः
परित्रातुं शङ्के परिहृतनिमेषास्तवदृशः ॥"

शक्ति की दृष्टि से भी देखा जाय तो शक्ति बिना सारा प्रपञ्च शवमात्र ठहरता है । अशक्त व्यक्ति, अशक्त समाज, अशक्त जाति, अशक्त देश भारभूत ही होता है, अतः शक्ति की पूजा सर्वत्र स्वाभाविक

> We [314] bow down to Kālarātri, praised by Brahmā, Vaiṣṇavī, the mother of Skanda, Sarasvatī and Aditi, the daughter of Dakṣa; they purify and are auspicious.

Bhagavatī's various guises have been described in this *mantra*; She has also been called Ātmāśaktirūpa (She whose nature is the power of *ātman*) through terms like "She is the power of *ātman*, the enchantress of the universe" and the like. Here, '*ātmaśakti*' is also interpreted as 'the *śakti* that has the nature of the Self' (*ātmārūpaśakti*). Furthermore, "who knows so, he crosses over" has been said; these words mean that in Her knowledge there is release from the grief of this *saṃsāra*, which is implied by the word sorrow [*śokopalakṣita*]. Further on, it is said "Her nature unknow by even Brahmā and the other deities, She is called the Unknowable; Her end is not found, and so She is called Infinite; everywhere She is known to be singular, so Bhagavatī is called One." She is endless, she is one, She is many, She is everything.

Using [315] beautiful words, Śaṅkarācārya has also described the two forms of Bhagavatī, both qualified and non-qualified: "O Goddess! The world comes into being and is destroyed when You blink Your eyes. Saints say that when Your eyelids close, the world dissolves into *pralaya*; therefore, it seems that it is for the protection of the world that You watch Your devotees unblinkingly."

> O daughter of the King of Mountains! The sages have said that the world is dissolved and created through the closing and opening of Your eyes. I have a doubt may be Your eyes have stopped to blink in order to save from dissolution this universe, which is born when Your eyes are open. [*Saundaryalaharī* 55]

Even [316] when seen from the standpoint of *śakti*, the entire manifest world, if made devoid of *śakti*, is as still as a mere corpse. A weak person, a weak society, a weak caste (*jāti*) or a weak country is a burden; it is natural that power is worshipped everywhere. Everything in *saṃsāra* possesses the power to perform its task; only then

है। संसार में प्रत्येक पदार्थ में तत्तत्कार्य सम्पादन की शक्ति है, तभी उसका मूल्य है। अनन्तानन्तकार्योत्पादनानुकूल शक्ति से सम्पन्न ही परमेश्वर होता है। न्यूनशक्तिसम्पन्न ईश्वर होता है। जितना-जितना शक्तिसाहित्य होता है, उतना ही जीवत्व आता है। अधिकाधिक शक्तिसाहित्य में ईश्वरत्व आता है। निर्गुण, निराकार, निर्विकार, कूटस्थ परब्रह्म अनन्त शक्तियों की केन्द्रभूता महाशक्ति से संवलित होने पर ही विश्व की सृष्टि, पालन, संहार आदि में समर्थ होते हैं। यदि शक्तिसंवलन न हो, तो शिव भी सृष्ट्यादि में असमर्थ, अशक्त, शवमात्र रह जाता है, अतएव ईश्वर का ईश्वरत्व ही शक्तिमूलक है। जिसके सम्बन्ध से ही कूटस्थ चेतन ईश्वर बनता है, उसके महत्व को कौन कहे?

शिवः शक्त्या युक्तो यदि भवति शक्तः प्रभवितुं
न चेदेवं देवः।

आचार्य तो कहते है कि संसार में बहुत लोग अनेक गुणों से युक्त सपर्णा (पत्तोंवाली) कल्पलता का बड़े आदर से सेवन करते हैं, परन्तु मेरी तो ऐसे बुद्धि होती है कि (बिना पत्तोंवाली बेल) एक अपर्णा पार्वती का ही सेवन करना चाहिये, क्योंकि उसके संसर्ग से पुराना स्थाणु ठूंठ (पुराणपुरुषोत्तम कूटस्थ महादेव) भी कैवल्यरूप परमफल प्रदान करता है। सारांश यह कि सपर्णा कल्पलता के सेवन से भी अपर्णा (पार्वती) का सेवन बहुत अधिक चमत्कारपूर्ण है। कल्पलता बहुत फल प्रदान कर सकती है, परन्तु वह मोक्ष देने में समर्थ नहीं। किन्तु अपर्णा का स्वयं तो कहना ही क्या, उसके संसर्ग से पुराना ठूँठ (पुराणपुरुष निष्क्रिय शङ्कर) भी मोक्षफल प्रदान कर देता है—

has it any value. *Parameśvara* is He who is equipped with the *śakti* to perform infinite tasks. *Īśvara* is comparatively less endowed with *śakti*. The more one comes into association with *śakti*, the more individuality (*jīvatva*) one comes to possess; 'sovereignity' (*īśvaratva*) comes when one acquires the greatest [possible amount of] *śakti*. The highest Absolute (*parabrahman*) — without quality, without any shape, incorruptible and transcendental (*kūṭastha*) — only becomes capable of creating, nurturing and destroying the world after being qualified by *mahāśakti*, the condensed form (*kendrabhūtā*) of infinite potentialities. If there be no union with Śakti, then even Śiva becomes a weakened corpse incapable even of creation: the very 'sovereignity' (*īśvaratva*) of *Īśvara* depends on *śakti*. Who can fully describe its glory, the one whose relationship with which the transcendental consciousness (*kūṭasthacetana*) *Īśvara* becomes the Lord?

> If Śiva is with Śakti, then he is able to rule,
> Otherwise that deity is really not even able to move.
> [*Saundaryalaharī* 1].

Ācāryas[317] go so far as to say: "Many people in the world consume with great reverence the leafy *kalpalatā* (wish-fulfilling creeper), rich with numerous qualities, but I believe that one should serve the leafless (*aparṇā*) Pārvatī because, by being in Her company, even an old, immobile leafless tree-trunk (*kūṭastha*) [that is, the supreme, primeval essence, the transcendent Mahādeva] grants the supreme fruit of the absolute freedom (*kaivalyarūpa*) [the form of 'isolation']. The essence of this argument is that consuming even the leafy *kalpalatā* is less miraculous for giving results than consuming the leafless (*aparṇā*) [Pārvatī]. *Kalpalatā* can yield many [kinds of] fruits, but it cannot give liberation. But how can one possibly give enough praise to Aparṇā; merely by being in Her company, an old withered tree-trunk can also give the fruit of liberation:

> Some[318] people in this world with respect resort to the creeper with leafs and spreaded, being endowed with some qualities,

सपर्णामाकीर्णा कतिपयगुणैः सादरमिह
श्रयन्त्यन्ये वल्लीं मम तु मतिरेवं विलसति ।
अपर्णैका सेव्या जगति सकलैर्यत्परिवृतः
पुराणोऽपि स्थाणुः फलति किल कैवल्यपदवीम् ॥

आगे चलकर आचार्य कहते हैं— भगवान् शङ्कर के पास तो वृद्ध वृषभ की सवारी, भाँग, धतूर आदि विषों का खाना, दिशा का वसन, श्मशान क्रीड़ास्थान, भुजङ्गभूषण आदि जो सामग्रियाँ हैं, वह प्रसिद्ध ही है, फिर भी जो उनमें ऐश्वर्य है, वह केवल भगवती के पाणिग्रहण का ही फल है । भगवती के सौभाग्य से ही शङ्कर का ऐश्वर्य है—

भवानि त्वत्पाणिग्रहणपरिपाटीफलमिदम् ॥

इन उक्तियों का यही अभिप्राय है कि शक्ति के बिना कूटस्थब्रह्म अकिञ्चित्कर है, उसमें ऐश्वर्य आदि कुछ भी नहीं रह सकता ।

शक्तयः सर्वभावानामचिन्त्यज्ञानगोचराः ।
यतोऽतो ब्रह्मणस्तास्तु सर्गाद्या भावशक्तयः ॥

इत्यादि वचनों से अनन्त शक्तियों का वर्णन है । शक्ति और शक्तिमान् दोनों का ही अभेद्य सम्बन्ध रहता है । भक्त कहते हैं कि देवी की महिमा अनन्त है, फिर भी जो वर्णन समाप्त किया जाता है, वह गुणों के समाप्त हो जाने से नहीं, किन्तु असामर्थ्य या थकावट से ही स्तुति समाप्त की जाती है ।

महिमानं यदुत्कीर्त्त्य तव संह्रियते वचः ।
श्रमेण तदशक्त्या वा न गुणानामियत्तया ॥

> but my mind enjoys like this: in this universe only the leafless creeper is worthy to be served by all; in fact also an old trunk entwined up by Her gives as his fruit the way to absolute isolation. [*Ānandalaharī* 7]

Further on,[319] the master says: "Lord Śaṅkara is known to do things like riding an old bull, eating poisons like *bhāṅga* and *dhattūra*, naked at play in the cremation ground, wearing serpents as His ornaments and the like, yet the prosperity that He possesses is a result of marrying Bhagavatī. Śaṅkara has prosperity due to the good fortune inherent in Bhagavatī."

> O Bhavāni, this is only the result of the arrangment of [marriage], having taken Your hand.
> [*Devyaparādhakṣamāpanastotram* 7]

The meaning of these sayings is that the transcendental, ineluctable Absolute is inoperative without *śakti*, and He is deprived of prosperity, power to control and the other characteristics.

> The śaktis inherent in all things are objects of cognition beyond the range of imagination.
> Therefore, from that *brahman* emerged every manifestation, the powers of the existence.

Words[320] like these describe countless forms of *śakti*; *śakti* and the possessor of *śakti* (*śaktimān*) remain connected and inseparable. Devotees say that the greatness of the Goddess is infinite, and that whatever can be said [about Her] is not limited by any complete enumeration of Her qualities, but rather by the incapability or exhaustion on the part of Her devotee, and it is due to these secondary factors that the hymn of praise comes to an end.

> Words are exhausted in chanting Your glory, not for a limit of [Your] qualities, but due to the fatigue or to the inability to do so.

प्राणियों की अभीष्ट वस्तुओं में रूप, जय, यश और शत्रुपराभव होते हैं, यह सब निश्छलभाव से माता से ही माँगा जाता है-माता ही देती है—

रूपं देहि जयं देहि यशो देहि द्विषो जहि ।

इसीलिये सुरासुर सभी अपने मुकुट-किरीट के रत्नों से माता के चरणपीठ का वन्दन करते हैं ।

सुरासुरशिरोरत्ननिघृष्टचरणेऽम्बिके ।

कृष्ण ने भी भक्तिपूर्वक उन्हीं की स्तुति की—

कृष्णेन संस्तुते देवि शश्वद्भक्त्या तथाम्बिके ।

शाक्ताद्वैत में भगवती

शाक्ताद्वैत की दृष्टि यह है कि अनन्त विश्व का अधिष्ठानभूत शुद्धबोधस्वरूप प्रकाश ही शिवतत्व समझा जाता है । उस प्रकाश में जो विमर्श है, वही शक्ति है । प्रकाश के साथ विचारात्मक शक्ति का अस्तित्व अनिवार्य है । बिना प्रकाश के विमर्श नहीं, और बिना विमर्श के प्रकाश भी नहीं रहता । यद्यपि वेदान्तियों की दृष्टि में बिना विमर्श के भी अनन्त, निर्विकल्प प्रकाश रहता है, परन्तु शाक्ताद्वैतियों की दृष्टि से विमर्श हर समय रहता है । यहाँ तक कि महावाक्यजन्य परब्रह्माकारवृत्ति के उत्पन्न हो जाने पर भी, आवरक अज्ञान के मिट जाने पर भी स्वयं वृत्तिरूप विमर्श बना ही रहता है । वेदान्ती इस वृत्ति को स्वपरविनाशक मानते हैं । परन्तु शाक्ताद्वैती कहते हैं कि अपने आप में ही नाश्य-नाशकभाव सम्भव नहीं है । यदि उस वृत्ति के नाश

Among the living, beauty, victory, fame and the defeat of one's enemies are all desired, and all these should be sought from the Mother, with a mind free from deceit. It is [only] the Mother who gives:

> Give me beauty, give me glory, give me fame, defeat my enemy.
> [*Argalāstotram*]

That is why both gods and demons worship the feet of the Mother, [to the very] gems set in their crowns:

> O you mother, whose feet are massaged by the crest jewels of deities and titans. [*Argalāstotram* 15]

Kṛṣṇa also sang Her praise with full devotion:

> O Goddess, O you Mother, O You who are so exalted with undecaying devotion by Kṛṣṇa. [*Argalāstotram* 19]

Bhagavatī in *śāktadvaita*[321]

Śāktadvaita believes that *śivatattva* [the principle of Śiva] is the substratum of the infinite world, the [divine] light (*prakāśa*) which is of the very nature of pure knowledge (*śuddhabodhasvarūpa*). The reflection (*vimarśa*) in the light (*prakāśa*) is *śakti*. It is absolutely necessary that a power of the nature of reflection (*vicārātmaka śakti*) exists together with this light. *Vimarśa* cannot exist without *prakāśa*, and *prakāśa* also does not exist without *vimarśa*. Although the followers of *Vedānta* believe that even without *vimarśa* there exists an infinite and unqualified *prakāśa*, *śāktādvaita* followers believe that *vimarśa* exists eternally — so much that, even when the mental modification that makes its object the highest Absolute (*parabrahma ākāravṛtti*) is born out of the Great Saying (*mahāvākya*), even then does *vimarśa* itself remain present in a condition of spontaneous mental modification (*svayaṃ vṛttirūpa*), even when the limiting (*āvaraka*) ignorance (*ajñāna*) is eliminated.[322] *Vedānta*[323] followers deny this residual modality, calling it self-destructive (*svapara-vināśaka*), but the *śāktādvaita* followers say that it is not possible for

के लिये दूसरी वृत्ति को उत्पत्ति मानेंगे, तब तो उसके भी नाश के लिये अन्यवृत्ति माननी पडेगी, फिर अनवस्था की प्रसक्ति होगी । अविद्या स्वयं नष्ट होनेवाली है, अत: उससे भी उस वृत्तिरूपा विद्या का नाश नहीं कहा जा सकता । विरोध न होने के कारण विद्याविद्या का सुन्दोपसुन्दन्याय से भी परस्पर नाश्य-नाशकभाव नहीं कहा जा सकता । जो कहा जाता है जैसे कनकरज जल के भीतर भी मिट्टी को नष्ट करके स्वयं नष्ट हो जाता है, वैसे ही विद्यारूपावृत्ति स्वातिरिक्त अविद्यातत्कार्य को नष्ट करके स्वयं भी नष्ट हो जाती है । परन्तु दृष्टान्त में कनकरज का नाश नहीं होता, किन्तु इतर रजों को साथ लेकर कनकरज पानी के नीचे बैठ जाती है, अत: यहाँ भी उक्त दृष्टान्तों से वृत्ति का नाश नहीं कहा जा सकता । यही स्थिति—

विषं विषान्तरं जरयति स्वयमपि जीर्यति,
पय: पयोऽन्तरं जरयति स्वयमपि जीर्यति ।

इत्यादि उक्तियों की भी है अर्थात् वहाँ भी विष या पय नष्ट नहीं होता, किन्तु दूसरे पय या विष की अजीर्णता को नष्ट करके अपने आप भी पच जाता है । अत: इन दृष्टान्तों से भी वृत्ति का नाश नहीं कहा जा सकता । इसलिये वृत्तिरूप विद्या से संलिष्ट होकर ही अनन्तप्रकाशस्वरूप शिव सदा विराजमान रहता है । इसी तरह यह भी विचार उठता है कि अविद्या निवृत्ति क्या है? कोई वस्तु कहीं से निवृत्त होते हुए भी कहीं न कही रहती ही है ।

यदि ध्वंशरूप निवृत्ति मानी जाय, तो भी अपने कारण में उसकी स्थिति माननी पडेगी, क्योंकि घटादि का ध्वंस होने पर भी अपने कारण कपाल, चूर्ण आदि कहीं-न-कहीं, किसी-न-किसी रूप में उनकी स्थिति माननी ही पड़ती है । यही स्थिति लयरूपानिवृत्ति की

anything to destroy itself, so the destroyer-destroyed duality is not possible. If we assume the [necessity for the] existence of one mental modification (*vṛtti*) to destroy a previous one, then we will have to assume the existence of yet another *vṛtti* to destroy that one, resulting in a regressus ad infinitum (*anavasthā kī prasakti*). *Avidyā* is self-destructive by nature, hence we cannot say that it destroys the *vidyā* in a form of mental modification. Since there is no negation, it also cannot be said that *vidyā* and *avidyā* are in a destroyer-destroyed relationship, as [according to the rule of] *sundopasundanyāya.*[324] It is said that, just as gold dust destroys clay inside water, and is then also itself destroyed, so similarly does the *vṛtti* in the form of *vidyā* destroys *avidyā* — which is other than it [in degree of reality] (*svātirikta*), and then too is it itself destroyed. However, in actual fact, gold dust is not destroyed [during this process], but rather it settles at the bottom of the water, taking the other particles with it; hence these examples do not prove that *vṛtti* gets destroyed. Similarly:

> A poison helps digest another poison and is itself digested,
> So milk helps digest another milk and is itself digested.

These words also say that poison is not destroyed, but rather it destroys the indigestibility of another poison and then itself gets digested. Therefore, these examples cannot prove the destruction of *vṛtti*; Śiva, who is of the form of endless light, therefore remains forever present only by being affiliated with *vidyā*, which exists in the form of *vṛtti*. Similarly, one wonders how *avidyā* is eradicated, because an object remains in existence somewhere or another, even upon being eradicated somewhere else.

If withdrawal (*nivṛtti*) be considered to be the form of eradication, then one will have to believe that an object withdraws into its material cause and remains in 'existence' there, for one has to admit that even when a clay pot shatters, it still 'remains' in the form of clay dust, and the pot's parts, or what have you. The same applies to the withdrawal that takes place in the form of dissolution (*layarūpānivṛtti*). If withdrawal (*nivṛtti*) is said to be totally devoid of its own self-nature

भी है। यदि निवृत्ति को सर्वथा निःस्वरूप कहें, तो उसके लिये प्रयत्न नहीं हो सकता। सही कहें, तब तो उसी रूप से शक्ति की स्थिति रह सकती है। अनिर्वचनीय कहें, तो उसकी भी ज्ञाननिवर्त्यता कहनी पड़ेगी, अतएव कुछ आचार्यों ने पञ्चम-प्रकारा अविद्या-निवृत्ति मानी है तथा उस रूप से भी विमर्शरूपा शक्ति का अस्तित्व रहता ही है। हाँ, उस समय अन्तर्मुख होकर शिवस्वरूप से ही शक्ति स्थित रहती है—

मुक्तावन्तर्मुखैव त्वं भुवनेश्वरि तिष्ठसि (शक्तिदर्शन)

इसीलिये शक्ति को नित्य कहा जाता है—

नित्यैव सा जगद्धात्री।

नहि द्रष्टुर्दृष्टेर्विपरिलोपो विद्यते

इस वचन से वृत्तिरूप दृष्टि को नित्य समझा जाता है। परन्तु वेदान्ती द्रष्टा की स्वरूपभूता दृष्टि को नित्य कहते हैं।

शिवपरात्पर

विमर्श, प्रकाशशक्ति का शिव में प्रवेश होने से बिन्दु, स्त्रीतत्व नाद की उत्पत्ति हुई। जब दूध-पानी की तरह दोनों एक हो गये, तब संयुक्तबिन्दु हुए। वही अर्धनारीश्वर हुए। इनकी परस्पर आसक्ति ही काम है। श्वेतबिन्दु पुंस्त्व का, रक्तबिन्दु स्त्रीत्व का परिचायक है। तीनों जब मिलते हैं, तब कामकला की उत्पत्ति होती है। मूल बिन्दु, नाद और श्वेत तथा रक्त बिन्दु, इन चारों के मिलने से सृष्टि होती है। किसी के मत में नाद के साथ अर्द्धकला भी हुई।

(*niḥsvarūpa*), then there can be no effort to that end. To tell the truth, it is [only] in that very form [that is, the 'formless' form] in which *śakti* can exist. If we call it 'indescribable' then we will have to admit to the eradication of [this] knowledge about it; for this some *ācāryas* have declared that the eradication of *avidyā* is of the fifth manner,[325] and in that way also does Śakti remains in existence as *vimarśa*. Of course, at that time Śakti remains in existence only through the form of Śiva, having become introverted:

> You, O Bhuvaneśvarī, withdrawn dwell in liberation.
> (*Śaktidarśana*)

That is why Śakti is said to be eternal (*nitya*):

> That sustainer of the Universe is eternal.

> There is no loss of the sight of the seer.
> [*Bṛhadāraṇyaka Upaniṣad* IV.3.23]

By this statement, the knowledge as a mental modification (*vṛttirūpa*) is believed to be eternal. But *Vedānta* followers say that knowledge is [as] eternal as the essential nature (*svarūpabhūtā*) of the knower.

Even beyond the Supreme Śiva (Śivaparātpara)

When [326] *vimarśa* — the *śakti* of *prakāśa*— enters Śiva, then arises the point (*bindu*) as well as the feminine element (*strītattva*) [known as] *nāda* (resonance). When they become as one, like milk [in] water, then *saṃyuktabindu* [the compound *bindu*] arises, and becomes Ardhnāriśvara. Their mutual attraction is desire (*kāma*). The [327] white point (*śvetabindu*) indicates masculinity and the red point (*raktabindu*) denotes feminity. When all three unite [that is, these two points with *nāda*], then arises *kāmakalā* ('the wiles of Kāma'). Creation takes place when all four unite, the root (*mūla*) *bindu*, *nāda*, the white and red points [together]. Some believe that the half-division (*arddhakalā*) also came into being along with *nāda*. *Saṃyuktabindu*

कामकलादेवी का संयुक्तबिन्दु वदन है, अग्नि और चन्द्र वक्ष:स्थल है, अर्धकला जननेन्द्रिय है, 'अ' शिव का प्रतीक है, 'इ' शक्ति का प्रतीक है। यह त्रिपुरसुन्दरी 'अहं' से व्याप्त है। सम्पूर्ण सृष्टि व्यक्तित्व और अहं से पूर्ण है। सहस्रार के चन्द्रगर्भ से स्रवित आसव को पान कर ज्ञानकृपाण से काम, क्रोध, लोभ मोह आदि आसुर पशुओं को मारकर, वञ्चना, पिशुनता, ईर्ष्या मछलियों को पकाकर, आशा, कामना, निन्दा, मुद्रा को धारण कर, मेरुदण्डाश्रिता रमणियों में रमण कर सामरस्य की प्राप्ति होती है। कुछ लोग चमकार का यही रहस्य बतलाते हैं।

शिवशक्ति संयोग ही नाद है—

यदयमनुत्तरमूर्तिर्निजेच्छया विश्वमिदं स्रष्टुम्।
पस्पन्दे सस्पन्दः प्रथमः शिवतत्त्वमुच्यते तज्ज्ञैः॥

शिवसंश्लिष्ट शक्ति विश्व का बीज है। अहं प्रकाश में शिव निश्चेष्ट, शक्ति सक्रिया रहती है, यही काली की विपरीत रति है। विमर्शात्मिका शक्ति जब शिव में लीन होती है, तब उन्मना अवस्था होती है। उसके विकसित होने पर समान अवस्था होती है।

सच्चिदानन्दविभवात्सङ्कल्पात्परमेश्वरात्।
आसीच्छक्तिस्ततो नादो नादाद्बिन्दुसमुद्भवः॥

विभव सकल से शक्ति, उससे नाद, उससे बिन्दु का प्राकट्य होता है। नाद में जो क्रिया शक्ति है बिन्दु की अहंनिमेषा है। सृष्टि

is the face of the goddess Kāmakalā; Fire and the Moon are Her breasts, the *ardhakalā* is Her reproductive organ, the '*A*' symbolizes Śiva and '*I*' symbolizes Śakti. This Goddess, Tripurasundarī, is full of self-hood (*ahaṃ*). The whole of creation is full of individuality and ego. By [328] drinking the distillate (*āsava*) flowing down from the lunar womb (*candragarbha*) of the *sahasrāra* [the thousand-petalled lotus at the back of the head], by using the sword of knowledge (*jñāna-kṛpāṇa*) to destroy the demonic beasts of lust, anger, greed, attachment and the like, by cooking the 'fish' of deception, treachery and envy, and by adopting the *mudrās* of hope, desire, and censure, and by dallying with (*ramaṇa*) with the beautiful young women residing in the spinal column, one attains equanimity. Some people say this to be the secret of the *pāñcamakāra* [the five objects revered in *Tantra* for accomplishment or liberation].

Nāda [329] (resonance) is but the union of Śiva and Śakti:

> This supreme form in order to manifest all this universe
> Vibrated out of His own will. The knowers of this say that the first vibrating entity is *śivatattva*.

Śakti joined with Śiva is the seed of this world. In the light of the ego (*ahaṃ prakāśa*), Śiva remains inactive and Śakti, active. This is the meaning of the upside-down ('woman-on-top') sexual union (*viparītarati*) of Kālī. When Śakti — whose nature is reflection (*vimarśātmikā śakti*) — becomes immersed in Śiva, then the supra-conscious state (*unmanā*) comes into being. When this state is further refined, then one attains the state of equanimity (*samāna*):

> Śakti arose from the Supreme Lord, from the majesty of the Being, Knowledge and Bliss natured, from His intention; from Her [arose] the supreme resonance; from the resonance there was the arisal of the point (*bindu*).

Śakti [330] appears from the majesty of the totality (*vibhava sakala*), and from it comes *nāda*; from it appears the *bindu*. Within the *nāda* is the power of action (*kriyā śakti*); *bindu* is the twinkling of the

की अन्तिम अवस्था है 'इदं' । 'अहं' महाप्रलय की पूर्व अवस्था है और शक्ति की उच्छूनावस्था घनीभाव है। ज्ञान प्रधानाशक्ति क्रियारूपेण रज:प्रधाना बिन्दुतत्व से तम:प्रधाना रहती है। व्यवहार में शक्तिमान् से शक्ति का आदर अधिक है। बुद्धि बिना बुद्धिमान् का, बल बिना बलवान् का, शिल्पशक्ति बिना शिल्पी का कुछ भी मूल्य नहीं रहता। मिठास बिना मिश्री का, सौगन्ध बिना पुष्प का, सौन्दर्य बिना सुन्दरी का, लज्जा बिना कुलाङ्गना का कुछ भी महत्व नहीं रह जाता। शाक्ताद्वैतदृष्टि से शक्ति शिवस्वरूप ही है, सच्चिदानन्द में चिद्भाव विमर्श है, सत् का भाव शिव है।

रुद्रहीनं विष्णुहीनं न वदन्ति जनाः किल,
शक्तिहीनं यथा सर्वे प्रवदन्ति नराधमम्।

अर्थात् कोई भी प्राणी रुद्रहीन, विष्णुहीन होने शोचनीय नहीं होता, किन्तु शक्तिहीन होने से ही शोचनीय होता है।

नायमात्मा बलहीनेन लभ्यः।

बलहीन प्राणी को अपनी आत्मा का भी उपलम्भ नहीं हो सकता—

गिरामाहुर्देवीं द्रुहिणगृहिणीमागमविदो
हरेः पत्नीं पद्मां हरसहचरीमद्रितनयाम्।
तुरीया कापि त्वं दुरधिगमनिःसीममहिमा
महामाया विश्वं भ्रमयसि परब्रह्ममहिषि॥

परब्रह्म महिषीरूप भगवती को आचार्यों ने तुरीया चिच्छक्तिरूपा ही बतलाया है।

ego (*ahaṃnimeṣā*). '*Idaṃ*' (that-ness) is the final stage of creation. '*Ahaṃ*' is the stage prior to the great dissolution (*mahāpralaya*), and the zenith of Śakti indistinct condition (*ghanībhāva*). The *śakti* in which predominates knowledge remains dominated by *tamas*, due to *bindu*, which is dominated by *rajas* in form of action. In daily practice we respect the power more than the powerful. An intelligent person without intelligence, a strong person devoid of strength, a sculptor without the ability to carve, none of these have any value. Similarly,[331] sugar without sweetness, flower without fragrance, a beautiful woman without her beauty and a good family woman without any sense of shame also lose their importance. By the viewpoint of *śāktādvaita*, Śakti is of the form of Śiva. In *saccidānanda*, the *cit* (Consciousness) is *vimarśa* and the *sat* (Being) is Śiva.

> People do not consider someone deprived of Rudra or Viṣṇu to be a miserable man, but all consider Him so if He is without Śakti.

That is, "No living being becomes worthy of pity by being devoid of Viṣṇu or Rudra, but does become so by being devoid of Śakti."

> This self cannot be grasped by one without strength.
> [*Muṇḍaka Upaniṣad* III.2.4]

That is, "A weak person cannot even avail of his own soul."

> O Queen, consort of the supreme *brahman*! Those who know the Scriptures call that Goddess of the Word the house-wife of Brahmā, call Padmā the consort of Hari and the daughter of the Mountains as the companion of Hara. You, indescribable fourth, the great Māyā, with Your own unfathomable, limitless glory, You delude the universe. [*Saundarya Laharī* 97]

Ācāryas have said that the queen of the Transcendant Absolute — Bhagavatī — is none other than embodied *turīya* [the fourth state].

शङ्करः पुरुषाः सर्वे स्त्रियः सर्वा महेश्वरी ।
विषयी भगवानीशो विषयः परमेश्वरी ॥
मन्ता स एव विश्वात्मा मन्तव्यं तु महेश्वरी ।
आकाशः शङ्करो देवः पृथिवी शङ्करप्रिया ॥

समुद्र-वेल, वृक्ष-लता, शब्द-अर्थ, पदार्थ-शक्ति, पुं-स्त्री, इज्ञ-इज्या, क्रियाफलभुक्, गुण-व्यक्तिव्यञ्जकतारूप, प्रथमनीति-जय बोध-बुद्धि, धर्म-सत्क्रिया, सन्तोष-तुष्टि इच्छा-काम, यज्ञ-दक्षिणा, आज्याहुति-पुरोडाश, काष्ठा-निमेष, मुहूर्त्त-कला, ज्योत्स्ना-प्रदीप, रात्रि-दिन, ध्वज-पताका, तृष्णा-लोभ, रति-राग, उपर्युक्त भेदों से उसी तत्व का अनेकधा प्राकट्य होता है । शक्तिशब्द से बहुत से लोग केवल माया, अविद्या आदि बहिरङ्ग शक्तियों को ही समझते हैं । परन्तु भगवान् की स्वरूपभूता आह्लादिनी शक्ति, जीवभूता पराप्रकृति आदि भी शक्ति शब्द से व्यवहृत होते हैं । जैसे सिता, द्राक्षा, मधु आदि में मधुरिमा उनका परमान्तरङ्ग स्वरूप ही है, वैसे ही परमानन्दरसामृतसार समुद्र भगवान् की परमान्तरङ्ग स्वरूपभूता शक्ति ही भगवती है—

विष्णुशक्तिः परा प्रोक्ता क्षेत्रज्ञाख्या तथा परा ।
अविद्या कर्मसंज्ञान्या तृतीया शक्तिरिष्यते ॥

यहाँ पर विष्णु और क्षेत्रज्ञ को भी शक्ति ही कहा गया है । यद्यपि शक्तियाँ अनेक हैं, तथापि आनन्दाश्रित आह्लादिनी, चेतनांशाश्रित संवित्, सदंशाश्रित सन्धिनी-शक्ति होती है । क्षेत्रज्ञ तटस्था शक्ति है, माया बहिरङ्गा शक्ति मानी जाती है । तत्वविद् लोग कहते हैं कि जैसे पुष्प का सौगन्ध सम्यक् रूप से तब अनुभूत हो सकता है, जब पुष्प

> All[332] men are Śaṅkara, all women the Goddess;
> The glorious Lord is the knower (*viṣayin*), the supreme Goddess the known object (*viṣaya*).[333]
> That Self of the universe is the thinker and Maheśvarī the object to be thought;
> The divinity Śaṅkara is the sky and the beloved of Śaṅkara, the earth.

It is that element that appears in numerous ways — as the ocean to waves, as a tree to its creepers, as a word to meaning, as a substance to power, as a man to a woman, as an action to its fruit [reward], as a quality to its capacity to describe the individual [for whom it is pradicated], as the first branch of diplomatic science to the victory, as awareness to intelligence, as righteousness to a pious deed, as satisfaction to satiation, as wish to desire, as the fire sacrifice is to the offerings (*dakṣiṇā*), as a minute to a second, as fire to a light, as day to night, as craving to greed, as sex to passion, and so on and so forth. Many people believe *śakti* only to mean *māyā* or *avidyā*, or the external *śaktis*. But the delightful power is the essential nature of the Lord, and the Supreme *Prakṛti* is the individual self; these too are intended by the word '*śakti*'. Just as sweetness is the absolutely inner nature of things like white sugar, grapes and honey, similarly the supremely intimate essential nature who is the Śakti of God, the veritable ocean of nectar of the supreme bliss, is none other than Bhagavatī:

> The[334] Śakti of Viṣṇu is called supreme, non-supreme is called the knower of the field, an another is ignorance denominated action, intended as the third śakti.

Here Viṣṇu and *kṣetrajña* ('the knower of the field') have also been called *śakti*. There are numerous *śaktis*. The delightful power (*āhlādinī śakti*) dwells in Bliss, the Consciousness is basen on a part of knowledge, and the uniting power (*sandhinī śakti*) is supported by a part of the Being. *Kṣetrajña* is a neutral *śakti*, and *māyā* is believed to be an external *śakti*. People who know about the essence of things

को घ्राणशक्ति हो। अन्य लोगों को तो व्यवधान के साथ किञ्चिन्मात्र ही गन्ध का अनुभव होता है। उसी तरह भगवती के सुन्दर स्वरूप का सम्यक् अनुभव परम शिव को ही प्राप्त होता है; वह अन्य दृष्टि का विषय ही नहीं—

घृतक्षीरद्राक्षामधुमधुरिमाकैरपिपदै-
र्विशिष्यानाख्येयो भवति रसनामात्रविषयः।
तथा ते सौन्दर्यं परमशिवदृङ्मात्रविषया-
कथङ्कारं ब्रूमः सकलनिगमागोचरगुणे॥

अर्थात् वस्तुतः निर्गुणा सत्या सनातनी सर्वस्वरूपा भगवती ही भक्तानुग्रहार्थ सगुण होकर प्रकट होती है। वैसे तो भगवती के अनन्त स्वरूप हैं, विशेषतः शैलपुत्री, ब्रह्मचारिणी, चन्द्रघण्टा, कूष्माण्डा, स्कन्दमाता, कात्यायनी, कालरात्रि, महागौरी, सिद्धिदा ये नव स्वरूप प्रधान हैं—

कार्यार्थे सगुणा त्वं च वस्तुतो निर्गुणा स्वयम्।
परब्रह्मस्वरूपा त्वं सत्या नित्या सनातनी॥
सर्वस्वरूपा सर्वेशी सर्वाधारा परात्परा।
सर्वबीजस्वरूपा च सर्वमूला निराश्रया॥
सर्वज्ञा सर्वतोभद्रा सर्वमङ्गलमङ्गला।

वैसे तो अनन्त शक्तियाँ हैं, फिर भी इनके अतिरिक्त और भी कुछ प्रधान शक्तियाँ है, जो पूज्य हैं। व्यवहार और परमार्थ में उनका परम उद्योग है। निवृत्ति, प्रतिष्ठा, विद्या, शान्ति, इंधिका, दीपिका, रोचिका, मोचिका, परासूक्ष्मा, सूक्ष्मामृता, ज्ञानामृता, अमृता, आप्यायिनी, व्यापिनी, व्योमरूपा, तीक्ष्णा, अनन्ता, सृष्टि, ऋद्धि, स्मृति, मेधा, कान्ति, लक्ष्मी, द्युति, स्थिति, सिद्धि, जड़ा, पालिनी, शान्ति, ऐश्वर्या,

say that a flower's fragrance can only be completely experienced if the flower possesses 'smelling-power', and the others experience only a little bit of the flower's fragrance — and that, too, with impediments. Similarly, only the highest Śiva gets to completely experience the beautiful form of Bhagavatī. [That beauty] is not an object of another kind of vision.

> Particularly[335] by those who taste things endowed with sweetness, like clarified butter, milk, grapes and honey, [their sweetness] is inexpressible. This is only an object of taste, so O You, whose quality is not even an object of any of the Scriptures, how we can express Your beauty, which is an object of the eye of the Supreme Śiva? [*Ānandalaharī* 2]

It is the non-qualified, eternally true Bhagavatī, the identity of all things (*sarvasvarūpa*), who appears with attributes to bestow grace upon Her devotees. Of course, She has endless forms, such as Śailaputrī, Brahmacāriṇī, Candraghaṇṭā, Kūsmāṇḍā, Skandamātā, Kātyāyanī, Kālarātri, Mahāgaurī, and Siddhidā[336] — these nine forms are the most important.

> You are qualified only in order to perform some activity, but in reality You are the unqualified itself. You are of the nature of the Absolute *brahman*, true, eternal and invariable, of the nature of all, ruler of the universe, substratum of everything, even beyond the supreme, the cause of everything itself, the root of everything, without any support, omniscient, by every side beneficient, who is of the selfsame auspiciousness in all the auspicious things.

There[337] are infinite numbers of *śaktis*, yet there are also a few other major forms of *śakti* that are venerable. They are extensively taken recourse to, [both] in matters of day-to-day living (*vyavahāra*) and for liberation.

Bhagavatī is the overlord of the infinite *śaktis*: Nivṛtti, Pratiṣṭhā, Vidyā, Śānti, Indhikā, Dīpikā, Rocikā, Mocikā, Purā, Sūkṣmā,

रति, कामिका, वरदा, आह्लादिनी, प्रीति, दीर्घा, रौद्री, निद्रा, तन्द्रा, क्षुधा, क्रोधिनी, पुष्टि, तुष्टि, धृति, चन्द्रिका आदि सृष्टि चिद्घनमहासमुद्र की अनन्त शक्तिस्वामिनी ही भगवती है ।

'अगस्त्यसंहिता' के वचनानुसार भगवान् शिव ने श्रीराम के प्रत्यक्ष साक्षात् करने के लिये बड़ी तपस्या और आराधना की । भगवान् राम ने प्रसन्न होकर कहा कि यदि मेरा तत्व जानना चाहते हो तो मेरी आह्लादिनी पराशक्ति की आराधना करो, उसके बिना मेरी स्थिति नहीं होती—

आह्लादिनीं परा शक्तिं स्तूयाः सात्वतसंमताम् ।
सदाराध्यस्तदा रामस्तदधीनस्तया विना ।
तिष्ठामि न क्षणं शंभो जीवनं परमं मम ॥

यह सुनकर श्री शिवजी ने भगवान् की आराधना की । भगवती ने कृपा कर उन्हें दर्शन दिया । उनके अद्भुत रूप को देखकर उन्होंने अति भक्ति से दिव्य स्तुति की—

वन्दे विदेहतनयापदपुण्डरीकं
कैशोरसौरभसमाहृतयोगिचित्तम् ।
हन्तुं त्रितापमनिशं मुनिहंससेव्यं
सन्मानसालिपरिपीतपरागपुञ्जम् ॥

करुणा तो शिव, विष्णु आदि सभी देवों में होती है, परन्तु परमकल्याणमयी, करुणामयी तो श्री अम्बा ही है । कुपुत्र पर भी अम्बा की करुणा ही रहती है—

कुपुत्रो जायेत क्वचिदपि कुमाता न भवति ॥

शत्रु से निष्ठुरतापूर्वक युद्ध करते हुए माँ के हृदय में शत्रुओं पर कृपा भी रहती है । उनको बाणों से पवित्र करके दिव्यलोक में भेजती

Sūkṣmāmṛtā, Jñānāmṛtā, Amṛtā, Āpyāyinī, Vyāpinī, Vyomarūpā, Tikṣṇā, Anantā, Sṛṣṭi, Ṛddhi, Smṛti, Meghā, Kānti, Lakṣmī, Dyuti, Sthiti, Siddhi, Jaḍā, Pālinī, Aiśvaryā, Rati, Kāmikā, Vardā, Āhlādinī, Prīti, Durgā, Raudrī, Nidrā, Tandrā, Kṣudhā, Krodhinī, Puṣṭi, Tuṣṭi, Dhṛti, Chandrikā, and so on.

According[338] to the words of the *Agastyasaṃhitā*, Lord Śiva performed much penance and worship to make the Lord Rāma appear before Him in person. Lord Rāma was pleased, and said: "If You wish to know My *tattva* (essence), then worship my Supreme Śakti who is the giver of delight (*āhlādinī*); I have no existence without Her":

> O Śambhu, you should exalt the giver of delight, the Supreme Śakti, who is celebrated by the devotees of Viṣṇu, She is always praiseworthy, and Rāma is dependent on Her. I cannot stay without Her even for a moment; She is My supreme existence.

Hearing this, Lord Śiva worshipped Bhagavatī. Out of Her grace, She appeared before Him. Seeing Her amazing beauty, He sang Her praise with great devotion:

> I bow down to the lotus feet of the daughter of Videha, by whose youth and fragrance the mind of the yogins is enraptured, always served by the sages as swans, in order to eradicate the three kind of pains; She is the mass of pollen constantly drunk by the bees who are the saints.

Every[339] god has compassion, including Śiva and Viṣṇu; but only Ambā is supremely compassionate and welfare-bestowing by nature. Her compassion even goes to Her unworthy sons:

> An unworthy son can take birth, but nowhere is there an unworthy mother. [*Devyaparādhakṣpanastotram* 3, 4]

Even while ruthlessly battling Her enemies, in Her heart, the Mother feels grace even for Her foes. She sends them to divine worlds by purifying them with Her arrows. In fact, all are the Mother's children; who is Her enemy?

हैं । वास्तव में सब माँ के पुत्र हैं, शत्रु कौन है?—

चित्ते कृपा समरनिष्ठुरता च दृष्टा ।

अत्याचारी रावण को भी माँ सीता ने कल्याणार्थ प्रभुशरणागति का ही उपदेश किया है । अत्याचारी के अत्याचार पर ध्यान न देकर उसको सत्यपथ पर ही लाने का प्रयत्न माँ की ओर से होना उचित है । माँ ने अपने तप से हनुमान् के लिये अग्नि को शीत कर दिया— "**शीतो भव हनूमतः ।**" जो अग्नि को शीत कर सकती है, वह रावण को क्या भस्म नहीं कर सकती है? अवश्य कर सकती है । परन्तु उसने स्वयं कहा है—

असन्देशात्तु रामस्य तपसश्चानुपालनात् ।
न त्वां कुर्मि दशग्रीव भस्म भस्मार्हतेजसा ॥

माता कहती है— श्रीराम का सन्देश न होने से तथा तपस्यानाश के भय से, हे दशग्रीव, मैं अपने उग्र तेज से तुझे भस्म नहीं करती हूँ । वही परम दयामयी है ।

लङ्का-विजय के पश्चात् हनुमान् ने जानकी को विजय का शुभ सन्देश सुनाया और माता को सतानेवाली राक्षसियों को दण्ड देने की आज्ञा चाही, परन्तु माँ ने कहा— "**कार्यं कारुण्यमार्येण न कश्चिन्नापराध्यति ।**" बेटा, सज्जनों को करुणा करनी चाहिये, अपराध तो सबसे ही होता रहता है । जब ये रावण के वश में थीं, तब सताती थीं । अब यह सब कुछ नहीं सता रही हैं, फिर भी इनपर कृपा करनी चाहिये—

मातर्मैथिलि राक्षसीस्त्वयि तदैवार्द्रापराधास्त्वया
रक्षन्त्या पवनात्मजाल्लघुतरा रामस्य गोष्ठी कृता ।
काकं तञ्च विभीषणं शरणमित्युक्ति क्षमौ रक्षतः
सा नः सान्द्रमहागसः सुखयतु क्षान्तिस्तवाकस्मिकी ॥

> Even if is seen the harshness in battle, in the mind there is mercy.

Mother Sītā even preached to Her oppressor Rāvaṇa to take shelter in the Lord for his own benefit. It is only appropriate that a mother should try to bring an oppressor to the path of rightousness and to pay no heed to his oppressive acts. Through Her power of penance (*tapas*), the Mother turned the fire cool for Hanumān — "be cool for Hanumān." She who can turn fire cool, could She not turn Rāvaṇa to ash? Surely She could. But She Herself said:

> O ten-headed one, I don't turn you to ash with my destructive power, because I have not the permission of Rāma, and to safeguard My austerity.

The Mother says: "Because Śrī Rāma has not sent any message for that reason, I shall therefore not turn you into ashes, O Daśagriva (Rāvaṇa), out of fear that I should destroy my *tapas*." She alone is supremely compassionate.

After Rāma's victory over Laṅkā, Hanumān told Jānakī (Sītā) the good news of victory, and begged Her permission to punish the demonesses who had tormented Her, but the Mother said:

> One noble person has always to be compassionate; there is no person that never sins.

That is, "Son, noble people should practice compassion; everybody sins from time to time. They tormented Me when they were controlled by Rāvaṇa; now they are not, so we should have mercy upon them."

> O[340] Mother, O Maithilī (Mithilā dweller) You made insignificant the assembly of Rāma, by protecting from the Son of the Wind the demonesses who use to torment You incessantly.
> In fact, with the words '[give us] refuge', He [Rāma] protected the crow and Vibhīṣaṇa; may Your mercy without cause grant us forgiveness, for our vehement, enormous offenses.

कोई भक्त कहता है— हे माता, आपने सदा अपराधवाली राक्षसियों की हनुमान् से रक्षा करके श्रीरामगोष्ठी छोटी कर दी, क्योंकि उन्होंने तो जयन्त और विभीषण की रक्षा शरणागत होने पर की थी, परन्तु आपने तो शरण होने की अपेक्षा बिना ही उनका रक्षण किया—

पितेव त्वत्प्रेयाञ्जननि परिपूर्णागसि जने
हितस्त्रोतोवृत्त्या भवति च कदाचित्कलुषधीः ।
किमेतन्निर्दोषः क इह जगतीति त्वमुचितै-
रुपायैर्विस्मार्य स्वजनयसि माता तदसि नः ॥'

भगवान् भी जब जीवपर कभी नाराज होते हैं, तब माता उन जीवों के अनुकूल करती हैं । भक्त माँ से कहता है— हे माँ! जब आपके स्वामी भगवान् जीवों पर हितबुद्ध्या कुपित होते हैं, तब आप "यह क्या? संसार में निर्दोष कौन है?" ऐसा कहकर समुचित उपायों से पिता को अनुकूल बनाती हैं, इसीलिये कि आप ही सच्ची माँ हो ।

नित्यं विश्वं वशयति हरिर्निग्रहानुग्रहाभ्या-
माद्ये शक्तिं विघटयति ते हन्त कारुण्यपूरः ।

भगवान् श्रीहरि जगत् को अपने वश में रखते हैं परन्तु आपकी करुणा हरि की निग्रहादि शक्तियों को भी स्वाधीन रखती है । भगवती ही सबसे अन्तर और महत्वपूर्ण हैं, इसीलिये भक्त कहते हैं—

त्वय्येवाश्रयते दया रघुपते देवस्य सत्यं यतो
वैदेहि त्वदसन्निधौ भगवता वाली निरामाहतः ।
नित्ये कापि वधूर्वधं तव तु सान्निध्ये त्वदङ्गव्यथा
कुर्वाणोऽप्यभितः पतन्नशरणः काको विवेकोज्झितः ॥

हे वैदेहि ! आपके सान्निध्य में ही रघुनाथजी की दया व्यक्त होती

Once, a devotee said: "O Mother, You surpass the status of Śrī Rāma by protecting from Hanumān the demonesses, who always offended; [while] He [Lord Rāma] had only protected Vibhiṣaṇa and Jayanta when they sought refuge in Him, you protected [the demonesses] even without them expecting any protection from You."

> O Mother, like a father with a benevolent intention Your beloved sometimes becames angry on some person full of offenses, but You say: "What is this? In this world who is without blame?" So with the right means, You, having made Him forget all, make favourable Him, therefore You are our Mother.

When God grows angry at some living being, the Mother then changes His mind to favour that being. The devotee says to the Mother: "O Mother! When Your Lord grows angry at living beings for their own good, then You say: 'What's this? Who in this world is blameless?' You use various means to change his mind in favour [of the erring beings], for this, You are a true Mother."

> Always Hari, through the controlling power and the power of grace rules over the universe, but, O primeval One, Yours flood of mercy also annihilates that power.

Lord Hari (Viṣṇu) keeps the world under His control, but Your compassion keeps even the powers of Hari under control. It is only Bhagavatī who is the most important and intimate, that is why the devotees say:

"O [341] Vaidehi (daughter of Videha)! The compassion of Raghunātha (Rāma) rests on Your presence; in Your absence, the innocent Bālī was killed, as was killed the wife of the monkey (Tāḍakā). But when Rāma was in Your company, then even the crow (Jayanta) who hurt You, being refugeless, falling down, who had abandoned discrimination." The devotee says to Mother Lakṣmi:

> Lord Kṛṣṇa is resplendent in the hearts of the possessors of a body: O Devi, You fill this heart as well; O Padmā, the

है, आपका सन्निधान न रहने से निरपराध बाली मारा गया और ताड़का मारी गयी। परन्तु आपका सान्निध्य रहने पर तो आपके अङ्ग में व्यथा पहुँचानेवाला जयन्त भी अशरण होकर गिरते हुए बचा लिया गया। भक्त माँ लक्ष्मी से कहता है—

गौरश्चकास्ति हृदयेषु शरीरभाजां
तस्यापि देवि हृदयं त्वमनु प्रविष्टा।
पद्मे तवापि हृदये प्रथते दयेयं
त्वामेव जाग्रदखिलातिशयां श्रयामः॥

सम्पूर्ण प्राणियों के हृदय में भगवान् कृष्ण विराजमान् हैं। हे माँ! उनके हृदय में भी आप प्रविष्ट हैं और आपके हृदय में भी दया विराजमान है, अतः आप ही अखिलातिशया हैं, हम आपका ही आश्रयण करते हैं। इन बातों से भलीभाँति सिद्ध हो जाता है कि ब्रह्म, परमात्मा, शक्ति, गौरी, लक्ष्मी,सीता, राधा, करुणा, दया आदि रूप से ही भगवती की ही आराधना होती है। ब्रह्मविद्या की महिमा सर्वत्र स्फुट है, उसके बिना प्राणियों की अन्तरात्मा होने पर भी, परमानन्दरूप होने पर भी, अकिञ्चितकर-सा बना रहता है। जो प्राणी ब्रह्मविद्या बिना कीटादि नगण्य जन्तु बना रहता है, वही ब्रह्मविद्या की कृपा से ब्रह्म हो जाता है। वह भी भगवती ही हैं। भक्ति की भी महिमा प्रख्यात है। भक्ति के ही सम्बन्ध से भक्त भगवान् को अपने वश में कर लेता है। वह भक्ति भी भगवती ही हैं। शक्ति, भक्ति ब्रह्मविद्या के अतिरिक्त परमानन्दसुधासमुद्र परब्रह्म की मधुरिमा भी भगवती ही है।

भावुकों की भावना है कि आनन्दरससारसरोवरसमुद्भूतपङ्कज व्रज है, पङ्कज के केसर व्रजाङ्गनाएँ हैं, मकरन्द कृष्ण है, मकरन्द का माधुर्य्य, मिठास, सौगन्ध्य आदि राधिका हैं। यही दृष्टि सीता, गौरी आदि में समझनी चाहिये। इस दृष्टि से भगवती का स्वरूप ही सर्वान्तरङ्ग और सर्वोत्कृष्ट रहता है।

> compassion also dwells in Your heart, we take refuge only in You, the excellence of the whole waking state.[342]

"Lord Kṛṣṇa is within the heart of every living being, O Mother! You reside in His heart, and compassion is [also] in Your heart, You, too, are the excellence in all; we seek shelter only with You." Such statements amply prove that Bhagavatī is worshipped as *brahman*, *paramātman*, Śakti, Gaurī, Lakṣmī, Sītā, Rādhā, Karuṇā (compassion), Dayā (mercy) and so on. The greatness of the Absolute Knowledge (*brahmavidyā*) is clear everywhere; without it, despite being the innermost Self of all the living beings, and though they are of the form of the Supreme Bliss (*paramānanda*), they remain confused. The same living being that remains a trivial insect, animal or what have you, by the grace of *brahmavidyā*, becomes the Absolute (*brahman*). This too is none other than Bhagavatī. The greatness of devotion is well known. It is only through the relationship established through devotion that a devotee can bring God under his control; that devotion, too, is only Bhagavatī. The sweetness of the all-transcending Supreme Absolute (*parabrahman*) — a veritable ocean of supreme bliss — is also none other than Bhagavatī, in addition to being Śakti, *bhakti* (devotion) and *brahmavidyā*.

Enraptured devotees think Vraja [the place where Kṛṣṇa lived] to be a pond-lotus, the pistils of the lotus to be beautiful women of the Vraja, the honey is Kṛṣṇa and Rādhā is the sweetness, the deliciousness, the fragrance of this honey. The same point of view should be held in the case of Sītā, Gaurī and so on. From this point of view, the form of Bhagavatī alone stands as the most intimate and the highest of all.

The wife of *brahman* (Brahmajāyā)

In[343] numerous places, Bhagavatī has been said to be the pleasure-giving wife of the Supreme Absolute Reality (*paramātman*):

> The unqualified Supreme Self remains Your support; You are, O Bhuvaneśvarī, His joy-giving wife.

ब्रह्मजाया

अनेक स्थानों में भगवती को परमात्मा की भोगदा भार्या बतलाया गया है ।

निर्गुणः परमात्मा तु त्वदाश्रयतया स्थितः ।
तस्य भट्टारिकासि त्वं भुवनेश्वरि भोगदा ॥

निर्गुण परमात्मा ही भगवती के आश्रयरूप से स्थित हैं, भगवती उसकी भोगदा भट्टारिका है, अतएव वही भुवनेश्वरी हैं । जीव, ईश्वर आदि अन्यान्य सभी वस्तुएँ भगवती की ही सन्तान हैं—

मायाख्यायाः कामधेनोर्वत्सौ जीवेश्वरावुभौ ।

(शक्तिसत्वदर्शिनी)

जैसे वह्नि और उसकी दाहिका शक्ति का नित्य तादात्म्य सम्बन्ध है, वैसे ही परमात्मा और उसकी शक्ति का तादात्म्य सम्बन्ध है—

तादात्म्यमनयोर्नित्यं वह्निदाहकयोरिव ।

भगवती की ब्रह्मरूपता

केवल शक्तिरूप से ही नहीं, किन्तु ब्रह्मरूप से भी अनेक स्थलों में उसी का प्रतिपादन मिलता है ।

अचिन्त्यामिताकारशक्तिस्वरूपा
प्रतिव्यक्त्यधिष्ठानसत्तैकमूर्तिः ।
गुणातीतनिर्द्वन्द्वबोधैकगम्या
त्वमेका परब्रह्मरूपेण.......... ॥

अचिन्त्य अमित आकारों की मूलभूता सत्तास्वरूपा भी वही है, वही गुणातीत है । निर्विकल्पबोध से ही स्वप्रकाशरूपेण भगवती की

It[344] is the non-qualified (*nirguṇa*) Absolute Self who is situated as the refuge of Bhagavatī. Bhagavatī is His pleasure-giving wife, as She alone is Bhuvaneśvarī. *Jīva* (the individual soul), *Īśvara* and the like are all the offspring of Bhagavatī:

> The individual self and the Lord are the two calves of the wish-fulfilling cow called Māyā. (*Śaktisattvadarśinī*)

Just as fire and its burning power are intimately and eternally related, similarly are harmoniously related the *paramātman* and His *Śakti*.

> Between them there is an eternal relation as between fire and its burning.

Bhagavatī as *brahman* (Brahmarūpa)

Bhagavatī[345] is found described not only as *śakti*, but also as the Absolute (*brahman*) in numerous places.

> You are one established as the Nature of the Absolute; You are the inconceivable and the Śakti whose form is infinity; You are the only icon of the pure existence that is the substratum of every individual being, You are knowable only through an intuition beyond the qualities and free from duality.

She is the one who is the primordial (*mūlabhutā*) form of inerasable, inconceivable shapes. She is the one who is beyond attributes (*guṇa*). Only through a comprehension of [one's essential] undifferentiated state (*nirvikalpabodha*) can one experience Bhagavatī, who is of the form of self-illumination (*svaprakāśarūpeṇa*); thus, Bhagavatī is famous as the non-dual nature of the ultimate Absolute reality (*parabrahman*).

In the *Kenopaniṣad*, we find a description of Bhagavatī as the form of *brahmavidyā*. By Her grace alone did gods like Indra came to know *brahman*. When *brahman* disappeared from before Indra, he became ashamed, stood up in that very place and began to do

अवगति होती है, अतएव अद्वितीय परब्रह्मस्वरूप से भगवती नित्य ही प्रसिद्ध हैं।

'केनोपनिषद्' में ब्रह्मविद्यारूप भगवती का वर्णन मिलता है, उसी की कृपा से इन्द्र आदिकों को ब्रह्मस्वरूप का बोध हुआ था। जब इन्द्र के सामने से ब्रह्म का अन्तर्धान हो गया, तब इन्द्र लज्जित होकर उसी आकाश में खड़ा रह गया और तपस्या करने लगा। बहुत दिनों की तपस्या से सन्तुष्ट होकर भगवती इन्द्र के सामने प्रकट हुई—

स तस्मिन्नेवाकाशे स्त्रियमाजगाम बहुशोभमानामुमां हैमवतीम्।

इन्द्र ने उसी आकाश में बहुशोभमाना हैम अलङ्कारों से युक्त ब्रह्मविद्यारूपा भगवती को देखा और उसकी कृपा से ब्रह्म को जाना।

शक्ति के उपासकों का तो शक्ति सर्वस्व है ही परन्तु तत्तद् देवताओं के उपासकों को भी शक्ति की आराधना करनी पड़ती है। यहाँ तक कि शक्ति की उपासना के बिना उन-उन देवताओं की प्राप्ति ही नहीं होती। संमोहन तन्त्र में तो स्पष्ट ही यह उक्ति है कि गौरतेज राधिका की उपासना किये बिना, जो केवल श्यामतेज कृष्ण की आराधना करता है, वह पातकी होता है—

गौरतेजो विना यस्तु श्यामतेजः समर्चयेत्।
जपेद्वा ध्यायते वापि स भवेत् पातकी शिवे॥

penance. After many days of such *tapas*, Bhagavatī became satisfied and appeared before him:

> He [Indra] in that space passed close to an extremely bright woman, Umā, adorned with golden jewels.
>
> [*Kenopaniṣad* IV.1]

In that very place did Indra see Bhagavatī, extremely radiant of the form of *brahmavidyā*, adorned with gold ornaments, and by Her grace he learned of the Absolute.

For Śakti-worshippers, Śakti is the pinnacle of everything, but even worshippers of other gods are forced by necessity to worship Śakti — so much so that, without worshipping Śakti, they simply cannot attain those other gods. In the *Sammohana Tantra* it is clearly stated that without worshipping the fair-complexioned Rādhikā, he who worships only the dark-complexioned Kṛṣṇa is committing a sin.

> Who worships, or repeats the mantra of, or meditates on the obscure power
> Without [worshipping] the bright power, he, O Śiva, is a sinner.[346]

Notes

Abbreviations: A.D.: Alain Daniélou; *JISOA*: *Journal of the Indian Society of Oriental Art*; *MCL*: *Le Mystère du culte du Linga*; ms.: manuscript.

1 In the 'adapted translation' made by A. Daniélou and published in *The Journal of the Indian Society of Oriental Art*, Calcutta, vol. XIII, 1945, pp. 139-195, the order of the paragraphs was completely rearranged in a very personal patchwork. Forty percent of the text was omitted. We have indicated in the notes the correspondence between the page of the Daniélou's translation (referenced as '*JISOA* XIII, 1945') and the page of the edition in Hindi of '*Śrī Bhagavatī Tattva*' in *Bhakti Sudhā*, 1982, pp. 86-144 (referenced here as 'BS'). Daniélou's translations (*JISOA* XIII, 1945) do not begin here, as they do in Hindi, but rather start from the second page of *Bhakti Sudhā*, p. 87.

2 See note n. 1 on '*adhiṣṭhāna*' in '*Liṅgopāsanā rahasya*'.

3 These three first sentences can be found in *JISOA* XIII, p. 141.

4 From here until the next note, the text was omitted in *JISOA* XIII.

5 In order to deepen the subject we refer to the *pratyakṣa pariccheda* of the *Vedāntaparibhāṣā*. Anyway, what is here to be known is that we translate the Sanskrit term *vṛtti* by 'mental modification' or 'modification of the internal organ', following the definition given in the cited text '*antaḥkaraṇapariṇamo vṛtti*'. For all the technicalities, see *Vedānta Paribhāṣā*.

6 Until the next note, this passage is found in *JISOA* XIII in a separate part intitled 'The avatars of the All-Powerful Goddess', p. 177.

7 This sentence and the following *ślokas* appear in *JISOA* XIII, pp. 176-177.

8 The sentences and *ślokas* until the next note appear in *JISOA* XIII, p. 167.

9 *Māyā* is the illusive power of the Lord, His unfathomable potency, called also ignorance (*avidyā*), falsity (*mithyā*), or undeterminable (*anirvacanīya*). This undeterminable entity is sublated by knowledge — the selfsame essence of the absolute — and it cannot proceed (*anugatī*) also in the state of liberation, due to the divergent nature of liberation and falsity.

10 The translation of A.D. starts from here in *JISOA* XIII, p. 139.

11 The fourth state of being beyond wakefulness, dream and sleep.

12 The sentences and *ślokas* until the next note appear in *JISOA* XIII, p. 167.

13 The *Gāyatrī* is one of the seven vedic metres and it is composed by 24 syllables. One quarter of it has six syllables. The *Sāvitrī* — chanted following this metre — is the *mantra* by which the twice-born worship everyday the Sun. In the daily worship they previously recite the sevenfold application (*viniyoga*) of the *mantra*. One of the parts of this application is the enunciation of the *bīja*, the seed-syllable

of that particular *mantra*. This seed takes the form of the deity who is believed to be the germinal essence activating the entire formula.

14 These sentences and *ślokas* until the next note appear in *JISOA* XIII, p. 168.

15 These sentences and *ślokas* until the next note appear in *JISOA* XIII, p. 141.

16 The sentences and *ślokas* until the next note appear in *JISOA* XIII, p. 140.

17 The sentences and *ślokas* until the next note appear in *JISOA* XIII, p. 168.

18 The sentences and *ślokas* until the next note were omitted in *JISOA* XIII.

19 The sentences and *ślokas* until the next note appear in *JISOA* XIII, p. 141.

20 Many vedantic works have been written on the concept of *mithyā*, but here we can briefly say that *mithyā* is neither completely unreal (*asat*), like the son of a barren woman, nor real, as the Supreme Reality, because after the realization of It she will disappear; so it is said: *sadasadbhyāṃ vilakṣanānirvacanīyam*, that is, "different from real and unreal; undescribable".

21 The sentences and *ślokas* until the next note were omitted in *JISOA* XIII.

22 This passage appears in *JISOA* XIII, pp. 166-167.

23 The *Antaryāmi Brāhmaṇa* is the seventh *Brāhmaṇa* of the third chapter of *Bṛhadāraṇyaka Upaniṣad*.

24 The passage until the next note was omitted in *JISOA* XIII.

25 The sentences and *ślokas* until the note *28* appear in *JISOA* XIII, p. 166.

26 The sentences and ślokas until the next note appear in JISOA XIII, pp. 171-172.

27 Here the compound indicates the *brahman* as decribed in the *turīya* condition, without the limitations who characterize the other three states. It is often used to underline that *brahman* is the fourth because in its real nature it is always beyond limitations. To clarify this doctrine, see the *Māṇḍūkya Upaniṣad* with the Gauḍapāda's *Kārikās*.

28 The passage until the next note was omitted in *JISOA* XIII.

29 The sentences and *ślokas* until the note *32* appear in *JISOA* XIII, p. 172.

30 *Cinmātra*: the original cause of the five constituent elements (ether, air, fire, water, earth), be they subtle or gross. *Cinmātra* means *jñānasvarūpa* that is *ātman*, who is the cause of all this universe. See *Taittirīya Upaniṣad* II.1.1.

31 The more *sāttvika* the accidental conditions, the more the form of the Supreme Being will show his pleasing, serene and peaceful nature.

32 The sentences and *ślokas* until the next note were omitted in *JISOA* XIII.

33 The sentences and *ślokas* until the next note appear in *JISOA* XIII, p. 168.

34 The sentences and *ślokas* until the next note appear in *JISOA* XIII, p. 139.

35 The sentences and *ślokas* until the next note were omitted in *JISOA* XIII.

36 These two chapters (until p. 197), whose translation and annotation were specially made by Dr. Gianni Pellegrini, were not translated by Daniélou. Following Dr. Gianni Pellegrini:

Under two distinct titles: '*Śakti khaṇḍana*' and '*Śakti samarthana*', these 13 pages, as for the *Bhakti Sudhā* edition, are one of the most technical parts of the entire book. As the reader will observe, the debate concerns the position of two important schools of Indian philosophical investigation: *Nyāya* and *Pūrva Mīmāṃsā*.

The logicians do not accept *śakti* as a new category (*padārtha*), remaining steady in the position of seven *padārthas*, as presented by the *Nyāya* school. They affirm that we can consider the believed function of *śakti* as fully accomplished by *svabhāva*, or the essential nature of an entity, hence there is no need to accept *śakti*.

The *Mīmāṃsakas* contradict the *Naiyāyikas*' opinion and lead them to contradiction, thereby refuting their point of view. They, in fact, demonstrate the existence of *śakti* as a separate category, through scriptural authority, reason and other means of knowledge.

Moreover, it will result clear to the readers that in these two paragraphs there is a considerable change of style, argumentation and subject. In the previous and next passages, the author focuses his effort in discussing the *śakti* as the Universal Power, the spouse of the Supreme Lord and his capacity to act, manifest, conserve and annihilate the world. Everywhere, except in these two paragraphs, the subject is the Divine Mother, conceived as the enchanting power of the Lord. Here, with the term *śakti*, we are no more in a religious context, but the author penetrates one of the most debated matters of Indian philosophical analysis: the number and division of the categories (*padārthas*). So, here, *śakti* is treated as a *padārtha*, a philosophical category, which is a quite different point of view than the previous one. Maybe the author thought that to establish the *śakti* of the divine sphere, it would be proper to treat her in an philosophico-empirical context. Having so established the presence of *śakti* as a distinct category, the discussion on her in a different level could appear more logical and pertinent.

Besides the intrinsic technicality of the subject, the translator had to face other difficulties as well. Firstly, the embarrassment of translating the philosophical terminology without betraying its original sense. Secondly, we could not find out the text originally published in the journal *Siddhānta* (February-March 1944-1945), practically unavailable. *Bhakti Sudhā* is only a reprint of some selected articles of the Svāmī, but unfortunately it has innumerable mistakes and misprints that make even more obscure the understanding of the purport of some statements.

37 The powers are not object of an ordinary cognition; only *yogins* can know them.

38 *Arthāpatti*, cf. Śrī Vallabhācārya, *Nyāya Līlāvatī*, with the commentaries of Vardhamānopādhyāya, Śaṅkara Miśra and Bhagīratha Ṭhākkura, ed. by Pt. Harihara Śāstrī, Chaukamba Sanskrit Series Office, 1991 pp. 54-56. Here *sphoṭa* is not the inner power that leads to the meaning of a word, as considered by *vaiyakāraṇas*. Here the author wants only to identify one effect of the burning (*dāhakriyā*) — that is the onomatopeic sound *sphoṭa* — as said in *Nyāya Līlāvatī*, commenting which Śaṅkara Miśra states that *arthāpatti* in the text means *anyathānupapatti*. *Sphoṭa* here is *kriyā*, an action, so the presumption (*arthāpatti*) will be like this: "if in the fire there would not be present the *śakti* who produces the crackling sound of the burning then, when the fire, due to the presence of a particular fuel, is supposed to produce that *sphoṭa* sound, in that situation also the crackling sound would not be produced. In general, if the fire is present somewhere, even so it does

not burn its fuel": this is the *anyathā anupapatti*. This point of view maintains the existence of *śakti*. But the *Naiyāyikas* deny this position.

39 Along with the main cause, fire, there are many other causes called secondary causes (*sahakāri*) to fulfill the aim, the *sphoṭādi kārya*, or the burning of the fuel. Among these, there is also the *pratibandhakābhāva*, that is the absence of something which, being present, obstructs the normal functioning of the process giving birth to the effect. Therefore, besides other causes, also the absence of the obstructing agent (*pratibandhakābhāva*) is necessary for the effect, the burning. If the obstructing agent is present, the burning (*dāhakārya*) does not take place.

40 Taking from *Nyāyabodhinī*, *Nyāyasiddhānta Muktāvalī* and other *Nyāya* texts, a typical situation is described here. The fire is burning, resting in this fire the *candrakānta* gem, the burning is interrupted (*anvaya*) and taking it away the burning starts again (*vyatireka*). According to the *Naiyāyikas*, this positive and negative (*anvaya-vyatireka*) relation is the proof for the causality (*kāraṇatā*) of the absence of the obstructing agent (*pratibandhakābhāva*). But the *Mīmāṃsākas* contrast the position of the *pratibandhakābhāva* as cause, because, according to them, a cause can be only positive in essence (*bhāvātmaka*).

41 For the answer of *Nyāya* to *Mīmāṃsā* see Udayanācārya, *Nyāyakusumāṃjalī* I.10, according to which just as presence and absence (*bhāva* and *abhāva*) are both effects, in the same way both can also be causes. Through *anvaya* and *vyatireka*, we determine the cause-effect relation (*kāraṇa-kārya-bhāva*) between two entities. In our situation there is no opposition to the positive and negative concomitance (*anvaya-vyatireka*) of the effect with the cause, the absence of the obstructing agent (*pratibandhakābhāva*): *yatra yatra pratibandhakābhāvastatra tatra kāryaṃ yatra yatra pratibandhakābhāvābhāvastatra tatra kāryābhāvaḥ*.

42 The proving of an entity occurs in two ways: 1) The presence of a favourable proof (*sādhaka pramāṇa*), or 2) The absence of an indesirable situation (*bādhaka-pramāṇābhāva*). Positive and negative concomitance (*anvaya-vyatireka*) is a *sādhakapramāṇa*, and undesirable effect (*aniṣṭa-prasakti*) is a *bādhakapramāṇa*, so its absence is necessary to prove a cause-effect relationship.

43 Here the problem is: does absence (*abhāva*) exist or not? If it does not, it cannot be a cause. Kumārila Bhaṭṭa accepts *yogyānupalabdhi*: (*pratiyogi-sattā-prasañjana-prasañjita-pratiyogikatva*) the capacity of non-apprehension is the fact of being that, whose counterpositive existence is assumed from the hypotetical existence of the object of that counterpositive. He says that *abhāva* exists, but it cannot be a cause.

44 Prabhākara for the erroneous perception accepts the theory of the lack of the erroneous perception (*akhyātivāda*). According to him every perception is truthful (*yathārtha*) and if we see the snake in the rope, it is due only to some *doṣas*, defects (obscurity, similarity of the two objects, distance, etc.), and out of them we cannot discriminate between two types of cognition. In *ayaṃ sarpaḥ*, "this is a snake", *ayaṃ*, 'this', is the result of a direct perception (*anubhavātmaka*) and *sarpa*, 'snake', is only a memory of such an animal seen previously (*smaraṇātmaka jñāna*). The lack of discrimination (*vivekāgraha*) between the two different cognitions determinates the illusion (*vibhrama*).

45 Here arose a question towards the *Naiyāyikas*. There are 4 types of absence (*abhāva*): 1) Prior absence (*prāgabhāva*); 2) Subsequent absence (*pradhvaṃsābhāva*); 3) Absolute absence (*atyantābhāva*); 4) Reciprocal absence (*anyonyābhāva*). So the absence of the *pratibandhaka* is one of these, but which one? According to the questioner, prior absence (*prāgabhāva*) and subsequent absence (*pradhvaṃsābhāva*) cannot be a cause.

46 The *uttambhaka*, as it is called in *Nyāyakusumaṃjalī*, but commonly known as *uttejaka*, the stimulator, is an object that nullifies the action of the obstructing agent (*pratibandhaka*) and lets the effect take place. In the example of the burning power of the fire (*dāhakatva*), the *candrakānta* gem is the obstructing agent which stops the burning of the fire, and the stimulator (*uttejaka-uttambhaka*) is the *sūryakānta* gem: by putting it in the fire, the burning takes place, even if the obstructing agent is present. There, there is not the prior absence of the obstructing agent, because it is there, though ineffective. Therefore the prior absence of the destructing agent cannot be the cause of the burning (*dāhakārya*).

47 The same situation previously underlined for the prior absence (*prāgabhāva*) is seen for the absence after destruction (*pradhvaṃsābhāva*): it cannot be also a cause of the burning when related to the obstructing agent. That is: when the fire is burning, and the gem that is the obstructing agent is not present, there is its prior-absence, and burning is going on. Therefore if the *candrakānta* gem is not present, how can it be destroyed? So, in that specific effect there cannot be destruction (*pradhvaṃsa*) of the obstructing agent. Until here the *Mīmāṃsaka*'s objection is presented. From the next paragraph, there is the answer of the *Naiyāyikas*.

48 The *Naiyāyikas* say *uttejakābhāvaviśiṣṭamaṇi* is the obstructing agent, not only the gem: only the *candrakānta* gem qualified by the absence of the stimulator *sūryakanta* gem can be obstructing agent. When the stimulator (*uttejaka*) is present, the obstructing agent cannot work, so the effect takes place because there the *candrakānta* gem is cooperating with the stimulator (*uttejakaviśiṣṭa*).

49 *Saṃsargābhāva* is a denomination under which three kind of absence are gathered: prior absence (*prāgabhāva*), absence after destruction (*pradhvaṃsābhāva*) and absolute absence (*atyantābhāva*), without specifying any one of them, so the *kāraṇatā* of one of these will be specified according to the conditions. So, where the obstructing agent of the *candrakānta* gem is not present, the *saṃsargābhāva* will have the form of prior absence. When one removes a previously applied obstructing agent (*pratibandhaka*), the *saṃsargābhava* will have the form of absence after destruction (*pradhvaṃsābhāva*). When the obstructing agent (*pratibandhaka*) is neither placed nor removed, there, the *saṃsargābhāva* will have the face of the absolute absence (*atyantābhāva*).

50 The flaw (*doṣa*) consisting in indetermination of the causal factor (*aniyatahetukatva*) is like this here: without the generalization of the related absence, we say that somewhere the cause is prior absence (*prāgabhāva*), or absence after destruction (*pradhvaṃsa*), and somewhere else absolute absence (*atyantābhāva*), without a precise rule. But generalizing with the wider appellation *saṃsargābhāva*, this defect also does not arise.

51 The followers of *Mimāṃsā* accept the means of knowledge (*pramāṇa*) called *anupalabdhi*, non-apprehension in the cognition of an absence. Here the *Naiyāyika* is asking to the *Mīmāṃsaka* which one of the *abhāvas* is understood in the absence of apprehension (*upalabdhi*). So here if the *Mīmāṃsaka* specifies the absence-type involved, the same defect consisting in indetermination of the causal factor (*aniyatahetukata*) will be unavoidable. And in the *śāstras* there is a codivided solution (*vyavasthā*), according to which when the same flaw arises in two different points of view, both must ignore it: *yaścobhayoḥ samo doṣaḥ, parihārastayoḥ samaḥ*.

52 An obstructed (*pratibaddha*) *śakti* cannot be a *kāraṇa*. Only a *śakti* free from obstructions and effective (*apratibaddha*) will be considered as a cause. But in the word '*a-pratibaddha*', the first '*a*' means 'no', 'absence', *abhāva*. So it can be questioned, which kind of *abhāva* is it? So the problem and the solution in both the sides are specular.

53 So 'the insufficiency of the group of causes' (*visamagrī* also called *kārana-kūṭābhāva* = *sāmagrivakalya*) is the obstruction (*pratibandha*), and *pratibandha* is the complex of all the causes (*samagrasya bhāva iti sāmagrī*) needed for the production of an effect (*sāmagrivighaṭana-kāraṇa*), and the causes of weakness of the causal complex (*sāmagrī*) is the *pratibandhaka*.

54 In the text, we have to understand an objection (*pūrvapakṣa*) of the *Mīmāṃsakas* from the word '*yahāṁ*' until the words '*ṭhīk nahīṃ hai*'. They underline the flaw of reciprocal dependence (*anyonyāśraya doṣa*) in considering the absence of the obstructing agent (*pratibandhakābhāva*) as a cause. But how is this reciprocal dependence (*anyonyāśraya*)? It is so: if there is no contact between the fire and the fuel, no question arises about presence or absence of the obstructing agent, the *candrakānta* gem. From one side *Naiyāyikas* maintain that the absence of the obstructing agent (*pratibandhakābhāva*) is a cause, on the other side the cause is effective only with the absence of the obstructing agent (*pratibandhakābhāva*); if there is no cause and there is only the absence of the obstructing agent (*pratibandhakābhāva*), how is possible the emergence of the effect? This is reciprocal dependence (*anyonyāśraya*); better, the *pratibandhakābhāva* is also a cause, and this *pratibandhakābhāva* needs a cause (*kāraṇasāpekṣapratibandha-kābhāva*), so here the absence of an obstructing agent is among the causes, so the result will be: the absence of the obstructing agent needs the absence of an obstructing agent (*pratibandhakābhāva-sāpekṣapratibandhakābhāva*). This flaw begins from another flaw called self-dependence (*ātmāśraya*), when only one absence of an obstructing agent depends on itself (*svāpekṣapratibandhakābhāva*). If the *pratibandhakābhāvas* are two — one that is cause and one that needs a cause — then we have a reciprocal dependence (*anyonyāśraya*).

55 Only considering the absence of an obstructing agent (*pratibandhakābhāva*) as a cause we can prove that the gem (*maṇi*), the *mantra*, etc. are not favourable to the production of the major effect, the burning (*dāhakārya*), but they are adverse to it. In addition to this we can generally consider that the absence of an obstructing agent is a cause towards an ordinary effect, on the basis of positive and negative concomitance (*anvaya-vyatireka*), and when we specify the *pratibandhakābhāva*

and the effect (*kārya*), such as *candrakāntamaṇi* and production of the major effect (*dāhakārya*), we have here to examine which particular *pratibandhakābhāva* is obstructing a particular effect, as when the *candrakānta* gem is present, then the burning of the fire does not occur. On this basis we will determine that the *candrakānta* gem is the obstructing agent (*pratibandhaka*). Therefore, first we have to generally consider the absence of an obstructing agent as a cause towards an effect, through positive and negative concomitance (*anvaya-vyatireka*). After, we must specify in a particular case that first consideration.

56 One of the possible definitions of the reciprocal dependence (*anyonyāśraya*) is *svotpattyadhīnotpattikatva*, "the giving birth that is dependent on one's own birth", if referred to birth (*utpatti*). If the *anyonyāśraya* refers to cognition (*jñapti*), the definition (*lakṣaṇa*) will be *svajñaptyadhīnajñaptikatva*, 'the exercise of the cognition that depends on one's own cognition'.

57 In one sentence there is the refutation of both the types of reciprocal dependence (*anyonyāśraya*). The first (*utpatti*) is that the *mantra* is not the cause of its own prior absence (*prāgabhāva*), but prior absence is the cause of the *mantra*; in birth (*utpatti*), reciprocal dependence would have been if *mantra* were the cause of prior absence and prior absence the cause of *mantra*. The reciprocal dependence by cognition (*jñapti anyonyāśraya*) also does not subsist. Also an unknown obstructing agent can obstruct the effect. We learn from the *śāstras* that cause is of two types: *jñātasat* and *svarūpasat*; the obstructing agent (*pratibandhaka*) towards stopping the effect is a *svarūpasat kāraṇa*, because there is no importance if we know its nature or not, in part there are also invisible obstructing agents, so also the cognition (*jñapti*) based reciprocal dependence (*anyonyāśraya*) does not subsist.

58 Objection of the *Mīmāṃsakas*: when *mantrādi* are present, the burning (*dāhakārya*) does not happen, so we must consider *mantrādi* an absence of cause (*kāraṇābhāva*), not a cause (*kāraṇa*).

59 In the *mantra* there is the absence of an obstructing agent (*pratibandhakatva*) and in their *abhāva* the *kāraṇatva*. Only when we have the knowledge of *mantra* as obstructing agent (*pratibandhaka*), then we can know its *abhāva*; when absence of *mantra* will be recognized as a cause, only in that point we can understand that *mantra* is or not on the nature of *kāraṇābhāva* or *mantra* is an obstructing agent. So again we are faced with the reciprocal dependence (*anyonyāśraya*).

60 The logicians reply that we can understand that *mantras* and the like are obstructing agents also before knowing the causality of *abhāva*, because we see that when the *mantra*, *maṇi*, etc. are present the burning of the fire stops, so we have to recognize their capacity to oppose to the effect. So we are obliged to consider *mantrādyabhāva* as a cause, so here the positive concomitance (*anvaya*) will be like this: *maṇi-mantrādyabhāve dāhakāryaṃ bhāvati*, and the negative concomitance (*vyatireka*) so: *maṇimantrādisattve dāhakāryaṃ na bhāvati*.

61 Here there is a new objection of the *Mīmāṃsakas*. We have here to underline one inaccuracy of the Hindi text, in which there is not the inclusion of the term *asaṃnidhya* after *saṃnidhya*. We say this because the term '*ubhayathā*' after both of them lead us to think like this. Here in the mere fire, nothing happens if there is or not a gem, etc.; only in the fire effect is the difference clear. Due to this

consideration, we must accept an invisible *śakti*, inherent in the fire, but different from it, such that the effect occurs when it is present, but not when it is absent.

62 With the indifference of fire it is implied the stopping of the fire to burn. We can understand this *audāsīnya* with an ordinary example. When we are engaged in a private conversation with someone, if another person comes, we change immediately the topic of our dialogue. This is our indifference, detachment from the private topic. The same occurs with the fire: "changes immediately the topic", that is, stops immediately to produce its effect.

63 We can say that if we accept *śakti*, in such a particular situation of the absence of effect (*kāryābhāva*) we have to consider two ways: one is the destruction of *śakti* when is present the obstructing agent (*pratibandhaka*); the other option is the suspension of *śakti*, its *pratibandha*, also due to the obstructing agent. If the *śakti* is destroyed, then how is the burning possible, even if the fire is present, and how is it possible that, after this, the effect goes on?

64 The *Mīmāṃsaka* says that another *śakti* arises, the same as the previous one, so the effect can go on after the departure of the obstructing agent (*pratibandhaka*). But this concept is also incorrect, because we are not able to find another cause (*kāraṇa*), or the new *śakti*, and without cause, she cannot come out by herself.

65 The cause-complex (*sāmagrī*) that was working for the production of the effect, before the arrival of gem (*maṇi*) etc., is not finished. We have also to consider *śakti* as a part of the *sāmagrī* (*dāhādīkārya-anukūlaśakti*), and she is also destroyed. So there is no cause-complex for the birth (*utpatti*) of a new *śakti*. In the text, we find in the beginning of this sentence *agnisāmagrī*, but we would prefer *agnyādisāmagrī*.

66 The followers of *Mīmāṃsā* consider that in the fire is present *śakti*, a power, a potentiality, that makes it able to burn something. When this *śakti* is lost, the fire becomes unable (*aśakta*) to produce its major effect, the burning (*dāhakārya*).

67 When *śakti* was present the production of the major effect (*dāhakārya*) occurred and even if *śakti* is absent *dāhakārya* occurs, so which is the reason to accept *śakti*?

68 The fire is able to burn up something also without *śakti*, so there is no need to maintain her.

69 This sentence is without any doubt expressed by a *Mīmāṃsaka*, but it is incomplete; according to us something is missing. In addiction, we can guess that it pertains to the next paragraph, were we find its reply.

70 If we consider the obstruction of a *śakti* by another *śakti*, we must consider the obstruction of the first obstructing *śakti* by another *śakti*, and so on.

71 From the beginning of the paragraph until '*āvaśyaka hai*' there is an argument of the *Mīmāṃsakas*. They say that also by the cause-effect relation is it possible to infer *śakti*, because only from milk is it possible to make curd; in fact inside milk only is hidden the power to generate curd (*dadhyadyutpādanānukūla śakti*). The material cause-effect (*upādāna-upādeya*) relation of curd is only with milk, because in other substances there is not such a necessary *śakti*.

72 In the text appears the word '*āpatti*', but we consider it as a misprint, preferring the more appropriate word '*upapatti*'.

73 It is only the natural tendency of milk to produce curd, nothing more. We see it from our elder people, that when we need to produce curd, we use milk and not water or oil. So it is more logical to accept *svabhāva* instead of *śakti*.

74 Denying *svabhāva* as criterium (*niyāmaka*) of the cause-effect relationship, we cannot prove either *śakti*, because both of them depend of the same argumentations.

75 In conclusion also the *Śaktivādins* have to accept *svabhāva*, when there will arise such a question: "Why in milk there is the potentiality to generate curd?" Even without wanting they will say that in the *svabhāva* of milk inheres the *śakti* favourable to the curd generation. In the end also *Mīmāṃsakas* will depend on *svabhāva*.

76 One *arthāpatti*, presumption (*anyathānupapatti*) is that of the presence-absence (*bhāvābhāva*), the other one is this last argument pertaining to the relation cause-effect (*upādānopādeyabhāva*). That is, *maṇi* being present, there is absence of effect; being absent *maṇi*, the effect occurs. The other one is: being present the cause, there is effect; being not present the cause, also effect does not come to be.

77 The matter under discussion is the argument through which we can or cannot accept *śakti*.

78 In comparison with the situation in which *agni* is not able to produce effects (*ajanakadaśā*), in the situation of the effect production (*janakadaśā*) something different, something more, is present in the fire. So, here, the sense of *atiśaya*, 'special property' is *śakti*. Because we note that in such a condition fire is effective, able to produce effect, like an axe whose blade was no longer sharp enough to chap wood, but having being re-sharpened is again capable of chapping wood, because there is a special property (*atiśaya*) in the sharp blade compared to the previous situation. When the axe is *kuṇṭha*, then it is not an actor, a performer (*kāraka*) of effects, or the axe is not in his effective condition (*kārakāvasthā*), but when its *kārakāvasthā* is present, then, some *atiśaya* also is there, and that *atiśaya* is called *śakti*.

79 With this inference the *siddhasādhana doṣa* is this: the *Mīmāṃsakas* want to prove *śakti* through this inference (*anumāna*) but *Naiyāyikas* say that this *anumāna* is also proving the abundance of the presence, and the closeness of the auxiliary causes is also accepted by them. So the *Naiyāyikas* maintain the existence of special property (*atiśaya*); as it is already proven, and this is the flaw of proving something already proved (*siddha*) into which *Śaktivādins* have fallen.

80 The meaning of generic attribute beyond the sensorial range (*atīndriya sāmānya*) is *śakti*. Criticizing it, the *Naiyāyikas* say that it is knowledge through *indriyas* only by an omniscient *yogin*, so the qualification *atīndriya* is useless. The flaw is called disestablishment of the probandum (*sādhyāsiddhi*). The probandum of this inference is like this: the *atīndriyatā* is also present in the atoms (*paramāṇu*) but they are all active (*sakriyā*). The *Mīmāṃsakas* here want to establish not a *sakriyā* entity, but an inactive (*niṣkriya*) entity, like *śakti*. In *śakti* no *kriyā* (*karman*) action can reside. If in the probandum (*sādhya*) the word *niṣkriya* will not be joined, we

will have '*atīndriya-sāmānyavan-āśrayah*', in which 'generic attribute beyond the sensorial range' (*atīndriyasāmānya)* indicates *atīndriyatva*, the atoms are *atīndriyatvavat* endowed with *atīndriyatva*, and if the fire —the locus (*pakṣa*) — is the ground (*āśraya*) of the fiery atoms (*taijasaparamāṇu*), then here are not comprised the earthly atoms (*pārthivaparamāṇu*), but fire, thus, also becomes their ground, and this will lead to the *siddhasādhana* flaw (cf. note 79). So the right *sādhya* is that *agni* must be the ground (*āśraya*) of such an *atīndriya* entity which is *niṣ-kriya*, without action.

81 In the inference cited, the example (*dṛṣṭānta*) is *gurutvāśraya*, in which the gravity (*gurutva*) is also beyond the range of the senses (*atīndriya*) for the ordinary man.

82 Here the doubt is such: the knowledge of the *yogins* is due to the contact of the sense organs, or not?

83 In an inference, the ground (*āśraya*) is the sight capacity (*cakṣu*), the locus (*dharmin* = *pakṣa*) in which must reside the probans (*hetu*) and the probandum (*sādhya*). The flaw pertinent to the *hetu* is so exemplified: *gaganāravindaṃ surabhi aravinda-tvāt sarojāravindavat*, "the sky-lotus is fragrant, because it is a lotus, like the pond lotus". Its definition (*lakṣaṇa*) is this: *pakṣatāvacchedakābhāvavat-pakṣakatvam āśrayāsiddhatvam*: the flaw called *āśrayāsiddhi* consists in having a locus which is without the quality that delimits the locus-ness. So the *pakṣa* here is *aravinda*, lotus, in which resides *pakṣatā*, the locusness, but the delimitor quality (*avacche-dakadharma*) of the locusness (*pakṣatā*) here is sky-ness (*gaganīyatva*), and in the lotus does not reside *gaganīyatva*. So this pseudo-reason (*hetvābhāsa*) stops the inference.

84 The expression *dharmigrāhakapramāṇa* means the mean of knowledge (*pramāṇa*) through which will be proved the existence of the divine sense of the *yogins*. That means that the *indriya* of the *yogins* are different from ours, because what is beyond the possibility of the senses (*atīndriya*) for an ordinary man is knowable for the *yogins*. The opposition (*bādha*) will be because on one side there is acceptance of a divine sense organ and, on the other side, we don't accept a *śakti* capable to perceive objects that are beyond the possibility of the senses.

85 In *Nyāya* there are two kinds of cognition; the first is *vyavasāya*, by which an object is grasped, such as "this is a pot" (*ayaṃ ghaṭaḥ*); after this the subsequent cognition is *anuvyavasāya*, which is a cognition that makes the first cognition its object (*jñānaviṣayakaṃ jñānam*) such as *ghaṭajñānavān aham*: "I have the know-ledge of the pot". So if some object can be beyond the range of senses (*atīndriya*) in the *vyavasāya*, this does not happens in *anuvyavasāya*, in which every thing is mentally knowable.

86 Here *aindriyajñāna* means *mānasikapratyakṣa*, mental perception that comes through subsequent cognition (*anuvyavasāya*) being mind and internal organ.

87 The objection of the *Mīmāṃsakas* is that the use of the word *atīndriya* was not for denoting the mental perception due to subsequent cognition (*anuvyavasāya*), because sensorial cognition is different from *anuvyavasāya*. In other words they say that what is object of the first perception (*vyavasāya*) is sensorial (*aindriyaka*), and things perceived by *anuvyavasāya* are *atīndriya*.

88 The *Naiyāyikas* reply by explaining that what *Mīmāṃsakas* consider as *atīndriya*, that also can be known in the *vyavasāya* through sense organs. How? Through one of the uncommon sensorial contact *(alaukikasaṃnikarṣa),* called cognition of the qualified by the apprehension of the qualifier (*jñānalakṣaṇapratyāsatti*). We clarify it with the example 'the fragrant sandal' (*surabhi candanam*). If we see from a certain distance one piece of sandalwood, that sandal is an object of visual perception (*cākṣuṣa pratyakṣa*) but it has the qualification '*surabhi*', 'fragrant', and we cannot perceive the fragrance through the eye, but being the *viśeṣaṇa* of *candanam* (*viśeṣya* = qualified) we must admit also that its *cākṣuṣa pratyakṣa* is not normal (*laukikasaṃnikarṣa*) but is due to the uncommon one called *jñāna lakṣana saṃnikarṣa*. Here the cognition *surabhi candanam* is the qualified one (*viśiṣṭajñāna* = *viśeṣaṇayuktajñāna*), and according to the *Nyāya* rules, if in a *viśiṣṭa-jñāna* the qualified object (*viśeṣya*) is directly perceived (*pratyakṣagāmya*) also its qualifier (*viśeṣaṇa*) must be so, may it be through *laukika* or *alaukika* contact.

89 The adjective in the probandum (*sādhya*) remains unestablished, because every object (*padhārtha*) can be directly perceived, in one or another way.

90 We prefer to read *atīndriyatva* against *atīndriya* because it is more akin to *aviṣayatva*.

91 The object of which fire is being called the ground, or better *agni*, is said to be the ground (*āśraya*) of an *atīndriya* generic attribute, that is also itself without action (*atīndriyasāmānya-vanniṣkriya*). So, if *agni* is its ground, that fire-sustained entity, by which relation is it present in the fire? As the fire on the mountain is present by contact-relation (*saṃyogasambandha*), or as the colour in the pot is present by inherent relation (*samavāyasambandha*)? By which relation (*sambandha*) is defined the substainer-substained relation (*ādhārādheyabhāva*) between fire (*ādhāra*) and the entity which is endowed with a generic attribute beyond the sensorial range (*atīndriyasāmānya*) and which is actionless (*niṣkriya*)?

92 Accepting the *saṃyoga sambandha*, there will be the flaw of the probandum not residing in the example (*sādhyavaikalya*). The probandum (*sādhya*) must somehow be established (*prasiddha* = *pramāṇasiddha*) in an inference and in this body of inference we see the example (*dṛṣṭānta*) that is otherwise called *sapakṣa*, 'the locus in which surely *sādhya* resides'. In the *sādhyavaikalya doṣa,* the probandum is not present in the example. Here the example is 'the ground of the gravity' (*gurutvāśraya*). Gravity is classified among the 24 qualities (*guṇa*) that reside in the ground with an inherent relation, but here the relation proposed between fire and the actionless entity endowed with a generic attribute beyond the sensorial range (*atīndriya-sāmānyavānniṣkriya*) is the contact (*saṃyoga*), so there is a clear flaw.

93 So the relation between fire and the entity substained by it would be inherence (*samayāya*), like between a pot in which inheres a colour — but it cannot be, because the *Mīmāṃsakas* do not accept it.

94 We can see the elasticity of fire when putting a pan on a gas burner. Setting down the pan, the flames spread horizontally; taking it away, the flames return to their upward flow. This elasticity impression (*sthitisthāpakasaṃskāra*) is also an *atīndriya* quality, and action does not reside in the qualities, so this also is actionless (*niṣkriya*). So in inference, not giving the name of entity to be proved, it is found

that the given description is equally applicable to elasticity. We accept such an elasticity in fire, therefore there is the flaw of proving what is already proved (*siddhasādhana*), because the *Mīmāṃsaka*'s inference is proving it. By another point of view we can see here the flaw of establishing a different thing than the desired one (*arthāntara*). We can exemplify this error like: someone wants to make a sculpture of Gaṇeśa but by mistake the trunk is cut off, and the figure resembles a monkey (*gaṇeśaḥ prakurvāṇaḥ racayamāsa vānaraḥ*). Here the *Mīmāṃsakas* wanted to establish *śakti* but they proved elasticity (*sthitisthāpaka*).

95 Here again the *Mīmāṃsakas* try to demolish the *Nyāya*'s view, doubting the existence of both *siddhasādhana* and *sthitisthāpaka*. The text here lacks the term *sthitisthāpaka*, but it is surely a misprint, otherways the inference will be logically unrelated to the context.

96 In ancient times mats were made from a particular type of straw, long and hollow in the middle. Every blade was broken into two pieces and woven to make the mats. When spread, they returned to their previous state. This was the example for elasticity, not as the modern mats. Here the proof about the existence of elasticity is given in this inference; as *agni* is endowed with colour (*rūpavān*), it has no elasticity, just as the straw-mat, in which both — *rūpa* and *sthitisthāpaka* — are established by direct perception (*pratyakṣa-siddha*).

97 When an inference is violated by an accidental condition or a conditional agent as an *upadhi*, it becomes flawed; or if the probans of that inference is endowed with the *vyāpyatvāsiddhi doṣa,* the non-establishment of the invariable concomitance, it is therefore counted among the pseudo-reasons (*hetvābhāsa*). *Upādhi* has this definition: *sādhyavyāpakatve sati sadhānāvyāpakatvam*, 'a non-pervasion of the probans (*sādhana* = *hetu*) qualified (*sati* = *viśiṣtha*) by the pervasion of the probandum'. Now we see if the *upādhi* is present in the inference, from the *Mīmāṃsā* point of view. First we try the pervasion of the probandum (*sādhya*), that we can consider only as '*sthitisthāpakatva*' to simplify. Our *upādhi* is *sthitisthāpakakāryavattva*, or 'the possession of the action due to elasticity', as we can see in the example of the straw mat. So we are able to build this invariable concomitance in which the *sādhya* will be the pervaded (*vyāpya*) and the *upādhi* the pervader (*vyāpaka*): *yatra yatra sthitisthāpakasaṃskāraṃ tatra tatra sthitisthāpakakāryam*; therefore the conditional agent (*upādhi*) is pervading the probandum. Now we see the second part of the definition, the non-pervasion of the probans: *yatra yatra rūpavattvaṃ tatra tatra na sthitisthāpakasaṃkārakāryam*; in fact, we see that the table, the pot, the building are all coloured (*rūpavān*), but in them, there is no action due to elasticity, therefore the probans 'possession of colour' (*rūpavattva sādhana* = *hetu*) is not pervaded. So, the said 'possession of the action due to elasticity' (*sthitisthāpakakāryavattva*) is an *upādhi.*

The *Naiyāyikas* reply, arguing that no flaw is present in the inference (*anumāna*). Why? The *Naiyāyikas* say that the pervasion of the probandum (*sādhyavyāpakatā*) is necessary for *upādhi*, but it sometimes happens that we produce something that is destroyed immediately after, as for example, if a straw mat is burnt immediately after it is made. The *Naiyāyikas* maintain that an impermanent (*anitya*) substance (*dravya*) lasts for at least three moments (*kṣaṇa*): the first when it is created (*utpatti*), the second whilst it endures (*sthiti*), and in the third is its end (*laya*). Besides this, the *Tārkikas* accept that, when created, a substance (*dravya*) remains for a moment without any quality (*nirguṇa*) and without action (*niṣkriya*). A quality like *sthitisthāpaka* can be present only from the second moment in the straw mat (*dravya*) — but the straw mat might be destroyed in the third moment: so then, in a substance already destroyed, how could be found any action due to elasticity, which ought to develop in this third moment? Therefore, there is the elasticity-impression (*sthitisthāpakasaṃskāra*), but not the action (*kārya*) due to it. So, there is not that said *upādhi* in that created and immediately destroyed straw mat: *yatra yatra sthitisthāpakasaṃskāraḥ tatra tatra na sthitisthāpakasaṃskāra-kāryam*. So in that particular situation, we don't find the necessary prerequisites for the conditional agent, the pervasiveness of the probandum (*sādhyavyāpakatā*).

98 In other situations, *Mīmāṃsakas* accept the flaw called *siddhāsādhanatā*, but here they are arguing against its existence. So, the *Naiyāyikas* are trying to cause the former to fall by their own theories, which will be included among the 22 points of defeat (*nigrahasthānas*), as the contraddiction with one's own theory (*svasiddhāntaviruddha*), because afterwards the *Mīmāṃsakas* try to use this flaw against their antagonists, the *Tārkikas*.

99 In order to avoid the *siddhasādhanatā* given by the *Naiyāyikas*, the *Mīmāṃsakas* propose to add the adjective 'other than *sthitisthāpaka*' in the probandum of the inference, making it '*sthitisthāpaketarātīndriyasāmānyavānniṣkriyāśraya*'.

100 In any event, the *Mīmāṃsakas* will fall into the flaw [expressing] a different meaning than that which was desired (*arthāntara*) in *karman*, according to Prabhākara. In fact, Prabhākara thinks action (*karman*) as *atīndriya*, and in *karman* there cannot be action. So, if *karman* is *atīndriya*, it is also different from elasticity, and it is *niṣkriya*; so, *karman* will be established and not *śakti*; then, this is the *arthāntara*. Therefore, *agni* will be the ground of action, and not of power.

101 At this point, the objection is from the *Mīmāṃsaka* side. They are saying that there is no *arthāntara*. In fact, what sometimes takes place and at other times does not, depends on some special property (*atiśaya*), on its occasional existence: when this *atiśaya* is found, something happens; otherwise, not. If that something would naturally take place without *atiśaya*, then why is it instead called *kādacitka*, and not fixed? So, we must accept that when the *atiśaya* is present, an action takes place, and when it is absent, there is no such action. That *atiśaya* is none other than *śakti*.

102 Here is given the example for this invariable concomitance. The actions that proceed from separation and union take place when some *atiśaya* comes into the ground of their separation or union. There, the *atiśaya* will be an action (*kriyārūpātiśaya*). For example, two hands create a motion capable of generating the union (*saṃyogānukūlakriyā*); they can unite, and when comes a motion favourable for their separation, the two hands will separate (*vibhāgānukūlakriyā*). Here, the *atiśaya* is the union (*saṃyoga*) or the separation action (*vibhāgānukūlakriyā*). The effect of the action generating union is the union with another place (*uttaradeśasaṃyoga*) and the effect of the action generating separation is the destruction of the union with the previous place (*purvadeśasaṃyogavināśa*).

103 From this point starts the answer of the *Naiyāyikas*. They say that what the *Mīmāṃsakas* consider to be *śakti* is for them action (*kriyā*), so again the *Mīmāṃsakas* fall into the *arthāntara* flaw.

104 Among the pseudo-reasons (*hetvābhāsa*), we find the *anekānta* flaw of the *anaikāntika* probans, which is otherwise called '*vyabhicārin hetu*' or, in view of the flaw, '*vyabhicāra doṣa*'. Its definition (*lakṣaṇa*) is *sādhyābhāvavadvṛtti*: 'the probans resides where there is not the probandum'. Here, the *Naiyāyikas* believe in the Lord's existence (*Īśvaravādin*) and in the invisible power of the retribution of the fruits of the actions (*adṛṣṭa*), a point of view shared with the *Mīmāṃsakas*. That *adṛṣṭa* is already a potentiality, a power, *śakti*. If in *śakti* there is another *śakti*, in the second *śakti* there will be a third one, and so on. However, there is no *atiśaya*, so in the cause, in *śakti*, there is causality probans (*kāraṇatva hetu*), and that same *śakti* is also present where it is not possible for her to remain, like in *adṛṣṭa*; however, in *adṛṣṭa*, we find causality (*kāraṇatva*). So, *kāraṇatva* is both where there is *śakti* and also where *śakti* is not found. Just as the fire is 'not always related to smoke' (*dhūma-vyabhicārin*): where there is smoke, there is fire, and where there is no smoke, there can be fire, as in a red-hot piece of iron.

105 That *śakti* possess the probandum (*sādhyavān*) means that, in *śakti*, there is also again *śakti*. This leads to *anavasthā*, as explained above in note 91.

106 This *anaikāntikatā* refers to the previous flaw.

107 The *Naiyāyikas* are saying that it is not possible to accept the possessor of potency (*śaktimān*) as a cause until *śakti* is established. Here, *śaktimattva*, the possession of *śakti*, is the causality; in that *śaktimattva* qualifier (*viśeṣaṇa*) is present *śakti*. Only when *śakti* is proven can we speak of *śaktimān* and *śaktimattva* (*śaktiyuktatā*).

108 Here, the *Naiyāyikas* tell the *Mīmāṃsakas* that there was no need for so much difficult discussion, if only they had decided to prove *śakti* through another mean of knowledge (*pramāṇa*).

109 The *anaikāntikatā* flaw also come in *guṇas* and the like because they are also causes. In them there is causality (*kāraṇatva*), just as the colour of a thread (*tanturūpa*) is the non-inherent cause (*asamavāyikāraṇa*) of the colour of the dress (*paṭarūpa*).

110 The supreme (*parā*) generic attribute, *jāti* or *sāmānya*, is *sattā*, 'being, existence', which resides only in the first three categories of the *Nyāyā-Vaiśesika* system: in substances (*dravya*), qualities (*guṇa*), and action (*karman*). This *jāti* is also motionless, *niṣkriya*, but this does not imply that she can only stay within *dravya*, because her presence is also proved in *guṇa* and *karman*. The non-eternal (*anitya*) *dravyas* are *sāvayava*, made of various parts, and also possessed with motion (*sakriya*).

111 Both *guṇa* and *karman* are dependent on *dravya* and are only perceptible when they are grounded, inhering to *dravya*, so the generic attribute of substantiality (*dravyatva jāti*) is the pervader (*vyāpaka*) of the other two *jātis*, such as qualityness (*guṇatva*) and action-ness (*karmatva*), because we can see this kind of invariable concomitance (*vyāpti*): *yatra yatra guṇakarmānyataraṃ tatra tatra dravyam; yatra yatra dravyaṃ nāsti, tatra tatra guṇakarmānyatarmapi nāsti*, because we cannot find *guṇa* or *karman* without their invariable ground, *dravya*.

112 Here, the *Mīmāṃsakas* are trying to establish that the cause other than the cause of crakling sound (*spoṭaḥ*) is *śakti*.

113 This part appears in the text after one and a half lines, when the reply of the *Naiyāyikas* is already begun. So, we consider it a misprint and suggest rather to put it after the words '*svīkāra kareṃ*'.

114 That cause other than the cause of *sphoṭādi* is *śakti* for the *Mīmāṃsā* side, and the absence of the obstructing agent (*pratibandhakābhāva*) is such for the *Nyāya*. So, according to the *Naiyāyikas*, the inference proves *pratibandhakābhāva* as a cause; therefore, this will be an *arthāntaratā* for the *Mīmāṃsakas* who wanted the causality of *śakti* and, from another point of view, a *siddhasādhana*, because the inference proves the causality (*kāraṇatva*) of the *pratibandhakābhāva*, already accepted by the *Naiyāyikas*.

115 The sense of the adjective is that the *Mīmāṃsakas* don't accept the cause as a negative entity, so by employing 'production by a positive entity' (*bhāvajanya-tva*) they hope to avoid the *arthāntaratā* flaw. So, the probandum will be *ubhayavādisaṃpratipannasphoṭa-kāraṇātiriktabhāvakāraṇājanyaḥ*.

116 *Naiyāyikas* accept nine common causes for all the effects; the first of them is *Īsvara*. So *Īsvara*, already accepted in *Nyāya*, answers the description of probandum (*sādhya*); therefore, there will be the flaw of proving what is already proved (*siddhasādhana*).

117 The *ādheyaśakti* is a power produced secondarily, on some ground, being previously not present.

118 All these sentences are evidence that things like grains, the sacrificial pole and the fire acquire some previously not-present special property after some action is performed upon them, which is the *ādheyaśakti*. So, for example, after being sprinkled (*prokṣaṇa*) the grains are so purified that they become worthy for something other, in them something new appears. In the same way, we must examine the other sentences.

119 *Tatbalāt* means that on the basis of the established special property (*atiśaya*), *ādheyaśakti* resulting from the purifications (*saṃskāra*), it is possible to infer a *sahajaśakti*, an innate power.

120 There are six auxiliary proofs for the *viniyogavidhi*, 'the injunction of application'. These are 1) *śruti*, when a word is expressed; 2) *liṅga*, the power of a word; 3) *vākya*, the sentence in which it is present; 4) *prakaraṇa*, the context in which it is placed; 5) *sthāna*, its place within that context, and 6) *samākhyā*, the word whilst retaining its etymological meaning. The strongest of these *pramāṇas* is *śruti*, the others following in succession, with *samākhyā* as the weakest.

121 Just as the village is the object of the phrase 'he goes to the village', similarly 'grains', 'the sacrificial pole' and 'fires' are the objects of their phrases. From this object-ness (*karmatā*) we can deduce that in them something new appears, due to their related actions. Otherwise, no other visible result (*dṛṣṭaphala*) can be found there, and we cannot say that a Vedic sentence is fruitless (*niṣphala*). This is sufficient ground to think of that special property as *śakti*.

122 All this discussion can be found in Udayanācārya's *Nyāyakusumāñjalī* I.45-50.

123 The *saṃskāra* produced by the sprinkling (*prokṣaṇādi*) does not awaken in the grains, but in the sacrificer who sprinkles them, because they are insentient things. How can it be possible for a quality such as *adṛṣṭa* which is specific for the sentient *ātman*, to arise in an insentient quality, inhering within it?

124 The thing that is worthy to be purified by the action called 'purification' (*saṃskāra*) is called *saṃskārya*. Within it inheres the attribute *saṃskāryatā*. There are four entities called parts of the sacrifice (*karmaśeṣa*): 1) those things worthy to be created (*utpādya*), like the sacrifical cakes (*puroḍāśa*); 2) those things worthy of transformation (*vikārya*), like *soma* and the like; 3) those things worthy to be obtained (*āpya*), like the *mantras* or villages and the like, and 4) things worthy to be purified (*saṃskārya*), like our grains (*vrīhi*).

125 Educated people (*śiṣṭa*) use the expression *prokṣitāḥ vrīhayaḥ*, 'the sprinkled grains'.

126 The *Naiyāyikas* say here that, as the cognition of a pitcher (*ghaṭa*) is created only within the knower (*jñātā*) and nothing happens in the *ghaṭa* through this condition, so, in the *jñātā* is created a special property (*atiśaya*) because what before he did not know, now he does: so also for the grains. Just as we can say '*jñāto ghaṭaḥ*', 'the pitcher is known', and if also the knowledge is related to the knower, then a *ghaṭa* is only the object of that cognition. Similarly we see in '*prokṣitāḥ vrīhayaḥ*', 'the sprinkled grains' [*tadīyatvapratīti*], where the *atiśaya* is created in the man who sprinkles, but as the grains are the object (*karmakāraka*) of that sprinkling, common people would say that the grains are 'sprinkled'. So, in conclusion, we cannot accept the grains as the ground of newly created *atiśaya*.

127 Here, the is a reference to *śakti*. The *Naiyāyikas* say that fire does not need anything other than itself to burn fuel.

128 This means that *śakti* is not merely the essential nature (*svabhāva*) of Īśvara, but something else. Also, the genitive term (*ṣaṣṭhī*) '*asya*' explains the relation (*sambandha*) of *śakti* with Parameśvara.

129 There are six means to determine the true meaning of a statement, largely of *śruti*: 1) *upakrama-upasaṃhāra*, the object treated in the beginning of a context must be the same as at the conclusion; 2) *abhyāsa*, the repetition of something many times in that given context; 2) *apūrvatā*, the subject must be original, and not treated anywhere else; 4) *phala*, the result; 5) *arthavāda*, the laudative passages extolling that same thing, and 6) *upapatti*, the logical support to that subject. Here, we find that *śakti* is used as a probans (*hetu* = *liṅga*) for Parameśvara.

130 *Arthavāda* are the laudative or critical passages in *śruti*, '*praśastinindānyatara-paraṃ vākyam*'. They are not intrinsically significating anything, but do so when associated with an action, thereby gaining importance. So, after a vedic sentence (*śrutivākya*) describing some *karman*, there might be some *arthavāda* to eulogize that action, or to prescribe someone from doing anything contrary to it. So their importance is subordinated to the action.

131 Here, the sense of the passage implies that the reasoning given by the *Naiyāyikas* in favour of *pratibandhakābhāva* as a cause can also be advanced by the *Mīmāṃsakas* corroborating the causality of *śakti*. Both are possible, since we

have no definitive proof (*vinigamakaviraha*). So, on the basis of mere reasoning, one cannot come to any conclusion.

132 Here starts the refutation of the *Naiyāyika*'s view. The *Mīmāṃsakas* say that it is impossible to use only reasoning in contrast with *śakti*'s causality; it is also necessary to clarify which shall be the concrete problems that shall arise whilst accepting it.

133 Among these two types of *tarka*, the first only explains one's own view, and the second tries to nullify that of the opponent.

134 The sense of the expression '*viparyaya-paryavasāna*' is 'if what I am saying is untrue, surely there will be some logical fallacies'.

135 It is not enough to demonstrate the possible flaws in the opponent's views; it is necessary to corroborate and demonstrate with proofs (*pramāṇa*) one's own view. Here, the *Naiyāyikas* are neglecting the causality of the power (*śaktikāraṇatā*), using it as a step for their critique of the selfsame *śakti*.

136 The meaning here is that in a base (*adhikaraṇa*), also called *anuyogin*, we can neglect the presence of something cognized, a *pratiyogin*, a known object established by means of knowledge (*pramāṇa*). The *Naiyāyikas* don't accept *śakti*, so she is not cognized (*pramita*) for them, so how could they negate Her? This means that we can negate the presence of a lotus in a library, for example, because the lotus is *pramita* for us, already cognized through *pramāṇas*. However, we cannot negate the 'sky lotus' from the same library, because it does not exist; so, it cannot be *pramita*. So, we cannot neglect only what is somewhere already cognized. So, how can the *Naiyāyikas* refuse the causality of power (*śakti-kāraṇatā*), if they don't accept *śakti*?

137 If *śakti* and her causality are cognized in a certain ground (*adhikaraṇa*), the *Naiyāyikas* can refute her in another *adhikaraṇa,* but not fully. "*Śakti* does not exist", they say.

138 In the text, three kinds or modes of discussion (*kathā*) are presented: the first is *vādakathā*, in which someone like a disciple asks something to another, like a master, with the desire to learn. The second *kathā* is *jalpa*, in which two or more debaters before each other argue, to establish one's own views and to nullify those of their opponents. The third *kathā* is *vitāṇḍā*, in which one of the two sides desires only to nullify the arguments of the opponent, without giving his own theories.

139 The original text presents the reading '*pratibandhabhāva*', but this is not tenable, so we prefer '*pratibandhakābhāva*'.

140 For the *Mīmāṃsakas*, the obstructing agent (*pratibandhaka*) is the entity that stops an effect when all the causes favourable to the production of that effect are present.

141 Here, the statement of Udayanācārya is contradicted, saying that it is also contrary to common experience.

142 We think that it is better to substitute the word '*pratibandhabhāva*' with '*pratibandhābhāva*'.

143 Here also in the text is the word '*kārya-pratibandhakābhāva*', but we prefer '*kāryakāraṇabhāva*', because if we maintain *pratibandhakābhāva* with *kārya*, the same *pratibandhakābhāva* cannot be *anyathāsiddha,* and also because *anvaya* and *vyatireka* are needed to confirm a cause-effect relationship.

144 Here, the *Mīmāṃsakas* contradict the *Nyāya* view. For the *Naiyāyikas*, non-apprehension (*anupalabdhi*) means the absence of apprehension (*upalabdhi*), so if the *Mīmāṃsakas* do not accept absence (*abhāva*) as a cause (*kāraṇa*), then how can the absence of *upalabdhi* be the cause of the cognition of absence? There is a contradiction. So, if *abhāva* cannot be a cause, how can the *Mīmāṃsakas* accept the *abhāva* of perception as a cause?

145 Opposite to apprehension of a positive entity (*bhāvopaladbhi*) is the *abhāvopaladbhi*. When this *bhāvopaladbhi* is not present, how can we use it for the positive concomitance (*anvaya*) or the negative one (*vyatireka*)? So ask the *Naiyāyikas*.

146 In the non-apprehension (*anupalabdhi*), there is no other cause than absence (*abhāva*), so the *Mīmāṃsakas* accept *anupalabdhi* as a cause (*kāraṇa*), but this does not mean that this acceptance of the causality of absence (*abhāvakāraṇatā*) is total.

147 The case under discussion is that of the fire, where it is possible to consider *śakti* a cause, against the superfluous absence of the obstructing agent (*pratibandhakābhāva*).

148 The *Naiyāyikas* also accept the direct perception of an absence; the *Mīmāṃsakas*, however, do not. It is not possible to catch the absence of anything through the senses. The *Naiyāyikas* accept six kinds of *saṃnikarṣas*, or union of the senses with their objects: 1) *saṃyoga*, union of an object and the sense, like a pitcher with the eye; 2) *saṃyuktasamavāya*, perception of what inheres to the object united with the sense, like the colour (*rūpa*) with a visible pitcher; 3) *saṃyuktasamavetasamavāya,* the perception of what inheres in the inherent entity of the perceived object, just as the generic attribute 'colour-ness' (*rūpatva*) is inherent in *rūpa* which is inherent (*samaveta*) in the pitcher; 4) *samavāya*, the inherence, the perception of the quality inherent in a substance, as with the sound in the ether: the faculty of hearing *(śrotra)* is said to be the ether (*ākāśa*) in the auricular cavity and the sound (*śabda*) is the particular quality of the ether. The relation established between quality (*guṇa*) and the qualified (*guṇin*) is *samavāya*, so the perception of sound in ether is possible for *samavāyasaṃnikarṣa*; 5) *samavetasamavāya*, the perception of what inheres in the inherent thing, just as the sound-ness (*śabdatva*) in sound (*śabda*), wherein the *śabda* is inherent in the hearing faculty (*śrotra*); 6) *viśeṣaṇaviśeṣyabhāva*, the relationship of qualifier-qualified, necessary for the perception of *abhāva*. So, the floor has the absence of the pitcher (*ghaṭābhāvavaddbhūtalam*); in this condition, the eye is united with the floor (*viśeṣya*), which is qualified by the absence of the pitcher (*viśeṣaṇa*). Here, the *Mīmāṃsakas* say that contact (*saṃyoga*) can only exist between two substances (*dravya*), and that absence (*abhāva*) is not a *dravya*, but the *indriyas* are. The scope of inherence-relation (*samavāya*) is limited to quality and the qualified, part and whole, and so on; it cannot be used to perceive *abhāva*. If

neither of them is useable, their union — *saṃyuktasamāvaya* and the like — cannot be used, either. So, five perceiving contacts (*saṃnikarṣa*) are eliminated in the matter of perception of the absence (*abhāvapratyakṣa*). The last is *viśeṣaṇaviśeṣyabhāva*, which is not a *saṃnikarṣa* according to the *Mīmāṃsakas*. Why? Because it does not correspond to the definition of relation (*sambandha* = *saṃnikarṣa*): '*sambandho hi sambandhibhyāṃ bhinnaḥ, ekaḥ dvīṣṭhaḥ viśiṣṭha-buddhiniyāmakaśca*'. Take the relation between a table and a pitcher. The relation, here contact (*saṃyoga*), is different from both pitcher and table; it is between them. First, *viśeṣaṇaviśeṣya-bhāva* is not 'one' (*eka*), because there is one qualifier-ness (*viśeṣaṇabhāva* = *viśeṣaṇatā*) and the other is qualified-ness (*viśeṣya-bhāva* = *viśeṣyatā*). '*Dvīṣṭha*' means *ubhyaniṣṭha*; the relation must reside in both objects related (*sambandhin*). But here, *viśeṣaṇatā* resides only in *viśeṣaṇa*, not in *viśeṣya*, and *viśeṣyatā* only in *viśeṣya*, not in *viśeṣaṇa*. Also, the first requirement, 'different from both the related objects', '*sambandhibhyāṃ bhinnaḥ*' is not present, because if we consider qualifier-ness (*viśeṣaṇatā*) as different from qualifier (*viśeṣaṇa*), all seven categories can be a *viśeṣaṇa*, and we would have to accept another category, *viśeṣaṇatā*. In fact, besides *viśeṣaṇatā*, there is no entity that we can find in all of the seven categories. Moreover, it cannot be included in any one of the seven. The same is true for qualified-ness (*viśeṣyatā*) if considered different from the qualified (*viśeṣya*). So, the *Naiyāyikas* must consider *viśeṣaṇatā* of the nature of *viśeṣaṇa* and *viśeṣyatā* to be *viśeṣya*-natured. So, if the definition (*lakṣaṇa*) of an entity is not harmonized with that selfsame entity, the result will be that, for example, a goat could be a cow as well. Here, the *lakṣaṇa* of relation (*sambandha*) is not connected to *viśeṣaṇaviśeṣyabhāva saṃnikarṣa*, so it cannot be a *saṃnikarṣa*. So, the *indriyas* cannot grasp an absence but can catch only a related object. If anyhow we accept the sensual perception of an *abhāva*, we must find a relation between the two; however, as we have seen, *viśeṣaṇaviśeṣyabhāva* cannot be that necessary relation. This is the reason why we gain knowledge of *abhāva* through non-apprehension and not direct perception.

149 There is an auxiliary explanation in the text. When we say '*daṇḍī puruṣaḥ*', 'the man with a stick', between them there is a *viśeṣaṇaviśeṣyabhāva*, wherein the stick (*daṇḍa*) is qualifier (*viśeṣaṇa*) of the man (*puruṣa*). Between them there is a contact relation (*saṃyogasambandha*). When we say '*sundaraḥ bālakaḥ*', or '*rūpavān bālakaḥ*', 'the beautiful boy', here as well qualified (*viśeṣya*) is the boy (*bālakaḥ*) and the *viśeṣaṇa* is the beauty (*rūpa*), but here beauty is a quality (*guṇa*), and so inheres in *bālaka* through inherence-relation (*samavāya-sambandha*). The author is saying that, if we accept the theory of the *viśeṣaṇa-viśeṣyabhāva*, we must determine which *sambandha* connects them, having eliminated already both *saṃyoga* and *samavāya*.

150 The text gives an example for inference, '*parvato vahnimān*', 'the mountain has fire', where the fire is in contact (*saṃyukta*) with the mountain, and it is also a qualifier of the mountain. So, here as well, the fire is perceptible because it is a connected qualifier (*saṃyuktaviśeṣaṇa*). However, we know that it cannot be so, because in this particular case *agni* is only *anumeya*, or cognizable through inference.

151 Here starts the answer of the *Mīmāṃsakas*. They say that, for a common man, it is compulsory for the senses to make contact with their object to gain direct perception. If we accept a direct perception (*pratyakṣa*) without the perceiving contact (*saṃnikarṣa*), then everything will begin to be directly perceived. So, if there is no direct perception of absence, there is no meaning of the positive and negative concomitances (*anvaya-vyatireka*) with senses, because here it is limited to the basis; the capacity of the senses vanishes in the ground (*adhikaraṇa*), so there is no *anvaya-vyatireka* of the *indriyas* with *abhāva*.

152 The *Naiyāyikas* accept that if an *indriya* is able to grasp one object, by that same *indriya* the absence of the object is also grasped along with the basis (*adhikaraṇa*) of that object. So, if every day we see a pitcher, it is appropriate to say that the absence of the pitcher and the table, on which is the pitcher, are also grasped by sight.

153 The pitcher is directly cognizable, Mount Meru is not before the eyes of a sighted man, so the pitcher upon Mt. Meru should be *pratyakṣagamya*. To this, the *Nyāya* reply that therein Mount Meru is the ground (*adhikaraṇa*) of the pitcher, but it is not directly perceived, so the pitcher and its absence of colour (*rūpābhāva*) are not perceived either, because the perception of the *adhikaraṇa* is compulsory in the perception of the absence (*abhāva*).

154 The blind man cannot see the pitcher or its absence of colour (*rūpābhāva*), so he knows it by touch. So, the visual sense is not grasping the pitcher, the ground (*adhikaraṇa*). He can grasp that *adhikaraṇa* and the counter-positive (*pratiyogin*), the colour (*rūpa*), only through the sight (*cakṣu*). In *Nyāya* there is a rule that an *indriya* can grasp an object as well as the *adhikaraṇa* of the absence of that object. Here the pitcher is known by the touch-sense (*tvāgindriya*), but the *pratiyogin, rūpa* or its *abhāva*, cannot be grasped by *tvāgindriya*.

155 The *Naiyāyikas* say that only the odour of a flower is graspable by the sense of smell, and not its basis as a flower or whatever; so, there the *pratiyogin* is odour (*gandha*), whose direct perception (*pratyakṣa*) is found through the sense of smell. But how do we perceive the *adhikaraṇa* (*anuyogin*) of the counter-positive (*pratiyogin*)? So, according to the *Nyāya*, there should not be any perception of the absence of odour (*gandhābhāva*) when someone takes the flower and smells it, saying 'it does not smell'. Through this reasoning, the *Naiyāyikas* vitiate the rule of the *Mīmāṃsakas,* according to which the *indriya* which grasps an object also grasps the ground (*adhikaraṇa*) of the absence (*abhāva*) of that object. In the same way, we can investigate the other example. We receive a perception of absence of colour (*rūpābhāva*) in the wind. The perception of the counter-positive (*pratiyogin*) of *rūpābhāva*, that is *rūpa*, takes place through sight, but its *adhikaraṇa*, the wind (*vāyu*), cannot be grasped by sight, so too *rūpābhāva* cannot be perceived.

156 The *Mīmāṃsakas* answer that the perception of colour (*rūpa*) is not by sight, so there is no problem: that knowledge will be gained through non-apprehension. Also, the *Naiyāyikas* say that only the absence of a counter-positive (*pratiyogin*) perceptible can be perceived, and definitely not the perception of the absence of an atom. So, they also say that not all the *abhāvas* are directly perceivable (*pra-*

tyakṣagamya). This is the same for the *Mīmāṃsakas*; some *abhāvas* are known through other means of knowledge (*pramāṇa*), as inference, presumption, or perception. But the *abhāvas* that the *Naiyāyikas* accept as *pratyakṣagamya* are seen by the *Mīmāṃsakas* as cognisable by non-apprehension (*anupalabdhigamya*).

157 Here, the other mean of knowledge (*pramāṇa*) is non-apprehension (*anupalabdhi*). So, *yogyānupalabdhigrāhya* means 'that what is worthy to be directly perceived is not so perceived'; so, the knowledge of this absence of perception is only possible through *anupalabdhi*.

158 To simplify, the *Mīmāṃsakas* are saying that if the pitcher were to be on the table, we ought to be able to see it; it is not, so we cannot.

159 Included in the concept of non-accessibility to sensorial perception (*indriya-grahanāyogyatā*), the worthiness to be perceived by the senses is also the *indriya*. So, if the *indriya* is the cognizer of the counter-positive (*pratiyogin*) and if it is not there, there will be neither the cognition of its ground (*adhikaraṇa*) nor the cognition of the absence of that *pratiyogin*.

160 Here, *vyāpakatva* and *vyāpyatva* are respectively called *niyamyatva* and *niyantṛtva*, on the basis that *vyāpti*, 'the invariable concomitance' also called *niyama*, 'rule'. When we consider the positive *vyāpti*, in the presence of two objects like fire and smoke, its shape will be "*yatra yatra dhūmaḥ (vyāpya), tatra tatra vahniḥ (vyāpaka)*". When they are absent, that is, in their *vyatireka*, the shape of the *vyāpti* will be just the opposite of the positive one (*anvaya*). The absence (*abhāva*) of what was pervaded (*vyāpya*) will be the pervader (*vyāpaka*), so the *abhāva* of what was *vyāpaka* will be *vyāpya: "yatra yatra vahnyabhāvaḥ tatra tatra dhūmābhāvaḥ*".

161 If there is no flaw, there will also be no absence of knowledge; that is, there will be right knowledge (*yathārtha jñana*). When there is flaw, then we have erroneous knowledge, not otherwise.

162 In our context, the effect is the burning of the fire (*dāhakārya*) and the cause is fire and the rest.

163 The mutual dependence is explained in the following lines. It is that before there is the knowledge of the obstruction (*pratibandhajñāna*), there is knowledge of the absence of effect (*kāryābhāvajñāna*). Not being *pratibandhajñāna*, there will not be *kāryābhāvajñāna*, either. So, on the basis of *kāryābhāvajñāna*, we start to seek an obstruction (*pratibandha*), due to which the effect does not take place, even if all the causes are present. When we ascertain the *pratibandha*, then shall we say "Due to this, the effect comes not". Moreover, the knowledge of *pratibandha* is included in the *pratibandhābhāva*, and *Naiyāyikas* consider *pratibandhābhāva* a cause, so the ascertainment of the obstruction (*pratibandha*) must be previous, but the *pratibandha* will be established only after the absence of effect.

164 When we know that *mantrādi* as obstruction (*pratibandha*) is there, we will understand that the causal complex lacks something.

165 The absence of the obstructions (*pratibandha*) like *mantra*, gem (*maṇi*) and the like is included in the causal complex (*sāmagrī*). The knowledge of the

insufficiency of *sāmagrī* will be next to the knowledge of the *pratibandha*. On the other side, we have that only knowing the insufficiency of the *sāmagrī*, we can understand that there is an obstruction.

166 *Naiyāyikas* try to nullify the mutual dependence given by the *Mīmāṃsakas*. The fire alone has both positive and negative concomitance with its burning effect: "*yatra yatra vahnistatra tatra dāhaḥ, yatra yatra vahnyabhāvastatra tatra dāhābhāvaḥ*". In the same way, we observe the positive and negative concomitance (*anvaya-vyatireka*) between the absence of the obstructing agent (*pratibandhakābhāva*) and the effect: "*yatra yatra maṇyādyabhāvastatra tatra dāhaḥ, yatra yatra maṇyādyabhāvābhāḥ (maṇyadiḥ) tatra tatra dāhābhāvaḥ*".

167 We will have innumerable absences (*abhāva*) of the same object, or an object homogeneous to that and of different kinds, all this expressed by the word '*ādi*', 'etcetera', after '*maṇi*'.

168 The second option is to gather all the various *abhāvas* of the multitude of obstructing agents (*pratibandhakas*) into one collective name '*pratibandhakābhāva*', in general. So, the question is in regards to the nature of the causality of the absence of the gem and the like (*maṇyādyabhāva*). In the texts we find this option expressed in two nouns, 1) *pratyekaparyāpta*, and 2) *samuditaparyāpta*. That is, the *kāraṇatā* must be accepted in all the single entities, or in their general collectivity.

169 As the *abhāvas* of only a single obstructing agent (*pratibandhaka*), like *candrakānta*, are innumerable, how can we imagine the positive and negative concomitance (*anvaya-vyatireka*) of the other kind of *abhāvas* of the obstructing agents (*pratibandhaka*) with the effect as well? So, in this option, there is a *gaurava* flaw, 'excessive heaviness'.

170 Here, *pratibandhakābhāva* has been said to be the cause, the insufficiency of the causal complex (*visāmagrī*) is the obstruction (*pratibandha*). In the compound *pratibandhakābhāva*, the qualifier of the *abhāva*, its counter-positive (*pratiyogin*) is obstructing agent (*pratibandhaka*), the nullifier of the causal complex. We know that there is a general rule '*abhāvajñāne pratiyogijñānaṃ kāraṇam*', that is 'in the knowledge of the absence, the knowledge of the counter-positive is its cause'. Here the knowledge of the *pratibandhakābhāva* is impossible without the knowledge of the obstructing agent (*pratibandhaka*). So, here, to understand the *pratibandhakābhāva* we need the knowledge of obstructing agent (*pratibandhaka*). But only when the causality of *pratibandhakābhāva* has been proven can we call it obstructing agent (*pratibandhaka*): this is a mutual dependence.

171 It has been said here that the reason to consider cause to be *pratibandhakābhāva*, *kāraṇa* can be only the disinterest of the cause in producing effect, just as, for example, a teacher who refuses to teach.

172 We see here the previously mentioned presumption that has the form of an otherwise inapplicability (*kāryānyathā-upapatti-rūpā arthāpatti*). If in the cause there would not be the *śakti* to produce the effect, then the arising of the effect could not take place. So, only by accepting *śakti* as cause have we the solution to the incongruity of the effect.

173 Only by accepting *śakti* is it possible to see a logical application of the cause-effect relation. In fact, to produce curd we need only milk, not water or the like.

174 *Naiyāyikas* accept essential nature (*svabhāva*) instead of power (*śakti*) as a cause. Here, the erstwile applicability (*anyathā upapatti*) is also like this; without accepting *śakti* we see the possibility of the cause-effect relation, just as it is the nature of milk to produce curd, and not of water. So, there is no need to maintain *śakti*. However, at this point the *Mīmāṃsakas* ask for the real intended meaning (*abhiprāya*) of this *anyathā upapatti* of the *Naiyāyikas*, furnishing two options and thereafter rejecting both.

175 *Mīmāṃsakas* state that if we must accept *svabhāva* extending greatly its field of action, many of the categories (*padārtha*) recognized by *Nyāya* will be substituted by that same *svabhāva*. The activity of categories like generic attribute (*sāmānya*), inherence (*samavāya*), particularity (*viśeṣa*) and so on, can be also performed by *svabhāva*, just as it is the nature of the pitcher to be endowed with colour. Or, as we have seen in substance (*dravya*), quality (*guṇa*) and action (*karman*) inheres the same mode of general attribute of existence (*sattā*), but how can we call *sattā* 'existent' '*sat*', for we must consider another existence (*sattā*) as inherent within the first one, and so there will be *regressus ad infinitum* (*anavasthā*). So, just as *Naiyāyikas* accept as existent *sattā* even without any other existence (*sattāntara*) inherent within it, they can also accept *dravya*, *guṇa*, and *karma* as existent even without any *sattā* inherent within them.

176 In the previous paragraph, the explanation was regarding 'the generic attribute' (*sāmānya*); now, the other two mentioned categories (*padārtha*) 'inherence' (*samavāya*) and 'particularity' (*viśeṣa*) are treated.

177 The essential nature of particularity (*viśeṣa*) is to be individually differentiated '*svato vyāvṛttaḥ*', so, the *Mīmāṃsakas* ask the reason out of which the *Naiyāyikas* don't accept that an individual self (*ātman*) like other eternal *dravyas*, is different from other *ātman*, of its own nature.

178 Besides other such categories, the *Naiyāyikas* accept time and space as common causes (*sādhāraṇa kāraṇa*) towards any effect. Therefore, an effect would occur in a given moment and place, not otherwise. If we accept *svabhāva*, we could also state that it is the *svabhāva* of a thing to arise in a particular time and place.

179 Here begins the dismissal by the *Mīmāṃsakas* of the second option offered for the question regarding the real intended meaning (*abhiprāya*) of the otherwise applicability (*anyathā upapatti*).

180 Where we have evidence concerning a certain *padārtha*, there the situation will be organized on the basis of that *padārtha* established by means of knowledge (*pramāṇa*). However, while there is no *pramāṇa* in accepting an entity, the *Naiyāyikas* insist we must accept the essential nature (*svabhāva*). So though *svabhāva* we will be able to give some logical order to the situation.

181 *Mīmāṃsakas* conclude, following the *Naiyāyikas* reasoning, by affirming that *śakti* is ascertained through means of knowledge (*pramāṇa*), so there is no need to take refuge in *svabhāva*.

182 '*Advīṣṭha*' means that *śakti* resides only in fire, not in any other connected object.

183 With this precision the *Mīmāṃsakas* avoid the flaw of proving what is already proved (*siddhasādhanatā*) and the flaw of the meaning different than the desired one (*arthāntaratā*). With the first definition, the flaw in uncommon perception (*alaukikapratyakṣa*) called *jñānalakṣaṇapratyāsatti* is avoided, with the second, in the common subsequent cognition (*anuvyavasāya*). So, except for those two kinds of cognition, the meaning of the term *atīndriya* is our intended *śakti*.

184 Praśastapāda was the commentator on the *Vaiśeṣikasūtra*, with his famous *bhāṣ ya* called '*Padārthadharmasaṃgraha*'. He also accepted the aforementioned entities like *atīndriya*. So, the *Mīmāṃsakas* prove that their given meaning of *atīndriyatva* is absolutely not uncommon.

185 From among the 24 *guṇa*, the *Naiyāyikas* also accept *saṃskāra*, 'impression'. This *saṃskāra* is tripartite: 1) *vega*, 'speed'; 2) *bhāvanā*, 'inner falling', and 3) *sthitisthāpaka*, 'elasticity'. Here, the word '*bhāvanā*' used by Praśastapāda indicated not only itself but elasticity as well.

186 The word *āśraya* in the inference means merely a ground of *agni* or a basis in which *agni* is related through inherence (*samavāya*).

187 Here is the critic of the *Naiyāyikas*. There are also different entities (*padārtha*) than *śakti*, whose ground is fire. Sometimes *agni* can be the ground of wind, as with the flames, or of atoms different from its own. So, wind and *pramāṇas* respond to the description given by the probandum (*sādhya*) of the inference; so, there will be the flaw of a 'meaning other than the desired one' (*arthāntara*) and 'proving of what is already proved' (*siddhasādhanatā*).

188 *Advaita Vedāntins* and *Bhāṭṭa Mīmāṃsakas*, instead of inherence (*samavāya*), accept *tādātmya*, 'identity'. So they cannot consider a ground related to the ground of *samavāya*.

189 From this point starts the answer of the *Mīmāṃsakas*. Its meaning is that the action of the *samavāya* relation of *Nyāya* is substituted by another relation (*sambandha*) in *Mīmāṃsā*; through that relation, fire is a ground. This *sambandha* is called *tādātmya*, as we have seen, or otherwise *vaiśiṣṭya*, 'peculiarity'.

190 Here, the *Mīmāṃsakas* refered to are the followers of Prabhākara. So, the *Naiyāyikas* can say that Prabhākara considers actions (*karman*) as the *Bhāṭṭa Mīmāṃsakas* consider *śakti*, not residing in two objects (*advīṣṭha*) and *atīndriya* different from elasticity (*sthitisthāpaka*), so there is a meaning other then the desired one (*arthāntaratā*). But the answer of the *Bhāṭṭas* will be that they do not accept the *atīndriyatva* of action, so there is no *arthāntaratā*.

191 Again, the *Naiyāyikas* ask 'what is the reason why, when the *mantra* or gem (*maṇi*) or whatever are present, the effect does not take place?' So, the position of the *Mīmāṃsakas*, according to which *abhāva* cannot be a cause, is sublated.

192 Still, the *Naiyāyikas* say that "if *śakti* is in substances (*dravya*), qualities (*guṇa*) and actions (*karman*), why then is there the division between them, since all should become *dravya*?" Because the *guṇas* cannot reside in the actions, as well as in the qualities, but only in the *dravyas*. This position is preceded by the refutation (*khaṇḍana*) of the *Mīmāṃsakas*, "*yah bhī kahnā ṭhīk nahīṃ hai*".

193 So, the *Naiyāyikas* say that if *śakti* is grounded in substances (*dravya*), as well as in qualities (*guṇa*) and actions (*karman*), and similarly as well for *guṇa* and *karman* will be possible to affirm their ground-ness in qualities (*guṇāśrayatva*). This position of the *Mīmāṃsakas* is not tenable, because if *guṇas* and *karman* are considered to be grounds for *guṇa*, it will be impossible to cancel the previously-mentioned inadequacy (*anupapatti*). We have to remember that in the beginning of this statement of the *Naiyāyikas*, there is the refutation of the *Mīmāṃsakas*.

194 The characteristic referred to here is the *śakti* intended in the inference. What is the ground (*adhikaraṇa*) of a quality cannot be the *adhikaraṇa* of *śakti* say the *Naiyāyikas*, and there is no other *adhikaraṇa* of a *guṇa* other than *dravya*, so *śakti* cannot be present in any other category. Here, the *Mīmāṃsakas* refute this. In the inference, the locus (*pakṣa*) is fire (*vahni*), but it has to be considered as an indirect indicator (*upalakṣaṇa*) of any positive entity. So there is a common rule for inference, according to which the entities that came inside the *pakṣa* cannot be example (*dṛṣṭānta*), for example. In fact, we have seen that another appellation of *dṛṣṭānta* is *sapakṣa*, "which surely possiedes the probandum, *sādhya*" (*niścitasādhyavān sapakṣaḥ*); both opponents accept the presence of *sādhya* in the *sapakṣa* and in the *dṛṣṭānta*. The definition of *pakṣa* is '*saṃdigdhasādhyavān pakṣaḥ*', in whose 'locus the presence of *sādhya* is doubted' and is not already established, therefore we cannot consider those things coming into the *pakṣa* to be examples. The *Mīmāṃsakas* say here that they accept *śakti* not only in fire, but everywhere, so it is not proper to posit one of those things as *dṛṣṭānta*; however, without *dṛṣṭānta*, there will not be any ascertainment of the invariable concomitance (*vyāptiniścaya*), so also inference, being based on *vyāpti*, would be impossible.

195 *Īśvara* is accepted by both the opponents (*vādin-prativādin*) like *Vedāntins* and *Naiyāyikas*, so we can consider Him as the example (*dṛṣṭānta*). However, for the *Mīmāṃsakas* who do not accept *Īśvara*, the probandum (*sādhya*) in their inference (*anumāna*) corresponds to *Īśvara*, so there is the flaw of proving something other than what was desired (*arthāntaratā*). But, the solution of the *Mīmāṃsakas* is to give a new adjective, 'born from a born existent entity' (*janyabhāvajanya*), which is not applicable to *Īśvara*.

196 The newest problem found by the *Naiyāyikas* is that by giving the other *viśeṣaṇa*, it will be impossible to confirm *śakti* in the external categories (*padārtha*). But the *Mīmāṃsakas* say that the establishment of *śakti* in eternal entities can be done by applying the example of the non-eternal (*anitya*).

197 Were we to find a part-whole relation (*avayavāvayavin*), we are before a non-eternal entity (*anityapadārtha*). In fact, whatever entity (*padārtha*) is endowed with parts (*avayavin*) is created, so is also non-eternal (*anitya*).

198 The atoms (*paramāṇu*) are eternal in *Nyāya*, so too are their colour (*rūpa*) and other qualities. But, the *rūpa* in non-eternal objects is as those objects, non-eternal (*anitya*). So too is *śakti* of two types, say the *Mīmāṃsakas*, eternal (*nitya*) and *anitya*. For them, the *śakti* in the *nitya padārthas* is *nitya* and that in the *anityas* is born from a positive existent cause (*bhāvahetujā*), which is the same as our adjective *janyabhāvajanya*.

199 Here, with the word *apramāṇa* used by Svāmī Karpātrī is a *bahuvrīhī* compound not used in Hindi, which means *apramāṇika*, 'not established'.

200 The *Mīmāṃsakas* are saying that they do not accept within the unsentient grains (*acetana vrīhī*) or such places the presence of invisible retributive power (*adṛṣṭa*) in the form of righteousness and unrighteousness (*dharmādharma*), but rather in something other than it. They call it *adṛṣṭa* — literally meaning 'invisible' — because that *dharma* is beyond the sensorial range (*atīndriya*). So, through the sprinkling (*prokṣaṇa*), the created special property is not *dharmādharma*.

201 The invisible new resultants (*apūrva*) produced by the secondary rites (*aṅga*) is summarized with the *apūrva* of the main rite forming the *pradhānāpūrva*.

202 We can conceive of an invisible result (*adṛṣṭaphala*) only if no visible result (*dṛṣṭaphala*) is present, and not otherwise. Here, the *dṛṣṭaphala* is not seen, so the *adṛṣṭaphala*, like the invisible new retribution (*apūrva*), must be accepted; otherwise, the vedic injunction (*vidhi*) regarding the sprinkling (*prokṣaṇa*) will be refuted.

203 Here is the *Mīmāṃsaka*'s answer to the *Naiyāyika*'s statement about the fact that the accusative word (*dvitiyā śruti*) in "*vrīhīn prokṣati*" ["He sprinkles the grains"] is subordinate (*gauṇa*). The *Mīmāṃsakas* affirm that when we have a clear logical applicability of the principal, literal meaning (*mukhyārtha* = *vācyārtha*), it is not possible to take recourse to the implication (*lakṣaṇā*) in order to furnish an implied secondary meaning (*lakṣyārtha*). In fact, the rule intended for the use of *lakṣaṇā* is only applicable when the *mukhyārtha* is not clearly and completely understood.

204 The following passage until the next note appears in *JISOA* XIII, p. 173 under the title of 'The Unborn'.

205 The following passage until the note *207* appears in *JISOA* XIII, p. 174.

206 *Bhagavad Gītā*, trans. Swami Gambhirananda, *op. cit.*, pp. 374, 376, 549, 570 and 570, for the 5 quotations of this passage.

207 The following passage until the next note appears in *JISOA* XIII, pp. 175-176.

208 These two *ślokas* appear in *JISOA* XIII, p. 173.

209 The following passage until the next note appears in *JISOA* XIII, p. 176.

210 The three following *ślokas* appear in *JISOA* XIII, p. 139.

211 This *śloka* was omitted in *JISOA* XIII.

212 These two *ślokas* appear in *JISOA* XIII, p. 140.

213 These two *ślokas* appear in *JISOA* XIII, p. 176.

214 The following passage until the note *216* appears in *JISOA* XIII, p. 175.

215 This matter is quite discussed in many vedantic treatises, in which the *Vedāntins* maintain that *ajñāna* is a positive entity, when the *Naiyāyikas* and other philosophers contrast this theory. They state that *ajñāna* cannot be a positive entity because the word is prefixed by 'a', that, grammatically, is a negative determinative compound (*nañtatpuruṣa*). For this reason the meaning of that privative '*a*' is absence (*abhāva*), therephore the term *ajñāna* means 'absence of knowledge' (*jñānābhāva*).

216 The following passage until the note *218* was omitted in *JISOA* XIII.

217 Technically speaking the definitions of counter-positive (*pratiyogin*) and its basis (*anuyogin*) are respectively: *yasya abhāvaḥ sa pratiyogin*, that is 'the counter-positive is an entity whose absence is present'; *yasmin abhāvaḥ sa anuyogin*, 'the basis [of the counter-positive] is the ground in which the absence is present'. Here the *Naiyāyikas*, differently from the *Vedānta* followers, mantain that knowledge (*jñāna*) is a property/quality (*guṇa*) of the self (*ātman*), which is a substance (*dravya*) where it resides through an inherence relation (*samavāya-sambandha*). So, for example, when the individual is in deep sleep, his self doesn't know anything, so in that moment knowledge is the counter-positive and the ground of its absence is the self. If we see the couple *anuyogin-pratiyogin* from a relational point of view, then the substained entity is the *pratiyogin* and its substainer, its ground is the *anuyogin*.

218 The following passage until the next note appears in *JISOA* XIII, p. 176.

219 This passage appears in *JISOA* XIII, p. 161.

220 The following passage until the next note was omitted in *JISOA* XIII.

221 The sentences and *ślokas* until the next note appear in *JISOA* XIII, pp. 165-166.

222 These two *ślokas* appear in *JISOA* XIII, p. 166.

223 The following passage until the note *225* appears in *JISOA* XIII, p. 156.

224 The *karma* who has already start to give the results of actions.

225 The following passage until the next note appears in *JISOA* XIII, p. 157. Daniélou makes a new paragraph here.

226 The following passage until the next note appears in *JISOA* XIII, p. 158.

227 This *śloka* was omitted in *JISOA* XIII.

228 The following passage until the next note appears in *JISOA* XIII, p 144.

229 The following passage until the next note appears in *JISOA* XIII, p. 145.

230 The following passage until the next note appears in *JISOA* XIII, p. 146.

231 From this whole paragraph, these four words are the only which Daniélou did not translate. Alain Daniélou, who was a known opponent of monotheism, became famous as the author of *Hindu Polytheism*, a book based on more than 150 quotations of Svāmī Karpātrī, in their 'adapted translation'.

232 The following passage until the next note was omitted in *JISOA* XIII.

233 This passage appears in *JISOA* XIII, p. 165.

234 Every mental modification (*vṛtti*) has an object, and this *vṛtti* dispels the ignorance relative to that object. But this kind of *vṛtti* is destroyed by another *vṛtti* whose content is a different object. There is one supreme and ultimate *vṛtti*, born from the hearing of the upaniṣadic great sayings from the master, which has *brahman* as its object. When this *vṛtti*, through a long practice become ininterrupted is called *akhaṇḍākāravṛtti*, a unique mental modification which has an uninterrupted flow.

235 This passage until the next note was omitted in *JISOA* XIII.

236 This passage until the note *238* appears in *JISOA* XIII, p. 142.

237 See the *Taittirīya Upaniṣad* II.8.2-4.

238 This passage until the note *240* was omitted in *JISOA* XIII.

239 *Mūlājñāna* is the ignorance attributed to *saguṇa brahman* by which he doesn't recognize his *nirguṇa* nature, and the *tūlājñāna* is the ignorance associated to individual objects.

240 The following passage until the next note appears in *JISOA* XIII, p. 146.

241 These sentences until the next note were omitted in *JISOA* XIII.

242 This sentence appears in *JISOA* XIII, p. 146.

243 This sentence was omitted in *JISOA* XIII.

244 The following passage until the next note appears in *JISOA* XIII, pp. 146-147

245 This passage, like all the others, is taken from the *Durgasaptaśatī*. Here, in particular, is mentioned the verse I.42 and following.

246 In *JISOA* XIII, A.D. makes here a new paragraph.

247 The terms *svāhā* and *svadhā* are the *mantras* which follow the oblations, respectively, to the deities and to the ancestors.

248 The following passage until the next note appears in *JISOA* XIII, p. 164-165.

249 The following passage until the note *251* appears in *JISOA* XIII, p. 177-178.

250 Innumerable passages of vedāntic texts affirm that the only method to realize the Supreme is through the instruction regarding the great-sayings (*mahāvākyo-padeśa*). Strinckly speaking this is *brahmavidyā*. Confront with *Kena Upaniṣad* III.11 and IV.1 with the commentary of Śaṅkarācārya.

251 The following passage until the note *255* appears in *JISOA* XIII, p. 148.

252 The sound in its four manifestations, as transcendant, intentional, mental and audible.

253 This episode is also narrated in the second and third chapters of *Durgasaptaśatī*.

254 The hymn of the deities to the Goddess is in the chapter four of the *Durgasaptaśatī*.

255 The following passage until the next note appears in *JISOA* XIII, pp. 150-151.

256 This deed is narrated from the chapter five until the chapter eleven of the *Durgasaptaśatī*.

257 This sentence was omitted in *JISOA* XIII.

258 In *JISOA* XIII, p. 151, Daniélou made here a new paragraph. The passage until the next note appears in pp. 151-154.

259 In *JISOA* XIII, A.D. makes here a new paragraph.

260 Till here the deed narrated is found in the fifth chapter of *Durgasaptaśatī*. Afterwards starts the narration related to the sixth and seventh chapters, in which, respectively, appear the slaying of Dhūmralocana and that of Caṇḍa and Muṇḍa.

261 Here the deeds related to the eighth chapter of *Durgasaptaśatī* are narrated.

262 The Devi's deeds narrated from this point, until the end of the paragraph, are related to the chapters nine, ten and eleven of *Durgasaptaśatī*, in which are described the death of Śumbha, Niśumbha and the eulogy of the gods extolling the Great Goddesses.

263 The following passage until the next note appears in *JISOA* XIII, p. 164.

264 The following passage until the next note appears in *JISOA* XIII, pp. 154-156.

265 The following passage until the next note was omitted in *JISOA* XIII.

266 The *Devisūkta* is composed in eight stanzas contained in *Ṛgveda* X.10.124 and following.

267 The following passage until the next note appears in *JISOA* XIII, pp. 191-192.

268 The Supreme Self is called also *samudra*, 'the sea', the resting place of all the waters, because *brahman* is the place in which every thing enters as do the rivers in the sea. Every modification of the internal organ (*antaḥkaraṇavṛtti*) has as its object the selfsame Consciousness (*caitanya*), but limited by some accidental conditions (*upādhyavacchinna*). So, also those modifications, as for waters, have their resting place in *caitanya*, which is like the sea. In this point of the text, a particular state of the intellect (*buddhivṛtti*) is compared with the waters, due to their common transparency and fluidity. In this sentence also an other important tenet of the *Advaita Vedānta* is hidden, that is the capability to grasp or to pervade *brahman* through the modifications of the intellect (*vṛttivyāpyatva*): as waters pervade the sea, the ultimate, undivided *vṛtti* (*akhaṇḍākāravṛtti*) pervades, that is, has *brahman* as its object. See also note 5 p. 334 and 234 p. 360.

269 Here we find a reference related to the the *darśana*, 'the seeing' of the vedic seers, according to which they were not composer of the *mantras* (*mantrakartā*), but seers of them (*mantradraṣṭā*).

270 The translation of this sentence appears in *JISOA* XIII, p. 165.

271 The following passage until the next note was omitted in *JISOA* XIII.

272 The following passage until the next note appears in *JISOA* XIII, p. 179.

273 The following passage until the next note appears in *JISOA* XIII, p. 186.

274 In *Vedānta*, *māyā* or *avidyā* has been said to be embodied with two *śaktis*: *āvaraṇaśakti*, through which the reality is concealed, and *vikṣepaśakti*, through which this universe is imagined above the concealed reality as substratum.

275 The following passage until the next note was omitted in *JISOA* XIII.

276 The following passage until the next note appears in *JISOA* XIII, pp. 168-170.

277 The following passage until the note *280* appears in *JISOA* XIII, pp. 180-182.

278 Names of Viṣṇu.

279 Names of Pārvatī.

280 The following passage until the next note, which contradict the Daniélou's theory about 'Śiva Lord of Tamas' was omitted in *JISOA* XIII and was never mentioned by Daniélou. See supra, *The problem of Daniélou's translations*, p. 42.

281 On this issues see *Sāṃkhya Kārikā* 12-13.

282 This sentence of Svāmī Karpātrī, which contradicts Daniélou's theories against mixed marriages, was omitted in *JISOA* XIII and never mentioned by Daniélou.

283 These *ślokas* appeared in *JISOA* XIII, p. 178.

284 This passage appears in *JISOA* XIII at the bottom of p. 182.

285 This following sentence was omitted in *JISOA* XIII.

286 The following passage until the next note appears in *JISOA* XIII at the top of p. 182.

287 The following passage until the next note appears in *JISOA* XIII, p. 183-190.

288 All these descriptions are taken from the *Tantras* and here mostly from *Śāktapramoda*.

289 A.D., *JISOA* XIII, p. 183 : "this Goddess made of the descending tendency (*tamas*)".

290 A.D., *JISOA* XIII, p. 184 : "The shape of this Arch-Power of Time Maha Kali is that Bliss beyond the beyond, which is the supremely transcendent Bliss-shape of the Principle, the *brahman*".

291 The following passage until the next note appears in *JISOA* XIII, p. 184.

292 A.D., *JISOA* XIII, p. 184 : "In the Night of Time, which is the state of universal dissolution, this light appears, like a star, giving both knowledge of the supersensible world and the means to this knowledge."

293 *Ślokas* omitted by A.D. in *JISOA* XIII, p. 184.

294 *Ślokas* omitted by A.D. in *JISOA* XIII, p. 184.

295 Sentence omitted by A.D. in *JISOA* XIII, p. 184.

296 This poison is the terrible one, which came out due to the *samudramanthana*.

297 A.D. in *JISOA* XIII, p. 185 : "who plays lustfully with him".

298 Sentence and following *ślokas* omitted by A.D. in *JISOA* XIII, p. 185.

299 A.D. in *JISOA* XIII, p. 185: "is called Shiva".

300 A.D., *JISOA* XIII, p. 186: "The Lady of Spheres (Bhuvaneshvari)".

301 A.D., *JISOA* XIII, p. 186: "The Three-mothered (Tri-ambaka)".

302 A.D. makes two more paragraphs: "The lady of the spheres", "Her marvelous radiance," *JISOA* XIII, pp. 186-187.

303 These *ślokas* were not quoted by A.D. in *JISOA* XIII, p. 187.

304 These *ślokas* were translated into Hindi by Svāmī Karpātri; we follow his translation.

305 A.D. in *JISOA* XIII, p. 188: "as the deceitful (Bagala)".

306 These *ślokas* were translated into Hindi by Svāmī Karpātri; we follow his translation.

307 These *ślokas* were translated into Hindi by Svāmī Karpātri; we follow his translation. *Ślokas* and translation were omitted by A.D. in *JISOA* XIII, p. 188.

308 These *ślokas* were translated in Hindi by Svāmī Karpātri; we follow his translation.

309 A.D. in *JISOA* XIII, p. 190 make here a new paragraph: "The Amourous, Lalita".

310 A.D. in *JISOA* XIII, p. 190 make here one more paragraph: "The lady of lust, Kameshvari", "the ten *Mahāvidyās*" becoming twelve.

311 This is only to underline that *śakti* is the inhabiting Consciousness inside them, who permits them to fulfil their respective functions.

312 In the *JISOA* XIII, paragraph moved by A.D. until the end of the article, pp. 192-193.

313 The following passage until the next note appears in the *JISOA* XIII, p. 170.

314 The following passage until the next note was omitted in *JISOA* XIII.

315 The following passage until the next note appears in *JISOA* XIII, p. 194.

316 The following passage until the next note appears in *JISOA* XIII, pp. 159-160.

317 The following passage until the next note appears in *JISOA* XIII, pp. 162-163.

318 The following *ślokas* were omitted in *JISOA* XIII.

319 The following passage until the next note appears in *JISOA* XIII, p. 159.

320 The following passage until the next note appears in *JISOA* XIII, p. 194.

321 This part called "The All-Powerful Goddess as Śakti" appears in *JISOA* XIII, p. 158.

322 *Prakāśa* is the result of successive sublations of the superimpositions, so it cannot stay without its reflection and, on the contrary, there cannot be a reflection without a light as its origin.

323 The following passage until the next note was omitted in *JISOA* XIII.

324 That *sundopasundanyāya* is an example of the reciprocal relation of destroyer-destroyed. In the *Mahābhārāta* we find that two demon brothers, called Sunda and Upasunda killed each other in order to gain the favour of the *apsaras* Tilottamā.

325 Here there is an allusion of the fifth definition of *avidyā*, *māyā*, *mithyā*, as presented in the *Iṣṭasiddhi* of Vimuktātmācārya, and again discussed in the fifth *mithyātva* of the *Advaita Siddhi*.

326 The following passage until the next note appears in *JISOA* XIII, p. 142.

327 The following passage until the next note was omitted in *JISOA* XIII.

328 The following passage appears with some changes and an interpolation in the end of the article published in *JISOA* XIII p. 195.

329 The following passage until the next note appears in *JISOA* XIII, p. 143.

330 The following passage until the next note appears in *JISOA* XIII, p. 142.

331 The following passage until the next note was omitted in *JISOA* XIII.

332 The following passage until the next note appears in *JISOA* XIII, p. 171.

333 We translate here *viṣayin*, litteraly 'possessor of the object' and *viṣaya* 'object' remembering the explanation made by Śaṅkarācārya in the beginning of his commentary on the *Brahmasūtras*.

334 The following passage until the next note appears in *JISOA* XIII, p. 158.

335 The following passage until the next note was omitted in *JISOA* XIII.

336 These are the nine forms of the *devīs* adored during the nine days-nights of Durgā *pujā*.

337 The following passage until the next note appears in *JISOA* XIII, p. 160.

338 The following passage until the next note appears in *JISOA* XIII, p. 163.

339 The following passage until the next note appears in *JISOA* XIII, pp. 161-162.

340 The following *ślokas* were omitted in *JISOA* XIII, surely because they are very close to Christian ideas of compassion, even in the vocabulary, and these ideas were not recognized by Daniélou as universal spiritual teachings, but as 'moralism' characterizing 'monotheism'.

341 Certainly due to the same reasons of similarities with the religious climate of Christianity, the following passage until the next note was omitted in *JISOA* XIII. We follow here the translation of the *ślokas* done by Svāmī Karpātrī.

342 The text of this verse present the reading '*jāgradakhilātiśayām*'. Even if we translated the word according to this compound, a more appropriate reading could be '*jagadakhilātiśyām*', that is 'the excellence in the whole universe'.

343 The following passage until the next note appears in *JISOA* XIII, p. 144.

344 The following passage until the next note, underlining the intimate relation between the Lord and His Śakti, was omitted by Daniélou in *JISOA* XIII.

345 The following passage until the end appears in *JISOA* XIII, pp. 143-144.

346 These *ślokas* concluding the whole article and underlining, one more time, the indivisibility of Śiva-Śakti and the similarities between Śaivism and Vaiṣṇavism, were omitted by Daniélou in *JISOA* XIII.

Selected Bibliography of Svāmī Karpātrī

Ahamartha aur Paramārthasāra (The meaning of ego and the essence of the supreme knowledge), Svāmī Maheśvarānanda Sarasvatī, Ara, Tha. Radhamohana Simha Prakasaka, 2019 (1962), pp. 280.

Bhagavat tattva (The principle of the Lord), G.S. Misra, Kasi, Mulacandra Copra Prakasaka, 1997 (1940), pp. 722.

Bhagavatsudhā (The nectar of the Bhagavata Purāṇa), III ed., Kalkattā-Vṛndāvana-Dillī, Rādhakṛṣṇa Dhānukā Prakāśana Saṁsthāna, 2054 (1997), pp. 391.

Bhaktirasārṇavaḥ (The ocean of the taste of devotion), Govinda Narahari Vaijāpurakara, Kalkattā, Bhaktisudhā Sāhitya Pariṣad Prakāśana, 2025 (1968), pp. 266.

Bhaktisudhā (The nectar of devotion), Dillī, Śrī Rādhakṛṣṇa Dhānukā Prakāśana Sansthāna, 2000, pp. 1060.

Bhramara Gīta (The Song of the Bumble Bee), Srimati P. Jhunjhun-vala, Varanasi, Visvadiyalaya Prakasana, 1999, pp. 191.

Caturvarṇya-saṃskṛti-vimarśaḥ (Reflections on the culture of the varṇa institution), 2 vol., Pt. R.G. Sukla. Srisantasaranavedanti, Puri, Govarddhana Maṭha, I part 2030 (1973), II part 2036 (1979).

Dharmakṛtyopayogi-tithyādi-nirṇayaḥ kumbha-parvanirṇayaśca (Decision about the lunar days and other issues to perform rituals and the Kumbha Parva), (with M.H. Ojha), Akhila Bharatiya Varanasi, Dharma Saṃgha, 2021 (1965).

Gītā jayantī aur Bhīṣmotkrānti, (khaṇḍa 1) (Anniversary of the *Gītā* and the departure of Bhīṣma), Kalkattā-Vṛndāvana, Rādhā--kṛṣ ṇa Dhānukā Prakāṇana Saṃsthāna, 1986, pp. 242.

Gopī Gīta. Dārśanika vivecana (The Song of the Gopis. A philosophical disquisition), Srimati P. Jhunjhunavala, Varanasi, Sri Markandeya Brahmacari Prakasaka, 1989, pp. 547.

Hindūkoḍabil pramāṇa kī kasauṭī par (The Hindu Code Bill in the light of proofs), Kalkattā, Akhila Bhāratīya Hindīkoḍabil Virodha Samiti, 2006 (1949), pp. 260.

Jāti, Rāṣṭra aur Saṃskṛti (Caste, State and culture), Svāmī Sadānanda Sarasvatī 'Vedāntī Svāmī', Varanasi, Śrī Karapātra Dhāma, s.d., pp. 64.

Karapātra cintana (Reflections of Swami Karpatri), 1st ed. 1994, Sadānanda Sarasvatī (Vedāntījī), Varanasi, Karapātra Dhāma, 2001, pp. 236.

Kyā sambhoga se samādhi (From sex to samadhi: Is it possible?), Sadānanda Sarasvatī (Vedāntījī), Varanasi, Karapātra Dhāma, 2032 [1975], pp. 112.

Mārksvāda aur Rāmarājya (Marxism and the Kingdom of Rāma), [5th ed., I ed. 2014 (1957)], G. S. Misra, Gorakhpur, Gita Press, 2053 (1996), pp. 860.

Nāstika-āstikavāda (The orthodox and heterodox points of view), Sadānanda Sarasvatī (Vedāntījī), Varanasi, Karapātra Dhāma, s. d., pp. 66.

Pūṃjīvāda, Samājavāda aur Rāmarājya (Capitalism, socialism, and the Reign of Rāma), Lakṣmaṇa Caitanya Brahmacārī, Varanasi, Sri Vedāntī Svāmī Rāma Rājya Pariṣad Prakāśaka, s. d., pp. 267.

Rāhulajī kī bhrānti (The error of Rahul), s.d.

Rāmarājya Pariṣad aur anya dala (The Rāmarājya Pariṣad and other parties), s.d.

Rāmāyaṇamīmāṃsā (Enquiry into the Rāmāyaṇa), 3rd ed., 1st ed. 1977, Kalkattā-Vṛndāvana-Dillī, Śrī Rādhakṛṣṇa Dhānukā Prakāśana Saṃsthāna, 2058 (2001), pp. 1049.

Rāṣṭrīya Svayaṃ Sevaka Saṃgha (R.S.S.) *aur Hindū Dharma* (RSS and Hinduism), Mahanta Vīrabhadra Miśra, Varanasi, Mahanta Vīrabhadra Miśra Tulasī Mandira, 1970, pp. 238.

Saṃgharṣa aur śānti (Struggle and peace), 3rd ed., Sadānanda Sarasvatī (Vedāntījī), Varanasi, Karapātra Dhāma, 1993, pp. 204.

Saṃkīrttana-mīmāṃsā evaṃ varṇāśrama-maryādā (Enquiry on the prac-tice of *kīrtana* and the dignity of the varṇāśrama), Sadānanda Sarasvatī (Vedāntījī), Varanasi, Karapātra Dhāma, s.d., pp. 112.

Sanātana saṃvidhāna. Rājanīti meṃ adhikāra (The eternal Constitution. The qualifications for politics), Svāmī Sadānanda Sarasvatī, Varanasi, Sri Karapatri Dhāma, s. d., pp. 21.

Śrīrādhāsudhā (The nectar of Rādhā), 3rd ed., Kalkatta-Vṛndāvana-Dillī, Rādhākṛṣṇa Dhānukā Prakāśana Saṃsthāna, 2054 (1997), pp. 313.

Śrīvidyā-ratnākaraḥ (The ocean of Śrīvidyā), 4th ed., Sampādakaḥ Dattātreyānandanāthaḥ (Sītārāma-kavirājaḥ), Varanasi, Śrīvidyā Sādhanā Pīṭha, 1997, pp. 533.

Śrīvidyā-varivasyā (The worship of Śrīvidyā), Sampādakaḥ Dattātreyā-nanda-nāthaḥ (Sītārāma Kavirājaḥ), Varanasi, Śrīvidyā Sādhanā Pīṭha, 2048 (1991) pp. 313.

Śukla-yajurveda mādhyandina-saṁhitā Karapātrabhāṣyasamanvitā (Commentary of Swami Karpatri on the mādhyandina-saṁhitā of the Śukla Yajurveda), *adhyāyāḥ* 1-40, 8 vol., Pt. Gajānana Śāstrī Musalagāṃvakara, Kalkattā-Vṛndāvana-Dillī, Rādha-kṛṣ ṇa Dhānukā Prakāśana Saṃsthāna, 2043 (1986-1992), pp. 3052.

Veda ka svarūpa aur prāmāṇya (Nature and authority of the Veda), 2 vol., Hariharanātha Tripāṭhī, Varanasi, Drama Saṃgha Śikṣā-maṇḍala, 2016 (1959), pp. 737.

Vedaprāmāṇyamīmāṃsā (The investigation in the authority of the Vedas), Dharma Saṅgha Śikṣā Maṇḍala, 2017 (1961), pp. 75.

Vedārthapārijāta (The flower of the essence of the Veda), 2 vol., Pt. Vrajavallabha Dvivedi, Pt. Paṭṭābhirāmaśāstrī, Pt. Mārkaṇḍeya Brahmacārī, Pt. Gajānana Śāstrī Musalagāṃvakara, Kalkattā-Vṛndāvana-Dillī, Sri Rādhakṛṣṇa Dhānukā Prakāśana Saṁsthāna 2055 (1999).

Vedasvarūpavimarśaḥ (Reflections on the nature of the Veda), Pt. R.G. Sukla, Kalkattā, Bhaktisudhā Sāhitya Pariṣad, 2026 (1969), pp. 451.

Vicāra Pīyūṣa (Nectar of thoughts), Sri Santaśaraṇa Vedāntī, Varanasi, Akhila Bhāratīya Rāma Rājya Pariṣad, 2032 (1975), pp. 667.

Videśa yātrā: *eka śāstrīya pakṣa* (Journey to foreign countries: A scriptural point of view), s.d.

* * *

Other books of related interest
published by **Indica Books**:

- **A Concise Dictionary of Indian Philosophy**
by John Grimes
- **Sankara and Heidegger: Being, Truth, Freedom**
by John Grimes
- **The Aphorisms of Shiva**
The Śiva Sūtra with Bhāskara's Commentary, the Vārttika
Transl. by Mark S.G. Dyczkowski
- **A Journey in the World of the Tantras**
by Mark S.G. Dyczkowski
- **Abhinavagupta's Commentary on the Bhagavad Gita**
trans. with introduction and notes by Boris Marjanovic
- **Vijñana Bhairava: The Practice of Centring Awareness**
trans. and commentary by Swami Lakshman Joo
- **Shaivism in the Light of Epics, Puranas and Agamas**
by N.R. Bhatt
- **Aspects of Tantra Yoga**
by Debabrata SenSharma
- **Selected Writings of M.M. Gopinath Kaviraj**
- **Exposition of Reasoning:** ***Tarkabhāṣā***
Transl. by M.M. Pt. Ganganath Jha
- **The Sanskrit Language: An Overview**
by P.S. Filliozat
- **The Hindu Pantheon in Nepalese Line Drawings**
Two Manuscripts of the Pratiṣṭhālakṣaṇasārasamuccaya
compiled by Gudrun Bühnemann
- **A Treasury of Traditional Wisdom**
presented by Whitall N. Perry
- **मीमांसा-पदार्थ-विज्ञानम्** (Sanskrit & Hindi)
काशीनाथ न्यौपाने
- **आगम-संविद् Āgama-Saṁvid** (Sanskrit)
कमलेश झा